RAILWAY CHARACTER
LINES

RAILWAY CHARACTER LINES

Mike Collins

ATHENA PRESS
LONDON

RAILWAY CHARACTER LINES
Copyright © Mike Collins 2006

ISBN 1 84401 580 7

First Published 2006 by
ATHENA PRESS
Queen's House, 2 Holly Road
Twickenham TW1 4EG
United Kingdom

Printed for Athena Press

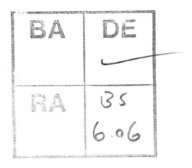

BA | DE

RA | 35
6.06

Dedicated to all who appear within, either by name or alias.
To Sandy for laboriously reading through the text,
and to Dr Stanley Pearson and the staff at Leeds Chest Clinic
who have, for twenty years, preserved me in a state in which
I am able to write all this.

Unless otherwise indicated, all photographs are by the author.

About the Author

Mike Collins joined British Railways in 1961, just before Dr Beeching (tree surgeon) cut off most of the branches. He spent his first eighteen months at the York Headquarters of the North Eastern Region in the Civil Engineer's Department. After completing a final year of his "thick sandwich" at Bradford University, he was despatched to the Leeds District Engineer's Office, a few months later joining the Area Assistant District Engineer at Huddersfield, before becoming permanent there as head of the Drawing Office staff of one. As his career progressed he worked alongside both men in the track gangs and members of management. With eight years' experience behind him he was gently edged into taking on permanent way projects of increasing magnitude, culminating in co-leading the civil engineering work on the York Environs Remodelling. With the onset of privatisation, projects hung in the balance, resulting in redundancy and retirement on health grounds.

Moving back into the Leeds Office in 1970, a change of premises six years later inspired the start of the unofficial *Leeds Civil Engineers' Annual Newsletter*, which detailed all the mishaps and unintentional mistakes of his colleagues, much to their collective dismay and amusement. The final edition, in 1993, was forty pages long. In a vain attempt to disrupt these publications, Mike was given the job of producing glossy full-colour official magazines of the *Leeds Civil Engineer* three times a year from 1990, while continuing with his project work.

Throughout his work Mike has observed the characters at all points along the engineering spectrum, many of them pictured in *Railway Character Lines*.

Mike is a fourth-generation railwayman, his younger son forming a fifth before being the first to realise that the financial grass is definitely greener outside the railway industry.

Foreword

> We need characters in life, for it is only in characters that worthwhile life exists.

Nathaniel Burrows (1768–1832)

"It takes one to know one" is not enough when it comes to spotting a character. This misses the statements on the reverse of the coin: "It takes a non-character to mistake a real character for a fool, a nuisance, a disruption and a total hindrance."

Yet from right across the spectrum, the railways of old were manned almost entirely by characters. This was before the rule of experience was replaced by the rule of economic integrity. In former days, the Permanent Way (PWay) Supervisor at Bradford, Dennis Durand, could always replace a broken shovel immediately, and have a man back working within minutes; today's accountant backs off in horror at the idea of a dead-money replacement bank of shovels, and requires notification of the damage. In due course he authorises a replacement from the manufacturers. In the meantime, our shovel-less man is put to other duties, regardless of the fact that shovelling is the engineering priority of that day.

Maybe Dennis was too extreme an example. Whereas most PWay Supervisors had a fairly sizeable room as a store, Dennis had the entire lower floor of a former goods warehouse. The two bits of his broken shovel would be sent in to Stanningley Workshops for repair on two different days. First the handle, which had come away from its blade, and a week later, the blade was sent in for a new handle. Ballast forks, picks and track key hammers suffered similarly and were also replaced on this pyramid-ordering basis. Track sluing bars were trickier, but given time a repeatedly bent and blacksmith-straightened bar would become two bars, each requiring replacement. To keep ahead, Dennis had to be devious, and to be that devious it helped by being a character. Today's characters are stifled.

Railway grading demonstrated the Orwellian principle that all men are equal; those who were more equal were the greater characters. Any man doing his allotted job to the best of his ability was as good as any other. It didn't mean that any two men could necessarily be placed on common ground to fight out who was the more equal. Cairo Bill in the Marsden track gang, who was convinced that his rechargeable wireless ran on distilled water, because that is what he knew was added to the rundown battery every time he took it in, went out onto the track twice a day and worked solidly and effectively. His District Engineer, Kieran Adams, talked, made decisions, and knew that a rundown battery had something else done to it besides adding water, but he would see it as a management right and requirement to spend the occasional working afternoon on the golf course with like colleagues. They were both characters, but there remains a doubt as to which was the most equal of the two.

But let's not allow ourselves to run away with the idea that characters need to be funny, good for a laugh, the office comedian, the lightener of dark times. Characters can be dark, troubled, peculiar and far from amusing at the time. Funny peculiar or funny ha-ha are opposites, joined by the common quality of eccentricity.

Take Naughton Grout, a technical man whose characteristics were obstinacy, awkwardness, pedantry, perfectionism, and an attitude that marked him out as being a good fifty years behind his time. He was a square peg roaming around a board lacking even round holes in his case. Grout was an acknowledged wizard in the science of curve realignment, but that was his absolute limit. Given charge of ten miles of route improvement, he designed some beautiful curves, and went out at night with the lining machines to put his paperwork into practice. Managerial panic set in when it was found that his budget was gone and only two miles had been completed. The reason – one machine was over-sluing by an inch throughout, so all of Naughton's six hundred-yard-long intended curve was exactly one inch further west than it should have been. Quite adequate for the increased speed now possible, but not perfect in the creator's book. As a result, Mr Perfect Pedantic goes back next night and tries again, achieving perfection, this time three-quarters of an inch too far east. So it's back again for another go, one night later. When faced with the financial implications, Naughton comes up with the aggravating line: "So you're saying that you don't want me to get it perfectly right, then!"

On the other hand there was the matter of Naughton's bodily functions. In the space of one afternoon he was seen to eat nine Mars bars one after the other. Intrigued by this we found him perfectly willing to be accurately measured from front teeth to rectum. Comparing this measurement to nine times the length of one bar, we found agreement within 5%.

He was also master of the art of the ventriloquial fart. With his six-foot-plus frame bent over curve calculations, Naughton could keep head and torso perfectly still whilst his fingers flitted over the figures and one buttock lifted an inch from his seat. With perfect timing he would wait five seconds before lifting one flaring nostril and eyebrow, to concentrate a saddened gaze upon a nearby innocent but reddening victim.

"Phucket" Dave, a most effective supervisor, was hounded by bad luck, but in one specific direction only. Dave must have had the most boring of weekly horoscopes, for every Saturday night was the same – he would lose or break his thermos flask usually at the start of the job. It dropped out of his bag as he leapt from the gang bus, it went under the caterpillar tracks of the digger, it rose into the air balanced on the end of a sleeper as the first length of old track was uplifted, it became a constituent part of the new track formation as the tamping machine pressed it deep into stone ballast, it was loaded with the muck, dispensed by the hopper wagon, crushed by an off-target hammer, or even run over by the train. Once, on a good night, it was found to match the guard's thermos to perfection, and was emptied in one before the guard admitted that sweet, strong, milky tea had slightly taken aback a palate expecting straight black coffee. Every flask disaster was accepted by Dave, with a tossed aside, "Phucket!"

Henry King, who went through life getting funny looks after filling in forms (Surname... First name...), arrived well late one morning, drenched and with a severely bruised right calf and a badly sprained back. Halfway to work his motorised cycle had packed up, so he'd had to push it along the gutter, each revolution of the fixed pedal striking him firmly on the back of his leg. Finally, after parking it, he began a limping gallop along the line of cars, noticed Peter White, the Assistant Engineer, climbing out of one of them, carried on running – now backwards, whilst waving and calling out an apologetic "Good Morning, Mr White", who then watched amazed as Henry collided with a projecting bonnet, rolled over the top and landed on the other side, still running, and without further comment.

Reggie Roberts, ganger to the six-man Honley track team, fearing the approach of redundancy due to the centralisation of all length gangs into two large ones, based in Huddersfield, decided to end it all, using a home-produced twelve-page universal pools plan repeated over three weeks, investing his entire earnings over that period at a farthing a line. Knowing he was bound to win at least one jackpot, and being quite incapable of the enormous task of checking the results, he confidently handed in his notice, took his fortnight's holiday allocation and waited for the Vernon's knock on the door. Three postal orders, adding up to a quarter of the stake, resulted. He returned to work on the third Monday to plead for his job back, only for Jack Senior, his older and wiser supervisor, to hand him back his letter of notice that Jack had filed behind the office clock.

Then there was Felix Ferris... no, Felix is worth a chapter to himself!

Characters all, never intentionally, but each in their own way keeping the great diversity of experience rolling along and making life worth living, and the act of going to work only a little less than a total pleasure.

List of Main Characters

Railway terms and work titles can be confusing, especially as with every reorganisation everyone becomes known as something else, and carries on doing the same job as before. There are many characters within and it might be useful to summarise who they are and what they are, were yesterday, and what they might be tomorrow.

Adams, Sydney

First seen as a clerk from CCE York on programme inspections. He moved to Leeds to become Chief Clerk, later called Administration Assistant, effectively, in Syd's case, chief over everything including the engineer. He was a wildly competitive man in our various ventures into sport.

Avery, Tim

Lewis's successor. Far more garrulous and mobile. Informally called "Tim".

Barnes, Elaine

A clerk who had as many office posts as she had sizes in dress! Elaine was a perpetual slimmer and sweller. She had a tremendous personality with a most offhand attitude to political correctness (not then invented). As an assistant she was extremely competent, eventually suffering like me at the hands of privatisation.

Bevan, Kye

Chief Draughtsman at Leeds and leader in many District PWay projects. He was latterly of poor health, made worse by the railway's tightening rules on drinking. A man of deep PWay theoretical and practical knowledge. Respected and feared amongst his Drawing Office technical lads.

Boyes, Bill

Formerly a driver in the Leeds PWay relaying section. Following a severe heart attack he was brought into the Huddersfield Area Office to work on light duties as linkman and clerk. Deceptively innocent and harmless. Very bad news for the pretentious and superior experience seekers.

Buckley, Ted

Area Bridge Inspector. Responsible for reporting to Albert Hughes and the Leeds Bridge Section on the conditions of all bridges, viaducts and "dead" tunnels on the Area. A gentleman with a great knowledge and experience in his field. Not supervisory material due to his gentle and amenable manner.

Clerk, Stompy (Bernie)

A messenger in the Leeds DCE Office. A messenger's job was to collect all incoming mail from the station in the mornings and sort and distribute it, doing the opposite at night. The messenger also acted as a most unlikely receptionist. Bernie was relatively

Collins, Mike — young in the part, usually reserved for those nearing retirement.

Senior technical engineer in the Huddersfield Area Drawing Office (there were rarely more than three there at any time). Later, was eased into minor then major projects working in the Leeds Office. A strong realist (pessimist); allergic to courses; far too much in awe of all others around him.

Ferris, Felix — Another amalgam of some of the technical assistants who passed through the Area Drawing Office.

Garner, Carlyle — Equivalent to Harry Hanson. For this character I have drawn together the worst of their kind, exact opposites to Harry, except in competence.

Hanson, Harry — Assistant PWay Inspector, one of three working for Jack Senior. His job involved walking the tracks allocated to him and initiating simple repairs. Like his counterparts, his bonus depended on the quality of his track. Harry was an honest and good man, working happily to his limits.

Holmes, Dave — A PWay technical assistant in Leeds Drawing Office. A good draughtsman with an unquenchable thirst for humour and mischief. Very popular.

Hughes, Albert — Works Supervisor under the AADE at Huddersfield. Responsible for buildings, bridges and tunnels. Another gentleman who had worked his way up from a labourer through a skilled artisan. Very fair and knowledgeable. Succeeded by Ken Oxley, who was mainly based on Jack Pinder, a pipe with a genial man behind it.

Kellet, Percy Chainman, ideal partner for Wilf. Similar record of progression into surveying. A fairly mischievous man who got worse as Wilf became sterner.

Lewis, J A Leeds District/Divisional/Area Civil Engineer. Responsible under the Chief Civil Engineer at York for all work within the ever-expanding Leeds District. Had two assistants – PWay (Tracks, etc.) and Works (Structures). Short and mainly silent Welshman, insistent on being called "Sir". Very rarely seen out of his office.

Midgley, John PWay technical assistant. Formerly of the York District, but amalgamated with Leeds during reorganisation, at which time he was in charge of installing the Selby Diversion. After a short while in the Leeds Office moved back to York jointly with me to carry out the complete PWay remodelling of the York Station area. John appears little in these earlier years, but I came to realise during the York work that I was in the presence of one of the railway "greats". John suffered and surmounted some personal tragedies while we were together which slightly affected his work. His true abilities were realised late in his career, as he was a frank and ferocious character when crossed. John was, in my experience, the finest PWay engineer I ever came across.

Milner, Elliot

Area Assistant District Engineer, Huddersfield. One of four AADEs. Responsible for all facets of civil engineering maintenance on his Area. Elliot would be known by his first name by the many who have watched him progress through the Drawing Office, or stubbornly as Mr Milner by the traditionalists.

Ryder, Irving

Assistant Works Supervisor to Albert Hughes. An excellent artisan, but rather out of his depth as a supervisor. Wielder of the mischievous folding three-foot ruler.

Senior, Jack

PWay Supervisor/Inspector at Huddersfield. Had grown through the ranks from platelayer to ganger into supervision. There were four such supervisors on the Area, all answerable to the AADE. Jack, like his counterpart at Bradford, Denis Durand, was a thorough gentleman and very fair employer and guardian of the men on the ground.

Stapleton, Eddy	PWay technical assistant. Started as a minor at HQ and sent to us on the Area to provide basic training. A most unpromising newcomer who triumphed over personal problems to eventually become a highly respected engineer. Amazed us all by becoming a leading figure in the team installing track in the Channel Tunnel.
Warbuton, Wilf	Formerly a platelayer or trackman, now a chainman or surveyor's assistant, based in Leeds. A chameleon-like character who could be absolutely essential and cooperative to those who respected his position, but rather surly to anyone treating him as if they were his better. To most a gentleman, friend and very experienced help, to a few, obstinate.

Contents

Peat	21
No. 23 Wellington Street, Leeds	43
Lavatory	71
Surveys	97
Dominoes	124
Illness	139
Harry	168
Tunnels	200
Some Exotic Surveys	232
Saturday Nights	256
Felix	282
Saloon, Part 1	310
Saloon, Part 2	342
Rules	366
Epilogue	391

Peat

Before we get bogged down in the tragedy of the peat saga, there are things need sorting. I'm really bound to provide an introduction to one essential element in the story, and many of those that follow. It's necessary, and I apologise in advance, and it won't happen again. There's this animal that'll keep cropping up, the species *homo correctus*, a very special and essential being in railway civil engineering circles up to the 1980s. He was traditionally known as the chainman, by definition a simple soul, but on examination a frighteningly complex creature, with unimaginable powers to make or break. This job has now, fortunately, been replaced by technology. Fortunately, because the source which supplied chainmen has dried up. True chainman material no longer exists due mainly to the policy of a full education for all.

For many middle-aged men in the gangs up into the 1960s, education had been a nine-year flirtation with hundreds, tens and units, weekly spelling tests, and the devastatingly boring saga of Janet and John. These two were a desperate couple of abnormalities whose daily interplay was told in excruciating detail as a means to sharpening reading skills. After struggling through any chapter of the pair's daily doings, the less than front-line reader must have thought hard and long about the advantages of learning to read, if this was the sort of thing dished up to satisfy the new skill. If young lads failed to latch onto any one of these three essentials of education, it became a case of "never mind, just give them a shovel or a brush for the duration, and they'll be alright". To settle this and make sure that no bright child was overlooked, they'd all have a single day of exams to sort out the quick from the thick. It was labelled "Scholarship" and later "11+", which in itself caused many to fall by the wayside, unable to get past this initial sum due to an apparent lack of information. "Plus what?" I heard one bewildered child cry. Just one short day out of a whole lifetime to decide a future!

Many were correctly assessed on that particular day as being unable to work out the price of apples and pears given two bits of information – two and three respectively cost 11d, whilst three and four cost 1/6d, because they hadn't yet grasped basic arithmetic. Some weren't able to do it because they couldn't read the question, proving that they were incapable of reading as well as arithmetic, and some were stumped trying to write down the answer if they knew it, and were therefore counted as being thick on all three counts. There'd be some who were off-colour on the day, and couldn't concentrate on anything, and there were a few, including my own father, who had worked out that to pass this exam meant losing your friends, and spending much longer at another, tougher school. All were labelled as failures, yet watch them fifteen years later working out the odds on an accumulator, or the theory of permutations on a pools coupon.

In fact, these one-day failures were bound to include many of above-average intelligence, yet they were, on the evidence of that fateful day, condemned to go down the snake rather than up the ladder. There were many suitable positions for them on the railway: shunters, sweepers, shovellers, porters and office messengers. Given time, they might manage to shine sufficiently to move into the lowest clerical level, or even to become supervisors, but it took years. This is why the high school leaver or university graduate would find himself working with middle-aged clerks and supervisors, in an office structure that insisted on making him, on grade, superior to these elders. This was a grave mistake, never graver than in the mix of a green Drawing Office graduate surveyor and the chainman, or surveyor's assistant.

"Assistant" won't really do, if I'm honest about it. Such a term suggests secondary or servile, and so many young grammar school lads, with a fortnight's evening classes in surveying behind them, have learnt the hard way that the chainman was neither a servant, nor a subordinate to the surveyor. He was a right arm! Just a hint of superiority or arrogance from such youngsters has condemned many a self-certainty to years of frustration and difficulty, as the "simple, slow and limited" chainman would undermine, and "straighten t'lad out for his own bloody good".

I suppose that's the essentials of this prelude, so if you want to jump ahead to where some talking starts, fine, but I'm going to hammer it home because you really need to appreciate that the chainman, who could appear to be an obstructive old man, was probably the finest educational element in a young civil engineer's career. Off you go, if you want, I'll catch you up later!

Ideally, the fledgling surveyor, after first explaining what the objectives were of a particular surveying job, should have contented himself with putting information down in his pocket-book, while the chainmen concentrated on the practical things such as setting out the survey lines, picking out relevant targets, and accurately measuring them from reference points. They would then convey that information to he who could almost be their secretary – the surveyor. A good team of chainmen could make an adequate surveyor exceptional. A hostile team, not credited by the newcomer at the outset with intelligence and superior experience, could make the path of the potential high-flyer more of a deepening trench, and five years longer than it needed to have been. It was sadly only a few who seemed to be able to appreciate the real equality of men of varying ranks in the achievement of a goal. First-time surveys could proceed in one of two directions:

Enter New Surveyor A, let's call him Ambrose, confident, superior, beautifully qualified on paper, and well aware of the difference between his wage and potential to that of the chainman. Enter also New Surveyor B (how about Brian?), able, nervous and in awe of the age and experience of his elders and betters, especially the chainman.

Surveyors Ambrose and Brian: "There's no need to pick up that drain catch-pit, thanks."

Chainman: "Why?"

Ambrose: "Because I don't want it! I'll tell you what I need!"

Chainmen to Ambrose: "Reet, lad. Fine bi us!" – immediately breaking off a partnership barely started.

Brian (in answer to the same query): "Because I don't think I'll need it, seeing as there'll be a completely new drainage system throughout when the job's done, and all that old stuff'll be ripped out. So long as we pick up a reasonable outfall, that's all that I should need. *What do you think?*"

Chainmen to Brian: "Mebbee, lad, but it might be an idea to have a look down 'em, just to check if there's any other drains running in from somewhere else, that tha'll need to tek into consideration when tha's designin' t'new one."

This is a lifeline to which Brian will react: "Yes, that's a point, of course, thanks, hadn't thought of that. Perhaps it might be an idea to pick every one up, after all. What d'you think?"

"Safest, lad, tha can nivver have too much in that book of thine, even if tha dumps aif on it later." And Brian is then accepted. Come dinnertime on that first encounter, he won't be left in a corner of the cabin with his wrap-up; no, he'll find the chainmen asking if he really wants his sandwiches, or would he like to sample "t'finest chip 'oil hereabouts?" From a willingness to realise and accept that experience might know best, Brian's practical education and his office reputation take off like a house on fire.

As for arrogant Ambrose, this first job turns out to be a disaster when he comes to try and plot it out back in the Drawing Office, and so is the return to site to pick up deliberately avoided details, and check on misinformation, such as the gas inspection flap, invisible the first time since it was underneath Chainman Percy's boot, or the fact that what Chainman Wilf identified as "just spray from t'engines", is actually a leaking mains service, or that the thick and dirty old signal cable, rather than "lookin' dead to me" (Percy again), is in reality the main link for the adjacent station complex. Life for Ambrose is an uphill struggle, from the first hint on his part that he feels himself to be on a different plane to his chainmen.

Ambrose may eventually alter his ways, and in time be pardoned, but he'd never be allowed to forget. Any failure to see where his problem lies, and he will return over and over again with threadbare or misleading surveys. Alternatively, the enemy may adopt the tactic of overwhelming cooperation. This will flood him with measurements recording details down to every small sod, alive or dead, on the dubious grounds that he "needs to show how much muck there is in t'ballast to be lettin' stuff like this grow". He'll be given precise offsets to old discarded bolts, half-buried in ages of track formation, as they become "a mains tap for t'gas heatin' system what de-ices track points", or a remote piece of signalling equipment. A stray redundant sleeper "could be owt, lad, you nivver know! Best get t'gang to lift it and come back later to check." Ambrose goes out to do track level surveys, using his mounted telescopic level to view and read off the chainman's graduated staff. This is stood on various points where relative levels are wanted, an operation which can put up to a hundred yards between the superior Ambrose and the "guileless simplicity" of Percy or Wilf. At this sort of distance he can't see Percy's boot stuck between the staff and the target point on the rail, or the same staff missing the rail altogether, and being carelessly lowered into a small hole at the side. All this translates to a decidedly exciting roller-coaster of track levels when plotted out later on the drawing board.

Ambrose also finds that he has "favours" done for him, such as finding a temporary benchmark – a datum level to which the whole survey is tied, which will be needed later as a reliable point of reference. It must still be sure to be in place when the tracks are torn up in the course of the renewal, six months later. It is your basis for the whole new scheme of track levels. But our obstructive chainman's "favour" is in electing the step of a redundant guard's van standing on an adjacent rusted siding, as the permanent point of reference, the van having "not shifted for years, lad. Look at t'wheels, virtually corroded to t'track; an' sithee – 'Cond' (condemned) painted on't side. Tha's safe wi' that, lad! That's goin' noweer, fast!" A guard's van which is known by a select few founts of all knowledge, namely the office messengers, typists and chainmen (Wilf and Percy), to be one of the hundred or so wagons at last to be hauled off to the breakers within the month.

Give the same levelling team the brow of a hill to go over and this surveyor is doomed! Once out of sight the chainman might kneel down, with the telescopic staff much reduced, providing a totally fictitious reading for the observing student. Alternatively, if the steepness is so severe that Ambrose's line of sight passes above the staff's measuring-scale limits, long, lanky Chainman George will hoist the foot of the staff to a position roughly in the region of his belly button, and helpfully advise Ambrose to "add four foot to that, lad, trust me!" In short, should you ignore and refute the superiority of the chainman's specialised knowledge and experience, you're done for.

In the meantime the initially nervous Brian is so well established by now that he can even drop the odd incautious remark, only to be gently cautioned with a "nah then, lad", whereas Ambrose will, for a long time, return with apocryphal surveys, leading to the production of excitingly unlikely drawings, and the notching up of the chief draughtsman's blood pressure one more peg. That valve will eventually blow, with references to tarts, trances and chocolate fireguards.

The chainman was an able, informed, mischievous, intelligent bundle, to be accepted as totally indispensable, or found steadily disruptive.

As it happened it was in my nature to be a very strong Brian-type, almost a traitor to my kind in the office. This arose from an inbuilt feeling of inferiority, which a desperate shyness amplified. I was, and still am, in awe of most men and women in the jobs they do, whatever those jobs might be. Also, I have always felt myself to be unable to do my job as well as they do theirs. I'd had drummed into me, at an early age, a natural regard and respect for my elders, under which heading Wilf, Percy and George qualified with honours. Immediately I met them, following three years of university, I felt that I was in the presence of a much greater practical knowledge of surveying than I'd so far accumulated, a knowledge brought about by experience rather than education. I'd been taught how to survey by the stars and measure the circumference of the earth; I'd the mysteries of tachometry and the cubic parabola totally sussed, but the chainmen had done railway surveys of track levels and alignments, which I hadn't, and what's more they'd done them without using the Pole Star, or worrying about how round the world was. I couldn't fathom how or why the Ambroses of my new world didn't share my admiration for these men, and how they could treat them with juvenile arrogance; but they did. As probably the Brianest of all Brians, I would take the advice of the chainmen at most times. As a result, I'd often return with a bit too much information, but rarely with anything missing. So much did I seem to be on a similar wavelength to them that the small gang would occasionally seek my help in their upstart cocky-bugger correction programmes.

★

After a year in the Leeds District Office, getting used to the earthier side of railway civil engineering, I was ready for the small satellite Drawing Office at Huddersfield, under the Area Engineer, Elliot Milner. There I was immediately appointed senior draughtsman, which took little effort on my part seeing as I was the only one there. I'd a regular turnover of juniors, some staying for a year or more, though in the main they'd be budding graduates (almost without fail, Ambroses) with great careers ahead of them, and needing only two-month stopovers to learn everything there was to know. Their brilliance can be judged when you consider that I left the Area after nine years, still with things to learn, whereas they had the skill to crack it in eight weeks. They had training programmes which looked like an American's European vacation schedule, sitting in as many seats as possible in the two years it took to make them junior management material. Clad in the most inappropriate suits and ties for the dirtier aspects of the work, they'd carry out these tasks with hurt expressions, or, demonstrating their managerial potential, would contrive to avoid doing them altogether. With bulging briefcases and matching egos, they were pure cannon fodder for the consortium of chainmen who could adapt their Chinese torture correction to a crash course in sadistic torment.

Introducing, at this point, Eddy Stapleton, one of the long-stay, modest-prospect juveniles, and most certainly a humble Brian specimen, but with an innocent naiveté that demanded that just a bit of leg pulling be performed on him at any appropriate moment. Eddy was to feature strongly in the peat saga. He was "nobbut a bairn", keen, inexperienced and vulnerable, and he was also learning to drive. (This happened to be a side of railway education I'd shied away from, without really knowing why, and as a result I'd got this sneaking admiration for the lad. It was years later before I fully appreciated my foresight in not fulfilling the railway's wish to teach me the skills required to launch yet another misguided missile onto the roads. It was a foresight once more born of inadequacy and a fear of failure. I felt fully justified in years to come when drivers acting as chauffeurs for technical staff became frowned on, resulting in the lads being landed with driving themselves to Saturday-night jobs, working continuously through to mid Sunday morning, and then driving themselves home – an exhausting and occasionally dangerous situation.)

We'd let Eddy have plenty of training runs in the car with Bill Boyes at his side. Bill was the office dogsbody by virtue of a heart condition that had curtailed his more active life in the relaying gangs. As a result he was both ideal and available to act as shotgun for the young learner. (Bill was another example of a man held back by traditional education; I wouldn't have liked to have taken him on in an IQ contest.) He was noted for a lifetime of mischievousness, and had been but briefly reined in by the heart attack. From working upwards of eighty hours a week, driving gangs to site and supervisors round their various jobs during the week, followed by long Saturday-night shifts, Bill was suddenly reduced to office hours. With his thick wavy silver hair, twinkling eyes and short stocky build, Bill would have made a perfect garden gnome, but the railway had all such jobs filled, hence his posting to the Huddersfield Area Office. Apart from office duties, Bill was available to run me to sites and pick me up at the far end. Also, I could help enhance his income by using him on a Saturday night, letting him go home after dropping me off, to return next morning at the end of the job. He was an honorary chainman in outlook, and I treated him with the same deference, respect and deep suspicion as I did Wilf and Percy. He would reward this veneration by getting me in and out of as many scrapes as he could. A rapid flight along a personal learning curve came to my rescue at an early stage, leaving Bill to then turn to the various Eddys that passed through our hands for his shenanigans.

With the boss, Elliot Milner, at a meeting at York Headquarters for the day, the office car was available for the junior staff, that's me. I knew that with Eddy driving, it would mean a nervous journey (for me at least), with three in the back – me being one of them, so I chose a fairly handy nearby job to tackle that day. Present was Wilf Warburton, Percy Kellett and myself in the back, and Eddy up front with Bill alongside. With five occupants it meant using the roof rack for the bulkier pieces of equipment, and forty-five minutes of argument and remedial tea breaks were necessary just to fix and load it. Still, a relatively early start and a short trip meant that we were all done and back in the office for dinner – always a prime objective. It was during the usual discussion on the imagination of wives, or lack of it, when it came to preparing their men's snap tins, and the various fillings of the sandwiches therein, that talk turned to allotments, home-grown vegetables, and gardening in general.

"T'soil's too heavy round here, that's the snag," Wilf observed, replacing an escaped lettuce leaf between the monumental slices of bread, first shaking off the ash and dust of the fireplace. "For missen, failin' 'oss muck, I could do with a load of that organic whatsit they sell at Halifax Sewerage. It's beautiful stuff, with bits of wool waste mixed in from t'mills. Breaks up clay a treat."

"Five bob a bag, though," Percy reminded him. "Goes no-where in a decent-sized garden."

"Tha gets it cheaper than that if tha can prove tha comes from around Halifax," Bill pointed out. "They reckon that living there, tha's sort of got a stake in it, so to speak, 'a contribution gratefully received' sort of thing. Brings it down to four and six a bag."

"Still no bloody bargain," said Percy, "considering that at our house there'd be aif a dozen of us stokin' up t'sewers every morning. Ah reckon they could afford to drop t'price a bit more sizeably. Ah'd refuse to contribute to it if ah couldn't get it for less than a tanner a bag!"

"Fancy collecting your own, then, d'yer?" asked Wilf. "Ah've got to admire t'idea, but ah reckon tha'd pretty soon get fed up; ay, and think on, they do tek t'smell out of it at Halifax, as it goes through t'works, it's not like that stuff they used to dish up at Esholt – d'yer remember it, Percy? Now that stunk. Took all t'polish off on mi coit buttons!"

"Oh ah remember, all reet. Ah'll say ah do! Aye, by gum!" said Percy, re-examining the contents of his sandwich. "(Why the buggery does she put fish paste sarnies along wi t'marmalade ones? Ah've been eating 'em in turn, and it dun't aif githee a shock.) You're back to comin' 'ome on t'Esholt/Leeds tram, aren't you? It were an interesting ride, and no mistake. What's more, ah were down ninepence, on t'deal!" He gazed into the middle distance, sadly recalling a financially depressing memory.

My nose for a story, added to the pair of them sitting back in their seats with their eyes flitting between each other and the ceiling, suggested possibilities. "What's this, then?" says I.

"Let's get this straight from t'start off, it were all dahn to him!" responded Wilf, with a slight degree of ferocity. "Thur's times when tha can't tek him nowhere! We'd this day, see, workin' at Esholt. Ivver bin theer? If tha has, it's summat tha wain't forget in an hurry, especially if it's a hot day, wi' t'wind in thy direction. I'n't that so, Percy?"

"Ay, by gum! We was working reet alongside t'shit farm's dumpin' ponds, weer they have them long bars wi' t'oils in 'em, them what trundle up and down ower t'cinders, chuckin' mucky watter out all day."

"Anyroad," continued Wilf, still in a slight state of breathless excitement, "there were nobbut t'river between us and them, and we were fair eatin' and breathin' t'stuff! Ah could barely touch mi dinner that day; fed aif mi sarnies to t'seagulls, and I weren't ower bothered about t'rest, I can tell thee! God it stunk! Middla summer and all, weren't it, Percy?"

"Aye, it were fair crackin' t'flags, that day, as ah remember. Tha could've fried eggs on thi cap after five minutes in that sun. Don't think ah'd've stuck another hour on it theer, though. You could smell nowt else for days after! It were on thi clothes, in thi hair, and stuck to t'back of thi teeth. I'd two baths that week, and ah weren't even mucky – t'wife thought I'd got missen a bit o'fancy on t'side, like, and then one what kept pigs, or summat!"

"Aye, it were certainly ripe! Nah then," went on Wilf, becoming more agitated and now on the edge of his seat, pointing the remains of a sandwich at Percy, "we'd had nobbut this pong all day. So why," finger now quivering, and scattering fragments of his dinner like confetti, "why does this daft bugger have to go and buy a sack on t'rotten stuff to tek home wi'us for his garden, eh? Smell alone were enough! After a day aht theer, tha could've just waved thi cap ower t'gardin fence, and tha'd've 'ad four-foot rhubarb within a week! So there we were, no transport, middle of nowhere, and he has to go an' get five stone on t'stuff in a sack to tek home, "cos it were cheap'."

"Good stuff. And anyroad, ninepence weren't all that cheap!"

"No, it weren't, as it turned out, were it? Nivver been so embarrassed in mi life."

"How come?" I felt a slight prompt called for, if only to give Wilf a moment to salvage the remains of his dinner. At the same time, though, Wilf's vivid tale had got me wondering whether my beef and pickle sandwich really did smell like that, or was it just something he'd said?

"Ah'll tell thee how come," went on Wilf obligingly, sitting back at last, but still underlining it all with pointed flourishes towards the ceiling with every phrase, "how come indeed. Because wi' 'avin no transport, we'd only to go back to Leeds on't ruddy tram, and him with aif 'undredweight of refined doings on his back! And in a leakin' sack! All this on a July afternoon, wi't temperature in t'eighties! That's why! Daft article! He climbs on t'tram and calmly slings t'sack under t'steps. Then we nips up on top t'get some fresh baccer fumes down us throats. Three or four stops later and we could hear rumbling noises goin' on downstairs. Another three and t'conductor's up two at a time. 'Anyone up here dumped a sack of summat downstairs, 'cos it's frigging ripe?' 'D'yer know,' says him theer, 'I thought I could smell summat when we got on,' he says, bold as you like. 'Could tha smell summat, Wilf?'"

By now Percy, helped on by Wilf's increasing agitation in the telling, was beginning to crack up. This was dangerous. I'd seen it before when Wilf got himself worked up. Things would usually just spiral away into a sulking silence, whilst Percy's stomach would start quivering, and odd muffled snorts would erupt through tight lips, along with his cheeks flooding a deep red. Worst of all, you could see Percy's eyes howling with laughter while his face stayed ten months pregnant with primed sandwich. Inevitably this wound Wilf up to extremes, until Percy's face would eventually burst, peppering the surroundings with remnants of whatever he'd last stuffed into it. All this was now in a critical meltdown state.

"So then," went on Wilf, back on the edge of his seat, and up both a tone in pitch and several decibels, "he starts on wi t'conductor, saying as how it were disgusting what some folk'd leave lyin' around, and how it were so bad, he was sure it'd be on his clothes for days. He even starts to crack on abaht a fare refund, would you mind! Conductor's going on, 'Well, someone must belong it, I don't know what I'm bahn to do wi'it. I'll be in bother if t'ticket snatcher gets on, that's for sure. Not supposed to carry stuff like that! I don't know what I'm to do'—"

"Ah, right!" butted in Percy, his volcanic face changing instantly like quenched steel from purple to a fearsome white. "So what does Mr Spotless, here, do then? Only tells t'snipper that if it were up to him he'd sling this stuff, what I'd paid good money for, off of t'tram at t'next stop! 'Well, I'm not touching it!' t'bloke says. 'Right,' says clever Dick here, 'I'll do it for thee!', and he drags it to t'step edge. Only goes an' catches it on summat, dun't he. Bloody stuff's pourin' aht on t'sack, an' flyin' off in t'wind. Theer's dried shit blowing all ower t'place, aif on it comin' back intter t'tram! No chance of picking it up later, oh no! He sees to that, alright! Nine bloody pence!"

Wilf had calmed down as fast as Percy had erupted. "Aye," he said, "and ah'll tell thee summat, tha can still tell, after all these years, where it were that we tipped it off. Yards and yards of t'greenest grass verges for miles. Tha were reet," to Percy, "it turned out t'be worth every bit of ninepence!"

Percy looked far from pacified. Then Bill, who'd been unusually silent for him, surfaced from behind his newspaper and climbed above his half glasses, to break into Percy's private wake for the lost fertiliser. "For heavy soils," he announced, "there's nothing better than natural peat, selected for its slightly acidic pee haitch value and its action in adding a fibrous texture to the fine particles which go to make up consolidated clay soils."

This stopped us all in our tracks. There was a total ceasefire in the assaults on our sandwiches, iced buns and mugs of tea.

"Tha what, says t'a?" Wilf descended into his broadest tones whenever faced with the pretentious. "What does t'a knaw abaht fibrous textures, an' what's a pee haitch, when it's at 'ome?"

"Bugger all, and no idea, in that order," replied Bill, "but while yor two were going dahn Memory Lane on a tram, ah've bin readin' this gardenin' bit in t'paper; and as it so happens, here they are, cracking on about exactly what we was saying... 'bout heavy soil an' all that... and here's us nobbut a stone's throw from t'biggest heap o' free peat in t'country! That's all!"

"What's he on abaht?" asked Percy, mentally comparing "free" with "ninepence".

"The moors above Standedge," I told him. "Just solid peat from toenail to horizon, and feet deep."

"It can't be free. Someone must belong it." Obviously, Percy couldn't come to terms with the idea that what he'd paid good money for, just to enhance the roadside between Esholt and Leeds, had something almost as good lying around for all to share, free and for nothing.

"Nah," said Bill, "it's common ground, up theer... belongs t'common man, like... like us, tha knaws, and the like... that's why it's called common ground... some's even called a common, aren't they? Like at Wimbledon, weerever that is, and," stretching his argument to tenuous limits, "common ground means somethin' or someweer what everyone's agreed on, and that means it can't belong anyone in particular." He did tend to trail off a bit here, apparently appreciating the vapid route of his reasoning. But Percy was aroused.

"Is it any good, then?"

"Any good! Weigh it up for thissen, sithee. Up theer it's all grass an' heather, wi sheep chowin' away at it all t'time. An' what d'we get from sheep, then?"

"Wool."

"Apart from wool."

"Legs o'lamb, and Barnsley chops."

"No, silly bugger, for t'garden?"

"?"

"Sheep shit! Years and bloody years on it, built up in wi' t'peat."

Percy still couldn't tie all this up with "free".

"Dust'a mean t'say that we can go up theer and just dig up what we want... and not pay nowt forrit? Won't someone miss it?"

"Ah, well, Ordnance Survey check up every ten years or so, they could easy notice a twelve-inch-deep hole... they'd need to alter t'next edition of their map a bit." My sarcasm was lost on those dead set on endless riches, and I was depressingly sure of how the natural progression of this discussion would be from here on in, and I didn't like it one bit. The "boss's car" wasn't strictly the property of Elliot Milner, it belonged to British Rail, but he looked after it like it was his own, and I knew full well that he'd be less than enamoured if it suddenly turned up with every nook and cranny filled with bits of peat and sheep muck. It wasn't going to be long before one of those present realised that the car was ours for the day, Milner was in York and would hardly come back to the Huddersfield Office just for half an hour or so, especially since his train had to go through Leeds where he lived. The roof rack was already in place, and there were plenty of empty sandbags in the PWay store.

"Tell you what," said Bill, "we've got t'car for t'day, there's no chance of Elliot coming back here for just aif an hour, seeing as he's to go through Leeds; we've already got t'roof rack on, and there's loads of empty sandbags in t'PWay store! How abaht it, then?"

"Hold on a tick." Here's me, Gypsy Rose Collins, trying to rein in the enthusiasm. "Elliot's not got over the cheese job, yet." Last summer, one of us who will even now remain nameless, left a carton of milk in the glove compartment, and forgot all about it. When dinnertime arrived the culprit was tempted away by the alternative attraction of two pints of shandy. Only a corporate willingness to blame one of the Leeds lads who'd had use of the car one Saturday night, diverted attention from us. The milk, long forgotten, had stayed put for at least a fortnight, with temperatures dipping into the seventies at night. It had left a six-month presence behind following its discovery and gut-churning rejection by Mrs Milner, while cleaning out the car one weekend.

But Bill was away now, enthusiasm and a chance of adventure were firing him up, and he saw no problem in collecting sufficient disciples to his cause to achieve a majority verdict. He rounded on me, who he sometimes saw as a bit of a drag.

"Tha's allus bloody frettin', thee! This is easy. We just nip up theer – twenty-five minutes – give t'young 'un a chance of a bit more drivin' – ten minutes dig – all bagged up – load up, an' 'ome. An hour, top whack! Dun't smell... not a lot. We'll even put it all up on t'rack if you want, out in't fresh air, no problems. Elliot'll nivver knaw! What d'yer think?"

"Reet! Ah'm in! T'job's a good un." Wilf and Percy in unison, slapping the table and already getting to their feet. Eddy looked to me for guidance as to what he should think, but I was broken. After years of experience in such arguments, I knew it was better just to get it over and done with. Besides which, my garden could do with a bit of freshening up as well. So "OK" it was. After all, enough for four of us (Eddy, as usual, didn't count), two bags apiece, all on top – neat.

"I'll just nip into t'PWay Office and get t'store key, to fetch some bags," said Bill. "Jack's in; I'll square it up. He'll be OK." This was true; I couldn't rely on our PWay Supervisor, Jack Senior, standing in the way, but I could see him wanting a couple more bags added to the load.

So while Bill trotted off, the rest of us horticultural pirates returned to livening up our tea dregs, with varying degrees of enthusiasm, and checking out the growing power of peat from the article in Bill's paper. He returned after ten minutes, just a short pair of legs topped off by a mound of sandbags.

"How many've you got there, for Chrissake? We only need eight!"

"Well, you know how it is," said the sacks, lowering themselves to the floor and revealing a somewhat dusty Bill. "Jack wanted to know what for, and decided he'd have a couple, then Horace t'shunter from Hillhouse come in, put his name down for four, Hilary on t'switchboard has a small plot – well, she rang through to book a couple..."

"How did—?"

"Jack said summat while he were phoning t'yard. And young Hilary misses nowt. We'll just have to put a couple of t'better bags in t'boot... I'll see to sweeping it aht!" – reacting to the look on my face. "Come on, look sharp afore any other bugger turns up wantin' some!"

So off we went, Eddy driving, and coping with the hills pretty well; Bill alongside, as required, and me in the back, sandwiched between Wilf and Percy, each of whom had failed to remove some minor pieces of surveying tackle from their greatcoat pockets. It was like sitting in a bath of wingnuts. To top it all, Wilf stubbornly tried to read yesterday's copy of Elliot's upmarket broadsheet that he'd found tucked away down the back of the seat. (I could tell that this impeded Eddy's rear view to the extent of completely, but the lad was far too timid to mention the fact. His ignorance of the presence of any other car behind him probably helped his confidence on the several hill starts, which Bill's route came across, on the way up onto the Pennine moors.)

"Down here," said Bill eventually, "it's a track to one on t'tunnel shafts. Don't thee worry, lad," seeing Eddy's startled expression as he turned onto Bill's "track", which looked about suitable for a written-off Centurion tank, and little else. "I'll turn it round for thee; I'll even bring it back up to t'road, when we've done. Just tek it a bit steady, that's all."

After a few hundred yards, which finally shaped me into a form sympathetic with the bottle bank of two lumpy chainmen, Bill announced that "This'll do", as we reached a small turning area. Despite the remoteness, there was plenty of evidence of human presence in the form of emptied ashtrays, discarded bottles, and a section of flattened heather. (Eddy also found a couple of balloons, but we let this pass.) As I'd told them, here was the peat and its accompanying heather for as far as the eye could see, which, due to the steady wind native to the moor tops and the accompanying wipe-outs of variable cloud-inspired fog, was not very far. Looking around, every detectable feature seemed slightly out of focus. In the circumstances, I could only think "bleak", which ideally matched my outlook at that moment.

"This is nowt like t'peat ah've seen in t'garden shop," said Percy, beginning to comprehend the "free" tag applied to it back in the office. "Theirs is brown and crumbly and squashy and light. This," picking up a clod of sodden, dense and very adhesive black muck, "ain't!"

"Shurrup, and get digging." Bill, on light duties due to his heart history, held the sacks, while three shovels filled them with large lumps of Yorkshire desert. Its appearance didn't improve in the slightest with depth, and the water content was adding to the weight more than Bill had foreseen, judging by the fading of his optimistic expression. Wilf and Percy together began the task of tying up the bags and lifting them onto the roof rack. The pair of them argued constantly in a low mutter, which seemed so in keeping with the desperate surroundings. They did, however, agree that any idea of tying down the sacks was unnecessary, due to the stability that their weight gave them. During an essential break for breath, Wilf's eye blankly surveyed the wilderness around us. A thought struck him.

"How come," he asked the world in general, "that if all this stuff what we're diggin' up and humpin' into sacks, and are goin' to haul home, and put on us gardens, 'cos it's so bloody wonderful for t'soil; how come that if it's so good, we aren't looking at miles and miles of pansies, and daisies, and crysanths and stuff? How come this ain't a paradise of plants? I 'aven't seen so much as a dandelion while we've bin up here." This struck a chord with Percy, who was still rumbling on about summer sunshine, Esholt sewerage and ninepence a sack compared with wet and cold, twenty yards of freezing visibility and for free.

"It's a point," he said. "Tha'd expect it t'be bustin' wi' stuff, if it's so brilliant. Nowt here but miles of manky heather!"

"Look," said Bill, obviously feeling the sympathy of his work-force slipping away, "tha's tekkin' it away to mix with heavy clay soil, aren't thee? So it stands to reason that if tha wants it to look like a bloody seed catalogue up here, then this stuff needs some heavy clay soil bringin' up and mixin' wi'it, dun't it? It's like chewin' a tea bag instead of mixin' it wi' hot water, i'n't it? Neither t'tea bag nor t'water's any cop on its own, but mixed up together they're gradely. If we'd brought a load of clay up wi'us, no doubt we could've planted a few rows of brussels and t'like. Tha's got to mix it wi summat, it's nobbut ower strong on its own. That'll be its pee haitch thingummy," he added, as a dubious afterthought. The labouring detail appeared less than convinced, but we returned to digging and loading, if only to get some feeling back.

Another spate of grumbling bubbled up as loading neared completion, Percy noticing that the clamps holding the roof rack down were "as slack as a ten-pint dick!", and accusations of incompetence blew up against whomever had fastened it on in the first place that morning, declaring that they were lucky to have kept hold of the rack itself, let alone the surveying tackle fastened to it. Wind-numbed fingers grappled with the hard knobs as we tightened up the four brackets hooked under the car's roof gutter.

Having satisfied ourselves regarding the security of the cargo, we found that however much we tried, we could only make room for the eight sacks so far achieved on top, without loading double, which I was more than relieved to find as not being an option. Bill, therefore, took it as being obvious that the remaining ten – ("Ten!" Again the born worrier. "Well, we may as well use all t'bags seeing as how we've brought 'em," urged Bill) – had to be stuffed in the boot, even though five of them hung out a bit. (More than a bloody bit! I thought.)

"Not to worry," said Wilf. "I've a ball of string in mi pocket." (Don't I know it, I thought). "We can tie t'boot lid down."

Loading the humanity proved only slightly less tricky than the peat. All available space was now occupied by a sizeable proportion of the Pennine Range, and the cosiness of we back-seat threesome was enhanced, for the return journey, by three ballast shovels, one of which had to be projected out of the rear window in an ancient jousting position. This by-produced an amount of ventilation which was at once welcome in the crowded atmosphere, and at the same time a little over-refreshing, consisting as it did of cold droplets of damp on a stiff breeze.

Bill took the car back as far as the lane as promised, keeping a thoughtful silence all the while. Normally an efficient, if casual, driver, Bill was concentrating rather more than usual, his nose pressed up against the windscreen. Reaching the relative comfort of the metalled surface, Bill stopped.

"If tha likes, lad, I'll tek it back t'whole way." This simple offer created a sharp surge of fear in me, that electric feeling that runs from your stomach to your throat when you sense a threat. While this offer turned me over, it merely came as a friendly challenge to young Eddy, a chance to handle a bit of a load for a change.

"No, you're alright, thanks, Bill, it's OK, I'll have another go, if you don't mind."

"Well, best take it steady, then. You've got a bit of a load on, you know; you might find it a bit tricky."

"Oh, I'm happy enough, leave it to me. I've done all that holding, using the gears and stuff."

I barely managed to catch "I'm thinkin' more of sort of turnin'" from Bill, meant privately for his pupil, trying to avoid our ears in the back. Mine were needle sharp by now. "It won't quite handle t'same as before. Tek it slow for a while till you get t'feel on it."

And off we set on the return journey to the office back down in the valley, and the security of town. Meanwhile, I was preoccupied with the menace I'd detected in Bill's concern; it may have just been me worrying in my usual way, but Bill's hypnotic stare at the road ahead was having all sorts of nervous repercussions within. Not that the rest of the company appeared to share my fears; Wilf and Percy were now engaged in a jovial discussion about the apparent merits of free peat against pricey sewage in the average garden, based on the drying samples lodged in their fingernails. This was only marred by the dawning of possible difficulties, yet to be solved, in getting their personal stake from office to home. Bill was not joining in, and I noticed him stiffen up as he advised Eddy to take the next left, to keep them off the busier roads. Eddy dutifully geared down in a faultless manner, and applied just the right amount of left-hand-down at just the right place.

The car went straight on.

"Lean forrard!" shouted Bill, bringing the whole back seat to a unison of alarm. As we shot upright, and over the seats in front – taking two shovels with us, and in the process adjusting the mirror into a position which would take account of low-flying aircraft – the front wheels of the car made spasmodic, but significant contact with the road, and the left turn was achieved in an unconventional series of short, sharp straights. That was it for me! Mild panic took over to varying degrees. Eddy, not yet fully understanding the problem, and obviously suffering shock at Bill's scream of panic in his left ear, sobbed a single sob. Bill did a panoramic survey to check for any official-looking witnesses, Percy and Wilf just shut up, and I, with recollections of my first-year degree course in civil engineering (principle of the lever) coming vividly to mind, announced that that was far enough, and that we would be dumping half of the load from the see-sawing boot. I was ignored.

"OK, lad, we'll change places," said Bill. "Don't fret, it's nowt tha did wrong, it's just a shade ower light on t'front, that's all!" Eddy was enthusiastic about taking up a passenger role now, no one having explained to him the art of steering in fresh air, and both front seats emptied in unison, an action which brought home to us in the tail section the true situation, as the road ahead slowly disappeared, to be replaced by sky.

Just to shut me up, Bill agreed to take a couple of bags out of the boot and shove them up front. This didn't go down too well with Eddy since it meant him nursing them all the way back. By the time the party hit town, and the busier traffic, a collective approach had been achieved, displaying admirable teamwork. Whenever Bill called out "Turning", we, the ballast in the back, would heave ourselves forward as far as the unit which we and the shovels had become would allow, then by swaying back and forth we were managing to provide Bill with a pulsing purchase on the road, sufficient to achieve the thru'penny bit effect of cornering. As we were pulling into the yard outside the offices, I'd to reluctantly admit to sense some degree of enjoyment, though I'd have argued strongly with Robert Louis Stevenson's theory about travelling hopefully being a better thing than arriving. He was probably on his donkey, not in a packed car, perfectly balanced on its back axle, rearing up and sniffing the sky. All sorts of relief accompanied my efforts towards disentangling myself from three shovels, two grumbling bundles and the unwinding ball of string, which had escaped Wilf's pocket during the journey's exertions.

Never more so than now, we agreed, did the railway owe us an unscheduled mug of tea, though considering the purpose and benefits it would see from the expedition, BR might have had other ideas. It was a nuisance, then, when the phone rang with a message from Hilary to tell us that Elliot Milner's meeting had been adjourned, and that he was coming through to pick up the car after all. This was not of great import, as the journey from York to Huddersfield took the best part of an hour, so we finished off our tea in comfort before tackling the unloading.

"Get it out the boot, first," said Bill, as we returned refreshed to the task of offloading. "Then I can start samming t'muck up – it'll stop yon whinging article from fretting himsen to death!"

Yon whinging article was far more occupied in finding a good storage point for the peat, so that it didn't prompt immediate investigations on our leader's return. I settled on the side wall of the PWay Office, and cleared a space. Offloading the boot was no great problem, and the car resumed a more alert posture as each sack was removed. Attacking the roof load was a little more tricky, since slinging sacks up was proving to have been an easier job than lifting them down (dragging the first, to see it steadily tear down the side, confirmed the need for a more careful approach). The operation was not helped by the passing of Brian Bolus, telecoms engineer, one of those folk who knows everything about everything.

"Where've you been collectin' that lot from?"

"From some scientific horticultural experimental laboratory specialisin' in soil and vegetable compatibility trials, t'other side of Meltham," replied Bill, surprising even himself.

"Bollocks," retorted Bolus, "that's straight off t'moors. Wasted your time there, you know. That stuff's lethal! It's raw acid, that is. Another hour in that boot and it 'd've burnt a way straight through t'floor. You want to forget it."

"Bugger off," invited Bill. "It just wants a drop of lime mixing in. Right as rain in no time!"

"Well, don't say I didn't warn you," replied Brian's back, as he wandered away.

"Wouldn't dream of it," replied Bill turning back to the matter in hand. "By, gum," he exclaimed, "we've ended up wi' a fair bit, haven't we?"

I'd just that moment been thinking the same. What had seemed a fleabite into the moorland, now took on massive proportions up against the side of the office, and the practicalities of sharing it out and carrying it home were beginning to hint at the impossible. The last bag had been dumped, and I was rolling a small lump of peat that had escaped in my hand, musing on the thoughts of Chairman Bolus, and working out ways of testing it, with a view to toning it down if necessary.

I suddenly cottoned on to a silence around me, a lack of grumble and mutter, and the back of my neck went bristly, cold and damp. I turned back to the car to see a sheepish-looking line-up of Bill, Wilf and Percy, along the side. "What's up?" I asked, returning to mild panic.

"Nobbut a slight problem, Mike, nowt to get excited about!"

This scared me more than a straightforward statement that the car had died a sudden death.

"What's up, then?"

Bill looked at his companions, who seemed united in voting him spokesman.

"Tha remembers as how that rack were a bit slack, while we were up theer? Well, seemingly it weren't until we'd got it loaded up that it started to work loose, what wi' t'extra weight pressin' it dahn, an' all, like. We really could've done wi' slackenin' it off a bit, afore we started to unload, tha sees…"

I could see. Where each bracket, now relieved of the load, was clamped onto the car roof, the gutter had bent neatly up in a graceful curve.

Reloading the peat until the fastenings could be unlocked worked well, but the resulting sight of an undulating roof, if anything, looked worse, once the rack had been lifted clear. Ten minute's amateur body repair work did little to improve matters.

The peat lay forgotten in its pile, way into the following summer. Half-hearted attempts to carry it home had given way to apathy, partly because all traces of the sacking had, as forecast, rotted away under the influence of the rich acids, and an orange stain was spreading from the heap through the stonework. The strength of the acid content had become patently clear during an experiment involving baking powder and Eddy's mug. Two years passed before the steady rains washed enough of the burning chemicals out of the heap for a solitary stem of rosebay willow herb to struggle clear, produce a twelve-inch spindly stem, and then keel over.

No. 23, Wellington Street, Leeds

Wherever you might have found yourself on the railway, whichever direction you might have looked, at whatever so-called level you might have been mixing, you could guarantee that within the assembled company you would be faced with a character; or was it just me that seemed to attract them like fluff to a navel? Originals, mavericks, eccentrics, defectives, or plain straightforward barmpots. Cyril Robinson, for example, could be standing, as he usually was, in the preserved thirties of the sixties' General Office, bent over a high clerical desk, when he'd suddenly yawn loudly, announce he was bored, and stretch out his arms in perfect synchronisation with his trousers dropping to the floor. This was followed by a heavy sigh, and a return to work without bothering to make any repairs. (Cyril was one of my great heroes, signing letters "R Supards", a signature that he bequeathed to me on his retirement.) Yet it wasn't until the Leeds District Engineer's mid-seventies' flit to Hutton House that I realised how, up to then, every building I'd ever worked in had also been a character. This move dumped us in the totally drab personality-free atmosphere of a "modern" building, a term of condemnation in itself.

Architects are sad pieces of nature, either totally daft, or depressing clones of banality. Railway ones crawled around amongst the second lot. When given a new office to fit out, they tended to model it on the pathos they saw all around them and would come up with a carpeted concrete field, sectioned into working units by canvas screens. Everything about Hutton House was about as stimulating as a hospital waiting area and completely void of hidden potential, from the lack of footsteps to the tiled sterility of the toilets. (Yes, they were toilets, now, soon to become loos! Gone were the traps, bogs, lavs, thunder boxes, khazies and shit'oils of old, replaced by Men's rooms and Ladies' rooms.) Whilst once investigating a break-in through the window of the Ladies one morning, I discovered the inside to be a tiled edifice, with boxed-in basins, green soap and a carpet on the floor. A powder room of great intimacy. The Gents, on the other hand, was dedicated to male bonding, almost open unto the fields, affording a standard of privacy one step back from a seat in a football crowd. Here you had to stand in stark exposure, instead of enclosed by three sides of porcelain, and be expected to pee to order into large ashtrays clamped to the wall, at the same time rigidly fighting off any neighbourly curiosity. Privacy means comfort that encourages relaxation and accuracy, and a better idea of when the job's completed. Beware light-grey flannels in a modern urinal. Not to mention the tension – many is the bladder that's come out of the unbounded wastes almost as full as it was when it went in.

All the way through Hutton House, ceilings were hung low to conceal all the things we'd come to accept as symbols of civilisation – dangling light fittings, fibre-wrapped plaited telephone lines in rusting conduits, impromptu washing lines, mouse runs, dust-coated spiders' construction lines, heating paraphernalia and assorted remnants of Christmas Past. Almost-new planed and varnished furniture replaced our old carved and undulating desks. Admittedly, we did have the novelty of swivelling chairs. But these could bite back as they turned out to be the last coffin nails following dinnertime jolly-juice sessions, and they were a fairground sensation that soon wore off. The mere action of a relaxed lunchtime typist leaping into your lap sent the thing spinning, launching a potential grapple into uncertain orbit. In the more sober occasional work-breaks, you might try kneeling up on them, and reaching out to the top edge of your drawing, like you used to do with confidence on the sturdy timber baulks of yesteryear, only to find your bum heading one way and your hand and drawing pen going the other in compensation. Results on the drawing board could be incredibly modernistic – almost like an architect's plans with added imagination.

There were perforated pegboards covering the walls, decorated with busy little job tickets and multicoloured pegs representing the plant required for each. A bit of keen dusting by the cleaners at night could basically rearrange jobs, placing unsuitably large cranes in tight-fitting tunnels. All this was taking the place of punctured plaster and peeling paint – weathered cream above slime green, separated by a fluctuating black line, which had been entrusted to a decorator suffering delirium tremens. It took us weeks, fuelled by nostalgia, before we reduced the new accommodation to a reasonably habitable slum, but no amount of personalisation could install character into it.

It was about then that I realised how lucky I'd been through the seventeen working years since leaving school. From that noble Edwardian building, I meandered into higher education at Bradford. I went along prepared for the serried ranks of lecture theatres, the communal campus and the sophistication of the union bar and café, and experienced the shock of finding myself attending some lectures in an old vicarage, of a socialising area made up of a main arterial road and four tributarial back streets, and of having to use an end terrace house for sophisticated debate. Upstairs in the house was the only catering within a bus ride, while down below was a fume cupboard occupied by a dozen or so habitual union activists majoring in smog production, with reparation of the ozone layer as a sideline. In fact the whole college was a haphazard collection of chance enclosures and reclaimed housing. But, during my first two years there, it was gradually being surrounded by the construction site of a new university, which was to slowly engulf and squeeze out the character of the old.

Take the old vicarage as an instance of buildings having character, hardly converted any further than having it de-vicared and replacing him with blackboards, except there was the wall. This was an exciting feature at the end of a corridor that had once led to the servants' quarters, now a grace and favour caretaker's flat. The linking doorway had been bricked up, but the fanlight above it remained, in dirty stained glass. By means of inventive construction work (a credit to us pupal civil engineers) using the old cupboards and assorted boxes strewn up and down the corridor, we were able to climb up to the fanlight for a direct view into a most intimate portion of the converted flat. Much lingering innocence was finally shed during observations made there in lecture breaks. This all came to a peak of learning for me and four of my course mates when, one day, we were straining to see through the coloured glass. We were just able to pick out the sixth member of our set on the other side, seemingly getting treatment from the caretaker's wife for whatever he must have phoned in sick with that morning.

Thick sandwich courses like the one we were on, allowed us eighteen months out of college between the second and final years "to experience practical situations, absorb civil engineering practices, and hone our intercommunication skills", according to the syllabus. In my case, the jam in the middle marked my start with BR, where I found myself designing bridge reconstructions that umpteen predecessors had designed before me, at the same time honing the art of always appearing to have something to do, and learning how to swear. All this before rejoining my similarly experienced mates for our final year at Bradford, in the now completed new university buildings. Here was another environmental shock for me, with the pristine surroundings invoking nothing but nostalgia for the old, decrepit and inadequate dump we'd left behind such a short time before.

Mind you, it was during that year and a half at the York Headquarters of the North Eastern Region of BR, that I was introduced to the exotic locations that the railway could offer up as a working environment. I turned up on my first day with a neat little document bag, a wrap-up bulging in one corner, and with orders to report to the original York Station buildings, replaced some eighty years previously by the splendid "new" station. It was there that I discovered the railway's great skill for making do.

My first proper office was a U-shaped shed stuck on the track bed in the area of the old station buffers. The middle sidings and platform lines had been shortened to accommodate it, and you stepped inside off the old station copings. You'd expect to get a fairly close view of trains when you joined the railway, but I hadn't bargained on how close. These sidings were still used for the storage of rail wagons, so the outlook could change during shunting from one of the reclaimed station buildings, to the sides of a high wagon, less than a foot from the window. There, on hot sunny afternoons, a distinct atmosphere was created as you worked alongside wagons of creosoted timbers, recently emptied cattle trucks or empty fish vans. It combined to put you in mind of everything you'd ever stepped in. My first desk was in a section built along one of the platform lines, looking out at the base of the U, which was built along the back of the repositioned buffer stops. Apparently, news that the sidings had been slightly pruned to accommodate our shanty town hadn't fully sunk in with the shunters who used them. I'd get a hint of this when the odd train of wagons passed my window at an alarming ten miles an hour, before hitting the new buffers, causing them to jump backwards up against the delicate walls of the Drawing Office. A permanent way gang would turn up next day to haul them back into position, without ever really bothering to fix them securely, as this was obviously a waste of time. After nine months I was moved into this base section of the U and experienced two such shunting miscalculations from the new and far more exciting angle of head-on rather than merely en passant. To remain seated with two-hundred tons of wagons coming straight at you, is like trying not to laugh when everyone else is. It all made for useful experience in gaining respect for trains when we had to go out on the track.

So, once I'd done with university, I settled into my first working home with any feeling of permanence, the Leeds District Office. I later made my move a year after to what was to turn out as my spiritual heaven in the bizarre water-tank offices amongst the sidings at Huddersfield Station, but I was still linked with this new home in Leeds, a pivotal point for my next fifteen years. Up to then, character in buildings was something I only appreciated in retrospect, but here it hit me from Day 1.

★

No. 23, Wellington Street, Leeds, can still be seen today, but only as a frontage to a redeveloped interior. This fascia, presumably listed, always looked incongruous, but never more so than it does now, as the new floors don't even try to line up with the tops and bottoms of the windows in the outside walls. All traces of character have now been removed by dedicated specialists, much as they do with asbestos.

In the old days, when it was something you could be proud to be part of, the interior was a thing of the most extraordinary ugliness with a quite haphazard layout. It was built in the shape of a square polo mint, with one edge, the main front facing Wellington Street, being considerably thicker than the other three. Ground floor and first completely covered the site, with the central hole of the doughnut starting at the second, and rising to the rafters of the fifth, where the Drawing Office was housed. Thus was created an artificial outer wall with windows facing into a deep well, drastically reducing privacy, and minimising ways of getting squat out of the way. If you can think along the lines of druids gathering at Stonehenge on Midsummer's Day, we at the top of No. 23 would comment on the midday sun reaching a certain spot down on the first floor roof at that one hour of that one day of the year. Decor to this internal shaft was in early-Dulux Dismal Black with a Hint of Desolate Grey. It was lined in timber panels covered in dull black tar with matching paint to the window frames, all set off by dramatic white strokes of seagull crap. (From the rows of minute lavatory windows at the back of the building we looked out onto Leeds City Station, built over the River Aire – the point of origin of the incontinent gulls.) This colour scheme of the central shaft ensured that the miseries of the Drawing Office could be passed down the rest of the building. But it was the room at the top where the extremes of weather-inspired discomfort peaked, under its iron truss and glass infill roof.

Looking totally daft, and completely out of place even then, was the Doric-columned entrance off Wellington Street. It surrounded a kind of dignity-reducing airlock of two sets of double wooden doors preparing you for a minute lobby which more than just hinted at the squalor lying above and beyond. Two features met you here: a staircase leading up into a 40-watt gloom and a flanking lift shaft.

Oh yes, and the mobile doormat, sometimes kicked into the lift or more often out into the street. Finding it engaged on this second journey would mean that one pair of doors were either stuck part open by it, or jammed shut with the mat rearing up halfway between the two sets. Alternatively, should the mat be heading inland, it would be holding the lift doors permanently open, allowing the contraption to default to its norm of "Out of Order".

Just sticking with the double doors for a moment; sturdy outers in a one-time heavy pine colour comprised of eight small panels each, and plain flush inners, neither pair sun-bleached as they faced north, but variously affected by years of multi-directional weather. All four doors would be clamped back open to the world in summer, in order to allow dust, traffic fumes and disorientated drunks to float up the staircase. For the rest of the year just the outer street doors might be left open. So the inner ones were in constant use, with the result that the hinges suffered a lingering death, and new ones had to be installed. Thinking in terms of the sometimes trapped doormat, rather than nailing the damn thing down, our powers hit on the idea of having the new swing doors made from invisible thick glass, so that you could look through them to see why they wouldn't open. This led to an unfortunate incident one autumn afternoon, when Ozzie Dean, an uncoordinated and tragically athletic clerk, was making a flying getaway down the stairs, two or three at a time. He completely remodelled an already distinctive nose, by mistaking the new closed glass doors for the ever-open old summer ones. Credit where it's due, though, to the Railway's material standards for the purity of the glass and the fact that it came out of the collision completely unscathed.

Action in the lobby would peak just before half past eight each morning, when the normally adequate entrance would be clogged way beyond its capacity. If you couldn't squeeze in beyond the inner doors, you knew you'd no chance of making the first lift. This desperate piece of equipment was a shuddering crate with theoretically sliding doors moving apart at both ends of it. One set operated on the ground floor, and the opposing pair served the various floor levels from two upwards – first in, first out sort of thing. When the lift arrived amidst groans, creaks, and disturbing metal to metal contact noises, the eight-twenty-nine panic invariably resulted in the front of the queue being catapulted into the cubicle, as soon as the doors jerked open and hard up against the control buttons at the far end. As a result anything intentionally programmed into the lift was of little significance following the random stabs already punched in from brolly handles, bulging pockets, wild elbows or those mysterious stiff lumps which used to be dotted about the person of older females. It was amazing – the transformation in the average male clerk in the space of just two yards. Out in the street, he'd raise his hat to a female colleague, with a polite greeting, whereas two paces later she became a mere bouncing board in his attempts to make the earliest lift. There was never quite the same congestion at night, since the stairs were a preferred ever-reliable option for the down direction.

Those lift doors were full of menace. They had much in common with the Great Whites of *Jaws* fame, but pre-dated the film by years. While they shared the ambitions of that big fish (known here in the North as a "special") they didn't have the smooth efficiency of the famous snapping jaws. In some respects they were superior. Where the shark would impulsively slam its cheek muscles into action, closing in a smooth high-speed snap, the lift doors came together in a series of angry jerks with speeds varying from zero to thrusts well in excess of its role model. Maybe a strategically applied jar of Vaseline would have helped, but this would have been yet another example of modern technology destroying character. What all this meant in practice was that high-speed last-minute entries were variously quite harmless or bluntly amputational.

There was a cast metal sign in the lift on which Messrs Otis recommended a maximum capacity of twelve. This had long suggested to us that the cattle crate had been diverted to us in transit from its intended location in a pygmy embassy. No way could you get twelve inside in any conventional manner. Once, out of purely experimental interest, the stated maximum was achieved by some lubricated clerks, taking advantage of minimal summer clothing. The record was contested since only five were actually in contact with the floor, and two of the number were being spectacularly held head-high and horizontal.

Wet days were particularly tiresome. While those at the head of the mob struggled to close umbrellas, they were under extreme pressure from behind, where the second front had the added incentive to get in out of the rain. Thus the lift would suck in an initial load of collapsed or still partially inflated brollies, the owners now wetter than they would have been without them, together with various component parts of the second wave in the form of unrelated limbs. Dignity was the inevitable loser on such occasions, with the exception of when The Engineer appeared.

J A Lewis, Esquire was a short unimpressive Welshman, once removed, easily mistaken as just a gap in a crowd. He was of limited vocabulary, particularly devoid of words like "good" and "morning", but he was the boss, and was always addressed as "Sir". Thus the appearance of JAL amongst the mass of early morning humanity would inspire a dash for the stairs, rather than sharing a ride. A journey alongside Him up to His office on the third, in the confines of the lift, would seem to take an age, being as it would be, enhanced by His oppressive and silent presence. Being the last of the chauffeured engineers, Lewis should have warranted a personal chauffeur-cranked lift, but instead, for a brief spell of every day, he was obliged to not only use the same confined crate as the common populace, but to have to share it with them as well. For thirty seconds his dignity slumped nearly as much as the morale of his companions.

It was also a worry about the thing that bits kept dropping off it. There's a draining of confidence about getting into a lift and finding yourself treading on the alarm button which has fallen out onto the floor. You get a crisis of faith when such things happen, usually focused on the strand of wire holding the wretched box in the air. When things that are visible can be rejected, you begin to wonder…

As you might expect, the lift suffered the usual idiosyncrasies common to its kind, and was often declared "Out of Order" by means of a grubby sign and sink-plug chain which someone regularly hung from a purposely fixed hook. The very fact that this hook existed at all only went to underline the depressing inevitability of frequent breakdowns, an impression enhanced by the fact that the notice itself was in manufactured etched steel. At such times, the stairs were rediscovered in the up direction, without the stimulation of trying to avoid Lewis. Climbing the stairs could prove as big an adventure as using the lift.

★

Each floor level had a small landing outside the lift doors, with the obligatory single light bulb. Some of these might even be working, though they seemed to have fairly short lives and observed exceptionally long periods of mourning before being replaced. This meant that intermittent stretches of almost total darkness could be encountered on the stairs. On these occasional platforms of gloom it was necessary to locate and avoid the single chair gracing each landing. These were there as a concession to the many bronchial and cardiac cases who found the stairs a major challenge, especially first thing in the morning. They also came to form the various camp sites populated by Stanley Mole.

Here we had a persistent Save-Your-Souls Evangelist, a Support-My-Cause Protestor and a Justice-for-the-Third-World Campaigner, all in one aggressively austere form. Oh, a pleasant enough bloke when talking about trivial matters, like the job he was there to do; jovial to borderline crackpot, in fact. A splendid ambassador for the railway to have as a communicator with outside parties like the Electricity, Gas and Water Authorities, which was amongst his duties, up to the point of parting company with them, where he might start handing out the odd leaflet, or try selling the latest bit of native junk designed to lighten the lot of his fellow man. He was blindly devoted to whatever mission currently appealed to him.

Overall, Stanley's ultimate intent was to save the world, and it has to be recorded that now having the benefit of forty years hindsight, he appears to have been pretty well successful in his aim, for here we still are. His journey towards his laudable goal had loads of side roads, like selling coffee and tea directly from African farmers to us. It cost twice as much as the exploitation goods you found in the shops and either hardly stained the water or tasted incredibly foul. There was a spate of selling ties made by a charitable old soul from his chosen place of worship. The product gave the appearance of having been cut from old curtains, in such a way that one curtain provided material for no more than two ties. These weren't just kipper ties, they were stingrays. We bought them, and wore them for daft. They became an unofficial, but variable, uniform accessory of the Leeds Civil Engineer. They were so wide that you could almost get away without a shirt, and you could recognise an approaching figure as a colleague long before making out his face, but the proceeds went directly to providing blankets for impoverished nomadic tribesmen. It would have been more productive to have sent them the unravaged curtains in the first place, but no! We had to be seen to be making some sort of personal sacrifice.

On the job, Stanley was a relaxed individual, easy-going and thoroughly amicable, but wind him up on human rights, or world famine, and you had a snarling, contemptuous, serious bigot. Campaigning and protesting were deeply ingrained in Stanley, so that any injustices or wrongs that might befall himself or his colleagues received the same treatment that the mooring of a nuclear submarine, manned by undernourished black slaves, in Leeds Canal Basin would have got. If you'd a grievance of any sort, Stanley was the man you should get behind you. Our lift, or rather the frequently static state of the thing, raised the Mole hackles to the point of red mist indignation. Come the third day of any continuous run of lift failures, and Stanley would act out a down-bums protest at every chair on each of the landings as they were reached on his way up to the fifth floor. Each seated demonstration lasted for the period of one article from his paper or magazine, and was accompanied by a grim, choked humming of something like "We Shall Not be Moved". Should there be no light on a particular landing, then he would perform a creditable mime of reading an imaginary piece, while turning up the violence and pitch of his anthem. All those who tramped on past him up the stairs were regarded as traitors to the cause, and would be severely ignored. He would even sit firm as the asthmatic coronary gasps of Drawing Office chief, Kye Bevin, were heard approaching from below, and he would remain solid despite gasped entreaties from his superior to "bugger off upstairs, you dozy do-gooding pillock".

As far as I can make out, the early sixties marked a high point for protest groups, and this was when Stanley Mole was at his fever peak of missionary fervour. It was an intensity that happily waned to an acceptable level in later years, but as it lost its infuriating edge, nostalgia for some of his dafter ventures began to creep in. One of his fads we particularly enjoyed was his running battle with a free American religious glossy magazine called *Plain Truth*. It was a revelation to us that infighting could occur within the missionary ranks, but this magazine seemed to get stuck right up beyond Stanley's flaring nostrils, to the extent that he took to kidnapping bundles of the monthly from Bairstow's newsagent's rack at the station exit. He must have studied them in great depth, in the revolutionary nerve centre he called home, for messages that he found at odds with his convictions of the time, and he would severely censor each copy in thick black pen. Next time he was passing the stand, all the amended copies would be reinstated, and a new batch removed for correction. He was undaunted by the impotent protests of old Bairstow, who could only put up a feeble fight, what with the things being free anyway. There came the morning when Stanley suffered a mild shock as he opened up his latest bagful on reaching his desk. Each copy contained an informal editorial revision slip done in Roneo stencil, bearing the rather personal message in dubious American prose of "Now then, Moley. What do you think you're playing at? Quit frigging about with our bloody magazine, you crusading wazzock! – signed YBA Pratallyerlife – Editor".

On a weekly basis, Stanley circulated a sawn-off Methodist collection box round the office with details of his choice of the week's good cause stuck on its side with Gloy. It was only natural that it should eventually be followed by a tin tea caddy with a rough piranha slot cut in the lid, begging contributions to Stanley Mole's Lobotomy Fund. Naturally the official box was abused outrageously, but still took in a tidy little sum in guilt money. Mole was tolerated most of the year, but would come in for some heart-rending abuse approaching Christmas, when he could be found pouring contractors' goodwill gestures down the sink, alcohol being one of his particular taboos. Time was to temper him, and dilute his attitudes, toning down his fanaticism about the health and wealth of mankind, his call to all nations to abandon everything from nuclear bombs to sharp pointy things, and the promotion of the True God. He settled down to become simply an affable, green, nonconformist teetotaller, operating from a brick garage temple to the east of Leeds, channelling his increasingly moderate campaigns towards the single aim of just saving the world.

All of which explains why we have just tripped over a twilit figure sitting on a staircase, going through the motions of reading a magazine whilst wielding an angry black crayon.

So, our backup lift, this front staircase, had a distinct role in our office life; emergency ups during periods when the lift's central nervous system took a break, and dignified downs in the evenings due to staggered train departure times. It was also held as a legitimate location for chance encounters and conversation as we moved between neighbouring floors. However, this staircase, on which luminous watches acted as beacons and a naturally polished handrail served as white stick and guide dog, was distinctly superior to its counterpart – the backstairs. There may have been a tendency to apply journalistic overkill in all the foregoing, which will now leave us searching for even wilder superlatives in order to describe the far less salubrious, and less legitimate, back door flight. The backstairs made the front flight look like a silver-screen ballroom entrance in comparison.

★

These were placed diagonally opposite in the building's layout, and were more of an internal fire escape than an intended route for regular use. (There was an actual fire escape running down the back of the offices which I never once saw used or tested in fifteen years. It relied for its effectiveness on there never being a fire in the back stack of lavatories, and as far as I saw could only be reached by struggling through minute lattice windows. Yet in a building relying on timber for the majority of its make-up, I suppose the rusted open steps provided some little comfort. At least, given either daylight or minimal street lighting, you didn't have to guess your way down.)

Dedicated mainly to the down direction, the backstairs were used for illicit escapes ten minutes before time, strategic disappearances between floors and away from probing telephones and as a venue for what passed in those days as casual sex. Baretimbered steps, which had been subjected to intermittent, but thunderous, contact, since the necessity for speed required only the occasional leaping touchdowns. Such hammering had left treads rattling loose and desperately hollowed out with protruding knots. No lino tiles, as on the front stairs, although these were a mixed blessing with their curled-edge similarity to traditional BR catering. Stairs creaked and cracked and on selected steps rattled loudly, which was a further obstacle for the rare users performing an upward trek to overcome. These were the really late, not the five minutes occasionals (train delayed – Leeds North points/body in tunnel/driver in personal crisis) who could indignantly refer the authorities to the next day's train log entries for corroborative evidence, when castigated. No, the backstairs (up) were for the morning after, failed alarm, forgot it was Monday, post nine arrivals, who had long run out of expiring grandmothers. Regular offenders like this had arranged a small cupboard of anonymous files and a coat hook at base camp, so that they could suddenly appear from the back doors of the various floors clutching important looking papers, although they had to rely on friends to remove their desk dust sheets earlier. Then there was the sex.

Here, on this darkened adventure playground, a secret grapple could be attempted in relative safety. If it was a welcome coupling, then it could carry on in the knowledge that any intruders had to set off a number of warning alarms, such as ill-hung doors on heavy springs and protesting floorboards rocking about a single nail. Unwelcome advances, and the standard of lighting was such that a later strong denial might generate doubt in the abusee. Contacts could be grossly intentional, but appear later in the light as completely accidental. A comprehensive knowledge of individual perfumes and footsteps was essential, otherwise you could find yourself exploring a structure owing much to and resembling in many ways, a dead whale. As to the lighting, it was from this staircase that replacement bulbs were taken for the front one. In danger of digressing again, it was on these stairs that the alien Thorpe-Gardiner had been dealt with.

Alien because he was simply out of place and out of depth amongst the likes of us; he just didn't fit in. Thorpe-Gardiner was never addressed by any of his first names – I don't remember if we knew them even; Thorpey sufficed should any geniality be called for. He was of noble middle-class birth, at a time when such things mattered and showed. This was borne out by the GBST-G embossed briefcase, always well padded out, and a rolled black umbrella. He was even seen to use the brolly now and then, so he wasn't only carrying it for show. It would protect a suit, dark, striped, with waistcoat. All this together with shoes of deep polished black, still having small areas of light-tanned, untouched sole visible on the underside. Real people wore the first clothes to hand in the morning, suits maybe, but not necessarily managing jacket and trousers from the same one. Shoes would be unintentional flip-flops that got wet inside and out if it rained, but not Thorpe-Gardiner. Personal appearance announced character, manners and breeding.

He was a good six feet tall, with his head pressed back into his neck in sergeant-major style, but in Thorpey's case this suggested a deep suspicion as to what might next be thrown in his direction. Black-rimmed spectacles that, as far as we could make out, were of plain glass. They were the sort that suggested studiousness and could well have been a judicious step back from a monocle. That would have meant death in Wellington Street.

I'd once come across Thorpe-Gardiner in my previous life at college. I found him standing alongside me when we were both amongst a party on a visit to the A1, Doncaster bypass construction worksite. All the rest of us were decked out in boots and donkey jackets, collecting more muck than the many site JCBs, but Thorpey was adorned the same as ever, shining from every angle. He almost managed to keep up this appearance right through the day, but for his shoes becoming a trifle tainted with mud.

He was a harmless sort, but his square attitude didn't fit into the roundness of the hole we all worked in, and just by being there he walked a knife-edge every day. His adventure on the back staircase happened on a day when frustration with him in the Drawing Office boiled over. Thorpe-Gardiner had butted into a conversation on class structure by declaring that it was useless trying to hide one's class as it was clearly stamped all over one, marking one out from one's inferiors. This offensive, though perfectly correct observation led to a crescendo of debate, culminating in a frogmarch onto the back staircase. Here an unceremonious stripping and real stamping operation took place with the aid of a tunnel Tilley lamp.

Drawings in those days used to be littered with inscribed forbiddances, disclaimers and circulation limits, and every rubber stamp available was utilised on Thorpey. They were placed as appropriately as possible over his writhing body, using an indelible ink: "Private", "Not For Issue", "Sign Below", "Passed", "Approved", "Superseded", and "Office Copy" were scattered fairly liberally, in part due to the unsettled nature of the recipient, but resignation to fate led to an angry calm, allowing precise placements of "Basis for Discussion", "Unspecified Enlargement" and "Not For Reproduction".

*

We've gone off at a bit of a tangent there, so let's return just once more to the authorised staircase, winding upwards around the lift shaft. Any diverted "lift-closed" victims would pass Mr Mole on whichever landing he was occupying at the moment, eventually attaining the fifth floor Drawing Office, top of the house. It was the obvious location for such a faculty, with its theoretical natural lighting, courtesy of the glass roof, bathing the drawing boards below in the purest of illumination. The artist's garret, and all that. It was therefore a big disappointment to a keen amateur scientist like myself, that this light, which had travelled untroubled some ninety-odd million miles from the sun, should fail so completely in achieving its purpose on arrival. This was solely down to the conditions it encountered during the final five or six yards of its journey.

Its first setback was in being confronted by a measurable depth of industrial grime on the outside of the glass. To my knowledge, based on fifteen years of observations, this muck was rearranged by a cleaning contractor no more than twice during that period. Where the glass did reveal itself, its quality was such that much of the light became confused by the swirling imperfections within, and staggered back out into space. Any remaining beams, intent on completing their mission, had to pierce a thick beige deposit of tobacco waste on the underside, and finally dodge in and out of the exotic structural iron truss layout, with its incidental decorations of cables, pipes, light fittings, rejected sandwiches and general long pieces of stored junk. The best that can be said about the embattled light, as it finally hit the drawing boards, was that it normally managed to enable us to distinguish between night and day, but little more. Side windows, facing out onto the central well of the building, fell short of providing any effective alternative to the roof lighting, since the ceiling pitched down into the central shaft, leaving the windows no more than two and a half feet high, and below the drawing board levels anyway.

Where the roof was a dead loss on the lighting front, it was more than adequate as a source of natural air conditioning. So good, in fact, that a light overnight breeze would dislodge enough fine dust from the trusses to turn any exposed drawings grey. Dust sheets were provided, and reluctantly used. Spreading one over your desk at the end of the day made a clear statement of a day completed, and when still *in situ* after eight thirty next morning suggested lateness. Both situations tempted vetoes from above. Removing them carefully each morning merely collected the dust (the sheets were never ever washed), to be saved until the end of the day, when you were left with the unmarked choice of two ways up to replace them. You could lose out anyway when morning latecomers burst in and whipped their covers off, sending clouds of dust into the filtered rays of the morning sun. Gales would cause a spectacular mess, surpassed only by the side effects of the annual truss-leaping ceremony, usually marking the approach of the three-day Christmas period. This was when 10%-proof gladiators would attempt a journey across the width of the office, swinging by hand from truss to truss. No one ever came to grief, since they were only a matter of six feet or so above the desks, but a year's serious muck would succumb to the vibrations set up by each festive gorilla, and fall en masse onto the desks and chairs below, reducing colourful paper chains to a universal grey.

★

…and now, a Historical Interlude:

On the day that George Stephenson tightened up the final bolt on his Stockton to Darlington railway, and sorted out the last little problem on the *Locomotion*, a niggling leak in the left cylinder, he looked round with complete satisfaction. It had been a successful day, from the moment he had brushed away a couple of large sycamore leaves which had settled on the rails, so getting the locomotive to move, through to the fruitful braking tests, but for the damage to the cow. Little Robert had produced an initial batch of Stockton Supersaver Awayday Returns to Darlington using his John Bull Ticket Kit.

Their refreshment car, hitched immediately behind the *Rocket*'s tender and superbly managed by Mrs George, was proving a money-spinner, serving hot tea direct from the boiler, and bacon and egg sandwiches straight from the shovel. George returned, tired but happy, to his workshop, a rented shed, later to become the third-class refreshment room on Darlington's Up Platform. He had furnished it throughout by himself, although he professed no great skill as a worker in wood. That said, the fitting out had hardly progressed beyond a shelf for the kettle and two nails in the back of the door. One was for his cap, and the other for the 1822 calendar of Messrs Steam-Personifieth-Us, Purveyors of the Finest Railway Paraphernalia for the Discerning Gentry, uniquely illustrated by a 12 x 8 signed print taken from an etching of Lady Hamilton in the buff.

Putting on the kettle, a memento given to him by Jimmy Watt, who had invented it as a by-product while perfecting a steam-driven pump engine, George settled down to fill the remainder of his day by working on his developing skills in carpentry. As the Stockton B&Q Depot had been giving away balks of solid mahogany with every ten own brand rails and fish-plates purchased, he had saved up an impressive haul of timber. Using construction design safety factors of x10, he fashioned the immense slabs of rainforest into long tables, finishing off the tops in professional grade three-eighths linoleum, acquired through his interests in Allied Oilcloths. For seating he utilised rejected sleepers, split lengthways into fours and fixed vertically; these he topped off with an empty cow, stuffed and stretched across the timber ends. Sub-standard rail fixing spikes secured the leather to the frame, with the irregular heads left projecting up to a quarter of an inch above the seat.

In the space of three weeks he had designed and built the furniture which was to end up in the Leeds Civil Engineer's Drawing Office.

A hundred and forty years later, the tables had now rooted themselves to the floors, and remained as solid as ever, whereas the broomstick dowels holding the tall seats together were beginning to work loose.

To achieve the seated position, an average-sized draughtsman was required to leap a little into the air, and hope for a safe landing on the leather, without lacerating himself, or his trousers, on the surrounding nails. Over the years this vertical take-off and landing approach, combined with the shuffling of position needed to line up your eyes with the current working section of the drawing, had caused the leather seatings to stretch and sag. This meant that within the clear outline of the supporting timber frame the seat itself was a depression of an inch or so in the leather material. It was a case of fitting round kegs in square holes as circular bums were presented with severely square accommodation, and sitting back led to a descent into the leather well. Intelligent minds had worked out that the now highly polished leather was creating a similar brilliance on their trouser seats. To counter this, many of the raw shiny surfaces were covered over with regulation railway chequered dusters. Further dusters filled the wells, so that a reasonably flat, padded seat was the result.

Thorpe-Gardiner was particularly faddy at preserving the condition of his trousering, and his allocated chair showed some distinction over those of his colleagues, in that the leather well was filled with a precisely fitting downy pillow, run up by Mama's little woman, and covered over with a piece of purple velvet left over from an evening frock.

This abomination to the senses was central to a near disaster, on one soberly remembered occasion, when The Engineer, J A Lewis (Sir), made one of his bi-annual visits to the Drawing Office. These normally occurred when the lift's foibles combined with The Engineer being distracted, so launching a confused Lewis out into the Drawing Office instead of the more civilised surroundings of his home territory on the third floor. However, visits became more frequent, and with some purpose, during the Thorpe-Gardiner period.

Although T-G spent only nine months in the Leeds Office before moving to the genteel surroundings of York Headquarters, he had the attention of this Engineer more than any other graduate before or since. Rumours of managerial ambitions towards golf club or free-masonry membership flourished, the T-Gs being well placed socially. J A Lewis, a stumpy Welshman of restricted manners, who would hardly stand out at a jumble sale, was not one who exuded suitability at first glance, and would have benefited appreciably from recommendations. On this particular rare visit, Sir was closeted in Kye Bevin's cubicle, a very unusual sight.

Normally a bell code system was used to summon heads of sections down to The Engineer's office that looked out over the front of the building through radiator-to-ceiling windows. (So good was the natural lighting in this office that drawings which had appeared OK up on the fifth floor revealed all sorts of embarrassing blemishes, from the traditional cooling towers produced by damp tea mugs, to inadequately erased messages.) This bell summoning system was controlled by a series of push-buttons on The Engineer's desk, and ambiguities of what distinguished two shorts and a long from one short and two longs, or even three longs, due to a lack of any sense of musical rhythm on Lewis's part, often resulted in a messy logjam of senior bodies assuming they'd been summonsed all at the same time.

Anyway, here He was, and an uneasy silence had descended on the whole floor. We were offering up a communal prayer to delay the return of Thorpe-Gardiner from a site meeting he was at, as it was most undesirable on this particular day, with Lewis on the floor, for T-G to have company of any sort at his desk. While he was out, his chair had been fixed.

No more than a simple substitution of the tailored cushion for a kettleful of water, an undetectable reservoir in the dip of the leather, with the velvet cover stretched back over the top, just clear of the water. We'd carefully arranged this during dinnertime, and then Lewis turned up. If Thorpe-Gardiner were to come back, the Boss was sure to stop and have a word with him, and

T-G was a big enough prat to invite Him to take a seat. Panic sometimes inspires, and it was Eric Gaunt's quick-wittedness that sent him tumbling down to the main door to intercept and divert the intended victim. He made up some tale about The Engineer wanting to see Thorpe-Gardiner in His office as soon as he returned, thus directing the lad into an empty room, and some confusion later. When things had quietened down a bit we drained off the water and resorted to the old favourite of filling Thorpey's rolled umbrella with all the little multicoloured holes collected in the paper punch. We got our reward that evening with a light drizzle, which T-G initially ignored, thus getting slightly damp, before resorting to the brolly and a fallout of confetti, which then stuck to his wet jacket. (A result considered even more successful than the last time we'd used this form of correction – one of the lads who stored his motor scooter at York Station before travelling in to Leeds by train, slung his crash helmet casually up on the luggage rack on his way home, to find that in so doing he had unintentionally decorated the three seats in front, along with their occupants to match.)

★

Any staff getting giddy and thinking along the lines of redecorating the offices in fresh, cheerful colours had only to be pointed towards the floor. Railway issue lino was the antidote to any tendency towards colour, but it was a perfect floor covering for accepting spillages. You've probably noticed that whatever drinks are brewed up in an office, either back then in the lino era, in large enamel pots, or as dispensed today from illuminated and computerised wardrobes, it always spills as a shade of brown. Now this matched the lino of old to perfection; all offices, waiting rooms, signal cabins and public toilets were embellished by this standard shade, not necessarily described simply as light brown.

Lino was a barometer of social activity; the pockmarking being abundant in the areas around the teapot, the towel, the calendar or the young lady tracer, as were the slight variations of colouring. Place mats on all the desks but one were yet another piece of off-cut lino (T-G had a laminated cork mat with an illustration of a cute Yorkshire terrier, occasionally being shagged by a crude mongrel in black drawing ink). Our scraps were regularly scrounged off the joiners called in to replace some of the more worn floor areas. Rather than preventing accidents as was the intention, many were caused by these new sections cut into the old, surrounded as they were by small, but significant, steps. Lino made the office a home, a fact that linked up with many others when the long-awaited move to the new accommodation occurred. Carpet tiles were no substitute; they marked the end of surround sounds, sounds of welcome and sounds of doom. Echoes disappeared, and flying abuse landed like soft dough. They combined with the polystyrene ceilings to bring about the death of ambience.

Yet we up in the old Drawing Office did have sight of opulent carpets. You only had to look out of the side windows. The piled extravagance of the fourth floor for instance, but we're getting ahead of ourselves again.

I might have given the impression that No. 23 consisted of railway offices, full stop, but this was not the case, and in these early days, we occupied only the third and fifth floors. Whatever our vertical neighbours thought of us, we certainly felt inferior to some of them – but only some. I saw a few changes during my fifteen years in and around Wellington Street, but not many as significant as those on the ground floor. Here existed one of Leeds's earliest Chinese restaurants. There was many a rendez-vous with their dustbins, carelessly arranged at the bottom of the rear staircase in the brilliance of the economic illumination. Many a five o'clock train was missed due to an unscheduled examination of the contents of the bins due to this lighting, combined with the steep twisting stairs, excessive speeding and a surprise new bin formation. Long before the court case, rumours abounded, arising from when these chance encounters disturbed an excess of catering-size cat and dog food tins. Further doubts built up along with the aromas that filled the stairway when the back doors were left open. We developed an innocent notion that the well-heeled were invited to take their pets along to eat. Thankfully, judge and jury were more worldly-wise, and the restaurant was closed down, to be replaced by a drawing office supplies shop of all things. We called in once, and only once, to enquire about the cost of replacing the ancient high chairs with steel swivellers.

Immediately above the Chinese was a carpet showroom of deep mystery. It had no access from the lift, so it was never likely that any personnel from the showroom would bump into railway staff on a regular basis, but no one was ever seen entering or leaving the door onto the stairs, and the place appeared forever closed. Maintaining our cosmopolitan theories, we had the place down as a smuggler's den, where illegal Asian immigrants were concealed in rolls of carpet.

Only slightly more active was the time-clock establishment on the second, and that only because it was the first floor to be visible when looking down the wall of death of the central well. Eric Gaunt had us convinced that it was a place where you took cats and dogs to be doctored. He was sure that such a surgery existed on the premises on the basis of some incorrectly addressed mail that had once found its way into the messenger's box. The second floor was, he reasoned, the likely site. His conviction grew stronger as we pointed out that all that was visible through the windows was a mass of time-clocks of every size and shape. There was even an organised display just within the doorway, off the stairs, of standalone and brass wall-mounted clocks. Putting all this to him, he responded by asking us just what we'd put on display if we were running a cat and dog neutering shop. One man was encountered, now and then, chatty only to the extent of a grunt sounding like "Good Morning", and he was hardly missed when the expanding Civil Engineer's department eventually took over that floor as well to house the Works element. Ah, but encounters between the railway and the fourth floor were very different, inevitable, and at times sensational.

It was home to a branch of a northern fashion house, in what seemed, from our point of view on the fifth, the most unlikely of locations. Looking around us, we could not see any way it might lend itself to being a place of glamour. Yet, despite having the same floor layout as us, and only a slightly different outlook, it managed to take the railway's accepted basics and transform them into a fairy-tale world. There was one occasion when three of us had to call on the fashion house, to discuss the unfortunate disintegration of part of their ceiling. This was not caused, as we explained at the time, by us testing some advanced surveying equipment on the floor above, but rather by the positioning of a table tennis board following the move of part of the office to railway-owned property within the station.

Going through the door on the fourth floor was every bit as dramatic as Judy Garland's "Wizard of Oz", stepping from the black and white of home into the Technicolor world of Oz.

There was exotic curtaining falling from lavish pelmets above the windows. You could only see it as a pretty edging from the outside, but it effectively diverted the internal eye from the monstrosity of the central well, and was reinforced by tumbling net curtains. A variety of decorative impedimenta kept visitors from getting too close to the windows, all combining to avoid them catching sight of us, the scruffy neighbours above and below. Their carpets had to be surfed through, though I fantasised an underlay of standard light-brown lino beneath. And there was furniture! Not just reconditioned jetties and reshaped barn doors, but real furniture. Telephones had handsets connected in neat curly plastic, instead of fraying purple/brown plaited twin flex, and they finished at the desk and didn't send out tentacles all over the floor. What staff we saw were dressed in a manner suggesting that they had never worn those outfits before, and would not be wearing them for work again. Everything just oozed posh without appearing o-t-t. Being sandwiched between railway floors rather obliged them to acknowledge us in the lift, but it was not grudging, and only happened between late arrivals of eight thirty railway and early nine o'clock fashion staff. But then, there were the fashion show days every six months.

You could tell straightway when these were upon us by the appearance of a chattering group of very presentable young ladies, arriving in the thick of the railway's morning lift assault, and filling the lift with erotic fragrances for the rest of the day. Here were today's models, not the coat-hanger jobs of later years, but real women, with lumps on them, especially when in the lift. Bravest among the lads would leap in ahead of them, to turn back in abject apology, both parties knowing that passing contact would be unavoidable on arrival at the fourth. Failing to gain this initiative, Plan B was to assist the young ladies to locate the correct button, ricocheting off various intervening points of interest. Treated with this mild sort of sexual harassment, the girls would demonstrate their professionalism, and leave many a young buck blushing, and occasionally in bollock-trauma, if contact had gone one step too far. Whatever else, the girls were always pleasant, and smiled constantly, not even changing expression as they stepped out at four with the lift doors closing on significant calls of "See more of you later!" They knew the score, and revelled in it.

My first show was a bit of a non-starter, due to my ignorance of procedures. At five minutes before ten o'clock, there was a spontaneous movement towards the small fifth floor side windows overlooking the well, right along one wing of the office. All eyes were trained on the small corner changing room where the girls quite happily dived out of one frock and into another, occasionally waving up to the audience, who would wave back, but withdraw slightly with the embarrassment of the acknowledgement. Blatant was one word for it, especially as it was apparent that the girls had deliberately pulled back the net curtains, on the face of it to improve the lighting for make-up checks. A northern fashion house required nothing more of their models than a strip down to bras and slips, but it was the sensuousness of the removing and discarding which raised the spirits and cockles of the lads. Nadine, the younger tracer, would occasionally demand a glimpse, but this was to look at the clothes, not something the lads could relate to. Her older, senior colleague would pass by, sniffing loudly, with threats of reprisal before noticing Kye Bevin, in his cubicle, also flattening his nose against the glass. Disciplinary reporting was unnecessary as the usual train of events would be discovery by the fashion house staff, abrupt replacement of the nets, a return to drawing boards, and five minutes later, the arrival of a red-faced Chief Clerk together with a well-worn copy of the riot act.

★

Apart from the lighting, our working conditions in the Drawing Office were only tolerable twice a year, late spring and early autumn. Should nature defy the railway laws that stipulated the precise beginning and end of winter, demonstrated by the dates when boilers had to be turned off or on, then even these two periods became uncomfortable. Uncontrollable radiators worked valiantly, and some degree of burns might be suffered by touching them in mid-winter. However, once radiated, this heat shot straight up and out through the single panes of roof glass, only slightly delayed by the lagging of grime. Rain was only a problem if the wind came from the north, or the west… and the east, come to think of it. At such times it could seek out slight flaws in the sealing of the roof components. Wind combined with rain left exotic patterns of soot swirls on all surfaces, any bit of which could be confidently entered for the Turner Prize for Art. Ventilation, or "the bleeding draught" as it was known locally, was via the small side windows overlooking the well. In summer, these could be swung about a central horizontal pivot to provide a placebo of ventilation, but nothing in practical terms. An atmosphere prevailed of dust, combined with humanity and incinerated tobacco, enhanced on occasions by overactivity in the Chinese restaurant or inactivity alongside an abandoned gas ring. For intermittent entertainment there were the birds.

We'd sparrows and tits fluttering in and out of the well in summer, seeking out small flies in the crevices of the wall cladding. We'd watch the blue tits, and occasional coal tits, noted as acrobats, hovering, probing and hanging from nothing, in their quest for some variety to their diets. Sparrows managed in their way, but looked wooden against the gyrations of the smaller birds; however for afters the bolder ones would drop to the well bottom, and clear up after our sport with the gulls. Having the River Aire flow past the rear of the block, before tumbling through the arches beneath the station, we'd flights of seagulls passing overhead now and again. By turning our small windows entirely over, the birds could sometimes be enticed down towards the shaft by well-timed fists of bread pieces. Once caught, they would wheel around just above the well, swooping whenever more chunks were torn off an old loaf. While we would wonder at the grace and ease with which they caught the bread before sweeping back down to the river, we were more interested in their by-product. By luring them close to the walls before banging the windows shut, we found we could worry them enough to cause them to crap all over the lower windows.

Space on the fifth started to appear as our lease approached termination and with the removal of odd sections to the station offices. This growing space we used at dinnertimes as a sports room. Centrally we had the table tennis which we had to nudge around until plaster falls on the fourth were minimised. It was set up over a blank in the lino from where the ancient slab desks had been ripped out. We found the games exciting in many ways, mainly due to the eccentricities of an exposed office floor, and its occasional lino holes, conduit runs and morning spills. Local rules governed hazards such as the low ceiling trusses and sloping roof, but none so bizarre as the boiler failure days in winter when rotational six-, seven- or eight-aside games were common just to keep ourselves warm. These invariably caused problems on the floor below, and never ran their course. Only men played games – that is until a young innocent miss from the Typing Pool Four announced that she would like to enter the Christmas table tennis knockout. She was a happy girl, convinced of purity in sport. This, mixed with her attempts to keep well up with the mini-skirted fashions of the day made for an unusually high spectator interest. Unlike most tennis audiences, eyes remained glued to one end of the table, and when it came to retrieving a ball for the lady, there was not a gentleman present to interfere with the game by offering to pick it up, rather allowing her do it for herself.

Crowd participation, combined with a most unlikely action game – a miniature ice rink, with players controlled on spinning rods – made for a Sports League. This was enhanced by dominoes, a very serious two by four snooker table, and a Yorkshire dartboard, with no trebles. Life was becoming really pleasant in Wellington Street, when everything changed. Only this dinnertime activity transferred well to Hutton House, in that we took over part of the windowless basement there. Recently refurbished, these offices, a good half mile further away from the station, came as a dream change for the sports activities, but that's as far as real improvement went.

Here, our small waist-high windows were exchanged for double-glazed walls. High glass ceilings and dust-laden trusses gave way to low warming polystyrene insulation panels. Light bulbs and green tin shades became concealed high-intensity fluorescent tubing. Drab walls were abandoned for pastel-papered room dividers. A haphazard timber yard, recognised as the office furniture changed into identifiably individual desks with swing chairs and stools. Draughty unheated lavatory cubicles were lost to warm, even hot, sealed rooms, with clean closets and hygienic wall-slung urinal bowls. Noise became muffled and almost unnoticeable, insults were lost in transit, and phone sites were extended to a host of convenient extensions, and the ripped, irregular, scruffy, stained lino was transformed into smooth, tight-fitting blue carpet tiles. Character was replaced by... (?)

Lavatory

"Y'know... when you really think about it... look at it from all angles... take everything into consideration... weigh up the pros and cons... all other things being equal... all in all... what with one thing and another... this is downright bloody boring!"

"This" was sunbathing. Not on some sun-drenched beach with palm trees and cocktail waiters waving above you, the sun streaming down and bouncing off the hot sand so as to strike you both directly and on rebound; no monotonous scrunching of the surf in the distance. Nor was it even the parochial heat of an upper-mid latitude sun piercing a bitter easterly to give the unprotected body a sensation of local heat amidst general cold while lying on irregular shingle, with the rattle of beer and Coke cans tossed back and forth on the edge of the incoming English tide. No, this was lying part-supported on a plank, thirty feet in the air, over the rim of a large water tank in the middle of Huddersfield. This sun was making one of its rare effective piercings of the colourful industrial West Riding atmosphere, and apart from the muted roar of traffic down below, there was only the occasional splash of stones plunging into the tank, delivered by two playfully deranged chainmen from ground level, with a view to dislodging myself or my current workmate, Vince Bell.

"Besides which," I added, "there's that bloody awful smell again. Have you copped it yet?"

I pulled myself up and looked around the PWay Yard, as if whatever I'd detected would manifest itself in a more tangible form. Vince remained in the rather unique position which he'd had to adopt; one that, though basically horizontal, could not be described simply as prone or supine. We were both on what we called the roof of the offices at Huddersfield; "offices" being perhaps a pretentious description for four rooms in terrace form, built out of an old pump house. Apart from which, its four-foot-deep reservoir water tank forming the entire upper layer of the terrace was hardly everyone's first idea of a roof. It did keep the offices remarkably cool, though, at this time of year.

The accommodation arrangement below had the PWay Inspector's Office at the sunny end, he being the first to take residence, with Elliot Milner's Area Engineer's room next door. Beyond that, via a corridor, we'd converted a store into a very comfortable Drawing Office a couple of years back. At the end of the corridor, between me and the yard, was Elliot's lavatory. We all shared it, but it was forever known as his, in much the same way as the Memorial is known as being Albert's. (Although Elliot was one up on Albert in his regular occupancy of the throne.) Outside in the yard, a vertical iron ladder attached to the face of the building passed in front of the PWay Inspector's Office window, and was topped off by three long runs of planks, allowing our two slightly contorted bodies to lie head and buttocks supported, with legs dangling in the water. Even the act of rising to a sitting position was not simple, and could be tinged with some danger.

We were both stripped to the waist in the midday sun, while the chainmen, Wilf and Percy, desperately sensible (older and wiser), remained seated and capped on a bench in the yard below, the bench consisting of a plank and two upturned buckets. Such a construction proved very adaptable. You could alter the spacing between the buckets, but had to dictate a strict code in seating patterns. What you also had to watch out for was the way you got up from the seat, either individually, or in unison. This demanded a degree of discipline; but we were all civil engineers of one sort or another, so the necessary calculations based on the principle of the cantilever were more or less second nature.

With the day starting cool, we foursome went for an early kick-off, before the heat of the sun made theodolite work impossible due to its exaggerating the dancing of targets in the shimmering air. Vince and I had first removed our jackets, followed by ties and then shirts at half-hourly intervals throughout the morning as the rising temperature passed each 10-degree mark (in those days in Fs). The last veil to be discarded was accompanied by cries of "You'll be sorrrreeeey!" from the capped and shirted wise ones. Their forecast was repeated as we started up the ladder at dinnertime. It was not a suitable ambience for the usual hour of social chat or a game of dominoes, the heat sapping any attempts at concentration, so nobody was offended by the team's pairing off in two directions. We'd once tried outdoor dominoes on a hot day, but the normally good-natured cheating had been replaced by anger and intolerance. Domino rage has turned many an old men's park shelter into a front-line war zone.

Up on the aerial lido Vince stirred himself, reverting quickly back to the status quo as one cheek slid off the supporting plank towards the beckoning water. "I'm convinced it's Elliot's drain that's smelling; it's been getting worse for months, now."

"We know it's Elliot's drain! It's the only thing around here that could smell like that! You realise that we're going to have to take a look into it some time soon, don't you?"

Vince spoke for both of us: "Ay, I suppose so, but we really need a cooler, wetter day for it, preferably with a strong wind. So p'r'aps not today, eh?"

Vince was one of the longer-term resident assistants to join me in the Area Office – before young Eddy Stapleton's time – and we'd become a formidable team. He was more experienced than most of the technical nomads briefly dumped on me, and had come with a multiple reputation, which was a first as far as I was concerned. Most comers-in would be anonymous character seekers, looking either for basic experience, or a quick, quiet passage on to the next tick on their management training programme, but Vince's technical skills were of immediate use. These were pre-CV days where a bloke could have a more bizarre reputation for skills, and before he joined us I couldn't see Vince's principle published attribute being of much practical value. This reported ability which travelled the grapevine ahead of his arrival was of being able to cut a fly in half using a flicked rubber band over amazing distances.

There had been no exaggerations about this, as Vince was more than willing to demonstrate. He couldn't go so far as to say whereabouts his rubber band would cause a split in the fly's personality, but even at eight paces, which was well outside any fly's visual ability, Vince could produce a clean amputation on his day. Off his day he would merely integrate the fly with whatever surface it had chosen as its final resting place. Today, with the sun at its height, and Elliot's drain at its most apparent, we had a gentle flow of potential targets, along with visitors eager to watch Vince at work. After getting over an initial personal natural awe in the presence of greatness, I'd had to curtail the demonstrations as the main office windows were becoming uselessly opaque due to a coating of fragmented flies, still ten weeks adrift from the regular six-monthly cleaning session.

There was a danger of me slightly idolising Vince, having developed a great admiration for him within a fortnight of his confident appearance one memorable Monday morning. Vince's arrival coincided with the bulk delivery of a new type of track chair-screw ferrule, made out of plastic, following a successful trial period in a variety of local conditions. (Ferrules are like a deep washer between the rail chair and its holding-down screw.) They were meant to replace the old wooden ones, which had limited lifespans, depending on their location. Vince showed great interest in the new multicoloured objects, and his inquisitive mind took less than twenty-four hours to find unexpected possibilities in them. A communal gas ring and grill stood in the corridor between Elliot's inner door and the outside world, and Vince discovered that by holding one of the new plastic objects in a pair of tongs over the gas flame, it would liquefy. If you now swung it all around the small area, it would produce an infinite web of invisible thread. And so it came to pass that the first supervisor to arrive around a quarter past seven next morning, coming to put the kettle on, was cocooned in a fine mesh of plastic filaments. After the initial spell of blasphemy, serious investigations were set in place, resulting in the earliest recorded carpeting of a new assistant by Elliot Milner. I was, quite understandably, much impressed.

Vince, like myself, was a modest hoper, one who would gently rise grade by grade throughout his career, ending up in some respectable position of pseudo management within the civil engineering set-up, whereas the whiz kids could fly from one organisation to another, gaining little knowledge, but apparently a multitude of managerial skills. The recognised principle was that if you could manage a bridge design office, you could manage a station operations office, or manage anything; you didn't need to have actually designed a bridge or worked on a station or to have really done anything to be an effective manager. On the other hand, to me, the Vince-types who passed through my hands evolved into effective support, capable of quickly taking on the same work that I did myself, and certainly giving immediate value for money in the time invested in their training. Apart from this, the management foetuses were usually a pain in the arse and a frivolous way of using up Drawing Office space, except for the grudgingly accepted duty of making Elliot and me tea three times a day. I quickly decided to share this duty with Vince, partly through my admiration of his reputation, but also knowing that if he ever got bored with tea-mashing duties, then experimentation with salt and pepper, at best, and such embellishments as HP sauce and Bisto at worst, would ensue. With his already well-developed skills, Vince could be relied upon as an intelligent and well-informed colleague, especially when it came to discussing technical engineering points in conjunction with delicate environmental matters of a complex and impenetrable nature like sinus-stunning smells.

"We might just try an arm's length examination, now that it's making its presence smelt, like. See if we can spot exactly where it's coming from."

"We might," agreed Vince, occupying himself in a casual study and comparison of the various passing fluffy clouds, "but I would submit to you that since we suspect it's Elliot's drain, and since that drain is on railway property, and was constructed to BR specifications, and built using BR materials and finances, and since we, or rather, you were the chief architect and designer of that drain, me just being the dogsbody that set it out and looked after the technical side of the installation... considering all that, I would, while humbly bowing to your acknowledged on-paper superiority in this team, suggest that we forget about it till we're back in railway time."

"Which, now you've shut up, we are! So come on!"

Climbing down the ladder, we both found that chance contacts between the metal rungs and the now tender area of our bare chests gave initial indications that the warnings of the chainmen were to prove justified. It was disappointing that on the positive side a mere pinkness was all that we seemed to have developed.

"Ooo, look," said Percy, "they're almost tanned in places, Wilf! Don't they look hard?"

Traces of rust from the ladder and landing had deposited a pattern of brown dust in various locations. "It's only a bit of rust," said Vince, rubbing it off; "Ouch! Bugger!" A verbal reaction meaning "it was beginning to hurt, and I'm annoyed that I've acknowledged the fact in front of these two clever sods".

"Had enough, has t'a? Reckon tha's turned thissens from off-white dollops of pie pastry inter irresistible golden Adonisisis, dust'a?"

"We've abandoned our worship of the sun god, partly because we were finding it mentally unstimulating, partly because two dozy pillocks were heaving half-bricks up at us, and partly because now that it's marking its presence at a peak, we're going to try and find out where that stink's coming from. We reckon that the bog drain there wants looking at, on account of the smells coming out of it, so we're going to do just that."

"What, now?" said Wilf, seemingly alarmed at the implications for him and Percy. "Have you sort of finished with our professional services, then?"

"I suppose so, unless you fancy giving us a hand with t'drain."

"Hi rather think," explained Wilf, "that Percival here would welcome a chance to explore the shops and thoroughfares of Huddersfield for a while, and hi will accompany him to make sure that he don't buy nowt daft or loss hisself, plus ah could do wi' an 'aircut, if that's OK by thee two."

"Suppose so." I expected such a reaction. "Leave it to the younger, fitter, dedicated lads, as usual!" adding, unwisely, some comments about haircuts and the dedication to railway time that Vince had been so keen to quote recently.

"T'bugger grows in railway time, so ah'll get it cut in railway time," replied Wilf, "and since tha's implying that this is not really suitable work for old has-beens like 'im and me, we'll tek our 'ook. Come on, Percy, this could get rough." With which the deserters wandered happily away to what they saw as being the safety of town.

This drain we were on about had been built about eighteen months earlier, when Elliot Milner, after his first winter at Huddersfield, decided that the existing toilet arrangements were unsatisfactory, and that he and his supervisors from the PWay and Works Offices, together with his technical staff (me plus Vince, at the time), were worth the cost and bother of installing a flushing lavatory within the office block. A visit to our offices by one of the Leeds typists, to copy up a lengthy report on Bradford Exchange station roof that I was preparing, underlined this need. Following my two courteous coffees and a tea in our least-chipped mugs, the young lady managed to pluck up enough courage to ask where "the facilities" were. The actual "facilities", a cubicle in the PWay store, were out of the question, and negotiations with Hilary on switchboard were necessary for the visitor to use her toilet in the main station building. This, along with the need to escort the increasingly embarrassed young thing to the obscurely concealed room, wait for her, and then guide her, now relieved but visibly distressed, back to her typewriter, confirmed to me that Elliot was right. We needed a handy, civilised, and humane bog.

It was interesting, in these late sixties, the golden age of chauvinism, that none of the menfolk for a moment considered the official staff toilet a fit place for a woman (unless, of course, she was in there to clean it!). Yet when the first suggestions were mooted that it might not be suitable for any form of humanity, there was muted uproar. It had been accepted for years, and a resistance arose from the establishment against the idea of any changes, accusing the posher end (engineering and technical staff) of being soft. Though to us barely approaching basic, the luxury of having three walls and most of a door provided unaccustomed privacy for those now occupying supervisory posts in the offices after many years out on the track, where "convenience" meant a tree or a wall as opposed to wild open countryside. So remarks about "being soft" were comparative and could be taken as referring to the natural air conditioning in the existing lavatory, which a casual observer might describe as the spasmodic lack of roofing to the building as a whole. That same observer would hardly count this as the only shortfall.

Summer presented few hardships, other than when it was

raining. It wasn't strictly true to say that a roof didn't exist; certainly there was no cover to the cubicle – there never had been, but there were still archaeologically satisfactory remains of the store's basic overall roof structure. However, what was left of it managed to direct rainwater towards particular spots within. This was only a minor problem for the storekeeper, who merely had to adopt an intelligent seating plan for susceptible items such as track salt and weedkiller. Not considered as part of his responsibility was the lavatory cubicle, where the fixtures were positioned in such a way that roof leaks in that area happened to coincide with the lavatory seat when vacant, or the occupant's head and shoulders when in use. It had been an early action of mine to arrange a sheet of perspex-like material over the cubicle. This produced an immediate comment from the supervisors regarding the amazing benefits of having a higher education, but it didn't prevent them removing it for the crucial months of winter, on the grounds that the summer's dust and pigeons had combined to make the cover cloudy, so creating difficulties in reading in the gloom of the darker season. (At no point in my life on the Area was there a dedicated light to the cubicle alone. Evidence that there had once been one remained in the form of a scorched flex hung from the main roof trusses, obviously a victim of rain running down it whilst lit up. All illumination came from a single 150-watt light fitting, central to the stores but casting a sharp shadow halfway down the cubicle wall, well above seated reading level. Any artificial aid to reading was only by means of reflection off the "white"-washed walls within.)

Winter, though, presented many more deficiencies apart from a shortage of daylight.

Open coal fires and stoves heated the various offices, at one of two regulo levels: either blistering heat or out – there was no in-between. This was the environment that had to be left behind whenever nature called. Thirty yards from the door and you could choose to use an old three-sided ash bunker as a urinal, though it was extremely difficult to pretend that you were doing anything other than the task in hand, as you nerved yourself up to stare over the vanity wall at the passengers sat on the Kirkburton train alongside, ten yards away. For the full services you required the key to the PWay store, a building which in another life had been the station's second-class Gents.

This housing for the staff lavatory was a large, heavily constructed stone building. In summer, the thick walls would retain the sun's heat, the vast space heavy in an atmosphere of old sacking, new wood and paraffin, plus whatever else had been introduced. In winter, the walls became running streams of condensation, knocking a good ten degrees off the perceived temperature. Old six-foot-tall slate urinal partitions ran down the full length of one side, eighteen inches deep, now providing excellent accommodation for the filing of shovels, ballast forks, pick handles and track sluing bars. There was the additional bonus of a channel cut into the floor that stopped the more unstable elements from slipping forwards. I had on occasional visits mused on the superiority of these old Victorian urinals as compared to the communal aluminium firing ranges and hung gutters of today, where you always manage to get the spot over the outlet, with three other bursting customers upstream of you. Avoiding these distasteful designs, but in many ways worse, are the exhibitionist buckets slung from a wall, with the average occupant, a compulsory show-off, standing back a good foot, combing his hair while performing – the same sort who, as a kid, rarely used the handlebars on his bike.

But I digress; back to the ancient powder room. Any remnants of the discredited store roof were of glass, half supported on terminally rusted metal bars, and given to spates of sudden death, betrayed by the discovery of yet another portion of blackened glass lying shattered on the storeroom floor. There existed no record of a partial roof collapse coinciding with a sitting tenant in the lavatory, but this may be down to experience adding caution during high winds, directing the urgent visitor several hundred yards down the platforms to the well-protected public conveniences. These were in somewhat better condition, due to the fact that customers were valued above staff, and that there were far more triplicated forms to be filled in if a paying traveller was damaged. On the downside there was in those times the ubiquitous penny to be spent. However, putting aside calculated caution as to the advisability of chancing the staff bog, nothing could alter the welcoming nature of the roof, so an additional hazard existed by way of the undisciplined incontinence of the ever-present brood of pigeons.

The one remaining working water closet from the former Gents was now our single cubicle, saved from removal. It retained the worn stone floor that guaranteed a puddle of varying size and origin at the point most used by feet over the last one hundred years. So, keeping semi-discarded clothing dry was an uncomfortable exercise, since it could be attacked by rain from above or rising damp from below. Privacy was afforded by a solid wooden door, starting twelve inches or so above the floor, a measurement that was steadily growing, as progressive rot increased the gap year by year. Open to the skies, there was but moderate protection from the rest of West Yorkshire, so that there was never a rush to be first to use it after a heavy snowfall. The only luxury within was the dubious one of having full use of the functional library, albeit cut into neat six-inch squares, hanging from a rusted nail hammered into the stonework at a very dangerous height. Flushing was, of course, by means of a hygienically corroded chain to a cistern way up over the pan. If the rain didn't get you, then the idiosyncrasies of the overflowing storage tank would. Concentration was never possible in winter; there were far too many inherent problems to contend with. Bitter damp, cold, pigeon guano, direct rain, roof collapse, an eccentric cistern and ill-placed puddles all went to keep the occupant literally on his toes throughout a visit.

Hygiene was preserved by the simple means of whitewashing the walls once a month, covering up disturbing skid marks and examples of very basic literacy. Inevitably the cubicle grew smaller with each application, and great lumps of deposited paint would come off without warning or provocation, adding to all the other hazards. These lumps of whitewash would be carefully collected and recycled.

Oddly enough, Elliot Milner, as one newly arrived from the fully appointed District Offices in Leeds, took immediate exception to the fact that for him promotion to taking charge of the Area Office at Huddersfield meant swapping centrally heated, running hot and cold facilities and the choice of four very private traps for something slightly inferior to the resources of a twelfth-century monastery. So a new lavatory, within the offices, was a priority for him. It was to be achieved by building it at the far end of the extended corridor between himself and our Drawing Office, and with the existing self-sufficiency of Area life, that very Drawing Office was to do the designs.

I was a little surprised to get the contract for such an intimate domestic job. Vince wasn't, though.

"Elliot's wanting something tailor-made, something that he can have total control over. I bet he'll want the bog pointing along one of his personal ley lines, or facing his zodiac sign or summat. Anyway, why shouldn't he give it us to do?"

"We've not exactly got a brilliant track record on inside work, especially you, since you buggered about with that plastic ferrule round the cooker. And what about his flue pipe? You can't claim that as an outstanding bit of engineering maintenance!"

"That was entirely down to circumstances; the ideas were sound, and it did work!"

Before we had the big gas convectors put in, Elliot's office was heated by a coke stove. A vertical flue pipe came out of the top, and after five feet going upwards, it did an L-turn towards the yard wall. There was a second bend when it reached the wall to go vertically up it, before turning again to pierce through to the outside just beneath the water tank. At the first of these turns was a removable plate for cleaning the flue out – removable by reputation only. When the wind blew in a certain direction (probably along Elliot's ley line) the fire belched smoke. Recently it had taken to doing it without preference to any particular wind direction.

"I wish we could sort that damn fire out," said Elliot. "I'm going home smelling like a stoker in a kipper factory!"

Vince was still, after several months, trying to reverse Elliot's first impressions of him. "I can handle stoves like that; we'd one in the Scout camp hut. Used to get blocked regular... sometimes on purpose. Bit messy, mind."

"See to it, then, preferably when I'm not around!"

I wasn't too sure about Vince's credentials in this area; there was a clipped upbeat note to his voice, and his eyes never settled on anything in particular while he was trying to convince Elliot. I quizzed him later back in our own office. "You sure you've unblocked a stove chimney like Elliot's?"

"Well, not precisely unblocked, as such, but I'm dead sure I can do it."

"So how much were you actually involved with this Scout hut chimney, then?"

"It was me that blocked it!"

"And that gives you the right to put 'unblocking chimneys' on your career record, then?"

"Look, it's simple. All we have to do is burn out whatever's up there. We set fire to the chimney and blast it out. Doddle! Nothing to it!"

For the next three days Elliot was off first thing to a conference in Manchester, half an hour on the train from Huddersfield. He'd only be calling in to look at the mail each morning, and then away. This seemed an ideal time for the job. Little Norman, a predecessor of Bill Boyes, who came in at six each morning to light up the fires and then stayed until three servicing the kettle, was put in the picture. He was a shrivelled asthmatic of about one hundred and four, with a permanent Capstan Full Strength between the two flaps of withered leather where his lips had once been. He'd light a new one from the last, mainly because he invariably blew out matches and lighters with his coughing. The first of the day was activated by the gas ring, as witnessed by the nudity of his eyebrows. We explained the situation to Norman, that we wanted the stove cold so that we could clear the pipe, and he wasn't to light it.

The next day was largely spent shoving anything and every-thing up and down the chimney from all openings, without drawing blood anywhere. We stuffed it with paper, set light to it, and succeeded only in disorientating ourselves in the intense smoke. It just wouldn't draw, and the paper simply smouldered. Vince's final plan was then put in hand.

"Stuff paper into this level bit, through the L-flap, keep that open until we've got a good fire going, then shut it. It'll be a bit messy at first, but I bet she clears." And so he with the preliminaries for a Scout badge in clearing stove pipes entered the second day.

One *Huddersfield Examiner*, a *Yorkshire Post*, a *Daily Mirror* and an ancient *Dalesman* were part shredded and loosely rammed along the horizontal section, since we'd clearly identified that the upright from the stove was clear.

"What's that smell?" It seemed like paraffin, but I knew Vince wouldn't be that daft.

"It's paraffin. Just a bit. I soaked the *Examiner* in it while you were getting the other papers!"

"Is this wise?"

"D'you want wise or effective? Can't do much harm, anyway."

The full fire, laid ready in the stove grate, was lit. The first snag, of course, was that it wouldn't draw, until Vince opened the L-bend flap, a window, and the outside door. Very little damage had been done before I managed to whip a cover over Elliot's desk.

It was a good fire. Within minutes flames were just reaching the open flap. At what he made out to be the critical moment, Vince closed the flap, using thick gloves at his second attempt, which followed a sort of ritual fire dance involving wildly shaking fingers and swearing loudly. A variety of expansion-cracking noises, and the strong smell of burnt dust along the top of the pipe confirmed that the paper had caught. Finally, a strong "phuddd" and shudder marked the paraffin-soaked *Examiner* going up, along with the stove suddenly drawing wildly. Norman put his nose round the supervisor's connecting door.

"Dust'a think tha's done it, then?"

"Looks very much like it!" said the Queen's Scout in pyrotechnics.

"Best close yon window, theer's a heavy drizzle comin' in, which is a bit of a shame, considerin'."

"Considering what, Norm?"

"Considerin' that Elliot's car is parked reet ahtside, d'rectly under t'chimney pot, and considerin' that tha two've just blasted t'blazin' ashes of t'best part of a newslad's sack up it, along wi' what looks like twenty-three old bird's nests, and had it mostly settling on t'car. It looks like it's bin thro' Happy Hour at t'crematorium!"

Never believe that black, as in Boss's black Anglia, doesn't show dirt; especially when it's virtually glued on in a combination of hot ash and cold drizzle!

In some ways, this episode gave me more confidence in tackling the lavatory drainage design. My experience of foul drains, though superficial, was to honours degree level compared to Vince's qualifications in towering infernos. I'd had plenty of practice around the neighbours' drains, possessing as I did the only set of drain rods in the street. I also had a peculiar satisfaction in successful unblockings. The achievement criteria of men differ strangely; some get it through macheting their way through their fellow man's insides, others climb impossible mountains for the reward of being able to just about detect their hands in front of their faces at the top. One of the lads in the Leeds Office used to get an immense kick running in the midst of six hundred similar barmpots through city streets and coming in a hundred and sixty-five behind the leader, a massive improvement on his hundred and seventieth the previous year. For me satisfaction is the belch and gurgle of a released drain following that initial slight oozing. Despite a super sensitive nose, I'd happily stand over an open manhole watching the released sewage until clear flushing water appears. I had now convinced myself that I was just the candidate for the Elliot Milner Lavatory Project.

When I was faced with designing this new effluent passage I had but two basic laws in the Mike Drainage Manual: 1. Water doesn't easily run uphill, and 2. It's not brilliant downhill either, if it's anything but unsullied, unless you can achieve a good slope. I'd a situation here which would have benefited from a repeal of the first law, and hardly lent itself to complying with the second. The small yard in which the pump house-cum-offices stood was built fifteen feet above Huddersfield, at the end of a half-mile-long viaduct, and was supported by the massive bulk of a blackened stone retaining wall rising from Fitzwilliam Street, below. A section of this wall extended upwards to form the back wall of our offices, so that the water reservoir on top stood some forty feet above street level. Three short sidings ran in from the main lines to offloading bays, at the far end of which stood the magnificent edifice of the PWay store – ex-second-class Gents – incorporating the existing staff toilet cubicle. It was magnificent, because it formed one bookend to the extraordinary classical architecture that is Huddersfield Station. The bays ran out up to the station forecourt railings, at the side of the famous George Hotel, birthplace of Rugby League. At the point where the main retaining wall adjoined the hotel there was a public urinal, the only possible outfall location for the new office sewer pipe.

A route for the drain was pretty well dictated. From the lavatory, through the massive pump house wall, and out into the yard, straight into an inspection pit. Textbooks on effluent shifting dictated a pit wherever the drain had to turn a corner. Thirty yards further on, into the middle of the yard, there was another bend and pit. This chamber was to become centre stage for the drama about to unfold, and its positioning was dictated by two major factors: any further and it would have gone bang through the sidings; any sooner and it would have been dangerously close to silly mid-off position, and occasionally the pitch of the ball, on the improvised cricket field, often used on cooler summer dinnertimes by the Drawing Office (which obviously included the scheme designer). From this point, the drain had to run a straight one hundred and fifty yards towards the public urinal, through another inspection pit built hard up against the retaining wall. Passing through the wall, it would then take a twelve-foot plunge, by way of a six-inch cast-iron pipe, into the main grate of the urinal that was covered by a heavy metal lid, central to the small floor area. Ideally, because of the materials it was to carry, the drain should have sloped throughout its length to such an extent that it would have been about ten feet deep by the time it reached the boundary wall, and therein lay a problem. This project was being supported by the esoteric manipulation of various financial authorities (done on the side), hence costs were to be kept to a minimum, and excessive excavation didn't fit into this concept, so the drain would have to manage with a much more moderate gradient, a recipe for trouble if it were not to be regularly maintained. Earnest intentions were there to do this, but that turned out to be yet another path to Hell as usual.

Back on the blazing afternoon, eighteen months after the completion of the toilet and drain – now accepted and enjoyed by all – it was well past the moment marking the change from "own time" to "railway time", and Vince felt he could now justify an investigation into the smell, with it being a railway smell. It would also delay having to return to an inside drawing board for the rest of the hot sunny afternoon. We both pinpointed the central inspection pit, not by smell particularly, but rather from a feeling that if anything were to go wrong with the drain, that was the most likely point. Traces of damp around one corner of the lid supported our instincts, indicating that at certain times the pit must gently overflow. As to us lifting the lid to check it out... well, attention to job descriptions, demarcation limits, expertise and simple fear, culminated in an unspoken agreement between us to go get the Works Supervisor. Off-track drainage was the responsibility of Albert Hughes, the Chief Works Supervisor, who was unfortunately out on the Area somewhere, but his vibrant deputy, Irving Ryder, was in.

We must pause here, have another mug of tea, and examine this supervisory manifestation now to take front stage. Irving was a fascinating character; mid-fifties, ever nervous, his small, five-feet two-inch frame would literally dance from foot to foot as he spoke, his eyes flashing around the room, sometimes independently, while never alighting on the person he was actually talking to. All the time he would be sucking in delicate traces of saliva escaping from an overexcited mouth. His speech could be likened to the progress of the infamous spider up the drainpipe, three phrases forward and two back: "Well, Mr Milner, it's like this, it happened this way, when I was measuring up the glass roof, up on the station roof – made up of panes of glass, like, I was measuring up with my folding rule, except it wasn't mine, because I'd had to borrow one, because I'd left mine behind, it being a Monday, and it being in my Sunday bag, and I got up on the roof, where the glass I was measuring was, and I measured it with this folding rule I had to borrow, because I hadn't got mine, as I say, so I unfolded the one I'd borrowed..."; an explanation which could continue until Elliot said, "That'll do, Irving!", deciding to wait until he could see Albert for a résumé.

Albert had to do this kind of "explaining after Irving" thing fairly often. Being far too kind-hearted for his own good to clearly lay the blame where he should, he would always begin with a little inward sigh, which substituted for "I know you're going to find this story hard to believe, and you know full well that I can't lie to save my life, but the poor chap tries his best, and accidents will happen". That understood, Albert continued in his phrase by phrase style: "Mirfield Station roof – you know we've a complete renewal of purlins and glass coming up soon – I got Irving to check the glass panel sizes for ordering – they're all the same so we only needed details of one. Send him on a measuring job – remembers his pencil – forgets his ruler." Albert inserted another of his apologetic sighs. "Borrows one from one of the joiners working there – trouble is, Irving's own is a folding three-foot – t'joiner's was a folding four-foot – Irving doesn't notice – (sigh) – panels are six foot each – one and a half ruler lengths with t'four foot which Irving puts down as four foot six – five hundred and twenty panels of glass ordered all eighteen inch short... they'll come in for summat, somewhere – (final sigh). I blame misself, really." (As usual). The glass never "came in for summat", and apart from one or two private cold frames, it stood around at Mirfield for a while, and then simply disappeared. Five years later it was dug up, when a remote railway yard became extinct and was sold for redevelopment.

Irving's folding rule was a legend in its own existence, a quarter of it tending to fold back at odd times, without him noticing. This usually showed up in having deliveries of materials arriving on site proving far too long, which is annoying, but not always disastrous. I've souvenirs at home from a bridge job that Irving measured up for and executed. Fifteen-foot longitudinal timbers laid end to end, twelve by six in cross section, all turning up eighteen inches too long, the famous ruler having presumably folded back a couple of times. Irving being Irving saved the Sunday by having a foot and a half sawn off each one, rather than put them in as they were, and cut the last one down to fit. Details of this incident will explain to my lass why she's forever negotiating six large blocks of creosoted timber in our garden which I've assured her over the last twenty-five years will come in for summat. (This plea, besides being Albert's only form of defence for Irving, is also the first line in the Procrastinator's Bible.)

Irving's ruler really let him down when it came to measuring up our new Drawing Office exterior door and frame during the refurbishment. What should have been delivered by van came on the back of a lorry, and no amount of sighing on the part of Albert Hughes could prevent Elliot going into one of his fuse-blowing explosions at the expense of poor Irving and his folding three-foot. Irving's doorway would have accommodated the Harlem Globetrotters in celebratory mood and still leave a foot to spare, and it was just short of being a garage wide.

And so, when the cavalry arrived at the oozing drain that blistering summer's afternoon, it turned out to be rather more Don Quixote with his donkey. Whilst Irving was an expert little worker in his trade with wood, he was not by a long stretch of the imagination supervisory material. He just happened to be senior artisan when the job came up, and for the railway, that was that. However, today was to turn out to contain his finest hour.

He trotted across from the Works Supervisor's Office to the yard, legs like tiny pistons absent-mindedly attached to a pair of multidirectional feet. In his eagerness to arrive and please he twice tripped over his shadow due to his eyes swivelling to pick up anything remotely approaching his flight path. Hand clasped below chin and now alternating his vision between sky and ground, he inspected the overflowing pit. "I think it'll be blocked, the drain that is, there's something blocking it. I think we need to unblock the drain. What I'll do, I'll get someone – someone to rod it, to unblock it, with rods. I'll go get someone… see who's in… if there is anyone… if there isn't, I'll… well, I'll go see anyway!" And off he trotted in his busy way. Only Chaplin could better Irving as a departing rear-view spectacle. He lacked the sway but compensated with his feet shooting out symmetrically at forty-five degrees from the direction of travel.

"This looks promising; a blocked bog drain and Ryder in charge! This looks very promising!" observed Vince, who had up to this point almost decided to chicken out of the lid-raising ceremony, not seeming too sure of his likely reactions.

It was obviously taking Irving some time to locate any spare men, and probably even longer to persuade them that what they needed to complete a hot summer's day, was a short matinée involving a blocked sewer. My curiosity was getting the better of me, in inverse proportions to my mate's. Vince had gone back inside, no doubt deciding that he could do so without losing face, on the basis that he felt we were wasting time. I was now quite fascinated, standing there watching the metal lid sweat.

I finally cracked and fetched out a couple of manhole keys, metal devices for lifting the lids off covered pits – which were a standard part of the survey bag tackle. I scraped out the gap round the lid, using a borrowed spade to remove the ingrained muck and weeds, and engaged the lifting keys. Raising it was a struggle, it was like trying to release a sucker pad, but eventually one edge eased with an accompanying "fflerrp", enough for me to get the shovel under and lift back the lid. In what must have been only a couple of seconds, quite a few things registered with me:

1. The pit was full to the very top.
2. The material filling it was so solid that the pattern of the underside of the lid could be clearly picked out as a mirror image in the top of the gunge.
3. Whoever was destined to probe about for the drainage pipe was in for a job they wouldn't quickly forget.
4. The stench was unbelievable.

I backed off as if I'd been blasted. The lid dropped back with a deep flop, fortunately more or less directly into position, but still managing to shoot out a starburst of grey-brown slimy fingers. I didn't stop to bother about adjusting it neatly into its slots, I just moved away as quickly as dignity would allow, back towards the office, and an emerging Vince. "The stench is unbelievable," I told him.

"No, it isn't," said Vince. "I'd believe it, and what's more I've no intention of questioning it. Listen, this'll interest you. I've had the plans out, and I've done a few calculations, and guess what!"

"What?"

"Well, I've worked out that in the year and a half that the bog's been in, considering the average usage, making allowances for staff fluctuations and holidays, and taking into account the volume capacities of the pipes and pits, I reckon it's been blocked to solids somewhere near the outfall since day one. How about that, then?"

He rounded with exaggerated self-satisfaction, proud of the

results of twenty minutes of railway time. I could see flaws in his reasoning, particularly in establishing how much was added to the bulk per sitting. My natural curiosity would at any other time have demanded some qualification of this figure, but my first-hand experience had rather taken the edge off any curiosity I might have had in the composition of the material. Certainly my observations had convinced me that a more distant watching brief was preferable. While waiting for further action, Bill and I were entertained by an open-air exhibition of fly-slicing by Vince, the Region's greatest, using rubber bands at five paces, since targets were presenting themselves readily. Every fly in Yorkshire seemed to be zeroing in on the slightly open lid.

Irving Ryder had found a selection of volunteers hard to come by, mainly because the works mess room had revealed only two candidates, Roland Brown and Ernie Kennefick. He knew that with them, what was to follow would be an uphill struggle.

Roland was a man skilled in his craft, that of dealing with gas and water installations. I'd felt it almost a privilege to watch him as he worked on fitting large gas heaters in the new offices, as well as the water supply extensions to the washbasins and new toilet. He was a tall, stern individual, with a long ebony pipe clenched between dusky teeth. His overalls were immaculate every morning, and only slightly less so by evening, due in the main to his precise definition as to where craftsmanship ended and labouring began. In common with his fellow artisans, he wore a trilby hat, as opposed to the common uniform of flat cap. The hat was his badge of competence, and just as the barber has his framed licence to cut hair, shave chins and provide something for the weak end, Roland had his diploma in the form of a hat. Therefore it had to be permanently in position, whatever contortions the job in hand called for. Roland was another of the inadequately educated great potentials, as his serious and informed conversation revealed. However, he showed no bitterness towards the young graduates of the Drawing Office, so long as their respect for his skills was acknowledged at an initial stage. With my painful hero worship of the utterly competent, I managed to strike up a very happy relationship with him, to the point of being invited to call him Roland as against Mr Brown.

Irving Ryder, however, had a difficult bridge to cross when it came to giving Roland instructions, for the latter harboured a polite regard for the position of supervisor, but very little for this particular representation of it.

It was by now a quarter to three, a time when most men like Roland would have nothing more on their minds than the train home, and tea (Tuesday, summer or winter, braised steak and kidneys, spuds and peas). To be invited to take part in an engagement with a heaving sewage pit at that moment was ill-judged and ill-timed, and of no interest to a skilled craftsman – the job having labourer written right through it. Fifteen minutes of argument was settled by compromise, despite the fact that Roland should really do as instructed if at all reasonable, and what with him still having a theoretical ninety minutes of working time left to fill. The settlement was that Roland would be present as acting supervisor, be paid as such, plus an allowance for working outside his specialist field, plus muck money – generally confined to tunnel work. He should also be allowed to call it a seven o'clock finish, and be transported home to his door on completion. On Roland's side he agreed to do it, in the full knowledge that there was maybe little more than twenty minutes' work, ten minutes washing down, and he'd still be home well before his normal train could manage it. As to his sidekick, Ernie, he would do as he was told.

Ernie Kennefick was a remarkable man. Four feet eleven tall, and much the same in diameter. He had a very high-pitched squeak of a voice, so that whatever he might say was always taken as being comical, and would get a chuckle, such that Ernie would join in. Thus, Ernie was a jolly little fellow, ever grumbling, but laughing all the while, giving out wildly confusing messages as to how he truly felt. However, if he were ordered to a job, be it pleasant or distasteful, he would always toddle off to do it to the best of his ability, with a grin and a grunt. He was a "green card" man, registered as having some sort of disability, and one of the percentage of such that the railway were obliged to employ. Whatever his registration said officially, Ernie's effective disability was that he had extreme difficulty in picking anything up, due to his body geometry.

Arriving on site, Roland carried the status rods – the ones with the screw on the end, the plunger, and the small wheel – whilst Ernie trotted behind with the standard linking rods wedged equally under each armpit. They set up base camp around the offending inspection pit.

I welcomed them warmly. "I've managed to ease the lid, Roland!" If I was looking for gratitude, I was not going to receive it from that direction.

"Oh, aye! So what stopped thee carryin' on, eh?"

"Expertise, or lack of it. Hadn't a clue what to do next." A blatant lie, which Roland's flue-brush eyebrows acknowledged.

First job for the master craftsman and acting supervisor was to set light to whatever mysterious substance it was that he pressed into the bowl of his pipe. Regardless of the expertise shown by his patron saint, St Bruno, the compost that eventually came to be fired up was accidentally augmented with many additional features derived from the more malleable components of his art, such as fibre washers, plumber's paste and putty. Over the years his habit had removed most of his sense of taste, and therefore smell. On the face of it this made him ideal for the present job. Ernie was a labourer, and therefore immune to everything, especially senses and feelings. It was, however, Roland's first drain clearance since his own labouring days, whereas Ernie had assisted at many in his time, but protocol did not allow him to offer any advice unless asked – not that that was likely or that he'd have given it anyway, as it was always refreshing to watch those placed in a superior role over you dropping themselves right in it.

Now, having lifted the lid, stepped back a little and considered the situation, Roland decided that the skilled part of this job would be prodding around with the first two rods to find the outlet pipe, and then screwing one rod to the next and pushing forward until the blockage could be located and dislodged. He explained to Ernie that his unskilled part in the operation would be withdrawing the rods from the mess on satisfactory completion, unscrewing them and washing them down. The consequences of this plan of action were obviously not lost on the little man, but that was life, he said, take it or leave it. It was probably this final boost to Ernie's apathy, plus his studied inferiority in the situation, which combined with Roland lacking his *Reader's Digest DIY Manual*, Chapter 122, "John Unblocks a Drain", that led to their basic mistake.

Lesson for the day: Where the waters are hid as with a stone, proceed from below, lest the waters roar and be troubled. Job 38:30, Mike 1:1 and Psalm 46:3.

That is, always approach from below and beyond the blockage, not downwards into it. This should ease the plug back, and allow the backed-up waters to start flowing gradually around it, thus avoiding a flood. To rod downhill will either compress the blockage further, or cause a sudden and uncontrollable release.

Admittedly, the correct way would have been difficult here, as the final pit was hard up against the retaining wall, just before the plunge into the public Gents, below. What's more, the pipe emerged at a fair depth, making the insertion of a rod difficult, adding to the problems of then bending it through ninety degrees. But this pit was empty, and the pipe was visible, in total contrast to the situation at the hub of operations.

Some intelligent prodding, together with a glance at the drawing, located the pipe opening, and Roland started threading his rods down towards the blockage. He had made the wise decision to dispense with the choice of probes, and to just send a bare rod end in first. Ernie fed him rod after rod, to be screwed firmly to the preceding one, all the time giving the extending length a slight clockwise twist to prevent the rods unscrewing themselves. A harmony of movement had more or less been established between the workforce, if the murmurings of Ernie could be ignored. Roland pushed hard on the rods ("Strike me! This is tough stuff; it ain't half bunged up down there!" – while from the background: "It's no picnic here, tha' knaws; it's bloody hard work bending down and picking these rods up!"). We were now joined by Bill, who had "rodded more drains in his time than he'd had hot dinners". He could see disaster looming, and wasn't going to interfere or miss it for anything. We'd all three, Bill, Vince and me, taken up a position at the final pit, overlooking the open-topped Gents urinal. It was no more than two minutes into the rodding before the first belch echoed down the pipe. It was like the noise you get when dragging a wellington boot out of thick mud. This was followed immediately by that sound so popular on exotic nature programmes coming from volcanic bubbling mud springs.

"I reckon it's abaht to... Bloody hell! Shift!" Bill was away, much faster than his heart condition should have allowed, fear and experience combining to outpace us two younger lads. Bubbling had given way to a most extraordinary rushing noise, and we just caught a glance of an enormous bolt of something shoot into the pit. It exploded in all available directions before taking the plunge down into the public Gents below. Now well placed, we watched fascinated as the drama was played out. The iron cover central to the urinal floor shot a good foot into the air, and eighteen months of concentrated sewage followed it, surging out of the urinal and across the main street of Huddersfield town centre. Solids were carried to the centre of the road, and fines made it to the opposite pavement, with liquids eventually lapping up along the shop fronts opposite. Up and down the road the tidal wave spread out, at the same time quickly losing its initial momentum. Soon it had reached its limits, with small reflected waves from street gutters and shop walls returning to the epicentre. Constituent parts were clearly distinguishable, new and old, while Bill imaginatively pointed out "Harry – definitely Jack – that'll be Elliott, there..." Once the more liquid element had dissipated by either evaporation from the oven-hot tarmac, or found itself a roadside drain to hide down, the remaining sludge reacted with the heat and slight breeze to carry the record of events that bit further afield.

The response of the general public was varied and absorbing, as they met, or were met by this sudden phenomena. There was not one of them could remember anything like this being mentioned on the weather forecast that morning. Some ran; some stood Canute-style fixed to the spot; some just turned their backs on it in the manner of a movie heroine. There were those who would obviously be embarrassed at any time by confronting anything slightly out of the ordinary in public; they either ignored events and quickened their steps away, or feigned to remember something they'd missed and turned to outpace the advancing complications. Others, reaching higher ground scanned the heavens in disbelief, but not a single one stayed around once the substance had slowed at its limits and started reacting to the power of the late-afternoon sun. My personal medal for stoicism in the face of attack went to the tall gentleman of West Indian origins who had been using the urinal at the critical moment. From above we could see him finish off the business in hand, button up, step delicately around the worst of the invasive mess, and then march steadily away without a backward glance, only pausing after fifty yards to examine the soles of his shoes.

Ranged along the parapet of the retaining wall above the street was a selection of mixed emotions as we admired our handiwork. Bill was giggling with happiness that his wildest expectations had materialised. Roland was realising that the pleasure was now his, to be able to return to his supervisor and tell him that it was he who now had a slight problem on his hands. Ernie was squeaking away an explanation as to where he felt they could have improved on their technique, while I was mentally assessing the extent of the spread which had now taken in both pavements, and some sixty or seventy yards of roadway. Vince was pointing out Wilf and Percy to me, in the street below, picking their way angrily through the spectacular mess. He'd been guided to them by recognising Percy's cries of "You dozy great pillocks! You want bloody lockin' up, t'pair on thee!"

With the arrogance of a skilled surgeon, Roland removed his untainted gloves and turned to his nurse (Ernie), instructing him to "finish off" while he made his leisurely way back to the Works Office, where Irving had wisely decided to remain. Ernie, now a muttering bundle of discontent, donned the discarded red rubber gloves and began the task of withdrawing and unscrewing the drain rods, now thickly coated with archaeological samples of a year and a half's sewage. Bill had recovered sufficiently to take pity on the sad balloon that was Ernie, and was unfurling the hosepipe which was permanently fixed at the ready against the office wall.

Vince and I were still taking in the settling scene below. All traffic had stopped. Buses were disgorging passengers who were obviously reluctant to remain in the hot confined surroundings of the upper saloon amidst the residue of a retreating tide of raw sewage. Windows up and down the street were being reluctantly slammed shut after balancing the heat against the stench. These were the anonymous offices of solicitors and finance advisors strung out along the first floors above the shops, all in the throes of entertaining clients in fan-aired waiting rooms or refined chambers, now all converted into heaving traps of choking effluent fumes. Worst of all, the bingo queue had found themselves on a small peninsular of normality, with the fetid mix marking a high-water limit along three sides of the converted cinema. A small area of the town, on a slightly over-hot summer's day, had been converted into a heaving oasis from hell.

Irving Ryder's finest minute of his finest hour was now at hand. He tiptoed through the scattered drain rods, looked down each of the open manholes, momentarily stuck his head over the parapet of the retaining wall and rapidly sized up the situation. He ordered a quick clearance of the rods, replacement of the pit lids, and a site evacuation. Then, using the nearest available phone, in the Drawing Office, he rang Huddersfield Council Offices, Sewerage. With a quite uncharacteristic calm and straightforward delivery, once he'd been passed through the maze of extensions, he informed the Council's Chief Inspector that he would be well advised to get some men to Fitzwilliam Street, outside the George Hotel, because "there seems to be something seriously wrong with your drains!"

Surveys

A state of harmony hung in the air, a combination of maturity, nature, and lad. Chainmen and surveyor had played their individual parts to perfection, Mother Nature had provided a jacket's worth of warmth and a fresh green pillow of new season grass on the railway cutting slope, and all the while the lad had been observing and learning with his determined dedication and appealing ambition, at the elbow of experience and in the footsteps of fortitude, absorbing expertise, like a tie in gravy.

Percy, Wilf and me, along with young Eddy Stapleton, were enjoying one of those average temperature days of late spring, doing a survey for a small renewal of some point and crossing work near Batley Station. For me, this was how it always should be – comfortable. None of your light rain in a steady winter northerly, when fingers seem to merge with survey book and pencil into a frozen lump, and having as much feeling as a TV soap extra in a pension queue, all with the nearest cabin a mile and a half away into the north wind. Nor should we have to suffer the weight of a summer sun on a sagging survey team, with the whole world dancing in an impossible way barely ten feet from the eyepiece of an impotent theodolite's telescope, the only resting place being the adjacent slope of nettles and brambles populated by a bugologist's dream of a hundred different kinds of miniature mobile hypodermics. In the perfect world, average is most tolerable.

For much of the time Eddy was quietly taking it all in, as the chainmen darted back and forth calling out measurements taken from a baseline to the running edge of the rail, a point end or a crossing nose. I was marking them down in the survey book.

Wilf: "At twenty foot!"

Percy: "Up cess rail, one foot six and a quarter... Turnout, two, eight an' aif... Down six foot, twelve ten... Little furry thing goin' like a concertina with St Vitus at thirteen foot six... seven... eight and aif... nine... is t'a gettin' all this?"

"Mr Kellet, this end of the operation would greatly appreciate it if you'd quit frigging about, like a certifiable prat!" I had Eddy looking over my shoulder, picking the idea up as we went, and Percy, as he would on such a day, was in his good-natured silly bugger mood, and there's me trying to keep it simple for the lad.

"Ah thought as 'ow tha were interested in nature, like!"

"I'm more interested in working with someone using their natural intelligence, rather than that of a retarded loofah!"

"An' ah'm not bent dahn 'ere fur thee to be dancin' aroun' singin' aht daft measurements," added Wilf. "It's time tha took a turn on t'dumb end 'ere. It suits thee better!"

"No pleasin' some… Up cess one seven and aif."

Eddy was coming along nicely, and got more out of a day on the ground than he would from me talking at him in the office. I'd far from perfected my teaching methods, which were much too jumpy for even me to keep track of. But although Eddy was taking it in well enough, and proving himself to be a handy little draughtsman, with a fairly secure grasp of the easier calculations, I could not in my wildest dreams have foreseen a future for this timid young lad, which would, in twenty-five years' time, place him as a leading consultant on a major railway construction job – only a tunnel under the Channel, that's all! I'd loads of paper geniuses pass through my hands at Huddersfield, but in all my time I reckon I only handled two such as Eddy. There was a deep inner pride in it for me in years to come, especially when neither of the two managed to develop an ego to match their progress.

By midday we'd done, and there was just over forty minutes to wait before our next train back, so the high spring sun and the new grass of the embankment beckoned. Batley rose up in local peaks and plunged into sharp valleys all around us, the level tracks of the railway looking incongruous in the surrounding hollows and hills. Thirty yards away was Batley Station signal box, and the occasional chimes of the communicating bells sprang from the open door.

Relaxation was a time for most of us to contemplate the meaning of life within the hundred-yard boundary around us, but for the keen young Eddy it was time to mull over what he'd seen, and ponder on anything which didn't quite tie up for him.

"I've often wondered," he began, anxious to see whether he would be tolerated asking questions during rest-time, "I mean, I know that steel tapes are more accurate than linen, so why do you use the cloth tape for measuring along the string line?"

"Because," I said, and I was a bit annoyed with myself that I hadn't already covered this, "we may have to lay it so that for a while it crosses the rails—"

"Bad luck, tha sees," Percy interrupted. "Nivver cross steel wi' steel; brings thee bad luck."

I noticed the faintest of winks from Percy to Wilf, though I reckoned Wilf was as baffled as I was at this gem from Old Percy's Almanac. However, experience had suggested that I should let them think I was up to speed with whatever was going on, and hope to catch on later. I was the same with the phone; any unrecognised voice who'd announced their name once and repeated it on request was never asked a second time out of simple embarrassment. I'd just hope to cotton on to who it was from the drift of the conversation.

"How d'you mean, bad luck?" asked the lad, just as Percy had wanted him to.

"Watch this, I'll githee a f'r instance," said Percy, rising from his head-back, knees-up position, and reaching into his survey bag. He pulled out the steel tape. "Come on, Mike! Gi'us hand!" With which he took the couple of strides or so necessary to reach the trackside cess, offering me the dumb end of the tape. "Now, Eddy! Just nip up to t'signal box and ask if owt's coming!"

Eddy dutifully trotted off to the box to enquire about any approaching trains while Percy sent me across the track with the tape.

"Are you going to let me in on this, or do I have to stand here like a spare part?"

"Hang on, just drop it across t'rails when I say."

Eddy was now about ten yards from the box steps.

"Now!" said Percy, and we dropped the steel tape across the lines.

I knew full well that this would show up as an electrical fault in the signal box, as our tape short-circuited the track detection current, but I couldn't work out what Percy's idea was.

Eddy reached the foot of the steps leading up to the box. Being a bright lad, he instantly caught on to what Percy had meant by it "bringing bad luck" when the bad luck arrived. In the opposite of a flash, yet in the instant of one, his whole world was plunged into darkness, as the signal box went into eclipse. The most enormous woman he'd ever seen burst through the box door onto the landing with a three-quarter attack one way, twisting to the same the other. This was the only possible approach for her, sort of screwing herself through the inadequate doorway. Even at fifty yards I was impressed, and at leisure later, I would work on the vision of this imposing "titanelle", and wonder at the bodily civil engineering that had gone into designing Isobel, for that was her name, a fact I gathered from Percy's gasp of "Oh sod, it's 'Idious Isobel!" His change of expression made it clear that he had not bargained on her being in the box on duty that day.

She was maybe no more than five foot four tall, but she must have tipped at eighteen stones. This bulk was incongruously supported by the most dainty pair of ankles, initially drifting into baseball bat shins, before disappearing up a regulation dark blue skirt hanging straight down from her impressive equator to a severely safe level below the knee. How the physical progression from slim ankles to global midriff was made in the limited space between hem and support system I couldn't visualise, and felt I could go blind trying. It took me back to a recent visit to the then newly opened Cathedral at Coventry, where the massive columns and roof were supported on delicate small blocks. Added to that, she had an uncanny facial resemblance to the mighty Sutherland tapestry. Later in the safety of home ground, Percy revealed that she was known to the lads in the local gangs as "Parlour Made", when they were safely out of earshot. Made like a parlour – a graphic reference to her enormous bay window, the most daunting of overhangs in the ascent of her north face, spilling over both to east and west. It was this last aspect of her layout that had spared Eddy from a view of her thunderous expression, which appeared to be fixed a good inch clear of her face.

Not that he'd hung around anyway. Completely ignored, Eddy had gone to earth beneath the box's balcony, and was doing himself no good at all by staring up in amazement through the gaps between the landing boards into the darker regions of Isobel's next week's washing. The lady herself was intent on declaiming Percy and me to the world, particularly Percy, whom she obviously knew from previous encounters. Eddy drew further back into the shadows away from the overwhelming mixture of emotions which sight and sound were apparently arousing in him. I too moved back onto the banking to marvel at the range and detail of Isobel's abuse that she was now directing solely at Percy. My assumption that they'd met before was more than true. Isobel recited in technicolor many minute details of Percy's character, whilst Wilf sat watching and occasionally nodding his agreement, or tutting a little if he'd not come across some point or other about Percy before. When she went on to thinly veiled references to Percy's family background, Wilf shook his head quite violently. "That's not true," he said to me, "not true at all. Ah've met Percy's dad!"

What was upsetting Isobel, if she could remember that far back, was that the business with the tape had shorted the track circuit and flashed up the impression of a train suddenly appearing from nowhere on her display board. She had obviously seen Percy's deliberate act of sabotage, and was mightily unimpressed. Then, in some clumsy way trying to mingle oil, troubled waters and old time's sake, Percy shuffled up towards the signal box in an attempt to placate the lady, overreaching himself to the extent of begging a mashing of tea from the infinite and eternal kettle common to all boxes. He managed as far as one foot on the steps before Isobel leaned over Percy as he put a hand on the banister, thrusting what looked like a dead-heat in a blue whale Derby at him, and threatening suffocation.

"Not one step further, Percy Kellet, not one step! You know the rules well enough... not another inch, d'yer hear?"

"Aw, come on, Isobel, luv! Me and the lads just want a brew!"

"Less of the 'luv'. I've a long memory, Percy Kellet, I've no need of you. You're no more than an apology for a coat hanger as far as I'm concerned, I can remember enough about you and your perverted mates. You get nothing here! You was in this gang when that Ibbotson Rose thing happened up here, so don't think you can come it with me!"

"That were nowt to do wi' me, lass, or any on t'lads – that

were just Ibbotson. Anyroad, it must have bin fifteen year ago, nah. Come on, lass, bygones, sleepin' dogs, live and let live... ah thought tha'd've forgot binow... old time's sake... old mates, an' such..."; hope dissolving; "How are we fixed for a mashin'? You're not bahn t'give us a mashin', are you?" Percy wisely recognising when he was beaten. "Right, ho! Come on, lad," he said to the cringing Eddy. "She won't eat thi!," adding unwisely, "She's obviously already had today's ration of raw meat for breakfast!"

This inspired a completely new line in abuse, which for inventive detail I could only find impressive. I was now back up the banking next to Wilf and our lookout man, both of whom had slipped into a sheltered hollow of obscurity. When I'd joined the railway, I'd taken up swearing as an accepted pursuit among railway males, but hadn't realised how effective abuse could be without resorting to everyday expletives. The lookout was explaining to Wilf that Isobel was the nomadic relief for a number of boxes in the area, and if she was in occupation, the box was impenetrable. Where you could normally rely on a readily offered scalding for your mug of tea leaves at any signal box, Isobel had forever had this determination that any man with an enamel container in his hand, mounting her steps, was intent on "having his way with her". Considering the nature of her topography and muscularity, the idea that any man might be in a position to embark on such a project without complete cooperation was ludicrous. Then there was the question of the simple ergonomics of such a procedure... I go dizzy even now just thinking about it.

Isobel was a leftover from the War, when ladies had been employed in signal boxes up and down the land. Whereas many had happily slipped back into a conventional housewifely lifestyle in the late forties, or been moved to more feminine station jobs on the return of the men, nobody had yet got round to discussing Isobel's placement elsewhere, due mainly to fear.

While Percy was returning to the relative peace of the banking, Isobel had performed a half-circle turn before returning to fill her small box, and Wilf was enquiring about the Ibbotson matter which had been brought up under "any other business" during Percy's recent diplomatic failure.

"Ah wasn't in this gang, then – before my time, tha knaws," said Pete, the lookout, "but Percy were; best ask him." It was apparent that Percy needed a little time and two marmalade sandwiches to recover his strength and nerve, while I suggested that Eddy might like to nip over the fence and up the hill for five bottles of pop in lieu of our refused brews of tea. Eddy was obviously still shaken up from his trauma in the underworld of the signal box steps, and was more than happy to distance himself from what was to be the lady of his bad dreams for a few nights to come. For my part, I could sense a story coming on, which might just add to the poor lad's distress, so he was better out of it. He trotted off up to the distant shop clutching my half crown.

"It were nowt, really," started Percy, "and it were certainly nowt to do wi' her. She just happened to be on turn that day – she nivver got really… sort of involved, or owt, like."

"I presume that this Ibbotson Rose is the same that's now linkman in the Works Office back in Huddersfield?" This was an "odd job" post that generally meant being stuck at the end of a phone to take and send out any messages. It also marked out the occupant as close to useless.

"That's him," said Percy, "great soft sod! What it were, that day, we'd a job up in t'tunnel yonder." (Morley Tunnel, starting a few hundred yards away towards Leeds from where we were sat – two miles long, dead straight except for the ends, and fairly clear – one of my favourites.) "It were 'bout aif past three, and we was walkin' out, back down to t'cabin, and Ibbotson suddenly reckons to remember summat what he's forgot, and sets off back inter t'hole. That were t'last we saw of him, that day. We knew what he were up to, though, 'cos we'd bin talkin' abaht it at dinnertime; he were off for a crafty eyeful!"

Percy's tale was long, and adequately filled the time until Eddy returned with the drinks.

Morley Tunnel comes out of the hillside at the Batley end, on a sweeping curve that starts about two hundred yards in the gloom inside – enough for the oval arch to appear as a pointed gothic when you're looking at it as you're on your way out. Through the cutting the curve sharpens up, bounded by some scrubby ground of no great distinction, except that it was well off the beaten track back in those days. During the course of the dinner break, on this particular day, discussions on pub politics, pigeons, rugby league, and similar religious topics, the local patrolman had mentioned that "it were good to tell it were spring" since the day before he'd noticed a lot of activity among the bushes up the banking, and on taking a closer look, he'd disturbed a couple "well and truly at it". Satisfying himself with a word or two to them about trespassing beyond boundaries, possibly lost on the pair who seemed to have no idea what boundaries were, he went on his way. Meanwhile, the lovers, failing to reconstruct the shattered fervour of their bodily fusion, scrambled back up the banking dragging an assortment of outer clothing behind them. Others in the gang remarked that it was a well-known spot for such sport, even hinting at a greater personal knowledge of it than they should have had. Throughout all this, Ibbotson had sat by quietly, taking it all in.

He was a large man in all directions, middle-aged, and with more hair up his nose than on his head. This was an immense dome, which a phrenologist could have read at thirty yards and would have seen as a three-volume novel, but for the fact that Ibbotson had no more than two or three points of remote interest which might be revealed in his bumps. He was perpetually encased in a light raincoat, in or out, summer or winter, originally fawn in colour, but later in its life reflecting brushes with tunnel walls, grassy slopes and past dinners. This coat would be replaced regularly every five years by the next one which had already served three years as best, followed by another two as pyjamas, throughout its probationary period towards becoming his current work coat. He'd a large active face, in contrast to the inactivity that lay behind it, though this mobility, together with the standard physical features, was concentrated in the middle third of the façade. The rest was quite vacant and he could have easily offered it up for advertising. Forever susceptible to tales and fables such as the present one, facial aerobics would abound as his imagination played out minor fantasies threaded into any salacious story he was currently taking in.

Ibbotson led what could only be described as a simple life. Every Thursday night he'd deposit an unopened wage packet and payslip on the scullery table, and Mrs Rose would open it without greeting, check it against the written details, and then hand back seven shillings and sixpence pocket money. Of this Ibbotson would return the sixpence as his chapel contribution. His allocation would rise to twelve shillings if pay for a worked Sunday was included, and to a regular eight shillings approaching Christmas. Her thinking here was that Ibbotson would need a bit extra for her present, whereas he would take it as a bonus to go towards his heavier drinking commitments around the festive season. As in communication, their approach to holidays was individual. She would take a fortnight off with her sister on a couple of coach tours, while he would go sit in a pub for the two weeks, permutating any one from four between Blackpool, Morecambe, Scarborough and Brid. This was his wife's arrangement, as she claimed that to have his bulk around on holiday went a long way to keeping her in a permanent shade. Ibbotson had never been consulted, and went along with the idea because he knew that any opinion he might have had wouldn't change the situation. Percy's summary of him as a "big soft sod" could hardly be challenged.

With the sun still high in the late-spring sky at four in the afternoon, Ibbotson had obviously decided to try his luck at a bit of voyeurism, thinking to find a place to hide on the hillside before the mills chucked out. His ideal spot turned out to be a small clump of bushes, near the top of the banking, where he was able to take up a position of all-round obscurity. There he sat and waited, staring fixedly uphill at the unofficial path leading down from the lane above the tunnel. So intense was his concentration, that the voices appearing almost in his ear took him by surprise. An adventurous couple had taken a completely different route to arrive on the railway side of Ibbotson's clump of bushes. This was ideal privacy for them, as the only nearby public exposure was onto the railway, where trains could be heard approaching with plenty of warning, adding an obligatory blast of the horn when entering or leaving the tunnel. They hadn't catered for the even closer bush-full of Ibbotson.

So there he was. In the front stalls for the cabaret, and it didn't disappoint. He eased himself into the best position, as quietly as a

Centurion tank in a small forest can do, and watched and watched, the raincoat adding to its decoration by taking on board a long unconscious dribble. Twenty minutes was enough. After that the pair decided to cement their romance with a pint and a gin at the local, back up the road. Ibbotson, very sensibly, waited, watching the couple make their way along the banking, until the distance was sufficient for him to make an undetectable escape. Rising in some discomfort, he was taken aback as he turned to find another couple among some thick grass to his rear engaged in Act Two, with Ibbotson coming in towards the end of the First Scene. Though this part of the stage was slightly more obscured than the setting for Act One, he watched on and used his imagination, topped up from the earlier performance, to fill in any details. A slight disturbance to his right made him turn sharply to find signs of activity in yet another circle of bushes, perhaps forty yards away. It soon became clear to Ibbotson that he was at the hub of a great wheel of passion, and the fun, for him, was beginning to wear off. If he'd been spotted at all, then the assumption would have been that he too was occupied in the pursuit of extras. Becoming the naturalist in his hide, he began to notice that when a couple had attained satisfaction it usually led to a quite unembarrassed retreat, hand in hand, studiously avoiding their uncompleted colleagues, in the general direction of the pub. It was obvious to him that he could hardly follow their example, in the same casual manner, without having the back up of a female companion. So there he had to stay. It was now five o'clock.

By the time the church clock on the hill had struck six, Ibbotson Rose was more than satiated in the field of virtual copulation, though he could at least take comfort from the fact that there were now more couples leaving than fresh starters. Dismay returned when he began to recognise the odd pair coming back for a second ride, now reinvigorated by the love potions of Booth and Tetley. Some pairs he was certain were even coming back reshuffled. By seven he was distinctly bored; way overdosed on the Prelude and F of copulation sufficient to sign up for a monastery, to get away from it for ever. Added to this were his occasional impromptu solos where he had to use his bulk and raincoat, plus a modicum of grunting, to divert any couple taking a fancy to his little nest.

If things had gone off the boil a little on the embankment of passion, elsewhere in the town things were beginning to heat up. Mrs Rose had graduated from annoyance over a spoilt meal, ready as usual at five on the dot, through a call at Ibbotson's pub, to an increasing panic as she dropped in on other members of his gang. Everyone lived quite near in those close-knit days of the small town, and by six she had covered all the team, more or less getting the same message. Ibbotson had last been seen walking back into the tunnel at around four. Not one of them was daft enough to suggest that Ibbotson might have taken off in a quite different direction to pursue his new-found hobby of hornithology. Mrs Rose was built frighteningly similar to her husband, with a subtle redistribution of lumps. That was where any similarity ended. She was not one to cross, and would have had little regard for the messenger, so nobody said any more than what they were certain of. Everything that was being revealed added up to a clear tragedy, and the railway and civil police were alerted. They all met up on the neutral ground of Isobel's signal box, much to the sulking fury of that male-hating Amazon.

A mass coitus interruptus spread throughout the shrubbery at the sight of the invasion of police, some of whom were on the railway line walking into the tunnel, and some coming down the field from the lane above. There was a lot of shuffling of bodies out onto the innocence of open grass. Ibbotson, on the other hand, withdrew deeper into his shrubbery, as he could only see discovery by uniforms at this point as being more personally damaging than if he'd revealed himself earlier.

Percy broke off from his tale to wet his thirst on the pop that had just turned up.

"Presumably he had to come out, or did he just wait till they packed it in?"

"No, it were the dogs what changed his mind!" explained Percy. "He was out like a rabbit when he heard the first yaps from 'em."

"How did he get aht of it, then, what'd he got worked aht to say to t'missus?"

"Nowt," said Percy. "T'bobbys got it aht of t'lads, put it to Ibbotson – he'd not thought up owt better, so it went straight back to their Ida. Ah bet that were some 'omecoming!"

"Did she chuck him out, then?"

"Nay, tha didn't do that in them days. No, it were t'back bedroom for him for best part on a year, well, at least up till Christmas. He weren't ower bothered, seemingly. Ida were one of the last women to go in for that tight curly hairstyle, and she useter start puttin' all t'block an' tackle work round her head shortly after tea every evening. Ibbotson used to reckon she looked like a busted sofa by t'time she were done, and 'e said it were not ower different to sleeping in a packet of cornflakes, lyin' next to her all neet. He were quite pleased wi't outcome of solitary, on the whole."

Time was getting on, and we should have begun making our way down to the station, a steady ten minutes away. This meant passing Isobel's box, which according to Percy shouldn't have posed a problem, if done without threat of rape or pillage. This wasn't enough for Eddy, though, and he insisted that we finish off our drinks so that he could take them back up to the shop and get our tuppences back on the bottles. Amidst a lot of induced burping, I told him I wasn't that bothered, but he got very short about it and said it was the least he could do seeing as I'd bought them. It was then that I realised that the shop could be seen as a long roundabout route back to the station, albeit up the hill and round the other side, but more importantly not going past Isobel's box. Pete, the lookout, asked us if we'd be OK on our own as he'd been pursuing his own version of Ibbotson's game, but with the sheep in an adjoining field.

"Just spotted another one on 'em tupping, ah'll just go mark it up." With which, he leapt over the fence, picked up a paint tin and brush concealed in the undergrowth, before galloping after the satisfied ewe.

"What's that all about, then?" I'd watched many eccentricities among the lads on the track, but had thought that chasing sheep was something they'd keep to themselves. We'd made the train and had just completed three minutes of intensive panting due to the cabaret delaying us enough to have to make the last two hundred yards in thirty seconds. We'd recovered sufficiently by Dewsbury to attempt conversation.

"Oh, you know," said Percy, "just a little job we've allus done for t'farmer. He can't be everywhere at once, so if we saw a sheep tupped we'd hop ower, like Pete, and dab some paint on its arse, so he knew which ones he might 'ave to see to himself, like, so to speak."

"We used to do summat similar in't park, when we was kids," added Wilf, "only it were fellers then, and we'd creep up and chalk a big white cross on t'backs on theer jackets. Packed it in after one of mi mate's father come home one neet wi' a big white cross chalked on t'back on his jacket."

"No," went on Percy, "we've allus got on well wi' this farmer. We used to drop him the odd scrap sleeper, or load on spent ballast, like, an' we kept his fences in shape an' all, and he'd allus see us alright around Christmas."

"It's our job to keep the fences up to scratch. Didn't he realise that?"

"Oh, he realised that, OK. It's just that we med such a gradely job on it that we sort of extended ussens a bit, and didn't allus notice whether t'railway were on t'other side of t'fence or not, if you understand mi meanin'. Tha c'n tell just how hand in glove we were wi' 'im. One of his beasts ran off down t'track, one day, while he were goin' ower t'crossing, and got itself killed bi a train. It made history, did that cow!"

"How's that, then?"

"It were t'only case of a cow being killed on t'railway, wi'out being struck dumb at same time! Right, I'm just off for a pee, that's another problem wi' having signalmen like Isobel around – one fly button an' she'd be ringin' in abaht thee for exposure!" With which he toddled off down the train.

Eddy was now intrigued. "What's he mean, about it not being dumb."

"Standard practice, Eddy, lad. When tha gets a beast knocked down on t'railway, tha can guarantee that even though tha might think tha's fust 'un there, that cow wain't have a tongue in its head. There's allus someone gets theer afore thee."

We had to elaborate a bit more for Eddy, not because of any

slowness on his part, but rather because he didn't believe what he was thinking. He looked at his potted beef sandwich a little more thoughtfully, before shrugging his shoulders and munching on.

★

Wilf was obviously still running over the events of the morning.

"There's summat familiar abaht that Ibbotson Rose story. Ah knaws for once Percy were tellin' it more or less reet, but dun't it ring a bell wi' thee, Mike?"

"Like how, Wilf?"

"Stanningley Tunnel, o'course! Not t'same exactly, in fact completely rahnd abaht, but there's a similar set of circumstances, dun't tha think?"

Percy returned refreshed and relieved. "What were this all abaht, then?"

"Wasn't it when we were in there doing one of those roof checks, Wilf?"

"That's it! Once a year, allus in friggin' February at first. Bloody awful job."

Stanningley Tunnel roof is an extraordinary shape, sort of warped and flattened. We'd had suspicions that it was moving, along with the ground and track, which was a bit disconcerting at the time, as you might expect. It was all right if they were all moving in the same direction, but if they started closing up… Well, Wilf summed it up in terms of ageing and having it away in later life. "Tha'll nivver be sure wi' each train whether it's going to fit, and even if it does it could scrape a bit!" I'd often thought of including this in my annual report, but management can be funny, so I didn't.

Anyway, I'd had these small brass studs fixed in the roof at every fifty-foot tablet mark, and on that once-a-year Sunday – always, as Wilf said, in frigging February – the pair of us would take levels through the length of the tunnel. All four rails (easy, just plonk the measuring staff on the rail head) and then on the brass markers. ("Bloody nigh impossible," said Wilf – this because it involved him lifting the fully extended fourteen feet of staff, and carefully placing it up to the brass stud in the roof – "Knocks the hell out of thi arms; and tryin' to get t'bugger reet on t'brass knob! Well, tha could be wavin' it abaht bloody ages".)

To cut a long story short, we found things were moving up and down, and not together. Only to a maximum of an inch, but at the time worrying enough. More scientific measuring coupled with better lighting has since shown up that many ground levels shift about, possibly due to fluctuations in the water table, but we were only looking at Stanningley, and had nothing to compare it with. Imaginative minds back in the Drawing Office had presented a case based on an idea that by hanging effective lighting in tunnels, you caused bulges in the walls, since sure enough, illuminate a tunnel, and there'd be the deformities appearing. Before any notice should be taken of these daft theories, the inventive ones declared the recently-lit-up Bramhope Tunnel between Leeds and Harrogate to be pregnant, as a particularly heavy bulge came to light. They claimed it was expecting a culvert, a proposition which finally got through to the eternally gullible.

Anyway, graduate bosses became nattered enough about Stanningley for them to demand a second set of measurements in July or August. I can't deny that the increasingly alarmist reports from mine and Wilf's graphic tales were rather directed at getting another soft Sunday out of it all, despite Wilf's arms, and such was the result. Having worked the oracle, there we were one July Sunday in the pleasant cool of the tunnel as against the heat of the midsummer Sunday morning outside. My fingers on the level remained in communication with the rest of me, unlike in February when all feeling would drift away as the ends turned an alarming purple before black. What's more, in July, I never heard Wilf complain once. We even took a break halfway through, and wandered out into that short pocket of comfort which always existed between the cool mouth of the tunnel and the trapped heat of the subsequent cutting.

It was just then that the emergency patrolman came through. A wiry little bloke, no more than five-two, unusually armed with just a shovel. We both knew John, or Point Four, as he was universally known. (I'd never queried this name, and had only found out a couple of weeks before that he'd picked it up on account of being the shortest of three brothers, all of them in the gangs. The other two must have stepped in something when they were kids since they'd both managed six foot.)

"Ay up, John, what're you doing out on a Sunday?"

"Heat patrol," said John, "and don't knock it! Bloody daft, mind! Ah'm s'pposed to spot a buckle in t'track as it's abaht to 'appen. Ah've six mile to walk, and tha's no idea but what ah goes rahnd a corner and t'bloody track goes twang be'ind me, and theer's me none the wiser. Still, that's not my worry, it's six hours Sunday-time, which can't be bad, tha knaws."

"Ah thought tha were tekkin' it a bit steady. An hour a mile isn't exactly stretchin' thissen, is it? Just be careful tha doan't break into a trot," advised Wilf. "Tha could easy knock an hour off over six mile!"

"No danger! Anyroad, it's what it sez on t'timesheet what counts. Reet then! Ah'm off afore ah see tha two start actu'ly doin' summat. Ah doan't want to get a sweat on bi watchin' thee do owt like work!" With which he set off into the blazing light of the high sun in the cutting.

Then something peculiar happened. As he rounded the curve, where the cutting changed to high embankment, he suddenly dropped into the cess at the side of the track. From there on he walked crouched down, occasionally looking across the tracks at rail level, as if checking the cross-fall. At one point he seemed to be particularly concerned, spending several minutes in a crouched position. From there he continued for about another hundred yards before clicking back upright into normal walking.

"He's spotted something wrong along there, and like he said, it's behind him now, so owt could happen without him knowing. Best keep an eye out while we're around."

Wilf was more positive. "We can have a look ussens in aif an hour when we're passin' – I tek it we will be passin' in aif an hour? Tha's nowt else up thi sleeve for today, has t'a?"

"No, as if! Come on then, if you're ready we'll get done. How's your arms, anyway? You've said nowt about them so far."

"Champion! Shoulders are a bit sore, like, but it's much easier this time of t'year. Mi arms're longer fer a start off, 'cos tha's not havin' to hoik up a bloody great heavy coit every time tha stretches up!"

When we'd finished, and were walking out a second time we could feel the heat now drifting into the tunnel. The temperature outside had gone up a few notches as the sun reached its peak. Sharing out the carrying of the gear, Wilf and I set off up to the level crossing where we'd left the car. At the point where the patrolman had started looking at the cross-levels from down in the cess, we both dropped down and started walking in a half crouch to look across the rails. We must have looked for all the world like Wilson and Kepple seeking Betty.

"Bit of a swilly up ahead, Wilf. I'll bet that's what was bothering him."

"Tek a look across when tha gets theer, then. Ah bet tha finds cross-levels've gone. Best place for a buckle that. Could go at any time in this heat."

A few more yards of Wilson and Kepple's sand dance, and we stopped, still crouched, and looked across the heads of the four rails. Sure enough, one rail was distinctly dipped compared to the others. We stood up to look at the line and see if there were any gaps in the stone ballast at the sleeper ends, suggesting some sideways movement of the track.

"Bloody hell!" said Wilson.

"Bloody hell!" said Kepple.

"You dirty buggers!" blazed Betty, an outstanding young lady in her early thirties, lying in the private garden at the bottom of the embankment, not twenty-five yards away. She was totally naked for all of two seconds, lying north/south from where we were standing with the two of us looking directly up her Antarctica.

She grabbed a nearby towel, and made a pretty poor job of covering herself up.

"Perverts! Seen all you want?" she screamed across at us.

"Can't be much more to offer, can there, luv?" called back Wilf, as she jumped up and shot off up to the house, forgetting that the towel was making only a fair job of protecting her frontage, but was doing little useful round the back.

We slowly recovered from the shock, and took in the surroundings. "Tha can understand her feelin' safe, can't'a? Sithee, two great panel fences eether side of t'gardin, ah'll bet t'neighbours cop for nowt, even stood on a chair upstairs. Thur's Duckett's crossing yonder wi' that bell wot rings whenivver a train's comin'. She's safe as houses theer – or was! Ah bet we've buggered up a nice little number for t'local lads, though!"

"Ay, and you can bet that this bit of railway's not been properly patrolled for weeks!"

We walked on to Duckett's crossing, where we bumped into the patrol man, John, again, who'd been having a break outside the cabin, sat on the side fence.

"Ah've bin watchin' tha two," he said, "creepin' along theer like a pantomime 'oss. Ah thought ah were t'only one as knew abaht that lass. Who telled thee?"

*

We were nearing Huddersfield by the time Wilf and I had finished our tale. Eddy, who'd been so unmoved and sulky as to be driven to drawing in the dust on the window, was sent down the train to try and collect a few newspapers for our dinner hour. The lad still hadn't fully recovered from his encounter with the dark underworld of Isobel, and despite some great discoveries, he still didn't seem to be sharing the enthusiasm of James Cook after the captain's exploration of a less daunting southern hemisphere. Eddy's brow was furrowed for days, and he didn't look like getting a good night's sleep for a while. Sympathy didn't stop us giving him a hard time when he returned from his paper chase with a mangled *Daily Mirror*, and a folded section of the *Telegraph*, turned to the crossword, with five filled in, two of which were wrong.

"Tha could've managed better than this on t'fust morning tram, lad. This i'n't stimulatin' material for an hin-depth discussion like as what we're used to, tha knaws."

"'S'all there was! The guard was going down in front of me."

"Look at this *Telegraph* what he's dug up. Business news, court circular and obituaries. What sort of use is that?"

"'Nother court circular on t'back 'ere, 'fact two. Someone's put a pair of horn-rimmed on t'Queen; can tha bi done for treason doin' that?"

"Ah bet if they took that manky tash she's got into account, along with t'sex change job they've done on t'Duke, tha'd bi gettin' pretty close."

I'd been focused on the middle distance knowing that I'd a bit of a problem to face up to when we got back to base. I was jolted back with this last exchange, sensing an opportunity suddenly made available for grabbing. I grabbed it: "I didn't realise you were so keen about upholding the dignity of Her Majesty, ER."

"Tha what?" Said with a deeply suspicious expression of furrowed brow and heavy eyes.

"What's up wi'im? Tha's changed thi tune a bit sin' last week, 'a'n't tha? Ah took it, and Percy agreed, that tha were less than enamoured bi t'royalty, after we'd laiked abaht on t'platform for t'umpteenth time on account of them comin' up 'ere."

"Just saying, I'm happy to see you're still interested in them, that's all. Although... funny thing that you should mention t'visit—"

"They've nivver changed thur minds agin! They have, 'aven't they?"

"There has been another letter, s'true."

In a month's time we were due for a royal visit to Huddersfield, to open something or other that had been up and running for months anyway, and She'd decided to pop up on Her train. If the Queen were to stop and think for a bit, she must find it a bit of a coincidence that when she comes to open a hospital, say, there always seems to have been a local disaster, combined with a sudden epidemic and the nine-month anniversary of a power cut, all going towards the amazing filling up of A&E and every ward, including maternity, with customers, before she's actually unlocked the doors. It's the same as when she cuts the ribbon on a new motorway, declaring that we now have her OK to use it, and when she drives through on what's supposed to be the first journey, she finds that already someone's thoughtfully decorated it with skid marks and squashed hedgehogs, as if it's been in full use for weeks. Then there's tree planting, when it must be forever apparent to her that new trees are supplied complete with a hole to put them in, and that it seems to take only one shovelful of muck to get them to stand up on their own, because that's all she ever sees of the job. And can you imagine the disappointed look on her face when she gets up in a morning and draws the curtains, only to find that there's no little brass notice stuck to the window saying as how it was her that's just done so? Anyway, here we were, in our little northern town, with something important like a bingo hall or a phone box to open, and finding her to be free that day, and just about up to slicing through a ribbon with a brand-new pair of scissors. In the spontaneous flash of three months of intensive preparation, up she comes with the Royal Train, since it's doing nothing special either.

On such occasions, it would seem that the mayor and council are delighted to meet her, and all want to turn out in full gear, along with the police, St John's Ambulance, hoards of polished Boy Scouts and Brownies, a few freshly painted soldiers, and the entire population of the township. Even the opportunist house burglars must view the occasion positively. In fact the only exceptions to the universal mood of delight are the Drawing Office staff of the local railway Civil Engineer's department. The whole event was always a total pain for us.

Just us, you understand. The rest of the lads are more than chuffed, with the one exception of he who is designated to the "long pole, with a hook and a bucket" duty. No? Answer in a minute!

Whenever the Royal Train travelled up from London to Huddersfield, or anywhere else for that matter, all level crossings and bridges, and even small rocks in an ideal sniping position, had to be guarded by a railwayman, usually from the Civil's Works and PWay gangs. They'd be dropped off a good hour before the timetabled passage of the train, and would take up a position of maximum surveillance potential, armed to the teeth with a rolled-up copy of the day's newspaper of their choice, and charged with specific instructions to prevent hurt, nuisance or damage to the Monarch. Thus, little Ernie Kennefick, for instance, hero of the office drainage clearance, would stand decorated with two high-visibility vests (one being insufficient to make the complete journey round his midriff), ready to fight off with his bare hands any marauding bands of Roundheads who might have been out of touch with current events since the mid-1600s. Should the armies of anti-royalists descend on Ernie's particular bridge or strategic sod, intent on foul acts of sabotage, he would have nothing but the power of verbal persuasion to put them off and enable them to see the error of their ways. He would remain alert and on his guard for as long as it might take, without any means of communication with the rest of the world, other than by possibly locating a handy hill and lighting a beacon thereon.

In the event, many an Ernie has settled down with his rolled-up weapon of mass destruction, devoured it from cover to cover, while waiting for the gang bus to return. This would often arrive as a bit of a surprise, and meant that the Royal Train had slipped by without him even noticing, perhaps maybe having momentarily had his eyes closed pondering on some issue raised by the paper.

On the other hand, it could be raining, snowing and blowing a gale, royalty being such, they are quite prepared to brave the worst of weather conditions to travel within the meagre protection of their luxurious eight coaches. Our Ernie could well be stood in a vast wilderness with only his small bridge affording any shelter, provided he could lash himself to some part of the wall to prevent him being blown down the track. Yet he would still consider his position as one of good fortune, since it marked him down as not having drawn the short straw of the long pole, with the hook, and the bucket. This was the poor soul appointed to attend to the Royal Train parked in a siding overnight. In common with all coaching stock of the time, it had simple, yet dependable toiletry arrangements – that is, a hole in the floor. Nothing passing through that hole could possibly be allowed to remain there – hence the bucket, the hook, and the distance afforded by the long pole.

It has been said before that the Queen and her family must have a conviction that small-town Britain smells universally of fresh paint. Certainly, as far as the railway was concerned, anything remotely close to the walking route that the royal personage would take, had to be painted. Days before, and weeks after, this corridor of resplendent colour would stick out like a sore thumb, until native grime toned it back into line. On the actual day, any signs or adverts that might cause distress to the oversensitivity of the nobility had to be covered up or taken down. Hence, for a while, there would be no indications for passengers as to where the station toilets were to be found. (It's just occurred to me: here's this royal party being protected from catching sight of any evidence of where the General Public secrete themselves in order to gain relief, when these actual facilities provided for them are arguably better than the hole in the floor that this same royalty has no doubt been hovering over within the last hour!) As to advertising posters, consider the plight of the female passenger caught up in an impulse to nip off her train and buy a new bra and not having the benefit of any billboard information to direct her to a particular brand, since it will all have been concealed as unsuitable viewing. Newspaper placards were collected up, and, of greatest importance, any graffiti, however innocent, would have been obliterated, if only by a carefully placed Union flag. It was commonly put about that the reason for all this corporate delicacy was that the Queen should not be in any way embarrassed by the sight of a direction to the Ladies, a brassiere, or the low down on a certain young lady from Oldham, but the truth was that no situation must be offered to the opportunist photographer for a combination picture of Queen and background which might prove palatable for the front cover of *Private Eye*, or the like.

Then there were the ludicrously incongruous horticultural displays. For a brief twelve hours, forty square yards of tarmac, backed by the large blocks of a millstone grit wall, itself decorated with a variety of fall pipes, redundant hangers and cables, were all transformed into an oasis of floral splendour by discreetly placed conifers, bins of exotic foliage, pots of marigolds, petunias, impatiens and bulbs in season, along with artificial grass and bonsai white paling fencing. All grown and laid out by our own nurserymen from near York, who used the same components in a different arrangement to enhance the gnomes, little helpers, windmills and perpetually running streams of the Christmas station displays. (Such festive scenes would centre around a sawn-off Christmas tree – sawn off to fit into the modern tight-ceilinged station concourse, but providing the by-product for the local Works Supervisor of the pruned top as an acceptable six-foot tree in its own right, for home.) For the royal visit the gnomes, and so on, were replaced by flags of unctuous loyalty, and the tree was replaced by *it*.

It was the reason for weeks of distress, aggravation, frustration, hostility, fury and regicidal leanings within the Area Drawing Office. *It* was the red carpet.

That's another thing about royalty, their feet must react badly with tarmac, such that whenever they get off something, be it a plane, ship or train, they need a transitional piece of carpet to break their feet in gently to the shock of walking on common soil. Popes are different; they can't get enough of it. Before the engines have wound down they'll be abseiling down the runway steps to get at the tarmac and give it a big kiss. But the royals need cushioning.

Now, whatever your views on royalty might be, and mine may have occasionally shown through this thin veneer of respect, the dignity of a royal arrival would be marred if the train were to run into the station and drop HM off at random. This could leave the local dignitaries having to trot down the platform, chains of office flying dangerously, to meet and greet her. So the exact position of the red carpet, laid from the station entrance, along the line of worthies, and then turning towards the platform edge, had to be precisely worked out beforehand. This done, it was a simple calculation to measure out and mark the point where the front buffers of the loco needed to come to a standstill, in order that the royal of the day stepped out from the predetermined train door straight onto the middle of the carpet. At the critical front loco buffer position, well away from the welcoming jumbo bouquet, there would be a clear paint line on the platform along with one of the more presentable gang lads, dressed in Persil-ised overalls straight from stores – betrayed by the neat chessboard of folded creases – and holding out a large red flag in a proudly extended fist.

All of which brings us back to the rumbling circle of hostility that was the chainmen. Over the previous few weeks three different lengths of dignitary line-ups had been sent to the Huddersfield Office, and three times Elliot Milner had sent me and the bemused chainmen out to mark the underside of the platform at the exact point where the royal foot should step onto native Yorkshire carpet. (I had tried to determine whether she led with her left or right foot, but Elliot had temporarily lost any semblance of a sense of humour, he being only slightly more enamoured about the whole thing than I was.) Then, a week later, the placing of Huddersfield's finest was swapped to the opposite side of the ticket barrier, so that the Queen would now walk forward towards the exit, rather than back along the train, thus generating a fourth letter of instructions. This move had been necessitated by the station porters having caused a small incident in their Platform 1 office, in which a simple meal of sausages and beans had erupted into an involuntary barbecue. Window frames looking out onto the platform had been cremated, and it turned out that extensive smoke staining of stonework was another thing that turns queens off. It meant yet another measuring and marking-up session.

Today's would be the fifth attempt at getting it right, and was just a matter of re-measuring along the platform from the new-determined point of regal unloading. Yet again the aim was to locate, and paint up, a further revision of the position for the flagman to stand, marking the stopping point for the front end of the train.

"What's it abaht this time, then?" asked Wilf. "Have they worked out that twelve Huddersfield councillors are wider than a dozen Londons, or summat?"

"No, we seem to have the chucking-off point right, at last. They've now found that due to engineering works somewhere down south, the whole train's going to be arse about front, so it's a new measurement to the buffers, but," I tried, brightly, "they've managed to incorporate two balls-ups in one this time, by suddenly realising that it'll be double-headed. So they've added the length of the second loco as well."

"How many times have we measured this lot up, now?" asked Percy. "And what's t'a bahn to use for paint, we've gone through aif a dozen colours already? T'end of yon platform looks like a cycle-dildo rainbow!"

"We're whiting them all out and starting afresh. They must have got it right this time."

So out we went again, same team as before, the same lookout man provided, he and the watching station staff drawing exactly the same conclusions of incompetence on my part – assuming that the one who carries the survey book must therefore be the one responsible for cocking it up every other time.

Having chalked up the loco buffer stop position, and painted over the four previous definitive statements, we walked back along the platform to the office. Percy opted to walk on the track, and on reaching the new indisputable royal jumping-off point, he paused.

"Are we absolutely dead sure and certain this time that they're hoikin' her off exactly here, now?"

"Definite," I said, hopefully.

"Reet, then. We'll just tidy all these marks up a bit," said Percy, dabbing around with his paintbrush for a while. After a meeting of the surveying committee, chaired by Wilf and Percy, it was agreed that this had been one of them jobs, where "beyond the call of duty" was mentioned more than once. Normally "them" jobs involved getting mixed up with a lot of muck or water, but the majority vote this time quoted mental taxation and aggro, so it was to the refreshment room next, where I was expected to put my hand down for teas and toasted teacakes all round, as some form of compensation.

Come the day of the royal visit, Elliot turned up in his inter-view suit. He was down to take up a privileged position in mid-field amidst the overnight horticultural explosion, with at best little more than his haircut and the knot in his tie visible. This privilege wasn't particularly due to his standing in the local railway hierarchy, but mainly because he'd let slip to Irene that he could get a couple of tickets for a place in the crowd, and she'd told him that he would. So to top off all the heartache, he was down one new hat for her as well. Ever the enthusiast, Bill made up a little Union Jack for him to wave, consisting of a postcard and a pick-axe handle. It lost much of its significance by being done in orange and purple, which were the only coloured pens I'd lend him. Black-inking the handle with "Aye up, love" took away any remaining dignity, but it didn't stop Bill putting on a show of hurt feelings when Elliot told him where he could wave it. Eddy and me, purely out of curiosity, took ourselves up onto the water tank roof of the offices, to watch the rather splendid train slide into the station. We couldn't see into the platform area because of the station roof, but did manage to make out a dot of red amongst the crowds outside the station front as the party climbed into cars for the short journey up the main street. It might have been the Queen, it might have been a bunch of flowers, or it might have been one of the Mrs Aldermans, demonstrating her husband's political allegiances. It really didn't matter. However, what did occur to me was that for all the intense meetings that Elliot had had with the local police, both civil and railway, and representatives of the royal household, here I was, unchallenged, in an ideal sniping position.

After the intense two minutes it had taken to move the Queen from QB2 (train) to KKt7 (car), Elliot returned to the office in a distinctly funny mood. I'd expected him to at least bring Irene back for a cup of tea, or more likely take her for one in the refresh. But no, he'd left her on the platform for the next train back to Leeds, and seemed to have something on his mind.

"Get out there! And don't come back until you can make out a full report. I want all measurements checked and double-checked. If you find a mistake, hide it, but don't think that's the last you'll hear of it from me!" No further would he go.

I recognised one of Elliot's rare black tempers, and knew well not to ask questions. Eddy and I wandered onto the almost deserted platform, plants and carpet now being removed with undignified speed, to be shifted on to Leeds where herself was to join up with the train in a few hours' time. I noticed Irene still waiting on a far platform, and had the brilliant idea of straightening things up with Elliot a bit by asking a posh suit near the Royal Train if she could have a lift back to Leeds on it. He said "No" but it took him a longer time than that to do so. We reached the critical open carriage door just as the carpet was being rolled up, and it immediately struck me that there was a distinct discrepancy between the position of the door and the bit of carpet she was supposed to have jumped out onto, amounting to about thirty yards. This rather gave me a clue as to the reason for Elliot's mood.

It turned out that the Queen had had to alight onto bare tarmac after all, and walk back to the carpet and the head of the queue of brass, so passing along them twice. I was considerably relieved to find the loco was also thirty yards past its mark, so it wasn't my mistake. We found that the flagman had been correctly placed, only to watch the loco run on past his outstretched flag. Proving material for a CBE, the determined lad had run alongside the diesel loco, banging his flag on the windscreen, before the driver pulled up at precisely the position he always did whenever he was bringing in the Liverpool express. I managed to question the driver on this point, and he claimed that his concentration had been shot to pieces by the sight of his neighbour and snooker partner, Councillor Harold Sykes, dressed up like an undertaker's runner, and standing amongst the line-up of notables on the herbaceous platform, amidst several similar. As a result, he'd reverted to a normal day, missing the flagman's signals, and running on to his usual stopping point at the top of the platform ramp. Consequently HM had had her unfortunate contact with a common bit of station tarmac.

I watched the train draw away, after studying the spartan luxury within. Contented and in the clear, I was in no rush to put Elliot out of his misery. My final check was on the underside of the platform, where I'd marked up and wiped out the various alighting points, just to make doubly sure on the position where the carpet had been. It was then that I caught Percy's bit of frustrated handiwork.

Fortunately too small to be easily seen from the opposite platform, four track widths away, Percy, venting his disenchantment, had arranged for the Queen to step over his own piece of undiscovered, but slightly confusing, graffiti which announced in bright yellow: "The king Queen gets off here"!

Dominoes

"Why haven't you played your double-six?"

"Tha's not supposed to know ah've got double-six!"

"We all know tha's got double-six. It's got a bit knicked out of t'corner."

I accept that home-made dominoes won't ever be perfect, but ours at Huddersfield didn't even flirt with perfect. They'd have had to improve some, just to make inadequate. Great slabs of hardboard, three inches long by one and a half wide; part drilled holes blacked in with Indian ink, set on a silver-painted face, and sprayed gold on the reverse. Back and front were almost equally recognisable, which was a pretty fair reason why the home side was never known to lose. Bill and I had made them from quarter-inch-thick hardboard packs, impregnated with something or other, one time popular with Harry Hanson for filling voids under sleepers at their bearing points. Two dozen dinnertimes of intermittent sawing, drilling and bandaging had gone into the production of a full set – "Why buy some when wiv got all that's needed to make 'em for nowt?" argued Bill. Double-six alone had demanded breaking into a second piece of board. Out of the twelve controlled drillings needed for the two sixes, it was almost inevitable that at least one would go right through, so seriously detracting from the integrity of the piece. The metal first-aid box, virtually empty by the time we'd finished, was sprayed gold to match, and used to house the monstrosities. Still, every winter dinnertime with Wilf and Percy over, out they'd come, and so would the same old complaints.

"Look," said Bill, detecting criticism of the combined skills which he and I had lavished on hand-crafting them, "we'd twelve dints to drill in that bugger, and we'd mebee a dozen goes at it afore we med one wi'out goin' reet through. Ah knaw it's not perfect on t'back, but bloody hell! A hole drilled reet though would've bin a dead giveaway. If tha's got double-six, tha should cover that nicked bit ower, or get rid on it sharp!"

"Look! A bloody octopus couldn't cover up all t'lumps and dints on t'backs on this lot. Why dun't'a just go aht and buy a proper set of doms? Ones wi' oils at each corner fer a four, 'stead of all ower t'shop; or three in a line fer three, not meckin' a bloody triangle, like thissun! If tha's landed wi' one of these sixes, tha's to count t'dots ivery time to mek sure, 'cos tha can't tell bi just lookin' at it! It's not as if him theer's got nowt, and can't afford t'buy some; ah knaw ferra fact he's done three Sundays on t'trot. You could get a set for a quid, anyweer!"

"That's pricey for just one dom. Ours is only a bit uneven along one of the short edges."

"What's uneven?"

"One-four."

"Tha knaws what ah mean, clever Dick, just tek it from me, these here're rubbish; ah'm knockin'!"

"Mebbee if tha'd painted t'dots on wi' different colours we'd have a better chance of tellin' a dodgy four from a scrappy five. Has t'a thought of that?"

"We couldn't wait while t'railway discovered that paint comes in more than three colours. They've not got beyond green, black and that ruddy awful magnolia. And they only have that because it looks like white what's already gone mucky."

"That's true. Elliot went for having his office done out in duck-egg blue last year. Threw t'Painting Bobby, Gordon Carter, into a right tizzy, and nowt happened fast till Elliot got him pinned down over it. He reckoned that t'stores couldn't find such a paint, so Elliot pointed out, like he can when he's crossed, that it was there on his colour chart. We managed to get hold of the requisition that'd come back from Central Stores stamped "Unavailable", and bottomed the matter. You'd to take it outside into the light, mind, but you could just make out the carbon copy. He'd only gone and ordered three gallons of Durex Eggshell Gloss, hadn't he!"

"Anyroad, even if we'd got tha duck-egg, we'd still only have had that, snot green and black to play wi'. 'Sides, ah reckon they're classy wi' these gold and silver sprays we used. They were from 'im trying to find summat for markin' up sleepers."

"Tha'll nivver get no change aht of yon thick berk, Carter. Gi'im more than one colour to use and he's buggered. D'yer know, when they wanted a zebra crossing paintin' on one o't'platforms at Leeds City, me and Percy had to go out and mark it up for him, like painting by numbers! 'One', 'Two', 'One', 'Two', all t'way across."

"Is this 'ere double-three or three-two?"

"Neether; it's two-three, and it won't go, anyroad!"

"Ah were only checkin' for later. Answer t'phone, Bill!"

"Hello! Wilf and Percy? Naaaw, they're still aht... shouldn't think they'll be back before three, earliest... And thee! Yon Gaunty seekin' yor two fer a quick job this afternoon."

"Cheers, Bill, one a day's enough, eh, Wilf? 'Specially if it's yon dopey pillock. Talk abaht brain donor!"

"Dids't'a hear about Keith Loach getting half've Normanton searchin' for Gaunty, las' week? It were after the barmpot had rung in from a phone box in t'middle of Normanton for some information on a job he were supposed to be settin' out..."

"He's a bugger fer goin' off wi' aif of what he needs. Coupla weeks back, we'd t'level, legs, staff, string-line, chalk, two tapes and a shovel between us, all t'way to Halifax, and when we gets theer he'd no survey book! Had to write it all dahn in t'stop press space of t'*Post*, wi' a run ower onto a fag packet. Ruddy useless when he's smitten wi' a new lass, is Eric."

"Aye, well, anyroad, he gives Keith t'number of this phone box weer he is, in Normanton, Queen Street, Cheapside area, tha knaws, and waits on a bit for Keith to ring back. Then he must'a reckoned it'd tek some time fer Keith to sort this info out for him, so he buggers off to t'caff fer a cuppa tea. Anyroad Keith's fund it and he's back to him in less than five, and he's ringing t'box fer ages afore this auld lad outa t'street answers it. Theers Keith askin' t'auld feller if he can see anyone hangin' arahnd. 'Aye,' says t'bloke, 'it's bloody market day, thurs aif've ruddy Normanton aht 'ere!' 'Well, can yer see anyone abaht wearin' an orange coat?' says Keith. 'Yup!' says he, 'thurs a woman in t'bun shop queue, and another ower theer wi' a pram, and theer's a poodle! Which one dust'a want?'"

"We'll have to start again."

"How d'yer mean? What's up?"

"There! Someone's put double-four up against a five."

"That's nivver double-four in this wide world, them's surely fives, aren't they!"

"Look. Double-five's over there among t'dead ones; you can tell it by that bit of red ink down one edge. See!" I turned it over, and proved it.

"Well, this'un mun bi double four and an aif, then."

"If it is double-four, then, what's it look like on t'back."

"It's near perfect as it happens, 'cept a tadge heavy on t'gold spray. Looks like what all the others should've done, but don't. Almost t'best domino we made, that, wasn't it, Bill?"

"Well, one or two on 'em had to come good out've seventy!"

"How d'yer mean, seventy? Theer's nobbut twenty-eight in a pack!"

"Ay, that's not countin' rejects."

"Yer not sayin that y'had to chuck away as many as that, is t'a? Dust'a mean tha med… what… as many as another forty-two worse nor these buggers?"

"There was a lot of hazards tha'd to tek into account; saw slipping, drill going reet through, him orderin' another six-three when we'd already done one. And thur were all them goes at double-six. Oh ay, and he even mucked up double-blank!"

"You can't've mucked up double-blank, fer Chrissake!"

"He did! Bled all ower it!"

"Ay, well I reckon I bleed longer nowadays. I was reading as how it's your diet that affects blood clotting. Alcohol's brilliant for that, and we don't get a drink now and again at dinnertimes, like we used to. Thickens your blood up, does a couple of pints."

"This new no drinkin' rule's mekkin a reet mess've things back in t'office. All t'lads what's on call aren't allowed to have any at all, tha knaws. Ken Lorriman got hisself in a reet pickle ower t'weekend – had to ring up t'gaffer, Colin Lamb, fer a rulin'. Colin were tellin' us all abaht it afore Ken come in Monday morning. Half six, Saturday neet, apparently, an' there's Ken on t'blower in a flat spin. 'Ay oop, Colin,' says he, 'ah've med a load o' Beef Bollocknaked ferrus tea an' t'recipe said to add three-quarters on a pint've watter, so ah slams in a bottle of Bugundee, like, juster liven it up a bit, like, burra suddenly thought on, like, as ah was on call fer t'weekend. Amm'a still OK, Colin, wi' t'new rulin's?' And Colin comes back sayin' as 'ow there were no problem, so long as he didn't eat none of it!"

"Mike went on a drugs an' alcohol course last Tuesday, di'n't tha? He teks that many pills he thought it were a launch party fer his auterbiography!"

"I'll tell you what, though, Frankie Ayres in Training took us, and I reckon he knows a bit more about it than he should! After we'd done with all t'official bunkum – you know t'stuff – long-term effects, and all that; how much is safe the night before, and all that… stuff what we knew already, Frankie comes round t'front of t'table, and leans back on it, t'way they teach trainers to do 'cos it makes 'em look more superior, or something. 'Any questions?' says he. 'I'll answer absolutely anything you want to know about the Drugs and Alcohol Policy document. Anything at all,' he says.

"So, someone comes up with 'What posts are going to be made Safety Critical?' – meaning where you've to keep off drink altogether at all times. Frankie comes back with: 'I'm afraid I'm not in a position to give a response to that. Any other questions?' Someone else asks: 'What safeguards will there be against victimisation of individuals picked out at random for screening?' Again, Mr Ask-Me-Owt comes back with: 'I've not been acquainted with any information on that point.' Then up comes another with 'What's going to happen to anyone prescribed drugs which affect performance on a long-term basis?' which I thought was a pretty basic thing to want to know. But, oh no, 'That is a matter for management which has not been transmitted down to me,' says Frankie.

"So I nips in with, 'How do you tell if someone's been smoking cannabis, Frankie?' 'Ah, right,' says he, 'you'll find it has a very distinctive odour, quite different from any tobacco, and you'll see signs in the smoker's behaviour consistent with him having this loss of reality as he drifts off into a dreamlike fantasy, and is overcome by this state of glorious euphoria. He'll be experiencing an overwhelmingly beautiful picture of vivid patterns floating before his eyes; then he goes off into talking about warm reds and yellows through to golden orange and a spectacular mauve, cracking on about it being a feeling you can't really describe, of complete whatnot…', and on and on he goes! I'll swear he didn't get all that from reading a book, or the like."

"Ah reckon they've got to be on summat to do that job. We was in t'same gang, me an' Frankie. Even way back then he could talk away an' knaw nowt, but I wouldn't swap wi'im now. Million years, ah wouldn't! Allus reet posh, though. Blew his nose wi' his back to thi, and on an hankie at that; used t'go out've t'cabin to fart, and allus went up agin' a tree to have a pee. Almost gentry were Frankie!"

"Are you goin' t'mek a move, or not? Tha's bin lakin' wi' that domino fer five minits, now!"

"It's jus' that I can't help feelin' it's a bit shorter nor t'others, that's all."

"Oh, six-two, aye it is. It were on its way to bein' a second six-three, an' we had to trim a slice off."

"Gerronwi'it, can't tha! Bloody hell, it's like playin' in't delivery queue up t'crematorium!"

"Ay, ah can tell thee. It's like bein' among t'dead in t'Leeds Office, nah. They've stopped t'lads havin' a go at t'women, wi' this sexual amusement thing; tha can't go out for a drink, an' theer's bugger all left to sing about! Theer's nowt left of life in t'place no more."

"It reet got to Kenny Lorriman las' week. Got hissen so wound up ower another set o'rules just aht. Teks hisself inter Kye Bevin's office and started sounding off abaht it all. Nowt t'do wi' Kye, but that dun't stop Kenny. Got proper aereated, he did, leanin' ower Kye's desk, wi't'finger waggin' an' all. Bloody dangerous, ah thought, what wi' Kye's temper, an' all – and tha could see as how he were a bit tekken aback at fust. Tha could tell bi his nose goin' redder, like – burree nivver rose to it like as how he normally would. We thought he were sickenin' fer summat, an' then he starts windin' Ken up even more, on purpose, like, an' Ken's nearly climbin' down 'is throat. Goes on fer a minnit or so, an' then Ken jus' runs outa steam, wi' Kye sat theer grinnin' at him. 'What's so bloody funny?' says Kenny. 'Ah'm bloody serious!' 'Ah was just wantin' t'see,' says Kye, 'how far up thi tie my tea'd go, whilst tha's 'ad it danglin' in mi pot!'"

"D'yer knaw, ah think mi hands're goin' inter cramp wi'

holdin' these bloody things. Ah'm goin' t'ave ter stand 'em up, it's like bein' in t'old bloke's shelter in t'park... Tha's med some awkard buggers 'ere, 'asn't t'a... look! They won't even stand up proper... gi'up kickin' t'table thi gormless article! Alright, that's it! Reshuffle! 'Cos tha's seen all mi flamin' hand, now, that's why! Sithee, it's no bloody wonder they tumble ower! All t'edges're rahnded so's they'll nivver stand up."

"'Aven't you got some yap! Ah thought tha were supposed t'be a champion at this 'ere. Tha were goin' on last week abaht winnin' t'month's cup at t'Mucky Duck—"

"Black Swan, pillock; and that were playin' wi' proper pot doms, them that's polished up black wi white faces an' little brass knobs inset in't middle fer shufflin', not gold-sprayed planks wi' oils in! An' summat else playin' championship stuff – tha can't tell what aif on t'doms are from t'back, eether!"

"That's not really fair, Wilf. Credit where credit's due. On a good day Bill can tell t'backs of every single one, not just half, can't you, Bill?"

"In a good leet, mebbee..."

"Talking of good light, did you heard about Steve Vertigans off Leeds area picking up Vinnie last Saturday night, to work in Morley Tunnel?"

"Vinnie lives up Manningham way now, dun't he? Along wi' all t'thirty bob ladies of pleasure?"

"Yup, that was mostly t'problem, 'cos Steve couldn't spot which road he wanted in t'dark. So he's driving along slowly, trying to spot street names as he's passing. He thought he'd found it, but he'd got Walk instead of Way or summat. Anyroad, he's about to set off again and this young lass turns up, wearing not much more than a belt an' vest. So she sticks her head through t'car window. 'Is there any way I can be of assistance to you?' she says. 'Yes,' says Steve, 'so long as you can handle a level staff,' which she naturally takes t'wrong way, and she's off with all t'professional chat, discussin' positions and price lists, and all. Steve's way out of his depth. Then this cop car comes sidling up, just as Vinnie comes out of his street end. Lass takes off and they're both left there, and stuck for half an hour trying to explain to these young coppers about surveying an' staffs."

"That's t'second time in as many months what Stevie's been in trouble wi't'bobbies. Got caught shop-liftin', week or two back. Them things tha's t'walk through what they've put up near to t'shop doors – they ring bells an' things if tha nicks owt an' try t'walk aht. Steve's in Emmaness, buyin' this new shirt, an' t'till lass forgets to tek that magnetic tab thing off what they have on all t'stuff now. Steve naws nowt abaht it, an' nowt goes off when he walks outer t'shop – machine can't've bin workin', or summat. But t'one at Littlewoods, when he walks in theer was, an' all hell's let loose, wot wi' t'bells goin' fifteen to t'dozen. Then these two grert g'rillas tek 'old; drag 'im off to t'office. Steve's tryin' to work out 'ow you get done fer shopliftin' when you're walkin' in to a shop, not comin' out!"

"He got off, though?"

"They couldn't pin owt on 'im, seein' as 'ow he were tekkin' stuff inter a Littlewoods, wi' a St Michael label, and had a proper receipt. Took some explainin' though. Them shoulder bandits what they have in t'security uniforms are a bit ninepence to t'shillin', tha knaws! Thick as bloody planks, some on 'em – ah knaw! T'wife's brother's one. Couldn't spot a shoplifter if he were pushin' stuff aht in a wheelbarrer, that 'un."

"Like these sixes. Ah've just twigged, all t'sixes're a bit thicker nor t'rest, look theer, feel t'bump when tha runs off that six-four onto t'four-nowt. See?"

"Tha's got a thing abaht us sixes, 'asn't tha? Tha wants t'try drillin' six aif oils in a bitter 'ardboard some time! Tha's reet through in a flash if tha's not careful. Wi' fund this sheet wot were a bit thicker nor t'others, and it were a lot easier to cope wi'."

"Meks fer a good matchin' set o'dominoes, though, dun't it? Aif a dozen thicker nor t'rest."

"Doesn't seem to've done thee no harm! How many matches has t'a nah, then?"

"Happen ah'm gettin' t'knaw t'backs an' all, like thee! Ah'd say some on t'backs're better nor t'fronts fer mekkin' aht what they're supposed t'be!"

"Ah'll tell thee a front what's as good as t'back – that's that theer lass in Typin', whatsername, Dizzy... nivver fund out her real name."

"Weren't thur talk of her an' Eric for a while? Ah knaw he fancied 'is chances theer."

"It were only tittle-tattle 'cos they allus seemed to come in together of a mornin'. Weren't surprisin' since they come on t'same train from Bradfud. They nivver come in together now, though, ah've noticed."

"Then they must definitely be on t'go, nah!"

"As a matter of fact there is something happening there. Eric was telling me that they were thinking of a driving holiday together with another couple, on t'Continent – one car – taking turns. She's put a lid on it though."

"Ah'll bet it were Eric – he'd 'ave big ideas about t'sleepin' arrangements!"

"No, apparently she were happy about that, or else they hadn't got round to what Eric's ideas might be in detail – no, she kicked it into touch herself. Said it were t'driving she didn't fancy. She's a bit short up top, at t'best of times, and Eric had been explaining about having to drive on t'opposite side of the road to what we do. Daft Dizzy gets up early one Sunday morning to practise driving on t'right between Bradford and Halifax. Only got halfway afore she turns round and knocks t'whole trip on t'head on account of it being too dangerous!"

"Bloody hell! Ah've fund another good 'un. Sithee, it's nigh on perfect! Square edges, stands up, got even spots, and look at t'back, no scratches, no blotches, no dints, no blood, nothing! Tha wants to get this 'un stuffed and mounted. Theer's no way at all on tellin' what this 'un is from t'back, what wi' all t'others bein' marked, like!"

"Double-one! That's the only one you can't tell from behind out of t'whole pack. Every other one, you can pick out, but that one's unique. Lay 'em all out upside down and you can label every single one bar that. I'd defy anyone to spot double one – it's got absolutely no marks on it at all."

"Bugger me! It is double-one an' all! Right! Ah suppose now that tha two's managed some sort of perfection, we'll be goin' fer a full range o' sports goods on t'production line?"

"Bill nicked a bit of round banister rail and sawed it up for draughts. But it were a boring game, and any king you made looked daft, and kept slipping apart, what with some of the cuts being a bit askew, like. They always looked drunk. He fell down a bit by colouring one set black, too – using creosote. It comes off on everything! Black ones were a sort of brown, and t'white's had brown fingerprints all over them. And we'd be playing while we ate our snap an' all – it was no fun lakin' with blacks."

"Reminds mi, ah've spotted a crackin' brush 'andle in t'stores, thicker nor usual. Dust'a fancy thi 'and at chess?"

"Bog off! We'd be a lifetime carving 'em, and you'd only go and creosote half of 'em again!"

"Put t'wireless on, let's see how they finished up dahn under."

"Work Study 'ad theer car radio nicked las' week. It were Charlie Ackroyd as usual. Reckons he went under a bridge, an' it just disappeared!"

"That reminds me, did you hear about Freddie Orton's long weekend in Spain, when he got caught up in an armed robbery? You know what he's like, Freddie. Soft as fog. Wife sees this posh bangle in a jeweller's and she has to have it, so in they go. They'd just about settled for it when these three blokes bust in, stockings over their mugs, all that stuff, and each with guns. It were hands up all round, while two of 'em goes through t'small shop like a dose of Andrews. Strip everything, chucking it to this other bloke with a sack near t'door. All t'shelves, displays and windows, and there's Freddie and Mrs Freddie, hands up against t'wall till they all bugger off as fast as they came."

"Bloody hell! I bet that put t'wind up Freddie, alright!"

"Funny thing, he told me, they took no notice of him at all, after the 'puttemup' bit. Him, his cash, and t'bangle his missis had fancied so much. All that was going through his mind while there's guns and masks and jewellery flying all over was, what was wrong with this trinket he was holding onto, seeing as how it was the only thing in the shop they'd let alone! Walked out wi'out buying it in t'end!"

"He were lucky theer, they can be funny buggers, t'Spanish. Ay oop! What's tha doin' wi' that spoon? I'n't theer enough ruddy scratches on these doms wi'out thee mekkin more!"

"Nay, I've jus' fund a spot of summat like putty stuck to this 'un. Jus' tryin' to dig it out."

"Bloody leave well alone, can't tha? It is putty. Wi' fund wi'd med two double-fives, so we bunged up one o't'oils an' painted ower it to mek it five-four. We'll 'ave t'do it all ower agin, now!"

"Put that one right way up, Percy, you've got it upside down."

"Du'n't matter, does it? It's double-blank anyway!"

"Bill and me know it's double-blank, but it doesn't mean that Wilf does. We don't want to be playing with an advantage, do we, Bill?"

"Knocks all t'fun art on it!"

"Yer like a bloody pair of kids, yor two!"

"Talking of kids, I bumped into Sam Simkins's missis and their two in Town Street, yesterday. D'you know, t'twins are nigh on three now. Doesn't seem five minutes since we had all that palaver looking for him when she was taken in suddenly."

"Ay, ah can remember us 'avin to split up to cover every pub in t'city centre. He said he were on a trainin' run fer wettin' theer heads. Fust time ah'd heard that Sam ivver needed a reason, or were short on practice. Ee, what's gone off in just three years! Them were t'good owd days then, when tha could aver drop at dinnertime, that shows how long ago it were – ah'm surprised t'twins are nobbut only three!"

"No, but ah could see young Sheila's got her hands full with 'em. They were chattering away just like their dad after five pints of sociable. I had to laugh; there's Sheila saying to 'em as they passin' a shop, 'What's that?' and one of 'em'd say, 'Butcher's'. She'd say, 'What do we get out of there?' and they'd be givin' her 'sausages', and 'bacon', and 'meat', and such forth. Then it were t'chemist's. Sheila's goin', 'And what does that shop have?', and they're giving it 'cough medicine', and 'plasters' and 'toothpaste'. Passing t'supermarket and they went daft with loads of stuff. Bright little buggers they are. Then we walked past t'pub, and Sheila's saying, 'And what do we get from there?', and both together t'twins said, 'Daddy!'"

"What's this reckon t'be?"

"Three-four. Why, what did you think it was?"

"Dunno. Could've been owt. Too much paint's come off, tha haster feel for t'bumps. It's like using that special writin' what deaf folk use."

"Braille, tha means?"

"Did you enjoy yourself with that one, Percy?"

"Nah, not when they fall straight in – you like to have to work at it a bit!"

"Don't remind me about hard work! I'm starting on our drive this Saturday, it'll be the big hammer and a pick for two days. Concrete's buggered, but I bet it'll still take some writhing up."

"You won't be makin' t'same mistake what Ernie Coombs med las' summer when he took his up – mind you, that were tarmac, not concrete."

"Oh, aye, he hired a kango hammer for his, di'n't he? I won't be going that far. It still took him the best part of t'weekend, and with the sun blazing down all the time. Decided to wait for his neighbour to get on with a job that he was planning, so as they could go halves on a skip. He were knackered all week after that."

"So? What went wrong?"

"Oh, didn't you hear about it? Well, he's proper done himself in towing with it two full days, nine hours a day, till it's broken up small enough to handle and pile up tidy near the gate to wait for t'skip. Bloody great heap of old tarmac, six foot high. Then this neighbour goes off t'boil, and they don't get the skip for a couple of months. It's September by then, and he gets out there to shovel it into a barrow and wheel it up into t'skip. But two months of hot sun, and running into autumn, t'tarmac's melted and gone stiff again. One solid pyramid he's got now. So it's back to the big hammer and pickaxe for another weekend!"

"Daft thing is, he comes in on t'Monday an' tells us all abaht it!"

"Best get packed up, I suppose. What d'you make it, Bill?"

"Must be comin' up two, now, can't quite tell—"

"You what! Have you two seen this watch he's got? Their kid's brought it back for him from America, there's nowt it can't do, is there, Bill?"

"Well…"

"You can dive up to half a mile deep, and it'll stand t'pressure; same with going up, it'll work nine miles high, keeps time to within a second a year; there's a button to light it up, tells the time in six different time zones; it's a stopwatch that works down to a hundredth of a second… what else, Bill?"

"Shock. It'll stand shock. Blurb says tha could drop it of t'top on t'Empire State, and it could land in t'road an' be run ower bi a tractor and still be OK!"

"Fifteen jewels, wasn't it, Bill? No, seventeen, little alarms as well, you can set it to go off up to five times a day, and then there's the countdown buzzer. You can't scratch t'glass, it'll stand up to 200°C, there's the date on it and it spots leap years, and there's him saying 'it must be coming up to two'! What's up with you? With that bit of tackle you can't be owt but spot on. Give us it right!"

"Ah can't. Minute hand dropped off last neet!"

"Never! You'r not fit to be let out with owt, you."

"Ay, less of it. 'Ave you said owt abaht thi gas leak, yet, eh? 'As he telled thee abaht week last Monday, and his famous gas leak back at 'ome? Virtually had Armley sealed off and evacuated while they dug it ower? Ah bet he's kept that quiet!"

"What's this then?"

"There's nothing to tell, nowt but a bit of trouble in our cellar; look, let's get these doms sided before Elliot cops us—"

"Dust'a want me t'tell 'em, then?"

"Alright, alright… we'd a gas leak at home, and it took them all Monday night to fix it. Kept some of t'neighbours up, so they were none too pleased. That's all."

"We was round his house Wednesday, and their Thelma tells me t'full story."

"OK… but I don't see why the fuss. It was this smell that started it. In our back room where we spend most of us time. I copped for it first… Got this nose, you know."

("Gerraway, so that's what it is!" – "Shurrup, do you want to hear it or not?" – "Ay, shurrup, Wilf! Go on.")

"Thought it was gas! Then a week later it'd got bad enough for our lass to smell it as well. Went into t'cellar, and it wasn't as strong there, so we didn't worry until after another week when we were having something like fish for dinner, and I decided it was well off. She says, 'No, it's that gas you can smell,' and it was, so that was that – straight on t'phone to Gas Leaks Is Us. Half an hour later, six o'clock, and there's two fellows with a van. Go down our cellar – they find traces, but decide it's coming in from outside."

"How do they test for it, nowadays? Didn't have a canary, did they?"

"No, silly sod, it's a probe-like thing and a meter. Anyway, they goes up and down t'pavement outside, and up everyone's gardens. By seven they've got us down as no problem, but next door's drive has to come up. More than that, they carry on down t'street and condemn three doors down as well, plus most of t'pavement in between. Nine o'clock and there's arc lights up, and they've started up with t'drills. All next door's concrete drive's up, plus them further down. We're OK for a while, no bother from t'noise, what with t'telly being in t'back. Both lads are in t'back bedroom, so they're alright. But out front, t'street's buzzing, light's on and folk coming out, talking to t'blokes, and they keep pointing at our house, so there's us keeping squat behind t'curtains."

"They won't let it go, once they've fund gas, them lads. Gas Board's worser nor t'railway when it comes to safety."

"I can vouch for that. We didn't get much sleep that night – drilling's off and on till half five next morning, when they all pack up and go. Got up at half past six and there's t'neighbour from across t'road looking like death and peering down one of t'holes. Next door's drive has been sort of put back, but there's no pavement for sixty yards, and three big holes. I was buggered for work Tuesday; went home early at four. At least t'holes were filled in by then, but there's still cones and barriers as far as you can see – nothing outside our house, of course, but there's two neighbours still with their cars out in t'street."

"Had they fettled it, then?"

"Oh, aye, got it all, no traces left anywhere. Came back and tested our cellar and it was clear. So we settles down to us tea. You wouldn't believe it, but while we're eating, t'smell's there as bad as ever. Our lass says it's got into t'curtains and things, so everything's washed, even t'carpets. Two days later we couldn't use t'room because of t'stink, so I says bugger this, and goes for t'big search in t'cellar. I could smell it quite a bit down there, now, and I follows my nose till it gets right strong. I'm kneeling down, next to t'vent on t'chest freezer, and there, six inches from my nose, there's this dead mouse trapped under t'motor, slowly baking away. Five minutes later it's out and buried, and t'smell's gone completely."

"I bet you kept that quiet!"

"Well, no, I thought it was real funny, so did Thelma, even though she'd washed t'curtains and things for nowt, but she said they needed doing anyway. No, daft like, I'm over telling t'neighbour – him that looked like death, and d'you know, I couldn't get a chuckle out of him; same with t'two what now have very bumpy drives. Isn't it queer what makes you laugh, and others can't see it?"

"Ay, well, that's folk fer thee. Ay oop, what's that doin' on t'floor?"

"What, that? Ah thought it were a biscuit, it's bin theer all dinnertime, ah think!"

"It's a bloody domino, tha great dollop! Dust'a mean we've bin one short all t'time we've bin lakin'? What is it?"

"Looks like five-one t'me. Kick it ower, let's see t'front... ay, theer y'are, five-one. D'yer know, I've missed that bugger once or twice, today!"

"What a bloody waste of time. What dozy wazzock's dropped that and said nowt? What's t'a findin' so bloody funny?"

I couldn't help but laugh, while Wilf blamed Percy and Bill, Bill blamed me, and Percy was sayin' he was out in the lav when we started, so it wasn't him.

It's queer that what might make you laugh, that others can't see, isn't it?

Illness

I was in the Leeds District Office, picking up Wilf and Percy to do
a survey over Bradford way, in Stanningley Tunnel. For me, starts
from Leeds meant an extra half hour at home. They also meant
the choice of bus if it was raining, or an hour's walk into town
along the canal bank, which was never a bad thing. A footpath
starting at the bottom of our street, going through the park and
down to the canal, from where you could walk right into the
centre of Leeds.

There was always a sense of nervousness, as you passed the
odd person in a very lonely situation. With all the stories you read
in the paper, each innocent passer-by was carefully examined
from the way they walked in the far distance, right through to
how close their eyes were together as they passed you. Each one
came into sight as the potential lone madman, intent on evil, and
it was only as you passed each other that you realised that they
were looking at you with the same nervous friendliness with
which you were weighing them up.

Yet, the canal bank, like all footpaths, was a "Good Morning!"
zone. I want to support notices that would make this clear: "You
are now entering a 'Good Morning' or a 'Good Morning Free'
zone." There was a clear line at the city end, as the path opened
up into the canal basin, where saying "Good Morning!" changed
from being the norm to the eccentric. It was as I crossed that line
on this fine sharp late-autumn morning that my thoughts turned
to the eccentric. I was lined up to take Morris Yeo out with us, as
he was involved in the overall job we were on, and Morris was as
eccentric as a circus bike. As it turned out, and was so often the
case first thing in a morning, Yeos were in short supply in the
Leeds Office. "Where's Morris, he's supposed to be out with me
today?"

"Having more tests!" said Keith Loach. "Waste of time,
though, he's bound to fail 'em! According to his diary, here, he's

up the Infirmary again – appointment nine o'clock, so you might just see him today."

"What the hell are they testing for now? He's spent enough time up there to have a vote, come the next election! I bet he's entitled to go to their staff Christmas party – cabaret time – 'Spot the disease!' Death and soul of any party, Morris! He must have had nearly every test going by now! Last time I talked to him he'd only to go for the smear, to get a full set, but I reckon there's got to be some serious groundwork done before he has that one!"

"Whatever it is, we'll know all about it soon enough, whether we want to or not!"

"I can hang on a bit and see if they've found a pulse, or anything. Assuming there's enough of him left to come out! We don't need to be off while half ten, and there's one or two things I need to see to downstairs."

"I wouldn't bank on him getting back at all; he was making notes, yesterday, and I saw 'toothbrush and sucking bib' on the list!"

"Sucking bib! What the buggery…?"

"Best not to ask, could be in old English, so you wouldn't want to know!"

Morris Yeo was a sad case. A well-built but lithe man, touching five nine or ten, in his late thirties, and the very picture of health. Gently rosy cheeks with a perpetual light tan over the bits not hidden behind an unabused beard – one of those that's allowed to cover all its natural ground, but is kept trimly pruned. It displayed traces of fair threads running down the dribble channels on either side of an even mouth, and was unstained by pollutants such as tobacco or strong tea. His head was a tight thatch of thick sandy hair, with no visible signs of fading. Unfortunately, on the down side, he was a very, very sick man; a walking miracle – death with batteries.

Superficial signs were all too evident; take the lightening streaks in his beard, for instance. He had worked out that these had to be a sign of rapid ageing, or even of the onset of early senility. The very thickness of his hair at an age when most men are showing some signs of loss worried him – why was his as thick as ever? Was it a male form of virilism, only ever before recorded in women? If so, was he changing sex to accommodate the disease? Take the reddening of his cheeks; could this not indicate all sorts of disorders, possible liver failure through excessive drinking (he'd had two pints of bitter and a whisky last Christmas)? Could it be a sign of contact allergies or dermagraphia? There was a possibility of folliculitis or shingles or even athlete's foot – a desperately serious disease when you get it on your face. Morris was forever anxious, and he had every reason to be so. He could never remotely be described as being in good health. His head and face were mere starting points… but, there, we could all start fretting for him if we were to know the whole truth!

Should any of us in the office cough, should anyone sneeze, should anyone groan slightly when rising from a seated position, should anyone scratch themselves more than once in the same place, should anyone visit the toilet at a frequency greater than Morris's accepted standard, then they'd be viewed with suspicion, and politely avoided. That is unless they could be gently questioned, segregating the diseased one from the interrogator with the sanitary safety of the green belt afforded by broad drawing desks – a belt wider than the leaping ability of the most athletic microbe. Any visiting stranger, with an unknown medical track record, would be treated with great wariness. Some innocent distinguishing feature like a mole or a blemish, and the newcomer had an unseen bell around their neck and a placard marked "Unclean!" – Disease and disaster were all around Morris.

The only bright spot in Yeo's sad existence was that back then in the sixties there were still a few diseases and disorders as yet undiscovered, like yuppy flu (he'd have gone a bomb on that!) so they were unavailable to him. Any air pollution in those days still had a visible component – and later findings of insidious imperceptible gases and particulates were at that time a threat to which he was still happily ignorant. A concept such as sick buildings, not yet a popular excuse, would have completely phased him out. Wellington Street's penthouse suite never looked particularly fit, even at the best of times. Smog could be avoided, and at that time ozone was still the smell of seaweed and seagull crap.

Life for Morris was a constant battle and worry, day and night.

(He'd got assurance that cot deaths were restricted to the first twelve months of life, but why, he would ask, did you hear of so many people "dying in their sleep"?)

Years later, at a get-together, all present agreed that Morris was the original sufferer of that seasonal thing – SAD – except he had it all year round. If it had been known of in those far-off days, Morris could have had a rubber stamp made of it for his sick notes. Apart from all the usual winter's lack of daylight symptoms, Morris was not over happy in summer (undue sweating, heat-stroke, ice cream allergies). Spring and autumn were both times of great stress for him, as he worried about the approaching onset of summer/winter.

Morris's fears sometimes overwhelmed him in the depths of the night. The local Samaritans had threatened to go ex-directory because of him. He very rarely went to see a doctor for obvious reasons. Surgeries are the worst places on earth for anyone vulnerable to copping for any disease going. Everyone in there's ill, and, therefore, a danger. From coughs and sneezes right through to legs in plaster. You could catch almost anything. If ever he did go, he spent the waiting time reading all the notices on the walls. By the time he got in to see the doctor, he'd contracted half a dozen new diseases, most likely at the expense of the one he'd gone in with in the first place. He'd be furiously noting down addresses and phone numbers of all the various support groups, even down to bereavement councillors. Later, him contacting these people would have them sending him what should have been reassuring lists and letters of other members' symptoms, and the various ways they had found of coping with them. Yet to Morris these helped him only in so much as to suggest new indicators that he could almost immediately replicate, so confirming that he had that particular disease.

He took preventive measures against everything, avoiding eating or drinking what was a danger one week, only to gorge on it later when it was declared beneficial in the fight against some mid-African swamp fever. He always regretted not smoking, since he couldn't give it up. Then there was his medical notebook. The slightest odd feeling was itemised, and a cross-referencing system would throw up, in his terms, not all the diseases it could be, but rather all the diseases that it must be! Furthermore, he would analyse his daily contacts, his diet, and any unusual environmental features he'd encountered during what he imagined to be any incubation period. For this reason Morris's drinking was minimal. His book could show him that a glass of sherry had once inspired in him some dizziness, which was an obvious indication of his having vertigo or Ménière's Disease... or both!

He was tolerated just so far in the Drawing Office, but that was only as far as he had any uses...

"Ay up! While I'm here," I said, "is there a sick book open this week?"

"Should be. Ask Duggie."

From round the corner of the office Duggie Lomax appeared with an official looking clipboard.

"Anything particular in mind, Mike? Leprosy's in this week at a giveaway 25 to 1."

Duggie was the office bookie, capable of raising all sorts of gaming interest. What with the building being the shape it was, where nearly everybody in it could be seen from the fifth floor, bets on what someone's kit would be for the next day was an obvious favourite. Years later, when we moved to Hutton House, we could see the *Yorkshire Post* electronic clock easily, and a daily book was run on the temperature showing at three each afternoon – that is until they changed from Fahrenheit to centigrade. This badly reduced the field, and the odds, to daft levels. But Lomax's illness book was always a good venture, what with there being such a wide range of runners. It was based on forecasting the first complaint Morris Yeo claimed to have on any Wednesday morning. Mondays and Tuesdays were "paddock days" when you could study the walking miracle for form. Punters out on the four Areas, such as me, got a bulletin sent out on Monday evenings, though bets were discouraged by phone, what with one -atitis or -osis sounding much like another. So here I was with a rare chance to place an on-course bet.

Duggie was more than happy to take another mug's money, and cheerfully set off running down the week's list of favourites. But leprosy! I ask you; and for a measly 25 to 1!

"Leprosy, for Christ's sake! Where the hell d'yer dig that one up from? And why only at 25?"

"Look, you've got to suss these things out. Don't play if you don't do your research. Didn't you see *Commonwealth Report*, Sunday evening on BBC? A whole hour about Africa's lepers. A magnet for morons like Yeo, couldn't stop talking about it, Monday. Just the sort of thing he'd only need three days to think about, and look up the symptoms. 25 to 1's bloody generous! I could let you have it doubled up at 1,000 to 1 against a finger dropping off by Friday, if you like!"

"No, come on now, what's the serious betting? What's the word in the stables?" I wasn't interested in these wildly speculative donkeys, I needed proper information.

"Well, you know, you can get a quote on owt you like, but here's the current form and field," said Duggie, handing me a roneoed sheet of paper. "I'd stick to that, unless you know summat we don't."

There wasn't much to choose from. Eight quotes, and 25 to 1 bar those. As usual, a cold was running at evens, with hypochondria at its customary 20 to 1 on, only because Duggie thought it a good joke. Morris Yeo had often maintained that this was the only common ailment from which he'd never suffered. I always found Duggie's line of reasoning behind the week's runners of interest, not having the Event himself present for a first-hand assessment. (He was as we spoke undergoing a vet's inspection at the Infirmary.)

"Bursitis. I've heard of that; what've you got that in for?"

"Remembrance Sunday week before last. Yeo's always at church that Sunday, because of his dad. A good hour and a half of up and down on his dodgy knee—"

"Housemaid's knee! Got you!"

"Good odds on that one, this week. You'd've only got 2 to 1 last Wednesday!"

"Laryngitis; that's always in; mmm… er-y-sip-elas, where's that come from?"

"Ah, well. We'd a bloke from Manchester in at a meeting last week, told Morris he'd had it once. Think he was trying to shut our lad up, but you know the form – he hears the symptoms, and next day he's got the first signs!"

"Depression's not worth a shout, either. Not at 3 to 1 on. You don't give owt away, Duggie, d'you?" I pondered my options. "Hey! What's this you've slipped in at 100 to 1? What the buggery's Gyn-ae-com-astia, when it's at home?"

"Oh, forget that 'un," said the punter's friend, "just a dozy gag of Gaunty's. Someone said Yeo was just a big daft tit last week... look it up, if you want, but it's not worth a shout, I promise you."

I had a sudden inspiration. "Tell you what, I'll leave it for this week, but will you give me a quote for next Wednesday on tunnel vision, 'cos we're off into Stanningley today, if he ever gets here."

"What that bloke wants," said Eric Gaunt in passing, "is a long night with a mucky woman. That'd sort him out, once and for all. Though," he added thoughtfully, "I've only ever had Yeo down as a flat out man; never had him as jump material."

"I'd close down, if he got a bird! God knows what he'd come up with! It'd be like the National, he'd have that many runners. He'd cop for everything!"

"Aye, but at least he might've enjoyed catching it!" Eric was the office joke book, and usually good for material I could recycle back at Huddersfield. Eric was easily the universe's anti-matter to poor Morris, and also one of the most unsympathetic to his troubles.

As it happened, the lift recovered from its usual morning sickness just then and sounds of it bursting into action echoed from out on the landing. It came back up five minutes later and decanted a serious-looking, and somewhat exhausted Morris Yeo out into the Drawing Office.

"Aye up, Morris, lad, you're the lucky one! You're the first that buggering lift's deigned to bring up today!" I should have known better; never call Morris lucky!

"The damn thing's just about done for me! I pressed for it at the bottom – nothing! Walked up to the third and I hears it going past downwards. Hit the button on three and the damn thing falls out and drops on t'floor, so I races down to two and I'm hammering the knob there as it sails by up and stops at three, so the button must have been working after all. I nips up to catch it, just as it starts dropping back down to two. There's no button in three now, so I gallops up to four. It picks me up there and brings

me all the way up from four to five. I'm bloody knackered, now."
All of which underlined Morris's second claim to fame; bad luck!
"Wouldn't care, but I've wasted an hour up the hospital. Fizzing
doctor's knocked sick! Oh, hello, Mike, can you hang on ten
minutes, and I'll be with you." Then conspiratorially, "I've
summat I want to have a quiet word about, away from these
gonks."

Bugger, bugger, bugger, I thought, I'm Mr Trusty again. This
had happened before. I must have "sympathetic mug" tattooed on
my forehead. Morris had once in the past mistaken me as a
willing ear for his medical ramblings, and had misunderstood
silence as being at least more responsive than the "Bog off, you
sick freak", which often substituted for "Hello, Morris" in the
Leeds Office. Admittedly, I didn't have to put up with Morris
day-in day-out like the folk here did, and I was always interested
in placing modest bets with Duggie, so any form from the horse's
mouth could hardly go amiss. But to be trapped by Morris with
small chance of interruptions was a heavy price to pay for a bit of
stable info. Where I must have made my mistake was in once
mentioning in passing that I'd two uncles who were both doctors.
The fact that they'd both a PhD, one in Agriculture and the other
in Applied Chemistry, was of minor import. To Morris, I was
virtually a medic!

★

I spent the ten minutes he needed sorting out Percy and Wilf.
They were less than enamoured to find that Yeo was going with
us, especially as he'd be a fourth for dinner in the close comfort of
the PWay cabin at the far end of Stanningley Tunnel. If the length
gang were in strength, and using the same cabin, there'd be five of
them, plus us four visitors; hardly enough room to open a paper
or have a quiet nap, and if the medical moron got going...

We'd one of the Leeds Office cars booked, and set about
packing up the tackle. With Percy sat in the driving seat, we
waited for Morris. Wilf was riding shotgun at Percy's side, and I
was in my customary back-seat position. I was, and never since
have been a good passenger, and always saw the back seat as being

a foot or two further away from the accident, should it happen. We were listening to Wilf's muttered threats as to what he'd do if the diseased anorak started on about his problems. When Morris eventually made an appearance it was evident that he didn't intend to let the November weather get to him. Apart from invisible primers and undercoats, which we knew from the past would be at least one thermal vest, a lumberjack shirt, a pullover and a jacket, there were signs of a greatcoat peeping out from beneath an all-enveloping waterproof.

"Bloody hell, Morris," said Wilf, "tha's got more skins on than a ruddy onion! Wheer dust'a think tha's sitting wi'all that on?"

"There's no need to go on, Wilf. I'm putting the mac in the boot."

"Better to put t'coit in here and thissen in t'booit! Here, get in t'back wi'im. If tha sits up front, 'ere, God knows what Percy's going to be grabbing to change gear wi'!"

Morris stuffed his rainwear in the boot with the surveying gear, and set about tackling the gap between the tipped-up front seat, now vacated by Wilf, and the door frame. Wilf helpfully held the door open, which partly compensated for his having slid the seat as far back as it would go so that Morris's sardine impersonation should be the more of a challenge. Apart from a vaguely waving hand pretending to push the most protruding bits of Morris into position, Wilf played no further part in the operation, other than the occasional remark about sheepdogs and cat flaps.

Morris finally hauled himself into the car, tugging at stray jacket pockets and coat tails, and finished up alongside me, half-facing forward, with his legs across mine due to the position of the seat in front. I can't quite describe how I now felt, other than that claustrophobia would have been a relief.

"Anyway, how are you keeping, Morris, owd lad?" said Percy, addressing the rear-view mirror while starting up the car and easing it out onto the road. He grinned mischievously at Wilf, knowing full well that they, sat in the front, wouldn't hear a word of the reply while the car was moving, but that I most certainly would.

Sure enough, on arrival at site twenty-five minutes later, Percy switched off the engine to "…all yellow, but the main thing they did say was that it was very rarely fatal in the long run… Are we here, then?"

With which the morning's job got going, to be satisfactorily wound up a couple of hours later. Here was an odd thing I'd noticed about Yeo; get him started on a job and he seems to have nothing to say, other than this and that about the work we're doing. No grumbles, no worries, no apprehension at working in the heavy confines of a steam-filled tunnel – nothing. It seemed like he was able to shut off, become human, and do a decent job, just when required. But come job done, and back would come the gloom and doom.

As it happened, when we got up to the PWay cabin, we found it cold and empty, so Plan B came into operation. Wilf and Percy dropped the two of us off in Bradford to meet Dennis Durand, the local PWay Supervisor, for them to return to base with the tackle, no doubt parking up somewhere and sneaking off into town for a while. We were left to make our own ways back on the train.

It was during this period of fifty-four minutes that our benevolent Company set aside as sufficient for us to have a meal and take relaxation that Morris brought up his problem. This immediately stuffed any ideas about the relaxing bit. I soon found out why Morris had felt things were too delicate for discussion within the Drawing Office. Also, as he churned it out, I reckoned Morris hardly appreciated the immense favour he was doing himself by keeping his worries under close wraps.

Despite his superficially comprehensive knowledge of all the downsides of medicine, Morris was still extraordinarily naive. Maybe this was due to him wanting to get down to his in-depth studies of diseases and symptoms without bothering about the basic workings of the human body, or more importantly the fact that there were one or two fundamental differences between the sexes. This had never dawned on me until today as he unloaded himself.

"I'll come straight to the point. I'm concerned, even worried, about one of the folk back in the office. Y'see, I started keeping a record after I'd noticed a pattern on the holiday chart: you know that they've got us putting down when we're off sick, now, as well as just holidays, don't you?"

"Out on the Area we don't bother too much about—"

I should have realised that I was merely the sleeping partner in this conversation. Morris ploughed on regardless.

"Well, I'll tell you something I've found very interesting, very interesting indeed. This particular person was—"

"Who? I can't get what you're on about unless you tell me who we're talking about!"

This put him out a bit, and he was obviously miffed. His audience was galloping when he wanted to tell the story his own way. "OK, but not a word to her, understand?"

Ay up! thought I. *Her*, eh? I'd not put Morris down as observing a "her". This narrowed it down to the clerks... or perhaps the two tracers?

Morris came in close, looking over my shoulder, and then over his, in true conspiratorial style – the sort of thing you see in one-star movies. He almost climbed into my ear. I hoped to goodness that I didn't look infectious with anything, because if he should catch owt in the next month, he'll sure as hell put it down to me.

"It's Nadine Kershaw," he said, so conspiratorially that he seemed to think that half of Bradford might be interested. Tracer, I thought, and the one of the two that was worth watching. Just fancy! Morris Yeo! This could be worth passing on. "She's one of the tracers," he went on, not crediting me with much memory. "She keeps having the odd day off, and the pattern is always a multiple of four weeks. Now here's the other strange thing; I've noticed that when she isn't actually off when the pattern might say she should be, she's not the same girl as she usually is at all. Proper snappy and short she is, especially when I try to ask her what's wrong with her."

"You mean to say that you go nattering her when she's feeling off it, like? Don't you realise—?"

"Look! If you're ever ill as often as I am, you'll know that you need a bit of consideration now and again, so I just go round and try and cheer her up a touch, that's all. Swap symptoms, and such. If anyone can help, it's me! I've most likely had what she's got, and could help, like."

I demanded attention, and ignored the flack of interruptions that spattered on. "Now hold on a bit. You're telling me that you're concerned about some problems that Nadine's having about once a month. And you've been keeping a record of her when she's a bit down! Good God, man! Why? For Chrissake!"

"The girl's suffering! It's regular, and has been for the whole year since I first noticed it. That makes it chronic! Besides...," and this was where the crux of the matter was, as Morris settled on a violently quiet hiss, "what if it's contagious?"

I wasn't ready for this depth of innocence, and I could see that I'd have to start at ground level.

"Look, Morris, how much do you know about women? What's she told you?"

"It's been very difficult to get anything out of her at all, but over the months I've gathered a few things. Most important, she thinks it's some kind of curse that's been put on her, that's how serious things are; she's got a mental thing about it. She seems to blame it on a visitor of some kind, probably a gypsy that she's not bought pegs off, or something. You know what some women are like about superstitions and such. (Thank goodness I've never been brought down by superstitions, touch wood. I'd be a nervous wreck!) Anyway, that's the sort of level of seriousness we're talking about! It's almost a psychosowhatsit matter! She needs to be talked out of it, and that's what I keep trying to do – talk her out of it!"

"Right." It was clear to me that the situation called for grasping bulls by horns, or horns by the balls or something. "You might find this hard to believe, but Our Lass at home has the selfsame problem; mebbee not as bad as Nadine, but it's definitely the same. It's absolutely nothing to worry about, and you can't catch it!"

"Good God! Your wife's got it too? What are the symptoms, then?"

I suddenly lost all interest, if there'd ever been any there in the first place. Even life itself didn't hold much attraction for me in the immediate future. I mean, it wasn't a subject we even discussed at home! The only thing I knew about it was that should I make any landing approach noises, I'd sometimes get a sort of "ah herrmmm" from the control tower, and that was it. We didn't exactly call a summit meeting about it, or have it embroidered over the bed. By now I was looking longingly at the clock, and willing it to get round to when Denis said he'd be back for the meeting. But Morris was like a ferret with a finger.

"You see, I can't help Nadine if I don't know what's happening. If I've ever had it, or anything like it, I may have found some easy way of dealing with it. And another thing, she says that she's never been to the doctor's about it, and I think that means she's too worried!"

"Look," I could see no way out, "it's no more nor less than a matter of passing a bit of blood, that's absolutely all; and there's nothing more to it."

"You *what*?" You could see Morris at once galloping off along a meandering trail through kidney stones towards the great unknown. That was it for me. Enough was most definitely enough, even though I reckoned that I may have done more damage than good. I ignored all further rantings and noticed with a vast relief the approach of measured boot treads on the lino corridor. For the moment I could breathe again.

★

During the discussion that followed with Denis, I passed him a breakdown of the job we were on about. At the bottom I'd managed to scrawl large "For God's sake, ask me to hang on a bit after this meeting!" As a result Morris was kicked out into Bradford to pick up a few idiosyncratic Asian diseases, while I was taken on yet another tour of Denis's store. The object was achieved and I'd managed to make sure that I travelled back to Leeds alone.

I'd been bitten once before like this – being out with a nutter on public transport – and I could see all the signs of a possible repeat of the most embarrassing train journey I'd ever had in my life, sharing a front seat with Ken Lorriman on a fairly busy diesel multiple unit.

That time Ken and I were coming back from Hebden Bridge, where the train originated, and we'd bagged the high-backed seats right behind the driver. On the way we kept half an eye on the track in front, and noted down any faults or rough riding. Pulling into Halifax and Bradford, and various other smaller stations on the way, I could tell the train was filling up, but Ken was oblivious. He was like when you see animals being got under control by slotting a sack over their heads – as soon as they could see nothing, they weren't bothered any more. With Ken it was tunnels, and there are loads on that line. Whenever we dived into one, he'd go on with this story about his most recent sexual adventure with his versatile wife. This wasn't unusual for Ken, he was proud of his exploits, and could see no reason for not boasting about them; it underlined his very precious masculinity.

Plunging into the first of the tunnels triggered some association in Ken, and he started up with a detailed report on his vasectomy, when it had taken six, "repeat, six!" return visits to the vet's before they'd declared him as shooting only blanks! Now that, he stated proudly, was what he called being up to scratch! Ken then went on to describe the last weekend at home, house full of kids, his "come meter" registering full (with here a slight tangential discussion on the imagined problems of monks in monasteries and similar vestal males, on whether their come meters worked normally and whether they regularly exploded, or not!).

Then came the inviting of wife into garage, details of the arrangement of the workbench and vice, the usefulness of a large block of timber on the floor, and the speedy "plugging in", before any of the kids could miss them. All described in vivid detail in the manner of a combination of the *Kama Sutra* and *Blue Peter*. He then went on to make it perfectly clear that there was a small collective of the community's couples, and that his experiences were of a broader nature than some might find seemly. Apparently they... well, more to the point was Ken's booming delivery of all these confidential secrets, with which even the diesel's roaring engines couldn't compete. All I noticed was the total lack of any other kind of conversation within the compartment. Ken had the window seat, and I could see better than him the reflections in the driver's compartment window during the various tunnels. It was not actually full, but was pretty close to being so. Ken, eyeballing me throughout, was quite unaware of the fact that we were not the only two people in the world.

As the driver changed ends at Bradford, there was quite a considerable turnover of fellow passengers, and Ken was as oblivious as I was aware of the few curious faces that walked very close to our window, staring in, and obviously wondering which of the two was the innovative Superstud.

★

Having managed to ditch the company of Morris Yeo, I went back to Leeds on a later train, which gave me twenty minutes of relaxed thinking time to mull things over. I'd been a bit KO'd at the ignorance and lack of worldliness that Morris had shown, and I reckoned that I was now probably apace with his regular colleagues in the main office on this point. They possibly would not have been at all surprised by the lad's reactions and innocence. There was already a plan of action clicking into place as I arrived back in Leeds, and I made my way up to the fifth floor, by way of the fourth and second due to innocently trusting the vagaries of the lift. But I wasn't at all prepared for my reception.

As I walked into the office I was leapt on from several directions at the door.

"What the hell have you done to Morris?" asked Keith, acting as spokesman. "He's locked himself in Trap Two, and won't come out! Keeps on about he might have caught haemorrhaging, or summat. Where've you had him? What the bloody hell have you been telling him? It's alright for you; just fill the retarded sponge he calls his brain with a load of boloney, and bugger off back into the woods at Huddersfield. We're left to deal with the yammering git!"

"It's nowt to worry over, it's just that he's had a bit of an instant education today, and it's taken him by surprise."

"Fine," said Duggie Lomax, "I can kiss goodbye to next week's sweep; what with Morris in the state he's come back in, he'll be a cert for whatever you've filled his head with for the duration. You don't know how to handle Morris; he's a delicate flower. Now just what's he picked up while you've supposedly been in charge of him?"

"He's just found out summat on women's troubles, that's all."

"And just how's he found that out?"

"It was in a woman's periodical," I said, purely for my own amusement.

"Well, he can't be thinking of copping for that... he can't, can he?" I'd been wrong previously. I was in fact ahead of the Leeds lads in discovering the depths of Morris's ignorance.

"He can, and is! Look, it's been a long day, and Morris has been most of it, just—"

"Hold up!" said Duggie. "There is life after death, sithee." He was nodding towards the corridor leading from the Gents, where Morris could be seen sidling back to his desk. He looked miserable to a new strength of miserability. "There's a challenge for you, Eric. You always reckon you could get a laugh out of a corpse – try cheering that bugger up a bit – tell us one of your latest."

This was a gauntlet thrown down as a result of an earlier argument. Eric Gaunt was the acknowledged comedian amongst us, and rather savoured it. He'd a bachelor-like lifestyle, but for the fact that there was a woman in his bed most nights. Never known to come to work from the same direction two days running, his evenings always started in the Dog and Gun, where he tended to pick up the best jokes and the worst women. We all wandered over to where Morris was sat staring at something midway between here and there.

"He reminds me," said Eric, in a slow drawl, "of this bloke that goes into t'baker's shop and says to t'lass behind t'counter, 'Can I have two brown loaves please, love?' and she says, 'Sorry, we've only got white left.' And he says, 'That's OK, I've got mi bike outside!'"

There was a stunned silence.

"You what?"

"Is that it?"

"I don't understand that," said Morris, suddenly focusing. "Why don't I understand it?"

"You dozy sod, Gaunty. Now look what you've done!" hissed

Keith. "That's going to make things a whole lot better! Is that the best you could come up with?"

"I laughed like hell, last night, when I heard it!" Eric responded obviously hurt, but clearly mystified that his story had now lost him, as well as the others.

"What time was it, then, when you laughed like mad at that load of old rubbish?"

"Be about quarter past eleven, just before we were chucked out!"

"Thought it might have been. You'd laugh at owt at that time! If you've any more like that, keep 'em!"

I found myself suddenly in uncharted waters here, as Eric's story had sparked of a recollection of something similar I'd picked up recently. "It just so happens that I'm in possession of the funniest joke that's ever been told... ever." I was already fizzling out and wishing that I'd not started. "Got it off one of the painters last month, in Huddersfield."

"Well go on, then!" Eric seemed unsure about someone trespassing on his territory, but he always needed fodder for the "Dog" that night.

"You've got to understand that it's pretty subtle, in fact it took me a couple of weeks before I got it, myself. Mind, once I had, I couldn't stop laughing!" I found a broken chuckle coming out, as if to demonstrate what passed for laughing with me. It was clear that I'd yet to win over the sympathy of the audience.

"Are you going to tell us it then, or not?"

"Right, well, it's about this bloke who comes up on the pools, and decides to build himself a really posh house. You've got to follow this very carefully, you understand, 'cos it really is a bit deep. So he finds out what the most expensive stuff he can buy is, looking through Harrods's Building and Plumbing Materials Catalogue, and comes up with these very special red bricks, with a gold stripe running right round them, at fifty quid apiece. Are you following this, OK?"

"Special gold-striped red bricks at fifty quid apiece," echoed a member of the audience.

"So, he gets plans drawn up... (the way I was told it, the plans were described in full, you know, each room, the size, arrangement of floors, number of windows, and all that, but I'm telling you the shorter version to save time)."

"It doesn't show," muttered Gaunt.

"Anyway, from the plans, he gets worked out exactly down to the last one how many special red bricks with a gold stripe running right round them he's going to need, 'cos at fifty quid each he doesn't want to waste money, right? House gets built and he's moving in, and when he's settled down, he takes a walk round the garden, and then he spots it! One special red brick with a gold stripe running right round it left over, lying in the middle of the back lawn! One brick's no good to no one, and he starts to wonder what the hell he can do with it. Now, this is the bit you've got to really concentrate on, and cop hold of." I was grinding towards the nub, and slowing down on delivery.

"He's a natural, isn't he? Has you in the palm of his hand, dun't he?"

"He'll be seeing mine, soon, if he doesn't gerron wi'it."

"Right." I was now spelling it out word by word, just as the painter had to me. "So he picks up this special red brick—"

"With a gold stripe running right round it," said my impatient chorus.

"Yes, right, so he picks it up and he looks at it and thinks for a while. 'I know!' he says, and gets into his car. He puts the special red with... the brick on the passenger seat beside him, and drives off. After twenty minutes, he comes to this bridge over a railway, and thinks, That's it! Perfect! So he gets out, looks around and dips into the car and picks up the special redbrickwiththegold-striperunningrightroundit, and leans over the bridge, and... then... he... drops... it... over... on... to... the... side... of... the... railway line!"

The ensuing silence was prolonged. Short of taking a lap of honour, I couldn't make it clearer that I'd finished, but it was equally obvious that the less than enthralled audience were expecting rather more details.

"You've a bloody nerve," said Eric quietly, breaking a disbelieving silence. "Fancy complaining about mine. At least it were short. So we're going to crease ourselves when we get it in a week or two's time, are we? What did you think of all that, then, Morris? Cheer you up a bit, did it?"

"I don't understand," said the stricken one, "what difference the colour of the bread made."

"Reckon you lost one of us early on there, Mike!"

I was a little reluctant to leave the Leeds Office that day, despite the concrete lifebelt effect of my story on Morris. There seemed to be scope for a few interesting developments in the area of Morris's phobias. Keith Loach took me to one side and explained one or two real problems that they'd had with their "special case" from time to time. He suggested that today was not a good day for progressing Morris's fears any further. In fact Keith, who was a qualified first-aider, more or less warned me off for the time being. From past experience it would be up to him to pick up the various pieces that Morris, following disintegration, broke into and attempt their reconstruction. So a final friendly "Now bugger off back to Huddersfield!" rather made up my mind for me.

However, I'd been mulling over this idea on how to rehabilitate Morris since leaving Bradford, and I was determined to make amends for what I couldn't actually pin down as having done wrong. Now that I'd got the measure of the problem, I reckoned I could sort Morris out a bit. Unless, of course, he actually managed to start menstruating!

★

It was maybe a week after Morris Yeo's eyes had opened up to the wider world of new diseases that women could bring to his portfolio that I was next up on the fifth floor of No. 23, Wellington Street. I could detect a certain amount of hostility still, and found this to be coming from two different elements of the previous Wednesday's events. Firstly, it was very ill-timed for Nadine to experience a particularly bad dose, which arrived on Thursday, causing absence on Friday, and the limpet-like Sherlock searching of Morris on the following Monday. Secondly, Duggie Lomax, as he'd expected, had temporarily ceased operations on the sickness book, since they'd never before experienced such a single-mindedness in Morris, funnelling all his attention into just one complaint. He was valiantly battling against contracting full menstrualitis (a term he'd concocted with the willing assistance of, and minimal reassurance from Eric Gaunt). He rashly continued a fruitless one-sided private inquiry, through the germ-barrier of a crumpled handkerchief, with the evasive and increasingly uncooperative junior tracer.

What these ungrateful tosspots did not appreciate was that I was the bringer of all-round salvation, now that I'd fully formulated a programme for a confidence reconstruction programme in Morris. I called an immediate council of war in the Plan Room round the back, pulling in Keith, Duggie and a slightly reluctant Eric Gaunt. He'd been unforgiving as regarded my harmless tale, according to Keith, mainly because he'd apparently been tormented by it all week, and feared another imponderable "joke", and the further humiliation of not understanding that either. (He'd tried it out in the "Dog", and had had to buy his own for the rest of the evening.) Added to this, Eric said he wasn't too sure that he wanted a solution to the Yeo problem, seeing plenty of mileage left in it still. He softened as I explained my proposals, when he could see even more promising possibilities within.

"Everything alright, Nadie?" asked Keith of the passing cloud of purple thunder, obviously on her way to the sanctuary of the Ladies for the fifth time in a short morning. This in itself would no doubt be having further adverse effects on the fanatically observant Yeo.

"Can't you get that frigging depressive off my back? Can't one of you take him out to play on the railway lines or something? Just what's he after? If he's chatting me up, I don't see it. I just don't need him around right now!"

"We think Mike here's got the answer; just ease up on going off to the bog so often – you're only making matters worse."

"What the hell's that got to do with you or anything? Besides, it's the only way I can get five minutes' flipping peace!"

"It's too difficult to explain just like that, Nadie," I told her, "and I promise you that you don't really want to know. I've had this idea on how to fettle him for you, though."

Nadine went on her way, no doubt even more confused. If she managed to get any solace from my attempted show of confidence, she didn't show it too well. It was a confidence that I'd have been more than happy to have been able to believe in myself.

Devoid of Nadine, Morris had wandered back to his desk, and the Relief Committee took an immediate silent vote to leave me to it.

"Ay up, Morris, lad; how's it going, then?" I tried. This was a question that would never have been posed in real life, but this next hour was not to be in real life.

"Glad you've asked, Mike. As a matter of fact I'm still quite concerned about this menstruitis of Nadine's. I'm positive I'm getting a touch of it! Only this morning, just after I got up, I noticed..."

Oh, no, no, no! Get in there quick, Mike! Whatever descriptive detail was coming next, I was pretty sure I could do without sharing it. "Hang on, Morris, lad, I reckon I might be able to help you a bit there. You see, I've not been altogether up front with you about all this. I didn't realise you were as worried about her as you obviously are. It's not really like you to worry overmuch about health, is it?" I couldn't help pushing credibility to, and beyond, limits, but it seemed as if I was still not even approaching Morris's boundaries of infinite credulity.

"S'true," replied Morris, "but this one's a bit naughty. I'm due to go away this weekend and I could do with being sure I've not copped for a dose of whatever it is with Nadine."

"Well, old love, I'm here to put your mind at rest. I've got these tablets, see." "These tablets" were some I'd knocked out by cutting three round pieces of white chalk off a stick I'd managed to scrounge from the Training Section. Each was about an eighth of an inch thick. I'd made a reasonably neat job with the Print Room Stanley knife, so much so that I'd got a bit carried away, and extended myself into carving a capital "M" (for Menstrachex) on one face of the "pills". I'd given them a sort of professional smoothness by rubbing them over with a damp fingertip. Four rejections left the three passable tablets I was offering up to solve all woes.

Morris bit immediately. "What do they do?"

"They test for not having what Nadie's got, that's all! And

what's more, they tell you whether or not you're even a possibility for getting it! Y'see, I wasn't completely honest with you, because I didn't want you to worry. I'd to get myself these on prescription when Our Lass went down with it. The vet insisted, for safety's sake you know, and they always give you too many for your sixpence, so I've a few left."

"What d'you do…? How do they work…? How d'you know if…? How will…?"

"Easy up! You mustn't get overexcited, or they might not work at all. Now look, this is how they operate – what they do is react with the bug, or whatever it is – if it's there – and with the gene – if you carry the gene that lets you catch it, if you follow – right? Now, inside here is a foaming agent – OK. Now if the bug's there, it neutralises the foaming action, and it turns your water blue at the same time. Now, if you're clear, and there's nowt up with you, and there's no chance of there ever being owt up, there's no colouring of the water at all, but the main thing is you should see some slight signs of foaming after you next go for a pee. Obviously the more foam the better!"

Already there was a brightening dawn breaking over the desk of doom. The dense black cloud hovering over the condemned one was turning towards a less-threatening grey. Morris's hand shot out to grab at the mind-saving drugs of classroom best.

"Give us one, then, let's get to be knowing!"

"Hold your horses, Morris, there's just one snag with 'em. There has to be a lot of acid strength in them, as you'd expect – just to hold in the foaming agent, you know, so you have to take them along with a lot of water; and I mean a lot! Plus side is, of course, that you get to know the answer sooner rather than later – much better than hospital tests – that 'Come back in a week' sort of thing."

"Right," said my impatient patient. "So it's lots of water, piss goes blue if it's bad news, and foams if it isn't. OK, OK… how much water?"

"Seven or eight pints! Take the tablet with the first."

"OK, s'easy."

And off trotted an obviously slightly relieved Morris to fill up the kettle. At least he had an optimistic side.

"Alright?" asked Duggie, sidling up.

"Going great; are the lads set up?"

"Ready when you are. Keith'll be banged up in Trap One, Eric in Two with the tackle, and Four's still knackered and locked. So he'll be forced into Three. I'll be ready to follow Morris in, and give the lads the shout."

"For Chrissake keep it subtle, we don't want him to tumble."

"No, sorry, figure of speech. If it's Morris, I follow him in and pull the roller towel three times, then twice. That's the signal. Ay up, here he comes; I'm off!"

Exit Duggie, enter Morris. They passed each other, both throwing a conspiratorial glance as they did. In Morris's case, there was a double take for a second, not understanding why there should be any such reaction in Duggie. Morris was carrying a very full kettle.

★

Morris sat down at his desk, and eyed the odd-looking tablets in their rather dubious confines of a Swan Vestas matchbox. He picked one up and tentatively threatened it with his tongue.

"It's a bit chalky; I thought you said it was acid. This isn't acid!"

I couldn't do with things falling apart now on a purely scientific technicality.

"There's a balanced alkali coating to neutralise the predominantly acidic nature of the active ingredients once it's done its job. With all that water, it makes a neutral solution. Just get it washed down!"

With the practised movements of a life-long pill-pusher, Morris slotted all three tablets down his throat, chasing them with his first mug of water.

"One would have been en... Ah, never mind, you can hardly overdose on 'em. Look, I'm off downstairs for a bit. Remember, bad news if your water goes blue, no problems if it foams. Try and knock it all back within the hour, if you can." Realising that an hour watching Morris getting himself steadily outside eight pints of water could prove a bit tedious, I drifted off. "All the best!"

Passing Nadine on the stairs, I told her that she should have at least an hour of untroubled time to herself; information which did not quite have her skipping up the stairs and clapping her little hands with glee. "And what after that, then?" she asked, glumly.

"You'll see. Troubles are over. Promise!"

I went on down to the third, and dealt with various clerical matters, better seen to directly rather than over the phone. I then checked through the Staff Section, on the pretext of an update on any holidays remaining, but really for a rare close-up of the blonde junior. She was usually only seen in the distance from up on the fifth, and was one of Duggie's clothes horses in the weekly stakes. I continued round the circuit of offices and wandered into the Messenger's for a real session of intelligence-gathering, they, the chainmen and the Typing Pool being the depositories of all knowledge. Finally, five minutes with the typists, and back up to the Drawing Office. There I found Exhibits A, an almost empty kettle, and B, an obviously overfull Morris – and an absence of Keith and Eric, presumably already in position.

"Where you been, for Chrissake? I've managed seven, and I'm busting. Is it OK to go one short?" Slight pause. "I'm going anyway." With which the distressed reservoir waddled away towards the Gents at a commendable speed. Right on dot, Duggie followed. I felt emotional in the way I reckoned Montgomery must have felt, as his troops moved around him, falling into perfect position in the desert. With a comfortable feeling of a job well done, I settled down to wait.

Out of sight, I found later, things were not going completely to plan. Morris, who must have been thinking how close his luck was running in finding only one of the cubicles out of four available, thrust open the door of Three. He shot in, unbuttoning as he went. After thirty seconds of intense relief, he began earnestly studying the lavatory bowl for any suspicion of blue, the flow now becoming merely urgent as opposed to desperate. While he was bent in deep analysis, Eric took his chance. Picking up from the energetic tugs on the roller towel that Trap Three was full of the swollen tanker formerly known as Morris, he peered over, and prepared to add a few drops of Fairy washing-up liquid to the overhead cistern. He then realised the snag – he couldn't reach to squeeze and tip at the same time. He struggled. Morris was giving him all the time he needed, but panic took over. Eric wrenched the annoying little flip cap off completely off the plastic bottle and stretched over again, as far as he could. At this point, soaped-wet fingers and smooth container combined to drop the full bottle in the cistern. He'd a sudden desire to get out, and it was a suitably flushed Eric, followed by a querying Keith and Duggie, that blundered back into the office. They were followed four minutes later by a transformed Morris.

If I'd had any doubts about the ethical side of the plan, the rare spectacle of a beaming Morris dispelled them. The lad was absolutely radiant, and bubbling as much as the lavatory bowl apparently had. "Oh, that was great," announced Morris, presumably on at least a couple of counts. Turning in a stage aside to me, he hissed, "No blue, and plenty of foaming, though I had to flush it first! I'm clear! I've not felt so good for years!"

It was as things settled down, and the committee met over a mug of tea, that Eric first mentioned that things had got a bit hairy during the operation, and that the best part of a full bottle of the most violent of washing-up liquids was loose in Trap Three. A casual site visit confirmed our worst fears. The floor was quickly becoming soft and tender, covered, as it was, in a thin layer of delicate bubbles. They were just beginning to ooze through the traditional gap at the bottom of the cubicle door. A slight opening of the door showed that the problem was far more acute within, as the lavatory bowl appeared to have entered Fairyland in more senses than one. Foam was piled up level with the seat.

Quickly shutting the door, another out of order notice was posted. While this gap between the door and the floor was handy when it came to setting light to various occupants' newspapers, it was letting us down badly now, at this moment of crisis. Eric found it impossible to recover the steadily emptying evidence from the cistern, and had unwisely tried a couple of hopeful clearing flushes, each considerably adding to, rather than relieving, the problem.

As so often happens, discretion and withdrawal, together with a combined willingness to lie like fury if cornered, seemed the wisest move, especially as Morris's silence could be relied on. He took the malfunctioning of the system as being entirely his own fault, through overdosing on the pills.

I received daily reports back on my home ground at Huddersfield. Problems with Trap Three seemed to improve during the day, but returned each morning, when activity in that area was at its peak. Things didn't get any better, and the situation reached a zenith by the fifth day, a Monday morning, which was particularly spectacular after a full two days of gentle refuelling from the leaking container. Flushing produced breathtaking results. Foam had taken control of all four cubicles, and was even managing to beat the barrier of the outer swing door. Any brave or desperate soul using the toilets would emerge to leave a paddling trail right through the Drawing Office. A major diversion of traffic down to the third-floor Gents was causing considerable congestion.

As to the justification for our actions: Nadine had rediscovered her life, and was never approached by Morris again, and Morris himself returned from his weekend in the country, happy to have only picked up a trace of hayfever – in mid-November, mind! This supplied Duggie with a considerable profit on the week's betting. For myself, there was a further advancement within the office pecking order, set back but slightly by memories of my joke-telling ability. A weekend visit to the office had allowed the lads to rescue the remaining evidence from the cistern, and the matter was eventually forgotten.

*

For the sake of completeness, in case we don't come upon Morris Yeo again within these reports, for he was a person with a rather singular claim to fame, it should perhaps be recorded that he lived only another nine years, suffering a fatal heart attack in his mid-forties.

Duggie Lomax was felt to have slightly overreached decency on that occasion, by opening a book on likely gravestone engravings, offering a reasonably generous four to one on "How's this for 'Just a bit off colour'?"

So it was RIP Morris Yeo, famous to the few; discoverer and

test-pilot of a number of ailments previously unrecorded. Housemaid's bum, a crippling ache brought on by shuffling round all the rooms in the house while mini-vaccing the edges of the carpets which are known to harbour fleas and bugs; Athlete's armpit, an itchy rash which forms after running and jumping with your vest on inside out; Tennis inner-ear, a rare stinging pain accompanied by several days of humming, picked up while doing net judge duty; and Yeo's hypochondria – a conviction that everyone you meet is suffering from some transferable disease or other.

★

I wasn't in Leeds again for a couple of weeks afterwards. It was obviously still my finest hour, or fortnight, as it happened. Nadine, now in mid-month bloom, came over especially to make me a rather excellent mug of tea. Morris, who had returned to the simple pleasures of the common cold, arthritis and a toenail threatening to in-grow, was still happiness personified. Duggie was back to running a steady book.

Eric Gaunt was still a shade distant, but I felt my star to be in the ascendant, and that I could walk on water.

"Got another story for you, Eric!"

"Bloody great. Better than t'last one, I hope."

The lads were gathering round, mid-morning pots in hand. I felt quite good this time.

"OK, let's be having it!"

"Right, a railway carriage, one of those old ones – no corridor – just compartments, you know the sort, where you can't move up and down the train, each compartment's got a door to it with a drop-down window on a leather strap, they have them up—"

"Yes, yes, yes. Bloody hell! Your attention to detail is friggin' admirable! Gerronwi'it!"

"Look, it's important you pay close attention. It's like before, it's the details that count. Miss one and you've no chance. When I was told it—"

"D'you have a particular fancy for hospital food, then?"

"OK, right, there's this closed compartment, trundling along. There's just two people in it, a middle-aged bloke smoking a big pipe, and a posh lady with one of them snooty little dogs with a bow round its neck, sat on her knee. Right? Right, OK. So this fellow stokes up his pipe, and there's clouds of smoke coming out, and filling up the compartment, and this little dog starts coughing, like. It's going 'Currgh, currgh, currgh...' that's a dog coughing, currgh, currgh, cur—"

"I take it there's some point to all this?"

"No, shurrup, let him tell it!"

"Well, while it's coughing, it starts spluttering over this bloke, and he starts shuffling about, and stoking up the pipe even more, and the dog's coughing and spluttering gets worse, like, and that makes the bloke even madder, so he's puffing away even more, which makes the dog cough and splutter over him again, and then—"

"Mike! You have our total undivided attention. Get to the bloody point!"

"Look. I've told you. You've got to follow me exactly or you won't get it!"

"OK, man in coach with pipe, posh woman in coach with dog, man smoking, dog coughing and spitting over bloke, currgh, currgh, splatter, how's that?"

"Yes... OK, then. So the bloke takes his pipe out, and says to the woman, 'Stop that dog coughing!' and she says, 'You stop smoking and the dog'll stop coughing.' He says, 'If you don't stop it coughing I'll make it stop!' And she says, 'Oh yer, how?'"

"As posh as that, were she, Mike?"

"No, you threw me, she says, 'You will do nothing to my little dog, just stop smoking!' 'Stop it coughing!' 'Put that pipe out!' 'Stop it spitting!' So they're at it hammer and tongs, and the dog's still spluttering all over the bloke, so he suddenly jumps up, opens the window, grabs the dog, and slings it out of the train, just as they're going under this bridge, and the woman's up, grabs the bloke's pipe and slings that out of the window as well. Train starts slowing down, and they're still fighting. Two minutes later, and they pull up at a station. They tumble out onto the platform, t'guard comes along, stationmaster, ticket bobby, the lot, and they're all shouting and screaming and jumping up and down, till suddenly a little lad says, 'Look!' and he's pointing back up the track. And there's the little dog, running after the train, and up onto the platform. And as it gets nearer they can see it's carrying something in its mouth… Bet you can't guess what it'd got in its mouth…"

"The bloody pipe!" screamed Eric.

"Nope! It was a special red brick with a gold stripe running right round it!"

Harry

"How come electricity's so intelligent?"

"How do you mean, 'intelligent', Harry?"

"It's nivver really struck me before. You tek it for granted, like; allus having it arahnd thi. If tha can think back to living in t'gasleet days, like ah can, it gets thi thinkin'."

There was no denying that. This thinking thing was beginning to grip Harry.

"That's t'problem wi' you young 'uns today; you nivver get to ask yersens questions abaht what's all around thi." The philosopher bent forward and his head went knowingly to one side. He went into a fit of winking with the upper eye, in time with a nodding tic from vertical to slant. "Tha's just got to be that bit sharper to think up that tha needs to think on abaht t'question tha's thinkin' abaht in t'fust place, like."

"That's very true," I said in my approvingly thoughtful vein, tiptoeing the knife-edge between sympathy and condescension. "But I don't see as to why electricity's got to be intelligent, as such."

"Well, nah," went on Harry, who wouldn't have recognised condescension if it had been gift-wrapped and labelled "For Simple Sods Only". "Think abaht it; you've some electricity running along that theer wire, up theer," pointing to the light fitting, "and it knaws, when it gets to t'bulb that it's got to leet it up. Ower theer there's thi wall heater; when tha pulls t'cord, t'electric knaws it's to warm up them bars, as well as leet 'em up a bit to show as how they're on! And sithee, that fan of Jack's theer; electricity comes along and fathoms it's theer to mek it spin; not leet up; and not get warm. How does it tell, eh, if it's not intelligent?"

This is Harry Hanson, Assistant PWay Supervisor. Time: around half past twelve on a typical winter's day. Place: a six-foot arc around the PWay Supervisor's roaring fire. Lights on and striking the high windows in such a way as to make the damp gloom outside seem damper and gloomier. Harry had been looking thoughtful for some minutes before opening up. Thought betrayed itself in the form of a ballpoint dangling from the relaxed corner of his mouth for at least the previous ten minutes, eyes fixed on some point within the space of the office, rather than on anything tangible, body rocking back and forth in the manner of a stressed-out zoo-bound animal. Now that the thought had transferred itself from the "Think" file to the "Speak", its passage marked by the biro dropping onto the table, the eyes focused and the rocking stopped.

On these quiet winter dinnertimes the *Daily Mail*, *Telegraph* and *Mirror* were rotated between Bill Boyes, Jack Senior and me, while the *Daily Herald* was clamped firmly beneath Harry's elbows, open at the crossword. As usual, Harry had been tackling the Coffee Time Quickie, not, fortunately, one that the rest of the syndicate favoured. It was impossible to take over once Harry had assaulted it. He'd a unique approach to the art of crossword solving, never really grasping the spirit of the puzzle. Harry on seeing a clue, say: "Large English city", with "L" in place for the first letter, would put in "Leeds". With the answer actually being "London", there'd be a square left over, so Harry would simply black it in. Similarly "Small burrowing rodent", with the first and second letters already in as "M" and "O", and Harry would fit in "Mouse", either by squeezing it up into the four squares available, or if it fell at the edge of the grid, he'd cheerfully add an extra square in the surrounding space.

Despite this inventive approach, he was ever vigilant and indignant about what he saw as cheating in others. Glancing over Jack's shoulder one day, he scoffed in disapproval. "Cop-i-lot? What the bloody hell's 'copilot' when it's at home?"

"Co-pilot, assistant pilot on a plane."

"Well, put a bloody dash in, then. There's no such word as 'copilot'!"

"You can't put dashes in crosswords, Harry!"

"Ah bloody can! And theer," stabbing the offending section, "tha's put 'Why'. Weer's tha bloody question mark, eh? What's up wi'thee? And me wi' no proper education t'speak of! Dun't tha want t'get it reet?"

And it was while chasing Harry's sudden interest in electricity that I later nailed it down to the day's crossword: "Originator of electric generation". After trying to plug the gap with something on the lines of "National Gridline" in a space reserved for "Michael Faraday", Harry had floated into one of his deep trains of thought – for Harry was a thinker, even if the train often got shunted into the dead-end sidings of his mind. We knew from experience that when Harry surfaced from one of these reveries, we would have to pack in our own reading in favour of the inevitable discussion that followed. This was not altogether a bad thing, even though the fifty-four minutes allowed for the dinner break were precious. (So much so, that we weren't inclined to waste it in eating sandwiches. These were usually downed while working, in the previous half hour, so as not to interfere with the social exchanges which might be born out of each other's reading.)

Harry's starter for ten had obviously been fermenting for some minutes – triggered off by the crossword clue. His face was a picture of thoughtful concentration, with his forehead crumpled and his upper lip pressed hard up against the end of his nose. This completely obliterated the slender moustache that he drew in every morning with Mrs Hanson's eyebrow pencil – an attempt to match the appearance of his male role model, Clark Gable. (Occasionally there would be a faint suggestion of actual bristles in this area, but Harry's ambition for a natural thin adornment usually disintegrated under the inartistic assault of the early-morning razor – hence the use of the pencil.)

I have to digress slightly, now that the subject of Harry's sub-nasal artwork has cropped up a little earlier than I'd anticipated. This feature was far and away Harry's greatest point of reference, and held him hard in people's memories long after the name and the rest of the Gable likeness had escaped their minds. "Y'know who ah mean; him wi' t'small bore snot gutter under his nose, t'Bette Davis eyebrow tache, him wi' t'black lipstick and lousy aim!" – I've heard so many descriptions of Harry, pointing me in his direction immediately. It must have been a labour of concentration to apply, and betrayed Harry's early-morning state better than any described headache or delicacy after the night before. Someone had once suggested that what with the effort involved it would have been simpler for Harry to have had it tattooed on, or even embroidered – anything rather than that bleary close encounter with the mirror and pencil every day.

One morning, I remember, must have been particularly harrowing, since it looked like a sneeze had interrupted him at the two-thirds point and the finished product looked like a BUPA logo.

But back to the debate. As usual it was going to be down to me to discover some common ground for the ensuing discussion, seeing as I was "educated".

"And thur's other things an' all. Tek yon phone. How does it know to mek itsen talk, and not burn your bloody ear, or send it spinnin', eh? And," this one looked like being the biggy, "how abaht that theer hand-lamp, eh? That's not even connected up to t'mains. Electricity's bin put in its battery, an' it has to think on its feet, like, 'cos it's got no feedback to t'power station, has it?" he ended triumphantly. Not quite; there was an encore – "And that self same battery could be put in a radio, and it stops givin' off leet, and starts talkin'. Explain how it knaws to do all them things, at t'reet time. Now that's how intelligent electricity is!"

There was going to be an awful lot of groundwork to cover here, which would not be helped by Bill Boyes being there. Bill's motto was "If you can help somebody as you pass along the way – don't; not if you think you can get some mileage out of it." I could just about manage without Bill adding his twopenn'orth, but I knew that he was already inserting his money in Harry's mental slot.

"Harry's reet, tha knaws, and that's only t'start of it! What about it being able to go uphill just as easy as down? Sithee, it's to run reet up theer to that lamp from t'switch on yonder wall. If that light were worked bi watter, you'd have to pump it up theer… by electricity, probably."

"Electricity can't have owt to do with water, Bill," explained Harry, in his "not a lot of people know this" voice. "It's bloody dangerous to mix up water with electricity like; they're two different things." In moments of seriousness, Harry's broad accent could all but disappear.

"Nivver heard of hydro-electricity, then? That's electricity made from water, i'n't it, and no one in theer reet mind could think of watter as bein' intelligent, could they, Harry?"

"It gets even more difficult to mek out, the more tha goes interit, dun't it? Come on, college lad, explain how electricity comes t'be so intelligent!"

"Look," desperately trying to avoid Bill's inane grin from outside Harry's eye-line, "when it goes through that light bulb, it makes the wire in it glow bright. In the heater it does just the same, but with it being different wire, thicker wire," – I'd tried to avoid the word "thick" but it slipped out – "that slows it down and it has to work harder to get through, and work means heat, doesn't it? It also stops it from shining too bright. In the light bulb the wire's very thin and the electricity races through, which makes the wire light up rather than get over-hot." I hadn't convinced myself, yet, and I knew I was right!

"You ever tried takin' a leeted bulb out?" said Bill unhelpfully. "Gets quite warm, y'know. Anyway, you're sayin' that if you put electricity through summat thick, it'll warm it up, reet? Reet! Wouldn't tha say that Harry's t'thickest of us four, built as he is like a shit-house door?" Harry bristled with pride at what he took to be a compliment. "Here, Harry, grab t'prongs on this battery! See if tha warms up like as how he says." Bill had taken a heavy nine-volt job out of the store cupboard at his side. That's just the difference between Bill and me. There am I trying hard not to use the word "thick", and Bill comes right out with it, declaring the man thick to his face – and then twinkling towards me for a reaction. I refused to satisfy him.

"Didn't you say you'd some shopping to do this dinnertime, Bill?" I tried hopefully, while simultaneously imagining Harry's brain spinning round as he gripped the terminals of the battery which Bill had handed him. I pondered mentioning this effect, but thought better of it.

"I'll just see this next bit through," said Bill, also studying Harry's expression of concentration. "I reckon we could be runnin' into a whole new minefield, here!"

Harry was again studying a chunk of fresh air floating somewhere between him and the wall. This indicated a further submersion back into deep thought. Eventually, coming up for air…

"OK, then, I'll let thee have that. Electricity running through thick wire's bund to get hot, but, sithee, what about mekin' things spin, then, how about that?"

"That's an electromagnetic motor where the wire's in a coil…"

"Like t'coil in that fire, up theer on t'wall," added Bill in his supportive way. "But there's not much spinnin' round goin' on up theer, so far as ah can see!"

"No, it's different, it forms a magnet that spins—"

"It's not thick wire, you see, Bill," explained Harry, "that's why it doesn't get hot. What wire is it, then?" turning sharply back to me, and almost catching the expression I was shooting at Bill. "Spinning wire, is it?"

"And," said Bill, wishing to widen both the scope and the confusion as much as possible, "we haven't mentioned electric trains yet, like what they have on the underground and over Manchester way. How is it that t'electricity in them and in clocks is the same, but clocks allus run on time, eh?"

"That is just about—" I was beginning to bite, despite myself, but was happily broken off.

"Best you lot can do," said Jack Senior, emerging from his paper and making his first contribution to the discussion, at the same time noticing Elliot Milner, the Boss, approaching across the yard, "is to watch telly tonight. There's a regular programme that deals with just this sort of thing, Harry, so we can carry on tomorrow, after you've watched it. *Panorama*, it's called."

"Right," said Harry, "you want to watch it an' all, Mike. Tha sometimes just can't see t'wood for t'trees, and it could clear it up a bit for thee. Easy to get confused, though, lad; could happen to anybody. Don't thee worry thissen abaht it."

I went back to the comparative sanity of the Drawing Office. I was sort of grateful to Jack for engineering a let-off for me today, but fearful as to what Harry was going to pick up in his cock-eyed way from *Panorama*, especially when he'd be expecting a programme specifically about electricity. But this was the beauty of Harry Hanson, forever blissful in his particular shade of ignorance. It was mid-afternoon before the penny dropped with me, twigging as to why Jack had recommended *Panorama*, when we were talking about electrical current affairs. While admiring his punning thought process, I was none too happy as to the consequences for me that would inevitably follow.

It was a case of déjà vu. Almost once every week we'd be in this debating circle, with me the centre of attention. Last time had seen me struggling, without any assistance, in trying to explain why there was snow on the top of Mount Everest. "After all, tha's got to admit that t'top of t'hill is nearer to t'sun than t'bottom, so it stands to reason that it should be hotter, so why's theer snow up theer and not dahn at t'bottom, eh?" One New Year had been particularly trying as Bill had entertained the family at Christmas with an annoying box of crackers with inane questions inside them. For weeks afterwards, if he thought that I was looking too comfortable, all the old favourites would be trotted out, like "Why did kamikaze pilots wear crash helmets?" "Who could have been daft enough to buy the first telephone?" "How do snowplough drivers get to work?" and loads more similar old favourites. Bill loved taking Harry apart mentally, and always dragged me in to sweep up the pieces.

Harry was a straightforward character, adequately equipped when it came to matters playing a major role in his life, such as permanent way maintenance, selective gardening and working men's club-room politics, but outside these limits he was a complete innocent at large. It was unlikely that he'd ever take on a position akin to Jack Senior as PWay Supervisor, although he substituted well enough during Jack's holidays – in part due to Jack's preparations and careful instructions to all. Harry's view of life was that he was extremely proud of himself at having got to the position of Assistant PWay Supervisor, thinking back to his early days in the Standedge Tunnel gang, when his only sight of winter daylight would be on Saturdays. He still had minor difficulties with reading and writing and reporting track faults other than verbally, yet he drew pride from his own comparison with a few of the men under him who were completely illiterate. He could only see his superiority to them, rather than any inferiority to others. It was no matter for shame to bring a form from home for me to help him with, which I gladly did, despite the irony of my own total aversion to form-filling. After all, in his eyes I'd had a university education, and he hadn't. It wouldn't occur to him that he might never have had the chance of a similar career to mine; to him it was simply a matter of being born before such opportunities existed.

I've always admired men like Harry, purely because they've worked hard to fully achieve their potential, and were good at their jobs. It was just this admiration I had for the Harrys of this world that placed me in a position that gave me personal satisfaction. I could never understand why others couldn't genuinely appreciate the competence of someone working up to his own limits, and so relate to such as the permanent trackmen of life, alongside the high-flying graduates, like the ones who passed briefly through my hands, and who returned later in life as my graded superiors. If anything, I suppose I was the sort of person that I'd no time for – the perpetual underachiever, on the basis of the ambitions that my seniors held for me. All this resulted in my one boast in life – an admiration for all who achieved in their field, which led to a natural ability to get along with most people I met in the working environment – seeing position as a point on a spectrum, rather than a rung on a ladder of competence.

Harry was a well-built man, or "thick", as Bill had mischievously put it. While he might hover around the six-foot mark in height, the way he carried himself gave the impression that he was having to look down to you. He was well turned out, ever careful to preserve his appearance to the point of vanity. No more so than as displayed by the constant variations in the decor of his famous upper lip. His ambition to achieve a close similarity to his film hero only came about after some fool remarked on his amazing resemblance to Clark Gable, and Harry had from that moment forward determined to reach a sort of perfection such that someone was eventually bound to come away from a Clark Gable film and remark that the star had an incredible resemblance to Harry Hanson. I only saw him deflated the once, when a visitor to the Area had been introduced by Elliot, only to stare hard and long at Harry. Bursting with pride, Harry's response was, "Ah knaw just what tha's thinkin' – I remind you of someone famous, don't I?"

"That's it! I couldn't put my finger on it," said the visitor. "Stan Ogden to a T!" This punctured Harry for the moment, but he explained to me later that the chap was wearing specs, and carrying a briefcase, which seemed to imply with Harry that the bloke was bright, but limited in his physical senses.

Harry's get-up was smart, so far as the job would allow. Sunday jobs would find Harry still deep in Saturday-night Brylcreem, which lasted the best part of the week before having to be augmented by lard from Wednesday onwards. Navy blue suit for winter, grey flannels and sports jacket for summer, both topped off by a neat trilby which was his badge of office. He did sometimes return to his roots with a flat cap, but its fine quality and pristine condition had more of the country squire, shooting with hounds, than the labourer about it. There was most certainly no resemblance to the uniform cap of the trackman, with its universal oil and grease-mixed texture and colour, inside and out. Harry's downfall was his extreme conservatism, a description which in his simplistic way he would have taken as a deep insult. This, combined with his pride in appearance, absolutely forbade that he should take to the new-fangled high-visibility vests when they came out. "Ah'm not walking abaht lookin' a bloody clown fer no bugger!" There were months of being the only person not wearing one, combined with Elliot Milner's veiled threats and the eventual mandatory appearance of the safety gear in the Rule Book. It was only then that he caved in and put one on. After a couple of weeks, though, he wouldn't take it off, in the office, on the train home, and at meetings when he deputised for Jack. It suddenly became a symbol of importance and signified the constant threat of danger under which he worked. It came to rank alongside the change of headgear, and swapping boots for shoes (or "low-ties" as they appeared in his Colne Valley dialect) on attaining the status of supervisor.

Conservatism was also a feature of Harry's approach to track repairs, and he would scorn many of the innovations that were to flood in during the 1960s. One, however, which he grasped with unexpected enthusiasm was the idea of hardboard track packs.

Before continuously welded rails, railway track was made up of short panels, usually sixty feet long. It may be obvious that the most vulnerable points under traffic were the joints between one panel and the next. Only the most over-maintained stretch could avoid the rail ends being hammered into the ground, causing the joints to dip, along with the pounded sleepers nearest the joint being thumped into the ash or slag ballast. This was repaired by laying a measured amount of stone chippings under the bearing points of the sleepers leading up to and beyond a joint. Then up comes some bright spark from Derby Research Laboratories with the idea of using treated pieces of hardboard instead of the chippings. Dips could be measured and the appropriate number of packing sheets placed under the sleeper ends. Up to a point, it worked well; that point was Harry.

Harry's bonus, like all permanent way supervisors, was paid on the basis of track-recording equipment traces, which, among other things, measured the ups and downs of the track. Dipping joints featured strongly in the equation, so that Harry and his like were intent on improving the trace counts, which was subtly different to adequately maintaining the track. Hardboard packing was a quicker and more accurate way of achieving this, so Harry set about it, to be rewarded by a much-improved trace, and a heavier wallet. This was all right until Harry sat himself down for a breather one morning, and watched the trains go by. He was immediately alarmed to see that although the joints were no longer bouncing, the central sections of the track panels were. When not under load, the panels reverted to their hog-back appearance, with centre panel sleepers floating clear of the ground. "Dynamic loading" was not in Harry's vocabulary, and if it had been it would have probably been related to weightlifting. What was happening was that the permanently bent rails along with the sleepers, were being lifted off their beds, because the ends were now raised and supported by hardboard. When a train came along, the track was pressed back into place under the dynamic load, and a smooth ride was being achieved, but all that Harry could take in was the bouncing mid-panel sleepers once the weight had passed by. Answer – get them packed as well before Senior sees 'em.

So – come the next run with the track recorder, and Harry's joints are showing dipped again, because he's packed the panel length throughout. Next answer – put more packing under the joints... and so his maintenance went on!

Some years later I was on a track-relaying job one Sunday, replacing worn-out panels with the emerging jointless long welded rail. It was on a section of Harry's patch, and I was mystified to discover, as we lifted out the old track, that the entire half mile had come to be laid on hardboard. Not only that, but Harry's policy of alternately treating joints and mid-panel sleepers had led to places where up to twenty-four packs had been stacked one on top of the other, making for depths of up to eight inches of unconnected laminated hardboard sheeting. There was no way that I could squat the evidence before Elliot turned up on his round of the weekend jobs. Seeing it, he demanded that Harry should be in his office as soon as he got back from the weekly Monday morning meeting in Leeds. I was to be the unwilling witness.

"The state that track was in was absolutely abominable," was Elliot's opening gambit. Harry replied as only he could.

"Thanks, Elliot, but it's taken me six years to get it like that!"

Harry's real practical strengths lay outside his working environment. A tradition of cottage horticulture was a strong feature of life in West Riding towns, and Huddersfield and Harry were no exceptions. Everyone grew prize vegetables, and everyone had their own speciality: Harry's was tomatoes and cucumbers. This was now to lead to another rung on my young pal Eddy Stapleton's Learning Ladder of Life.

Harry was getting himself outside a typical dinner of a quarter of cheese, one very large raw onion (which would print an impression on any stranger on a par with the famous upper lip artwork on a first meeting with Harry), and three average tomatoes.

"You wait till t'back end on August, young 'un. Ah'll show thee what tomatoes can look like!"

Eddy had always been a bit in awe of Harry. I'd been there myself in my early days. It was the overpowering appearance and loud confidence that did it. So Eddy was both surprised and pleased to have been invited into the conversation. In actual fact, Harry was merely directing his swaggering boasts towards the only target left in the room that he could impress.

"Harry grows 'em – tomatoes, tha knaws," explained Bill.

"Mind, they're nivver nowt more than ordinary, as far as I've seen! I reckon tha could easy slip up bi taking them for little green ping-pong balls!" As he expected, he'd scored a bull's eye on Harry's blue touchpaper.

"What's t'a mean, Boysey? Tha'd nivver seen a tomato till ah brought some in furthee last summer. Ah'll stand a Drop o' York t'anybody as can better my tomatoes!" (This "Drop of York" was something I'd never seen or supped in my long time at Huddersfield, but I came to recognise it as the ultimate gauntlet in male statements of assurance.)

"Why dun't'a prove it, then?" said Bill, intent on devilment. "Let's sithee grow some here."

"What's t'a mean, daft bugger? Wheer canna grow any here?"

"That windersill! It gets the full midday sun, and theer's ten foot of winder uppards! Tha could grow 'em in concrete in a spot like that. Even Eddy could grow 'em theer, from him knowin' nowt, an' all!"

"Reet, Buggerlugs! How abaht it, young 'un? What's t'a say to this cocky pillock? How's abaht us two showin' him who c'n grow tomatoes?"

The cocky pillock was wriggling with glee, since what he'd started as a bit of modest mischief was turning out very nicely, thank you! Eddy, for his part, had grown six inches in stature, now being taken into partnership with Harry.

Harry took charge of the impressionable youth in exactly the same way as he would approach his dozen or so men on a Saturday night. "Reet, lad, fust job's a good strong winderbox. Any ideas?"

Eddy had only recently helped me complete a plan filing cabinet in the Drawing Office, from Dexion-style angle iron and heavy ply, so there was only one way open in his mind. "There's some of that shelving angle and thick plywood left over from Mike's plan cupboard," he volunteered. Which buggers up it walking in the direction of home, I thought, where it had already been planned in as greenhouse staging. In fairness, Eddy did turn to me for approval, which Bill readily gave, to save me the trouble. Anyway, I could wait and Bill had a number going here without me being involved – perfect!

"How dust'a see it, exactly?" asked the troublemaker.

Harry, now planner-in-chief, with a limpet-like audience, put pencil to paper. What appeared to me as a rough-up of a sinking ship seemed to mean something to Eddy, and he set about the following dinnertime constructing the window box. All this was made a lot easier by Jack Senior being on a fortnight's holiday, since he might have had some views of his own about the creation of an allotment on a level with his right ear. Jack, Senior by name and rank, obviously had the desk which was flanked on this side by the window in question, with another one facing him.

Eddy was a novice to civil engineering theory, and Harry was a complete stranger to it. A construction taking a line of material economy similar to that in the Forth Bridge took on a horrific shape within a couple of days. It looked like the inspired work of the giant steel spider after a night on the nectar. Light from the window was severely reduced by several per cent, and lights burned in the office despite the growing strength of the mid-spring sun. Harry brought in six spare tomato seedlings, and placed them in the lesser light of the east-facing window, pending completion of what now had to be accepted as a structure.

It was probably a little ahead of its time to be awarded the Turner Prize, but from what I'd seen in the Arts Section of the *Telegraph*, if we'd called it something like "The Metamorphosis of Reason" we'd have been likely to have got an Arts Council grant for it. I applied my knowledge of structural design and analysis born of three years' study at university, and however I looked at the basic framework, I could barely raise my opinion of it to the level of deep apprehension. And it only got worse as Harry happily went along with every helpful suggestion that Bill saw fit to make, at the same time dismissing, with advice to "quit whinging", any drawbacks that I might see. As a sort of senior partner in what would undoubtedly be put over as a group endeavour, the realist in me had come to accept that whatever the final outcome, I would be to blame in some way. I was becoming increasingly concerned as to Jack's attitude to this Meccano Kit 24 explosion, on his return. My natural pessimism once more making me alone to be the one viewing the horrifying construction from his likely point of view.

Aiming to reduce the disaster potential a degree or so, I added my twopenn'orth.

"You do realise that it's now eight foot high, with a centre of gravity at least halfway up, and that it's resting on a base of only twelve inches width."

"So?" said the Inigo Jones of vertical gardening.

"Well, it's set to topple over!"

"What sarky bugger were it yesterday reckoned it to be on t'lines of Blackpool Tower, then? Has t'a heard owt abaht that tumblin' ower?"

"No, but that's fastened down at the base; this needs anchoring way up."

This was one of those occasions when I realised too late that I hadn't yet bottomed the depths of Bill's devilment. In a much faster time than a heart case should have been capable of, he was up the ladder we'd had to bring in with four nails of the six-inch category, braying them into the fine window surround. He swung on the upper levels with a nod of satisfaction.

"Reet, lad!," said Harry, admiring the steel trellis of curtaining which now, at midday, was casting the room into a late-evening gloom. "What we need now is muck!"

"Sort of soil, do you mean, Harry?" queried the 'prentice boy.

"No, my beauty," (Harry was slipping into a Long John character faced with his eager little helper) "I mean muck, God's own muck, Nature's very best – sheepshit muck. We'll have a trip up yon moors t'get some!"

Déjà vu again! I felt it well up in me, helped along by Harry having pointed to the famous heap of peat round the back: "That'd do nicely for a base, like." Not one for another moorland safari, I watched happily as Harry took Eddy out that afternoon to "a spot he knew". They returned with four buckets of rotted sheep droppings, along with a bonus bag of chicken manure obtained from a mate of Harry's in Honley. This he'd swapped for two decaying sleepers. As ever, the railway had proved generous with its time and materials. We now had the basic recipe for Harry's success with tomatoes, the mix producing a concoction which could be summarised as horticultural caviar, if Harry's eulogising was to be correctly interpreted. Not surprisingly, the job of making up the tomato bed was firmly delegated down to Eddy, using the small fireside shovel.

"Come on, lad! Frame thissen! Let the dog see the rabbit! It's no use faffin' abaht wi' that bloody spooin thing; get thi hands in, get it packed dahn solid!"

Eddy's enthusiasm began to ebb as he set about installing the mess in the twelve-inch-deep boxing which formed the ground floor of the Tomato Hilton. This had been made out of what I'd hoped would become my spare plywood sheeting, along with some of Harry's famous hardboard packs. (I had to admit that they seemed far better suited to the bounds of an indoor compost heap than as the raw materials for dominoes.) Eddy's enthusiasm was now in free fall. With eyes closed and head turned aside, he plunged deep. In the longest five minutes of his life he achieved a boxed-in rolling plateau of a medley of sheep and chicken dung. He didn't turn a hair when Harry handed him the six plants one by one, scooping out small depressions for each, and knuckling each one in firmly. It was all finished off with a dousing of water. Then the sun came out.

There was at first what Harry claimed to be a faint whiff of the moors. Sure enough, I could detect crushed bracken and the iodine of peat; sheep and rabbits, and wet grass in the spring breeze. However, Bill and I reserved judgement on the effect for half an hour, by which time it had become necessary in a casual sort of way to prop open the outer door. This was about the same time that Eddy returned after a serious hand-scrubbing session, using every aid available in the cleaner's locker and the PWay store. He brought with him the sweet smell of glycerine, acquired from the liberal use of Swarfega, and a niggling complaint that he could not get his fingernails clean. He'd attacked them with loofahs, cotton waste, Brillo pads and a yard brush to little effect other than producing what looked like ten charred carrots. Harry tried to console him with the observation that he'd no need to worry, as eating any of the trapped muck would more than likely make his hair curl. This Eddy had found to be a frequent bonus, oft quoted by his seniors, when it came to contact with something unpleasant, and it was always presumed that he wanted it curly.

We all left the office a bit earlier than usual that night, with some apprehension as to how we'd find things next morning. Not to worry, as it turned out; our fears seemed to be unfounded. Certainly I could detect a new ambience within the office, but it was nowhere near as bad as I'd anticipated; that was until the sun got round again, needing the door jamming open once more.

"I reckon it's easin' off now," said Harry, who had most unusually stayed out with one of the gangs over dinner, and well into the afternoon. His opinion was not shared by the flies of Huddersfield. Pioneers among them, who had discovered the delights of this gift-wrapped oasis the previous day, had apparently been in touch with their many relatives overnight. Together with a number of nomads who had travelled down with the buckets from the moor, they were holding a grand reunion centred on Jack Senior's desk. There were now only three days before Jack was due to return from holiday.

Luck was on our side, on two counts. Jack returned with a spring cold, and the weather turned dull. Neither of these phenomena went any way to improve the appearance of the labyrinth of angle iron and string, but Jack was spared the worst of the smell. As something of a gardener himself, he felt he could put up with the temporary loss of light in the name of progress.

Harry maintained that you could almost see them growing immediately. He kept lining them up with the top of some scaffolding, two hundred yards across the goods yard. It was Bill who had to point out that rather than the plants showing formidable growth, the scaffolding was actually being slowly demolished.

After a week, the plants started moving. While they were actually achieving their first foot of growth, the weather had remained dull. This may seem a long time to have dull weather in late spring, but in reality it was more of a short time for tomato plants to achieve the twelve-inch mark. Harry's mixture had an amazing effect, and progress could now be seen on a daily basis.

At three feet, Bill was moved to remark on the speed of growth, combined with the spindly nature of the stems and the meagre production of foliage on them. But he had to admit that the rate of progress up the bamboo and brush-handle supports was impressive.

"These plants, Harry, did you really grow 'em thissen?"

"'Corse ah did. Gorra 'nuther dozen at 'ome. They're champion, an' all, jus' like these here!"

"And tha got thi seed from your usual shop, dids't'a?"

"Ay. What ist'a gettin' at?"

"Just thought tha might 'ave got 'em off've some feller as a swap for a cow what you was takin' to market, on the promise of 'em bein' magic, or summat?"

"What's t'a bloody on abaht?"

"Well, ah'm sat here waitin' fer some big bugger wi' a golden chicken t'come climbin' dahn one on 'em any minnit, shoutin' 'Fee Fi Fo Fum!' or summat!"

"Yer bloody puddled, you are," was Harry's departing assessment.

There were grounds for adopting Bill's theory. Not content with the evil foundations to the enterprise, Harry was applying a daily liquid fertiliser, Bill was emptying out the swills from the teapot into the compound, and Jack was tapping out his frequent pipes into the soil. Sideshoots began to develop wildly, twisting among the scaffolding, and we had no way of reaching up to nip them out. The gloom in the office, which we had now got used to, was turning into night. Nature was taking over with a vengeance.

An interesting occurrence took place in mid-season during a casual visit by Horace, the shunter from Hillhouse yard, during one of his twice-daily trips to the station from the far end of the viaduct. Horace had long been regarded as a raving religious freak due to his regular church attendance (Good Friday three-hour afternoons and Christmas Eve midnights). He came in one bright morning, looked at the rainforest on the window sill and staggered back with a sharp cry of alarm. He swore he could see amongst the twisting and turning of the stems and shoots, the form of the body of the risen Christ, and with the one shaft of bright sun penetrating the jungle forming a brilliant halo round the figure's head. He foretold that blood-red tomatoes would appear in all the significant places. The rest of us tried in vain to catch this effect, much to Horace's great frustration, but it didn't prevent him phoning the *Huddersfield Examiner*, *Church Times* and

Catholic Herald with his story that Jesus had appeared to him through a tomato plant. Nothing came of all this, neither did our suggestion that he tried *Psychic News*, since he maintained that they'd know already. Bill continued studying the shrubbery into that afternoon, finally deciding that the four o'clock sun was projecting a tenuous image of Noddy and Big Ears onto the opposite wall.

At around this time in my life I was little more than a mere beginner in the realms of horticulture, and could only look in awe at the plants as they raced towards the ceiling. I had no greenhouse at that time, and little knowledge of what tomato plants should look like, yet still the abundance of copious leafing and diabolical knitting of hundreds of anorexic branches stuck some chord of doubt in me. All evidence of the steelwork and brush-handle supports had long since been swallowed up, yet of actual tomatoes there was no sign. Then suddenly, one Monday morning, there they were; bunches of small yellow flowers, about a foot below the ceiling.

Vindicated in his own mind, Harry cracked on about the importance of restricting each plant to only four trusses. Bill observed that the support that lot needed was going to be far beyond the capabilities of any truss he'd ever come across. He added that at the present rate of growth, the second bunch of flowers would be hammering on the base of the water tank, never mind the third and fourth. As I was no stranger to the under-drawing, for reasons which might be explained elsewhere, I was persuaded to go up into the extensive loft area beneath the tank, and remove a couple of panels of hardboard ceiling to allow space for the expanding truss to venture into the darkness, were it so inclined. Between the ceiling and the tank base there was enough room to stand up, but no light. Before clambering up, Harry gave me a rabbit's tail to ensure pollination of the small yellow blooms. I did this, hanging through the hole in the ceiling, watched by a diverse group of horticultural gurus, each providing his own individual formula for the act of procreation. Curiously, I felt a slight embarrassment committing such a pseudo-sexual act in public.

By careful manipulation, the stems were encouraged to run back across the ceiling towards the central light fitting, which was to become integral to the lattice of string which emerged. Jack, resigned to the seasoned smell and the dark, and by now compellingly curious as to the eventual outcome, could be found examining the forming tomatoes with the help of his track binoculars. They were disappointingly small, but plentiful, by the time they reddened.

"Beats me why they haven't grown in pods!" said Bill. "They're a bit bloody small, aren't they, Harry?"

"It's because they're reet up yonder," suggested Harry. "Mike, d'yer fancy nippin' oop theer again and sammin' up a few?" I didn't, but curiosity gave me a leg up, and I went back up into the loft. To my surprise, I found that on closer examination, the tomatoes seemed even smaller. Collecting all I could, I returned to base. The company peered into the saucepan I'd gathered them up in.

"Should ah cancel t'lorry ah booked from t'market to tek away all t'surplus, then?" asked Bill.

"I reckon it has t'be that muck what went in fust," said Harry, who was still ignorant as to the history of the peat.

"It's just that ah'd warned Horace that he might have to run an extra train down to tek away what t'market couldn't handle!"

As autumn took over, the plants reacted badly to the coal fire, and began dropping leaves and stalks all over the office. Added to this, there was a living blizzard of tiny white flies. An imminent visit from The Engineer prompted Elliot to order the demolition of the experiment, which I was happy to do with an eagerness only matched by my seasonal willingness to rip down Christmas trimmings at the earliest opportunity.

*

Like many such failed ideas, there was a concerted lack of enthusiasm when Harry suggested a retrial the following spring. As demolition of the box and structure neared completion, I discovered that nature had presented us with a final tribute in the form of a completely rotted window sill, with traces of grass growing up through the cracks as tomato roots penetrated downwards.

We ripped the offending remnants out ourselves, ready for the Works department to fit a new sill. This proved to be the only positive thing to come out of the venture, since in common with many other structures of the late 1800s, some Victorian clown had left a time capsule buried there. Apart from some newspaper cuttings, and a full list of the members of Huddersfield Town Council and the London and North Western Railway Board, there was a coin. It was in mint condition, and I later traded it in at a dealer's for an expected colossal share-out. Proceeds covered precisely the initial cost of Harry's packet of tomato seeds.

"So it's turned out all reet, in t'end, on balance, like," remarked Harry, standing with his back to a gaping hole beneath a window covered in green stains and decaying leaves, surrounded by collapsed plaster. "Y'know, weighing it all oop, I reckon cucumbers could be a safer bet next year! Or a vine; it were close to bein' a vine, 'cept it were toms instead of grapes. Or happen a—"

"I", interrupted Jack, "will settle for a window sill."

★

Harry Hanson could never be subdued for long, and his natural enthusiasm and bonhomie were never far from the surface. Take one memorable journey for Wilf and Percy, the chainmen, and me, along with Harry, in one of the old railway gang buses. This was a typical vehicle of the time with five forward-facing seats, and benches behind them running down the sides. You could get six men per side in summer, and five plus clothing in winter, with room being slowly created as the intense vibrations of the vehicle consolidated tackle, clothing and man. We were travelling through Harry's homeland of Honley, and benefiting from a running commentary from our giddy guide. He spent the entire trip leaping from one side of the bus to the other. Sliding the windows back, which made up the top six inches of the sides, there were hoots of "Ay oop, 'Ubert!", "How do, George!", "Alright, Arthur?" from as much of Harry as could be slotted through the gap with his head turned sideways. As we left each new friend behind, Harry's head performed 180-degree turns back into the bus as it continued its journey at a maximum of 20 mph, to issue a potted history of Hubert, George and Arthur. And the way Harry put it over, every one of these mates was a local celebrity, having some unique quality, ability, or claim to fame:

"'Ubert is t'one what starts up ivery whip rahnd if any on t'lads comes a cropper, or owt. Hasn't two awpnies t'rub t'gether isself, buree allus chips in!" (Trans. – Hubert is noted for his generosity, despite his straightened circumstances.)

"George theer; can lay a wood on a tanner at thirty yard, nine times out've ten!" (George was extremely competent at crown green bowls.)

"Arthur's grandfathur were t'first bloke in Honley to get knocked ower bier tram. Gorris bike wheel fast in t'lines!" (Arthur's grandfather was unfortunate once.)

Harry hadn't a bad word to say about anyone... almost. Carlyle Garner, colleague, and fellow assistant to Jack Senior, was the exception.

I reckon that Harry's only disappointment with regard to his station in life was that Carlyle Garner was his equal on paper. I could see Carlyle as Harry's balancing matter within the grand universal plan. Where Harry was a fine erect figure, Carlyle was a thin, sinewy, and a partly constricted individual. Little round glasses and a pair of flaring nostrils beneath a global tip combined to remind me of the Olympic logo. Harry was straight as a die, unable to be at all evasive, and intellectually limited; Carlyle was inventive to extremes, a stranger to the truth, and bright enough to fabricate the fantasies that were his hallmark. These he would make up for no reason other than to gain attention. He was the epitome of Uriah Heep to his superiors. Elliot was addressed by all his supervisors, and many of the lads, by his first name, but to Carlyle he was ever Mr Milner, accompanied by that slight stoop forward, with his head at a "will that be all?" angle.

Carlyle detested Harry for his pomposity and ignorance; Harry could not do with Carlyle for his pretence and crawling, and superior learning. No assistance was ever asked for, between them, or ever offered. So the astounding generosity of Harry towards Carlyle, in the matter of the chrysanthemums, took everybody by surprise.

One day, Jack Senior was openly considering his options for the rapidly approaching summer, with occasional reference to Harry. In a normal environment, Harry was considered very sound on gardening, just suspect when it came to window boxes inside high windows and virile tomato plants. Near home he had a small allotment as well as a plot around the house, and often brought in samples as gifts. Carlyle was finding himself left out of the conversation, not something he tolerated for long. As I wandered into the office the conversation was in full flow, and I was surprised to find it a three-cornered affair including both Harry and Carlyle.

"I fancy some of they thur crimson thumbs this year." Carlyle, to no one in particular.

"Tha wot, says t'a?" said Harry. "What's a buggerin' crimson thumb?"

"Big, spiky flowers, come up to here, lots o'colours."

"Chrysanthemums," said Jack.

"That's what ah said. Missus likes 'em. Thought ah'd bung a few in this year."

"You should try and get 'em as young plants, locally," advised Jack, "rather than send away for 'em. Where would you go, round here, Harry?"

Harry would normally have leapt in with helpful suggestions at such a point, but this was for Carlyle, which was different. You might normally expect it to generate no more than a couple of grunts, but, totally out of character, he broke out into a wide grin.

"Nah then, tha dun't need t'go buyin' none, 'cos ah've a few plants spare tha can 'ave."

It was at this point that the world stood still. I sidled out to catch Bill at his desk in Elliot's office, next door. "Summat's up with Harry, he's doing Carlyle a favour!"

Bill, intent on some paperwork, shook himself and followed me back through to find Carlyle offering Harry money, and Harry blankly refusing. When Carlyle nipped out later, we fell on Harry for an explanation, but he would only remark that things was coming to a pretty pass if a mate couldn't do a mate a favour, without all his other mates making a fuss.

Next Monday morning, Harry went out with the gang at half

past seven, returning an hour later in the bus. He was carrying a wooden tray filled with small cuttings. Even with my superficial knowledge of plants I could recognise the undulating oak-like leaves of the baby chrysanthemums. There must have been at least forty plants, which was a bit more than a few. Carlyle accepted them with as good a grace as he could muster, and even mashed a pot of tea for Harry.

I noticed Jack and Bill exchanging eyebrow-launching glances at the sight of the plants, and the glowering flash that Harry shot at them both, which demanded no comments.

"I can't do with this," said Jack to Bill and me, coming through to the Drawing Office. "They're discussing t'best feed for 'em now, and Carlyle's listening! It's just not natural."

Carlyle took the plants home on the train that evening, and placed them in his small greenhouse. Mrs Garner was out all the following Saturday, so, with forecasters suggesting that any dangers of frost were now gone, Carlyle took to planting out his crysanths in neat rows. He did it methodically, all the time explaining his spacing, packing material, and liquid mixture with which he doused each plant, to a neighbour, two doors down. Arthur Sykes, one of the local gangers, was taking it all in, unable to dissect fact from fiction, since his knowledge of gardening stopped around the "green side up" stage. He did move now and then to pass Carlyle one of the long canes that were being carefully spiked next to each plant, giving them an optimistic five-foot target to aim for.

I'd been wrong in my estimation; there'd been fifty-seven young plants in all, less one that had got damaged. Nearing the end of an afternoon's observation combined with trying out the sturdiness of Carlyle's gatepost, Arthur looked up to see the lady of the manor approaching along the row of cottages.

"T'gaffer's here, Carlyle, tha's nobbut just finished in time."

"What've you two been up to?" she asked her husband as he rose from his two and a half hour backbreaking position.

"Planting you some crysanths, what someone at work has sold me."

"Where?"

"Here, woman! What d'yer think all this is?"

"That," said Mrs Garner, "is common chickweed! Where's the crysanths?"

Carlyle looked back at his handiwork of the best part of the afternoon, thought to protest, but sensibly desisted.

There is an inherent need in some people to publicly demonstrate their gullibility or incompetence in public – take church bell-ringing for instance. Make a balls of that and everyone for miles around knows. In common with most idiots who have a grievance about being made a fool of, Carlyle just had to broadcast the fact, complaining bitterly to Jack about so-called mates. Jack, who'd already had a tear-jerking report from Arthur Sykes, tried to console him by suggesting that it must have taken Harry considerably longer to find and uproot all the small chickweed plants than it had taken Carlyle to put them out in his garden, though they both knew that Harry's pleasure would have far outweighed the trouble.

★

Curve design was a particular interest of mine, and therefore a strong point for me. Without going into too much detail, it involves carrying out a detailed overlapping survey along one rail, listing the readings, and working through a smooth proposed design on a special form. Calculations through a number of columns then give the setting-out details for the improved curve. This was yet another thing which contributed to supervisors' bonus pay with the passing of the track-recording trolley.

Harry would come to me with his worst patches, and get me to do designs that he could put into effect, primarily to boost his bonus, but as a side issue to make for a better ride and railway. Carlyle, to his credit, attended all the educational classes for track workers that were run out of hours by Drawing Office staff, and had fully taken in the survey method and a simpler form of calculation that helped to improve alignment locally rather than over a long distance. As a consequence, he would watch me doing the far more complex calculations with interest, eventually deciding that he too could do them.

A few weeks after some deep questioning of my methods, he

turned up in triumph with a thousand-yard-long scheme for realigning the track to a perfect single radius throughout the tricky little tunnel at Berry Brow, known as Robin Hood. My best efforts had led to a scheme that involved two sharp radii going in and coming out of the tunnel, with a flatter curve in the middle, so I was initially impressed. Then I was carried back to an incident from way back in my early weeks at grammar school, during our second-ever music lesson. We'd been shown how music was written down; black or white circles, with or without tails, sprinkled with dots and sharp and flat symbols, all on two sets of five lines. One keen kid amongst us, or greasing little sod, as we had quickly come to know him, presented the music master with a full exercise book, ruled out in staves throughout, and splattered all over with haphazard musical notes and symbols. It had obviously taken him all week to do, and he smooched up to the teacher with a superior smirk and a request for him to play it to see what it sounded like. I saw my first music teacher lost for any sort of response. So it was with Carlyle's curve.

"What's t'a think to that, then? More than thee could manage, i'n'tit! Y'see tha might have t'learnin', but tha can't beat experience! Reet through Robin Hood wi a steady curve, nowt like them ower lumpy efforts you've come up wi'! Now you can show me how ah mark it out on t'ground from this paper!"

Unlike the rough and ready method taught in track classes, and intended for lads a little more limited than Carlyle, the technical calculation leaves you with a figure in the final column of the actual track slue required at each point to achieve your designed curve. Starting at the top, I noticed that Carlyle's scheme was distinctly exciting, rapidly moving up to slues of over a couple of feet.

"Where's the tunnel on here, Carl?"

"Dunno exactly; do it matter? It'll be someweer baht here!"

I was now faced with explaining gently to Carlyle that the slues which he'd built into his "perfect" design not only missed the tunnel mouth completely, but managed to go right round the outside of the rock outcrop which made the tunnel necessary, leaving the track hanging from sky hooks. By the end of the scheme, Carlyle's railway was heading for Manchester rather than the intended target of Sheffield.

He, of course, had told Jack, Bill, even Harry, and most of his gang that he was going to show t'college lad a few things.

★

Carlyle insisted on telling fairy stories for no reason, other than to impress.

There was this day we were on a trip out with Elliot in the car, going round Carlyle's patch, with me in the back seat, behind our star. We were examining a variety of problems, and listening to a constant stream of amazing facts from the tour guide. In deference to Elliot, Carlyle's commentary was devoid of his usual accents.

Passing the recently erected Emley Moor television mast, Carlyle had to air his "knowledge": "You see the top part, Mr Milner, where it's thin and straight? Made of papier mâché that is, all hundred foot of it, to mek it lighter... mind these chickens, Mr Milner, they're very special chickens these, worth fifty guineas apiece, they are... see that oak tree yonder, Mr Milner, I planted the acorn for that, with a dose of weedkiller – if you use it strong enough it acts like an immunisation jab, and becomes a fertiliser; that's why it's forty feet tall now... did you know, Mr Milner, that the old Newtown Branch between Mirfield and Huddersfield was built using pirate's gold... that's why the viaduct over Leeds Road's built in special blue brick..."

For a moment I thought I'd heard this one before, and wondered if each brick was going to have a streak of gold running through it.

Carlyle demonstrated his actual true skills as we went from site to site, detailing problems and solutions, and fully justifying his ranking, yet in between we were treated to a constant stream of fantastic "facts". "Did you know, Mr Milner, that Wordsmith, the poetry bloke, wrote a poem about tulips based on that garden over there... that doctor's we've just passed, Mr Milner, he still uses leeches... this rock cutting, Mr Milner, I once dug out a dinosaur bone..."

Elliot, when he got the chance of nipping into the conversation, suggested that Carlyle seemed to know his patch and neighbours pretty well.

"Every inch, Mr Milner, and everyone on it. Chap that belongs that house there, Mr Milner, came up on the pools and won half a million pounds, and he's insulated his roof with one pound notes… You've really got to know your way around if you're going to be any use at this job."

Around half past two we had a café break enriched with a dozen amazing things Elliot and I didn't know, and forgot on the spot. As we walked back to the car, Elliot turned to me. "Where was it you wanted to go, Mike?"

This was a spot I wanted to show where I was proposing a big realignment during a track-singling operation, sluing one line into the other to make use of the best of the materials. I'd been using the office's large-scale ordnance maps; those that are so detailed that they virtually named individual sods. But mainly, I hoped to have set things up so that I could floor Carlyle, and expose his persistent falsehoods. Normally I would have just directed Elliot to "the far end of Denby Dale Viaduct", but as I climbed into the back seat again I looked at Carlyle and thought, Right, pal, get out of this one.

"Ash Well Shrog, Elliot. Carl'll show you the way."

There was a great deal of satisfaction in seeing the back of the navigator's neck redden over, and the short hairs that decorated it stiffen.

"Where was that, Mike?"

"Ash Well Shrog, Carl!" This was actually a spot where an occasional stream ran through a few trees, pausing momentarily on its way to form a small puddle. On the large-scale map it was Ash Well Shrog. It was far too insignificant to make its mark on the car's Ordnance Survey map; in fact it was quite unlikely that the inhabitants of the single detached house, nearby, were aware of the name.

"Ah, right," said he to whom nothing was hidden. "Ash Well Shrog, is it? Now let me think what's the best way to get there from here." This was followed by a lot of thoughtful "Umms", and "We mights", and "It could be bests".

Elliot eventually turned again to me, strangely suspicious of my obstinate non-cooperation. "How would you get there from here, then?"

"I'd just get out of the car. It's up that banking there. That's why I chose this café."

"Well, Carlyle?" said Elliot, now in no doubt about the rules of the game.

"This isn't Ash Well Shrog any more, Mr Milner. They had to change the name so as not to confuse it with the Ash Well Shrog up on Emley Moor, because there's secret plans for the Americans to set up a Polaris missile base up there, Mr Milner, you see. So they had to change the name here, to avoid confusion, you see. No, this used to be Ash Well Shrog as well, but they changed it a year, or maybe fifteen months ago."

"Polaris, Carl," I began to protest, "up on the moors? I thought they were submar—"

"Do you really think it's worth pursuing any further, Mike?" asked a bemused Elliot.

"No, not really." I knew when I was beaten!

★

Elliot and I often travelled back together to Leeds in the car at night; it gave us an extra half hour of good discussion time, and many a plan was formulated and developed on that stretch of road. Over the years we made some useful discoveries such as the farm shop selling eggs like rugby balls – often triple-yolked. We sought out the sweetest bags of stable manure, and the garages currently offering the best free gifts. Together with this, there was a constant challenge over the years we were together to find the quickest route home, especially with the M62 opening up a bit at a time.

However, after our day of listening to Carlyle's fantasies as we covered his patch, I reckoned that Elliot was ready to hear one of the Dreamer's longer tales on our way home. One that he'd recounted to me and Bill a month or two before. It all happened on the day of the cloudburst up over the Pennines, in the Standedge area. Reports had come racing into Huddersfield of floods in the small town of Diggle, at the far end of the tunnel. Trains had been stopped, pending track inspection by the engineers – that being Elliot, with me in tow – and we were soon speeding out to site in the car. From Marsden, at the Huddersfield end of the three-mile-long tunnel, the road climbs steeply, criss-crossing the three parallel bores, which you can follow by way of the ventilation shafts appearing first on one side of the road, and then the other. Just over the peak of the hills, a minor road branches off to the left, down into Diggle. It was quite clear that this little lane had been the main route of the floods from the hills.

There was little evidence of trouble at the top, but as we went further down into the valley, the sides of the road had been torn away, with two clean, deep channels cut into the tarmac edges. Nearing the bottom, a small mill, about a hundred yards from the road, had been ripped apart, as the gathering waters had swept through the building, bursting through the uphill-facing double-delivery doors and taking the opposite lower side wall with them. Approaching the first houses of Diggle, we could see small trees that had been ripped up and thrown against walls and fences, often flattening them. Roads were still awash in the valley and the journey to the station was fraught with problems. We finally reached Diggle signal box, where the tracks were still under water, only the rail top being visible. Elliot told the signalman that we would be walking into the tunnel to inspect any damage, at the same time picking up from him the news that the water level was in fact falling rapidly. Sure enough, by the time we reached the tunnel mouth, the flood had receded enough for the track to be visible, yet the small stream which ran under the railway just short of the tunnel mouth was still a raging torrent. It was clear that this was the main source of the flooding as far as the railway was concerned.

We must have walked half a mile into the tunnel before we reached the limits of the flotsam of the flood, left high but not yet dry. Whole gardens had been swept away by the torrent, and dumped along this length of the tunnel, as the crazy salad of uprooted vegetables showed. By the three-quarter-mile mark it looked like we'd reached the high-tide point, so we began to make our way back, carefully examining the tracks for any signs of the stone ballast having been undermined. At around the quarter mile, I was amazed to find bales of cloth, obviously picked up from the mill way upstream, far too heavy for me to lift, but which an augmented gang were already clearing along with much assorted rubbish. For quick clearance they were throwing it to one side, up against the tunnel walls for future collection.

Coming out into the light again, the flood had indeed continued to back off, and considerable minor damage to the track formation was now exposed, especially around the bridge over the stream. Just as the sides of the lane down the hillside had been gouged out, so here the supporting stone ballast had been eroded from under the sleeper ends, mainly in the direction away from the tunnel mouth, but to a lesser extent into the darkness. Elliot decided to allow traffic to resume, but at a drastically reduced speed. He also arranged for the immediate despatch of a trainload of fresh stone from the District depot fifteen miles away and sought volunteers among the men to meet and tip it. A final necessity was an order for sandwiches for them from a local shop. Both of us had seen the extent of the damage at first hand, but this did not prepare me for Carlyle's stage-play of the events. I took great pleasure in recounting edited highlights to Elliot, as we made our way home, putting the icing on the overdose of Garner we'd had that day.

At the height of the flood, Carlyle was there! He actually lived about a hundred yards from the tunnel end and the normally placid hillside stream. His cottage was at the very centre of activity. He it was who had seen the approaching clouds, had witnessed the opening of the heavens in the hills above the town. It was he who had rushed round all his neighbours warning them, and, at the same time, the emergency services. He had alerted the local hospital, warned the police of possible looting from ripped-out shops, and had pressed the fire service into action so that they would be prepared for any electrical fires and the pumping out of houses. He had also forewarned the distant coastguards for some reason better known to him. The local vicar had been startled into action by our hero, opening the small church and community hall as a possible refuge and temporary morgue. All this Carlyle had achieved in the space of the five minutes that it took for the clouds to burst and the resulting downpour to materialise in Diggle as a raging wall of water. He had watched from his bedroom window as a man was caught up in the torrent, further up the hill. The poor unfortunate had lost his footing and was being tumbled down the slope by the violent waters. Carlyle had leapt for his front door (which previously in the story had been holding back four feet of water) and had seen the man being stripped of all his clothing as he was swept along the line of cottages. He had caught a glance of the man looking wildly for help as he was tossed in the torrent, and after hearing Carlyle's call, he saw the man grasping the palings of Carlyle's fence with his fingertips. Carlyle, with amazing presence of mind, had lashed a rope to the banisters of his staircase, tied it firmly around his waist and then half waded and half swum out and pulled the man into the safety of his cottage. He had then closed the door (against the aforementioned four-foot wall of water), and had administered the kiss of life. This had proved so effective that when the ambulance arrived, the rescued man was sitting in the kitchen, decked out in a spare suit, and enjoying a cup of tea.

All this Carlyle had seen with his own eyes and done with his own hands.

And all that time I knew for a fact he'd been stuck in a train at Marsden Station at the other end of the three-mile-long tunnel, prevented from proceeding further pending Elliot's inspection. His entire story was a complete fabrication, but I'd been entranced by it. Our emergency track closure had taken effect before Carlyle ever reached the tunnel, let alone his home in Diggle. But as if all this had not been enough for our superhero, he'd even more to tell me.

Somewhere in between ringing the church bells, and helping a housebound elderly neighbour to the safety of her upper floor, he'd suddenly realised the peril that faced the goldfish swimming around the stone sink which was set into his front lawn. Now at this point you've got to bear in mind that Carlyle was the man who'd once convinced some of the least likely potential brain surgeons amongst his old gang that he bred house-trained rabbits. This was demonstrated to them by having thrown a handful of currants into the lavatory pan. Such delusions had spread into his relationship with his pond fish. He'd realised that they would soon be covered by four or five feet of swirling waters, probably to be lost for ever. With the wall of floodwater approaching rapidly, he insisted that he'd knelt down at the side of the pond with a fingerful of the fish's favourite food. Thus attracting their attention, he'd fixed them with his masterful gaze, and ordered them to "Stay!"

And next morning, according to Carlyle, when the floods had subsided, those five little fish were still there, swimming happily around their sink.

*

It was a couple of days after our outing with Carlyle that I found myself back on the firmer ground of coping with Harry Hanson, still gnawing away in his quest for reasonable truth.

"Didn't mek much sense of that theer *Panorama* thing, t'other neet," he said. "Dids't'a watch it? Some old biddy crackin' on abaht animal welfare and battery chickens. No help wi' what we was on abaht a day or two back – 'bout electrics, tha knaws!"

This was one of those unsettling moments for me, when I'm set wondering who was pulling whose plonker. Jack, on the subject of electricity, had directed Harry to a current affairs programme, only for Harry to appear to counter one better with battery chickens. Bill added that he'd found that shocking, but Harry led us back to the norm.

"Nah then, less of the friggin' abaht. This business wi' t'electricity. Ah've bin thinkin'. Tek your cooker and your fridge. How come it meks one hot and t'other cauld, eh? Then theer's t'telly; same electric's goin' inter t'wireless as is goin' inter t'telly, so why's theer no picture on t'wireless wheer thur is one on t'telly? An' what about t'tea machine at t'side on't bed, t'same bit on electricity goin' in has a clock tickin' rahnd, a little leet t'see wi', and a ringin' alarm what weks thee up, even afore it meks a cup o'tea; nah doan't tell me that's not intelligent!"

We were shell-shocked; even Bill had nothing to say. Then suddenly...

"And another thing, tek aspirins. Wot abaht them! How d'they know weer t'pain is, eh?"

Tunnels

Have you ever tried real darkness? Where you can't see so much as a trace of anything, not even bits of yourself, like a finger three inches from your eye? And where five minutes later, after your eyes should have got used to it, you still can't? (In the sort of darkness I'm on about you don't even know when your finger is three inches away, and you could easily have your eye out. Do not try this at home.)

It's nothing like the sort of darkness you get when you're lying in bed at night, trying to drop off. There's still something there – street lights through slits of uncovered window ("I wish you'd draw them curtains properly! I don't know; I can't leave them like that!"), security lights across the road – left on so that Chummy can better see what he's doing, often a blazing moon picking out the stitching in the curtains and how we're going to need new ones before long; the little red stand-by light on the TV – subtle by day, a lighthouse by night, or the bedside clock visibly screaming at you that you shouldn't be still awake at this hour.

What's more, you don't find it out in the middle of nowhere, dead of night and no moon. There's still starlight, even clouds or pollution reflect a glow from distant town lights. Maybe even static flashes from a disturbed shirt, if you're lucky.

I suppose you could get it in a coal mine; but whenever I've been down one it's been more like Blackpool Pleasure Beach in late season. And it's no use just shutting your eyes tightly; all sorts of little lights and images flash around when you do that.

No, the full monty black oblivion of nothingness is really to be found when you're totally alone in the middle of a three-mile-long railway tunnel, six hundred feet below ground, with concealed airshafts, about two minutes after you've turned off your hand-lamp. At such a moment the only thing to strike the senses is the varied dynamics of monotonous drips from the roof. This was never something I'd try in the days of the paraffin Tilley lamp – there was a desperate fear that you'd not be able to get the thing going again. You only muck about with total darkness when you've got the security of the modern hand-lamp, fitted with two fresh batteries that day. Mind you, the Tilley was a much more friendly lamp in the long run. It gave you an all-round womb of light, providing some sort of a personal existence, whereas the battery inspired beam only shoots away from you like a gunshot, the light darting from point to point in a tight probing cone surrounded by an uncomfortable black void of which you're a part.

This darkness: it's a matt-finish black. An echoing tomb of black. A fire-back black, with nothing of the comfort which that suggests. Shine a light into this black close up to the tunnel walls and there's a sparkle reflecting from millions of tiny bright crystals. Without the torch beam these same crystals are quite impotent. The darkness has a spatial volume, either enclosing or endless, depending on which phobia you lean towards. An agoraphobic will sense an infinite expanding space and a total loneliness, whereas the claustrophobic will find the blackness holding him and slowly tightening its grip. Any evenly balanced individual will be able to stand in this darkness and mentally sway between the one phobia and the other, an uncanny feeling similar to looking at an Escher perspective drawing where reversals of perception can flood over you as you stare at it. Now that I'd got the Guinness list of phobias open (in order to check some treacherous spellings), I couldn't help looking up one or two other individuals who'd have varying reactions to life as a troglodyte.

Presumably the photophobic and phengophobic (strong light and daylight) will both be at peace. Not too sure about the gymnophobic, who has a horror of nudity; it doesn't make it clear whether it's his or someone else's, but I don't suppose that matters down there. Anyway, in the steady temperatures of cool in summer and cold in winter, he's going to have other things on his mind. I've no hope for the pantophobic, who fears everything, because this darkness is a store of all the imaginable unknown goings on around you, but I would be sure of the relief felt by any keraunothnetophobic, who, with six hundred feet of solid rock above him, should feel inaccessible to the targeting of falling man-made satellites! But how will my friend the satanophobic react? For here we're so much closer to the object of his fear, and there are a few idiots around who only go to make things worse for him.

Standedge Tunnel under the Pennine range is where I imagine myself closeted with all these sad phobics. Here we have two single-line tunnels, now disused, a spacious live double bore, and a totally forbidding narrow-boat canal tunnel hewn out of solid rock, and rarely lined. It runs at a lower level, down the middle, and extends well beyond the railway tunnel mouths at both ends. Although reasonably secure from trespass, the idea of the two empty holes running dead straight for three miles under hundreds of feet of rock is a magnet to the lunatic dare element. At the centres of the single bores, one and a half miles in, a large cavern joins the two, known locally as "The Cathedral". Since the tracks were lifted, it has been decorated in mystical signs, and has been the site of animal sacrifice. Iron arches rise into the darkness of the roof, providing these "religious" freaks and dozy articles with a monumental Gothic sanctuary for their antics.

Denied light, the senses sharpen to sound, smell and touch. The first two are obvious, but in the steam days they were only secondary when you were alone and on guard against the approach of a train. Touch was the first sense you were aware of, in that the caresses of a soft draught on your face or the back of your neck was most likely to be the first warning you had of an approaching train. This is a sense you don't have when you're out in the open, and so provides an extra feeling of security, peculiar to life underground, which is why I would generally say that for safety, I was happier in a tunnel than outside.

But what nature of train approacheth? Always the draught, but with a sensation of intense pounding and dull heavy piston noises, the steam loco would finally come to the eye as a pulsating red glow on the tunnel roof. (Oil headlamps were as useless as a candle in a disco.) If the driver could see your light through his smoke, there'd be a piercing scream from his whistle, which you'd acknowledge by waving your light from side to side. The roaring bulk and swirling steam, together with the fierce thrust of fire, combined into a mechanical avalanche. It thundered past as you stood clear in a wall refuge, a momentary blur of thumping pistons and immense unstoppable wheels passing within a yard of your face. Carriage lights would then strobe past, each an individual shape depending on the passengers' positions, or what they were doing. As the red tail light was quickly absorbed, the world turned grey in the beam of your light, swirling violently, to settle into a bundling stream of steam racing, then flowing, then drifting, after the train, and finally just floating haphazardly in that general direction. If you were lucky, an unnoticeable steady draught would take the steam away to the nearest downwind airshaft; if you were not lucky, you would be stuck until a train in the opposite direction set up a counter draught.

Digressing slightly, let me point out that there were those who could turn the darkness to their advantage, if they wanted. At the risk of being declared racist, the West Indians in our gang were best suited. Is it racialist to point out that if you stood a West Indian next to a washed Yorkshire miner, one would show up in darkness better than the other? It can't be, because it's a fact.

In the 1960s there would be banter between all men, often involving personal features, but more strongly, territorial origins. So that when the gang at Todmorden had to work up to the border with Lancashire, quite a bit of almost serious discussion would take place based on the physical appearance of each member, ancestry and ability. Those with Caribbean origins fared no better and certainly no worse.

At that time, there were a smattering of immigrants absorbed in the gangs, and the West Indians were the best represented. Generalising, they'd a temperament very much along the lines of the northern Englishman, and both got along better than any other mix in my experience. We did have Big Tony at Huddersfield, a giant of a man, and deeply Italian. Tony had the strength of two, and this was often used – "Don't thee two touch it, tha's faffin' like tarts in a tarance. Go fetch Big Tony, and doan't stand around watchin' 'im, 'cos tha'll both get t'bloody flutters seein' 'im hoik it abaht!" Tony would have gone far if in the twenty years I knew him, he had mastered basic Yorkshire. Tony's native accent was such that you could have put a thick sauce on it and twiddled it up on a fork. To complicate things, he'd adapted to the lad's language but not to their accent.

"Cumma onna you larza bastardas; pulla tha bladda saxo uppa! It'sa aisya to platta da sawdasta nora gaitta yoa lotta moavin! Ahsa mahkina upsa Sundah lista an tha'sa noana bahna t'mecca it if tha doan'ta frammah tha bladda sensa!"

The lilting tones of the West Indian lads, and these were proper West Indians, born and bred there rather than third-generation dusky tykes, slotted in with Yorkshire so well. Abuse from one of the darker lads was so much more effective with a singsong uplift at the climax, rather than the native drop into bottom of the chest. And what's more, they had exactly the same approach to work as their blanched mates, if a little exaggerated. They were individually inclined to either work harder than anyone else in the gang, or divert their energies to doing as little as possible. Take John Ford, for example.

John was a worker, and spent most of his time in the drainage gang, rising to ganger. Even when in this position of licensed go-easiness, he practically did the gang's work due to sheer frustration at the way the others didn't meet with his standards. "Gettasen out, lemme in. Yo's the use ovva choccolait taypot!"

His sense of dour humour was such that when we were tackling the drainage in Standedge he would use sunglasses, he said against the glare of the gas-bottle flares. I could see that his natural expression of tight-lipped disgust at the lack of energy around him, added to the shades, made him blend completely with the tunnel. Many a supervisor would take his frustration out in John.

"Fordy! Why the bloody hell can't tha smile now an' agin? Ah can nivver spot thee when ah want thi."

At which John would fling his head back, remove the glasses and roll in tearful laughter. "Yo Limey eyes no work. Yo's blahnd as bats, all on yo... doan't wop ma boss, ah's a gooood darkie!"

John's opposite was Black Round George. He piled out of the cabin one night with unusual enthusiasm, and got lost. We were relaying a large chunk of point and crossing work near Sowerby Bridge, and kept well to schedule until it came to testing. Obviously, with levels being not quite perfect, we'd expect a bit of trouble with the signalman at first as he tried to pull his lever-activated rods to haul the point ends across, but tonight, no matter how we tried for perfect levels, he could not get any movement. It was difficult to spot damage in the dark, but we kept on at it, sending the lads in for breaks on a stagger so that we could keep going all night. Eventually, the signalman went down below box to check the rods at his end – quite unnecessarily since nothing had been done there.

"This yours?" we heard from the bowels of the box.

Lying down to look through the gap where the rods left the box to run along the ground to the points, we could spot a large sack of something or other stuffed between rods and cellar floorboards. After a lot of prodding, the sack turned into Black George, who had been well away there for most of the night, lulled by the gentle movements in his bed on the rods as the signalman fought to get any play in them.

Back on track again after that diversion and stepping forward a few years. Now it would be a diesel loco, not steam, bearing down on you, through a much clearer tunnel. If you're alert, you may well catch the piercing headlight before the draught on the face. Soon after comes the crescendo of a throbbing roar, interrupted by the fanfare attempts at "Ilkley Moor Baht'at", and that's it! Then the Doppler drop in pitch, followed by the same carriage lights, but with now a long look at the dazzling red tail as it rushes away from you.

Try as I might, it takes more words to deal with steam than it does with diesel; it's that old "romance of steam" bug that some crack on about. (Steam, dream, cream: diesels, weasels, measles; or am I getting too deep now?) Anyway, as to those raving cravers who eulogise over the days of steam, I'd just like to be able to dump one or two of them in a long tunnel, with one of their objects of steam and fire when they go all nostalgic about the "good old days". Give them a Tilley lamp each, with its finite amount of fuel, and see how romantic it gets when they find they can't take a single step with any degree of safety, encased as they can be for hours in a prison of steam and smoke. They'd soon find out what truly blind devotion was.

And it's that smoke which lingers on in today's tunnels.

They're still lined with the residue of the steam age, and this affects both sound and smell. A train's horn, travelling with the rushing air towards you, is loud and strident, yet it doesn't have the same resonance as the playful scream of the child under a clean brick bridge or in a subway. It is dulled by the century of soot. In Standedge, where the airshafts are offset from the line of the active tunnel, placed as they are over the central canal, the sound of the tumbling water, common to varying degrees in all such, travels only a short distance down the tunnel. It does not reflect well from the tunnel walls. Yet when you get to the shaft, the torrential downpour is deafening.

Tunnels are now more often than not laid in continuous welded rail, and this sings loudly to herald a train's approach from a great distance away. Sounds are either absorbed or enhanced in this underworld, depending on their source and the transporting medium.

Smells have changed little. There remains the memory of steam in a slightly damp sulphurous odour. I remember walking through Standedge once, and getting a bus on to Staleybridge so that I could ride back through the tunnel. As we hit the tunnel end, an elderly lady opposite – all tweed and camphor – jumped up and went through the coach shutting everyone's windows, brushing aside protests with declarations of tunnel gases and foul poisonous air. With me being obviously of the railway, some of the disgruntled turned on me to rebut the aged one's science of doom. I just mentioned that I'd spent an hour and a half walking through this same tunnel.

"And what respiratory devices did you wear?" asked the old dear, now sure of proving her point.

"None at all!"

"Well, you're a very foolhardy young man, and should seek medical attention the moment we reach the next station! Oh! Guard!…" The unfortunate had been summoned by one of the protestors. "This young man needs urgent medical attention for detoxification. I was a nurse in the trenches, and I've seen it all before, so please see to it!"

I knew the guard; the guard knew me – he was based at Huddersfield, and had spent many a night working in tunnels with the likes of me – so I felt it might add to the hour if I slumped down in the seat and lolled with my tongue hanging out. Meanwhile, Florence Tweedy Nightingale went into a more determined gear, explaining the nature of my distress to the guard. We suddenly struck daylight, and she flew into reverse on her window run, opening ones that had been shut before, "To rid us of any contamination this young man might have brought in with him."

My mate, the guard, took his chance to put his face up to my unconscious ear and explain that he'd be immensely obliged if I'd get up off my arse and accompany him to his compartment, underlying the request with frequent "pillocks, dozy young buggers and daft young prats!" I decided to trot along with him, unable to come up with a suitable reply and busting to laugh.

Diesel hardly seems to have made a mark, though it is vile enough when the tunnel has captured it on a still Saturday night, belching from two or three locos and several diggers. Personal damage is being done, and that feels to be the case, whereas steam engines smelt friendly, even if you didn't appreciate it at the time.

★

"By gum, but I wish I could be going under instead of you! It's a fantastic feeling!"

Jack Senior to me as we were running up to Standedge Tunnel End at Marsden, with Elliot, in the car.

"It's my wrists, you see, they just won't let me grasp owt like a bar, at the moment. It's only in winter, you understand, but t'job really wants doing now. I bet you wish that the gear they sent us was in your size, Elliot, don't you? I reckon you'd have been in there like a shot!"

It was the first I'd heard that Elliot and me were noticeably different in size and shape, but I let it pass. Elliot confirmed his deep regret, alongside Jack's.

"After the meeting I've had in Leeds this morning, it would have been just the ticket to liven me up, but Mike here's won the toss, fair and square."

I didn't remember the toss, let alone winning or losing it, but there was little point bringing the matter up for discussion, as I was perfectly aware that I'd been chosen for some special mission, and should feel honoured and excited at the prospect. Instinct told me that the prize was not one to cherish anything like as much as these two would have me believe. They were obviously wetting themselves waiting for me to ask what it was, and I wasn't going to give them that satisfaction. It was Bill, back in the office, that'd convinced me that I didn't want to know what I'd won without buying a ticket. He popped his head round my door, with: "You jammy bugger! How dust'a manage to wangle all t'best jobs?"

"I'm going to get mucky, aren't I, Bill?"

"So lucky, you wain't sleep toneet!"

"I said 'mucky', and you know it! You might as well tell me, then I'll know what to take."

"All tha'll need's thi wellies, and I'll guarantee no muck! Guides' honour!"

We pulled up in the canal workshop's yard, at the tunnel end. Jack and Elliot had their wellingtons too, so we were all square at the starting post. Jack lifted a large sack of something, and slung it easily over his shoulder, leaving me to carry a five-foot track sluing bar, while Elliot struggled along burdened down by a notebook and pencil. I hadn't worked it out, but the bar looked ominous.

As usual, we took the safest route in, using the old Down Fast single bore tunnel, by now dead. This end of the live double Slow Tunnel curved sharply, making the most dangerous bit of any tunnel – the mouth – that bit more so in this case. There was a train-operated gong at the beginning of the curve, but I'd looked it over once and decided it was about as reliable as a Durex on a hedgehog. After about a quarter of a mile, we crossed through into the live tunnel, by way of one of the frequent spacious cross-headings, with planks over the canal. I had suspicions about these, too, but they'd never given me cause. As they got me further from the car, the pair of them began to open up on how they were to make this a day to buy a diary for.

"We'd a look at this flooding around the Flint Shaft area last week, Mike. It looks like the drain through to the canal's badly

made up, and we need to make a temporary release for the water."
Elliot was telling me nothing I didn't already know.

"We've had this trouble before, and with a bit of luck you can just strike right and get shut of it in no time." Jack was telling me something I didn't know, without overreaching himself on the details. We trudged on, mainly in silence, concentrating on where we were putting our feet. Suddenly, the sound of rushing water was upon us, if a bit distant. This was the trick of sound from the shafts – you would hear them as if far off when only one hundred yards away. During that distance it would grow in an alarming crescendo, until you stepped into the area of a vast offshoot to the tunnel, twenty yards long, with, at the end, the incredible sight of the foot of Flint Shaft.

Built for and over the canal tunnel, the shaft has an enormous diameter of eighteen feet, and rises five hundred-odd feet to the Pennine moors above. Whatever the weather has been like for months before, a steady torrent of water pours down the shaft, bouncing off the walls as it falls, creating a circular waterfall. It literally comes down in rods, there being no factors to alter its course, with the water entering through fissures in the lined rock throughout the depth of the shaft. Watch any high waterfall with its pulsating patterns constantly repeating themselves like the monotonous "real flame" effects in rotating electric fires, and you have the same at the foot of a deep shaft. It is both breathtakingly magnificent and unstoppably terrifying in the darkness, as it is picked out by the torch beams. In that enclosed environment, such an opening and deluge appear immense. It has never lost its fascination for me, standing as you do just a couple of yards from this raging torrent.

Water was playing about six inches up our wellies, and not getting away as well as it should.

"Right, now what we want you to do, Mike, is to slip into this new wet-weather gear, and pop into t'shaft. Prod about a bit wi't'bar, and see if you can make some sort of opening into t'canal, like."

All they wanted me to do was climb into these untested waterproof trousers, steely stiff with newness, add a matching bright yellow overcoat, equally inflexible, so that just bringing my arms together proved a great effort, and top it off with a hat for all sizes, certainly several larger than me. An overall effect that could only be summed up as "Grampus on the port bow, Cap'n Ahab!" "Scott's Emulsion" was Jack's aside to Elliot, who now openly displayed an inane grin. I was expected to step through concealed rubble, into this storm from hell, onto the top of the canal tunnel roof. To protect bargees of old from the anticipated drips from the shaft, a single skin of stone arch had been stuck over the canal. Here I was expected to probe the foot or so of this arch that lay between me and the inaccessible canal, and try to break through the very spot on which I stood! So I did. Having come this far, there seemed no reason not to.

As I stood there, wet in the face, but fully protected elsewhere, I conjured up a comparison with those dire storms you see on TV dramas, where you can imagine powerful hoses pointed at the set and surrounding six feet or so. Outside this circle, you knew there were all the trappings of cameras, lights, best boys, gaffers and directors, following perfectly dry scripts and admiring their idea of a heavy shower. What later appears on the small screen is the most unlikely barrage of howling rain, suggesting imminent death by drowning. The bottom of Flint Shaft was the same, but real.

You get a lonely "What the hell" sort of feeling, deafened by the pounding of the stair-rods on your head and shoulders. Five-hundred-foot waterfalls hit your plastic coating with heavy slaps that echo around the confines of the shaft bottom. Your whole world is concentrated into an eighteen-foot circle. So there's nothing left to do but start picking away at the floor between your feet with the iron bar. This takes up a rhythm from the relentless beat of the waters, and the most extraordinary thing happens. You find yourself singing! And singing at the top of your voice. The beat inspires a march, whatever the proper rhythm might be, and it comes out as a shout, and it has to be "Singin' in the Rain" – you just can't help it.

Once before I'd found this same urge. Real rain, this time. Late December, the longest night of the year, and nearing the end of a nine-hour shift in a deep ditch, as the relentless rail-mounted trenching machine carved out an excavation for a new drain. Ordinary waterproofs that time, with a hundred secret places for water to creep in over the length of a night, and more modest rain than in the shaft, but just as wetting as the artificial stuff. Half past eight, and the first hints of reliable daylight, cold, sodden, hungry, tired, and to the regular grinding beat of the trencher bucket chain, there you have it. Full belt, yelling out words you didn't even know you knew, and a daft feeling of cheerfulness.

★

Bill and I were standing at the window, looking out onto the station at Huddersfield, watching and waiting. Yet another management trainee foetus was to be dumped on us that day, into our tender care, for instruction and experience over the next eight weeks. We always tried to catch an initial look at what was to fall from the Leeds train, in order to make a quick assessment of the challenge that lay before us. I don't know why I bothered, they all looked total doylums at a distance and got worse as they came nearer. Bill, on the other hand, looked deeper; had he got a gullible lump of naive putty coming or just a sullen sulker? Was the world presenting him with material for eight weeks of evil delight and torment, or just something that might have no potential for sport whatsoever? Officially, my objective was that of instilling a complete knowledge into a half-interested being, intent only on getting through his two years of training, before he really showed us what he was made of, as a manager. Practically the best I could hope for was that we had someone who could be taught how to make tea, and then go and sit in the corner and read up on coffee. At worst I'd land a questioning academic who imagined that a degree in civil engineering gave him even a foothold in railway work. (I used about 10% of mine, and for half of that the chainmen had a better way.) Oh, and at the very worst he'd be a train-spotter as well.

"You don't think that's it theer, dust'a?"

"Can't be, it looks totally gormless, and look at the length of it!"

"Well, it's comin' this way, wither tha likes it or not!"

"Oh God! Looks like you're right, Bill. Briefcase, first suit, shirt cuffs, bored look… and a ruddy brolly!"

"Bloody hell, Mike, tha's gotten thissen a reet dollop theer, by t'look on it. And tha was reet abaht t'length of it! He'll be well out-of-gauge for these doors, and ah'll bet thee he hasn't learnt duckin'. Right then, best o'luck!" By which I knew that Bill had resigned himself to two months of mischievous drought, and that I was well and truly lumbered.

Scott was six foot something, unstarched and fragile-looking, wire spectacled, and with a handshake akin to embracing four recently defrosted nondescript sausages and a pilchard. More worrying, he wore this dark blue duffle coat over his college interview suit, and – I froze – had a copy of *Trains Illustrated* stuck out of his pocket. This was the pits – a railway freak, a gricer, a nerd! Bill's summary, as I introduced them, was obviously on the same lines as mine, and his contribution of "'Ow do, lad?" before immediately returning to the morning's mail nailed his attitude for the duration.

To his credit, Scott didn't push his addiction to trains beyond limits, but his reactions to a lookout man's warning varied from an alert jumping aside, should the approaching train be belching out smoke and steam, to a grudging sidle off the track with a contemptuous sniff, and some remark about it "only being an 08 shunter", or "Oh my God! A flipping Type 40!" I tried to persuade him that if hit by either steam or diesel, he'd be hard put to distinguish between them, as would those shovelling up what was left of him afterwards, but he remained unimpressed.

It was a quiet first fortnight with Scott, with the only signs of life in my charge coming when he saw a "Black Five" or a "Gresley K4" puffing up the viaduct. (Don't bother writing to tell me that either or both of these never went through Huddersfield – I've made that bit up, besides which I couldn't care less!) This sighting by Scott would inspire a leap for the outside door, to get a better and closer look. It was a bit like a dog who sees another one across the road. They've no idea of perspective, haven't dogs; any other sort of whatever size is always smaller than they are when it's across the road, and they'll set off at speed, only to brake hard as the actual situation dawns on them. Scott was like that. He'd bounce out of the door, only to pull up at the first siding, the object of his desire still way out of reach. So it was of interest to me to see how he'd react to a night's track relaying in a tunnel, nose to piston, and encased in the fallout of three or four of these beasts.

Eddy Stapleton and I were to share the night in Beacon Hill Tunnel, which emerges from the said hillside at Halifax Station. This also happened to be the location of Scott's home shed, so Elliot decided that he who was supposedly thirsting for experience could accompany us in a strictly observational capacity for the night. (Young "managerniles" were expected to do this, on an expenses only basis – something Eddy and I could never come to terms with.) Once we'd propped Scott up against a wall and told him not to touch anything, we were theoretically free to dash up and down between the four diggers loading old ballast into three trains of wagons. This meant having four steam locos distributed up and down the tunnel, so one should get close to our spotter at some time during the night. Our side of the operation was to keep a check on the dig levels, making sure a cross-fall towards the central drain was produced. Scott's role was to stand back, experience and learn. This he managed for ten minutes, before wandering off, obviously bored with the fume-spewing diesel diggers. He'd turned up earlier in the evening, courtesy of a lift from Bill, wearing a second, older duffle coat and a black bobble hat, but still with the bloody briefcase.

Beacon Hill is a fairly friendly tunnel. Straight, eleven hundred yards long, with usually a slight draught taking steam away in those days of old. It was quite damp in places, by which I mean that if you were stood in the wrong place you got wet from the water dripping through the roof. It was a reasonably uneventful night, livened only by the derailment of three wagons, which we decided to try and get back on the track ourselves, rather than call out the breakdown. (So much paperwork and so many tiresome enquiries.) This was usually achieved by getting a loco attached close to the affected wagons and shouting a lot. It worked again here, though at the expense of an hour's work. Eddy and I were totally engrossed until the end of the shift, when we wandered out together into the welcome daylight of half past seven.

"Where's Scott?" said Eddy.

"What Scott? Oh, bugger, I'd forgotten about him."

"Wheer's thi mate?" said Bill as we reached him on the platform.

"Lost him!"

"Good, let's go. He'll be alreet. Probably a homing pillock anyway, and he's not far off his loft."

"We can't just leave him in there, can we, Mike?"

"Give him ten minutes; we told him what time Bill'd be here. Let's just go wash off a bit."

We returned to Bill on the station end a quarter of an hour and a mashing later, just as one of the muck trains was emerging from the tunnel. Leaning out of the loco cab was a duffle coat and black cap. It waved to us, climbed down and walked towards us.

"What's he walking backards for?" Bill asked. "Silly bugger'll tumble!"

As he got closer, what Bill had taken as the back of a black bobble hat turned out to be the front of a budding young manager.

Eddy and I had managed to get our hands and survey books a bit grimey as usual, needing only minor repairs. But here was Scott, a mere observer, who now seemed intent on taking the best part of the tunnel lining home with him as a souvenir. What we could see as being a mouth appeared stuck on in minstrel-style, while no expression at all could be gleaned from the area where his eyes must have been. There was no clue as to the end of his black cap and to where the rest of him began, and the only bit which seemed to be coming out in much the same condition as it went in were his boots, still cleanish from having plunged into every water-filled hollow in the tunnel.

"There's no way I'm tekkin' that back home in Elliot's car. What bloody state's it goin' to be in after ah've dumped that pit 'eap back on its doorstep. He can get a bloody taxi. Ah'm 'avin' nowt t'do wi' gettin' that back!"

"There's no taxi driver going to look at him twice, Bill!"

"Nowt t'do wi me. Ah'm noan havin' that in t'back, and that's that!"

"Two hours for cleaning the car out afterwards, Bill?"

"Three?"

"Right!"

"OK! Come on, Al Jolson, let's fin' some rags to put thee on – thee two wait here, ah'll be back in a couple of ticks. Bloody hell, lad! What's t'a bin doin'? Ah doan't knaw whether to put thi in a sack, or shuvel thi in t'boot!"

"That," I said to Eddy, as Bill took the sooty beanpole home, "should cure our enthusiast of the romance of steam, and if it doesn't, his mother soon will when she sees him! You know what that muck's like on a bath side."

"My dad actually once hosed me down in the garden before letting me into the house; and even then I'd to get undressed in the garage!"

"No! I bet steam trains have taken on a different light for our two-metre mate there!"

Nothing of the sort. Next morning, back in the office, could we stop him telling us about being allowed to stoke the boiler and blow the whistle, or relating the tender capacities, the steam psi, the wheel arrangements, what was in the fireman's sandwiches, who the driver fancied in the cup? Could we, hell!

Any fond feelings I might have had myself for these belching hulks of sweating steel, burnt out for good after walking through Bowling Tunnel, a mile or so outside Bradford. It is positioned at the peak of the steep climb out of the city, and in my day Low Moor engine sheds were at its farther end. If it wasn't straining locos gasping in after a one in fifty haul out of the station, along with banker engines, it was locos running fresh from shed and heavy on smoke to take up duties at the bottom of the hill. I first walked through with the Bradford PWay Supervisor, Dennis Durand, a gentle giant with a wealth of intelligent conversation. This was just as well since our one-mile walk through the tunnel took us four hours in all!

Most of the walk was spent standing in the wall refuges, waiting for a bit of clearer air. When anyone goes on about the old pea-soup fogs, and tells you that their hands could not be seen in front of their face – don't believe a word of it. I've been through such fogs, and I've also spent what seemed like half a lifetime in Bowling Tunnel, and there's no comparison. I tried it, in the tunnel; putting my hand about twelve inches from my nose, and it simply wasn't there. We'd Tilley lamps that day which caused us to be enclosed in a thick cocoon of light, but it was no more than a yard deep. If we strayed any further than that apart, we lost each other. Engines could be heard approaching, and could be sensed passing, but all that changed was that our pods of light got smaller. During the long periods of immobility, Dennis ranged over loads of topics linked to our situation – questions mixing an intelligent mind and sparse education, and aimed in a friendly way at the young hopeful out of university. It was another spell for me of admiration and respect for the desire for answers, but he fell far short of getting much out of me that day.

"Why is it that we haven't invented a spray to clear steam in tunnels, like they can cause clouds to make rain in tropical regions by sprinkling salt on them?

"What's the make-up of all these tiny crystals mixed in with the soot on the tunnel walls? How've they been formed?

"Why do sleepers decay in some tunnels and rails corrode in others? Why don't both go together? Why aren't the effects from being in a tunnel the same in all cases?

"Why can't an emergency lamp be developed worked by energy created through the movement of walking, like those wrist watches with no batteries or winding bits?

"How is it that I can grow concrete in here?"

This was a baffler! The central drain of U-shaped concrete units had lids that seemed to expand in the atmosphere peculiar to this tunnel. So much so that Dennis would take out the odd one when two were cocked up at 45°, and add it to the rest he'd saved. What I couldn't help wondering was what effect was this having on other things in the tunnel; me, for instance?

In those days, all the shorter tunnels had a small stockpile of stout twigs, like walking sticks, at the ends. I'd find these being used by a patrolman suddenly appearing in the middle of a tunnel without a lamp of his own. (It begged the question as to how much use was a patrolman in a tunnel without a lamp. About the same as a meter reader lacking the ability to see through a vacuum cleaner, a carrier bag full of more carrier bags, a set of bowls and a piece of something that once came off something and might yet come in useful for something.) The limited track examiner's stick would be running along the rail head to keep him from tripping over, though it was no help against the odd badly spaced sleeper. I tried it myself a couple of times, out of interest and youthful lunacy. I think it was in Hipperholme Tunnel (a quarter of a mile in length and dead straight) and Sowerby Bridge (a bit longer – and under a cemetery which gave it that little bit more piquancy). I managed to hit the frequency of sleepers at a regular spacing of twenty-four to the sixty-foot length of track, but you then needed to concentrate hard. Catch the rhythm and you were off with confidence, until the back lighting of the receding tunnel mouth faded sufficiently to induce doubt, loss of confidence and the inevitable stutter and stumble. Oddly, out in the open, you could walk continuously without glancing at your feet, but get in the dark and you were lost. From my experience of many miles of track walking, I can still measure out distances of a couple of hundred yards with a 1% accuracy, purely on the twenty-four to a length basis. Is this all I carry away with me from thirty-three years of railway experience? An ability to measure a field without a tape!

To get through these shorter tunnels, without a lamp, you would walk in steadily, picking up the spacing of the sleepers, at the same time running your stick along the rail head. A full confidence at one hundred yards would drop off rapidly beyond the hundred and fifty mark, to complete failure by two hundred, by which time the increasing glare from the other end would be hampering things further, until it too began to pick out sleepers. But all that was for straight tunnels.

I've said here that the three miles of Standedge, and some-where else, that the two of Morley were favourites of mine. Both dead straight but for the beginnings of curves at either end. Leaving aside the two plus miles of Bramhope Tunnel, a hateful hole, with its twists and turns and regular downpours, my two least favourites were a short popular suicide tunnel just beyond Halifax, and a real sod at Esholt, between Baildon and Guiseley. This last was little more than five hundred yards long, but in its heyday as a double liner, it was treacherous.

It lay under wooded ground and leaked like a sieve. Sleepers were slippery throughout, and the track gradient was steep. Worst of all, it lay on a sharp curve. Since today it's been singled, there's plenty of room to walk alongside the track, with only the minor disadvantage that you have no idea which direction any train might be coming from (on double tracks you always walk the line facing oncoming traffic). Before singling, should there be anything coming, the jointed tracks gave no warning, and sighting was limited to the last few yards. Warning horns of trains entering the tunnel were late for the walker, and meant a scramble over the greasy sleepers to very tight walls. There was rarely time to seek out a refuge, so an unceremonious crouch at the foot of the wall was called for. This leads me to the throwaway remark that the notice referring to not flushing toilets in stations should apply to tunnels as well. If you were unaware of the fact, then let's just say that it's only recently that a few trains have begun carrying their sewage with them. Remember the special duties man attending to the Royal Train overnighting in a siding? He with the supply of buckets and a very long pole and a fund of gags based around a royal flush? Well, stood or crouching alongside a line, along with wind, speed and bad luck could occasionally combine to douse you in a fine spray, while a train flashed past.

"Mmmm," said Danny Grant on one such occasion, lightly smacking his lips together at speed in the manner of the wine expert, "a lady!"

★

I hate getting dirty; tunnel-type dirty, that is. Probably the mixture of soot and diesel has produced the current superior quality of muck, but it's considerably stronger and better covering than soot by itself. It's water- and turps-resistant, and even survives attack from Swarfega. This is high-grade top-calibre muck, so strong that once you've decorated yourself in it, you have to grow out of it before it drops off. It is British muck – wear it with pride! As I say, I could well manage without it, but seemed destined to attempt tunnel jobs that led to a deep attachment to the stuff.

On a drizzly day which made the assured conditions of the tunnel more welcome, I set off from Diggle to walk through

Standedge on my own, dropped off by Bill with a cheerful, "See you week on Tuesday, then!" I had been assured by ancient diagrams that there were twenty-four or so possible access points into the canal, all of which we would need to use for a complete renewal of the track drains in the dead-level tunnel. Some were overgenerous in size, like the Niagara theme park of Flint Shaft, others were pleasant little slight-stoop adits between the tunnels, crossing the canal. Two were even small cabins, complete with fire ranges, coat pegs and kettles, set into the tunnel wall. They had short chimneys from the stoves, through the wall and into the tunnel. This seemed at odds with the absence of doors, allowing the same smoke, backed up by the passing trains, back in. But the rest of the canal accesses you could easily walk past and miss.

Small eighteen-inch openings at the foot of the wall needed flat wriggling to get through into the sizeable chambers beyond. Man-made pot holes I struggled into, on the dubious assumption that I'd be able to get out again, all with a fading enthusiasm as the day went on. Had these been real potholes I wouldn't have thought twice about going through. Once would have been more than enough to persuade me that there was no way I was going any further, even if accompanied by experts and with a cave rescue service back-up. So why, on my own, was I prepared to crawl into these minute black holes? Goodness knows, though I have to admit that the gaps were bigger coming out than going in, by virtue of the layers of soot I'd disturbed.

That walk took three and a half hours; four to reach Marsden Station, where a mirror in the PWay cabin prompted the decision that I could not possibly transport the soot-caked figure reflected back at me on a public train to Huddersfield. Hence a rescue call to Bill, who, on arrival, expressed a preference to me travelling back on the roof rack, or even better, running on behind. His reluctance to know me evaporated once he got me back to the office, where he nearly crippled himself rushing in to get Jack to come out and see "this stick of Spanish what I've found!"

Another way I discovered for getting myself disgracefully filthy was really down to Elliot initially, though it was my brilliance in design work and complete lack of forethought which nailed it. He wanted to get more out of the tunnel examinations we went on together, and it was for me to work out how to do it.

Tunnel inspections were carried out using a sparingly converted cattle truck. As a support vehicle at the sharp end of modern technology, it would have needed considerable expense to bring it up to the standard of laughable. In appearance it was a large crate on and in which men stood with iron-tipped lances tapping the tunnel roof and walls to locate any hollow-sounding patches. It was pushed steadily along through the tunnel, normally done manually, as was the braking, but occasionally a small loco was attached, which contributed to the overall purpose of getting me as grimy as possible. The jousters were placed four atop the crate, covering the arch of the tunnel roof, with two more inside jabbing at the walls. Up to Elliot going on the management course "Sadism and Your Junior Staff", my job was merely to take notes. Inspired by the week's instruction, Elliot came up with the idea of adapting the wagon so that I could take readings of the haunch clearances, these being around the area where the edges of coaches come closest to the tunnel walls. Strangely, through transmitted enthusiasm and a total absence of thought about personal consequences, I was quite excited by the prospect, and both designed the equipment and supervised its knocking together.

The wagon (or Inspection Unit, as it was euphemistically called – having all the design ingenuity of a simplified plank) had two sets of steps to take you up onto its roof via manholes in the upper platform, at diagonally opposite corners. As it was pushed along in the direction of traffic, the opening was always at the trailing end, close to the tunnel wall, so it was there that I had a mounting made for each end of the crate. On it I could extend calibrated rods horizontally at roof level, vertically up the wagon side, and at 45° between these two. My rods were in beechwood, sliding through brackets, with twelve inches of flat brass at the ends, pivoted on thumb screws, so that a sudden change in the wall's shape would just knock them aside, without smashing the wood. I surveyed the minimum dimensions on all three rods through each fifty feet between tablet numbers on the wall, which even at walking pace, proved a job and a half. My position was about as dignified as a haemorrhoidal judge. I was standing

Wilf Warburton – one of the indispensable chainmen.

Don Newell, on the left, the basis for 'Elliot Milner'. On the far right is Works Supervisor, Albert Hughes, with Jack Senior at his side.

Dave Thornton, the basis for 'Eddy Stapleton', ten years after his period at Huddersfield. Here as site manager in Woolley Tunnel.

The Huddersfield Office under the water tank. Doors left to right; Drawing Office, Elliot's Office, P. Way Supervisor's Office.

The Office from the road, showing the area affected by the 'cleared drain.'

Huddersfield Office roof, and sunbathing boards.

Dinner hour for Bill Boyes and Jack Senior.

The front face of No. 23 Wellington Street, after refurbishment, but still unoccupied after thirty years.

The former drawing office on the fifth (top) floor of No. 23. Taken just prior to moving out, with the table tennis board in place.

The central shaft of the square doughnut that was No. 23. Notice the curtains on the fourth – the fashion house.

Photo: Kenneth Field. Batley end of Morley Tunnel, with Ibbotson Rose's sexual observation banking on the right.

Homemade dominoes with slight imperfections.

Harry Hanson, philosopher and gardener.

Photo: British Rail. 'The romance of steam'. Enthusiasts getting a dubious view of the countryside travelling behind a steam loco.

Photo: Alan Blower. Diggle end of Standedge Tunnel. The flash floods emanate from the small underbridge at the tunnel mouth.

Photo: British Rail. Standing in front of the 500-feet deep Redbrook shaft in Standedge Tunnel. The central figure is John Midgley, who, coming from York Area, had never experienced a tunnel before.

Photo: British Railways. Tunnel Inspection Wagon at the Marsden end of Standedge Tunnel. Probing rods operated from the roof, the body and by men walking alongside.

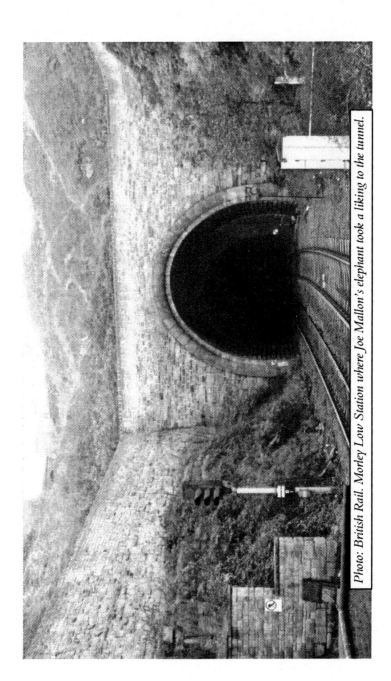

Photo: British Rail. Morley Low Station where Joe Mallon's elephant took a liking to the tunnel.

Huddersfield Slow Tunnel after singling the tracks, showing the effectiveness of lighting the site. A lining machine is in use.

Photo: British Rail. Result of setting out new alignment with a teapot full of paint.

Denise Collins (no known relation!) on whom 'Elaine Barnes', the culinary saviour of the inspection saloon, is based.

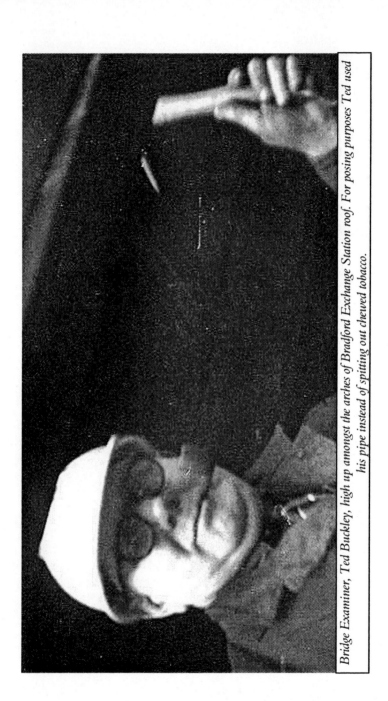

Bridge Examiner, Ted Buckley, high up amongst the arches of Bradford Exchange Station roof. For posing purposes Ted used his pipe instead of spitting out chewed tobacco.

Bradford Exchange roof examination. The lift is 'stabilised' by the platform on the right and a rail wagon on the left.

Stanningley Stores Keeper Johnny Bass.

Tapping a Thermit Rail Weld – the highlight and climax of a rail stressing job.

Re-opening of Slaithwaite Station, with synchronised dancers about to wreak havoc on the slender platform supports.

halfway up the ladder, with head and shoulders poking through the manhole, adjusting and reading off the rods as we went.

Now I did point out that these ladders were at the trailing corners of the wagon nearest the wall. So I trust the imagination can take aboard four men, standing on top of the truck, hammering poles into the soot-caked tunnel roof, knowing that they were being pushed clear of any falling material, all of which landed towards the rear end of the wagon roof, mostly close to the tunnel wall. I was at the rear end of the wagon roof, close to the tunnel wall.

This method of getting clarted up was more spectacular in that my lower half was always within the protection of the truck. I can still recall Elliot's uncontrolled laughter the first time I emerged at the end of a run with an inverted tidemark.

Whereas Elliot had to be taught how to get me filthy, a final method involved Wilf and Percy, the chainmen, and it came as second nature to them, and an objective of this particular job – tunnel profiling.

To get a picture of the rough shape of a whole tunnel profile, a series of measurements to two fixed reference points were taken, from various points round the arch of the lining. These ranged from the base of one wall, right up the side, over the top and down to the bottom of the other. We did this using three or four drain rods fastened together, with the dumb (zero) ends of two tapes fastened to the tip that one of the chainmen would poke up to the tunnel. Measurements were taken all round from both tapes to two of the four rails. By surveying along the tracks and across at each measuring point I could then draw out the profiles by compass, back in the comfort of the office. (I've just read that through and can hardly understand it myself. Just trust me – this way I got a true picture of the shape of the tunnel at regular intervals.)

This system made the gap between me and my shirt a target for collecting large lumps of tunnel grime, and for my survey book to become what Percy would refer to as a "mucky book". Taking off my shirt at night was impressive, as was the bedroom floor. If I remembered in time I'd undress in the bath; either way there'd be domestic trouble.

Wilf (or Percy) would swing the pole round to the various points, Percy (or Wilf) would read off the measurement to one rail, and I would do the other. In between, I would record both sets of data, while Wilf (or Percy) would watch out for what Percy (or Wilf) was doing with the pole as it was swung to the next point. They could see danger coming, and avoid it. I couldn't. They stayed untainted, I didn't. These were days long before the hard hat came about.

"Oops, has tha copped for it again, Mike? Sorry, lad!"

"Y'know, Wilf, we should have summat to shout out, like, when we've knocked a lump've muck off t'roof, so as Mike, here, has time to get outta t'road, like! It really upsets me when ah land him one, tha knaws!"

"Such as?"

"Well, ah'm thinkin' on t'lines of like 'Timber!' or 'Fore!', but not them."

"'Look aht', wain't do, 'cos he'll just think it's a train comin', tha needs summat distinct."

"Soot?"

"Nah, theer's no ring abaht 'Soot!'"

"How's abaht 'Below!', then?"

"Definitely not! That'd scare t'pants off 'im. He'd think a brick's come loose, or summat."

"'Lump of muck comin'!'?"

"It'd've landed afore tha'd finished!"

"'Old on a sec, while I shift up a bit. Shit!" Percy stumbled over a large piece of ballast, and released a small cloud of strategic soot.

"That'd do nicely!" said Wilf.

(Profiling in latter years has been done photographically, which is worrying, like adopting electric lighting. When we lit up tunnel work using only hand-lamps and flares, and did profiles using two tapes and a pole, they remained very safe places to be in. As soon as continuous electric lighting and generators made an appearance, illuminating the tunnels with startling brilliance, frightening bulges appeared in the walls, as I've mentioned elsewhere. On the basis that they were very rarely seen before, the only logical conclusion has to be that electric lighting causes tunnel walls to bulge.)

★

I've checked through this, and detect a suggestion of crudity in the method of tunnel inspection using the crate on rails. Just stand back from it a moment and watch two or three blokes shoving this truck uphill, while their mates knock seven bells out of the roof with poles, with an enthusiasm inversely proportional to the length of the tunnel. Then again watch the lad on the long brake lever as they work downhill. His expression changes from a doddle grin for the steady stroll, shifting a look of apprehension as he finds himself pacing out a bit while leaning hard on the brake. This turns to shear panic as he has to swing his whole body on the lever in an attempt to regain control – you've got to see it as dodgy, at best. Yet, this is all pretty sophisticated compared to some shaft inspections I've been on. To climb to the brow of a windswept hill, take a ladder onto the top of a stumpy circular stone tower, and then to climb into a bucket with two other idiots, takes the biscuit. This is rounded off by the bucket being winched down the inside of the shaft, giving the impression of tunnel crocodile fishing.

Shafts come in a variety of sizes; some are large, wider than the tunnel below, whereas others appear in the tunnel roof as a five-foot circular hole. My first go at communal abseiling was in one of these smaller ones, a two-hundred-foot shaft down into Thurstonland Tunnel up in the Pennines. Despite plenty of tunnel experience, I found the sensation of being lowered down into one in a tub unnerving compared to just walking in from the end. It was like being in a Ding Dong Bell rescue team, bumping from one brick face to another, trying desperately to keep some sort of balance by sticking to your own third of the space available. Any invitation to "Ay up, look at this!" produced a lurch and an unsettling tip of the bucket. That trip leaves little memory in me of the shaft condition, but plenty as to my dedication towards self-preservation. I'd usually felt a sense of security in tunnel work, and this was underlined by the few hairy experiences we had.

Such as, for instance, the Channel Tunnel tests in Standedge.

This might come as a bit of a shock to many of those who've

shared my most recent years on the railway, but this dull unimaginative writer was involved in preliminary design and feasibility investigations for the Channel Tunnel, no less, and was also injured in the course of the field tests. I should leave it at that, since the kudos tends to fade away as explanatory padding is added. But here goes regardless.

Back in 1968, Farnborough Research was looking for a ready-made test bed for the current vision of what the tunnel under the English Channel was to look like. They were involved from the wind tunnel aspect of the project, before there are any cracks about very low flying. In those days, the proposals looked much like any old tunnel, that is, not much bigger than the train. At this same time, one Dr Beeching was toward the end of putting the railway system back on its feet, by turning most of it into footpaths. These two events had come together when Elliot and I took a couple of government research stereotypes, most probably Fortescue and Carruthers – I can't remember, if not, then they should have been – up to Marsden to have a look at Standedge's two recently closed single line tunnels. Only the fact that they couldn't run a test train in, through and out at something like 100 mph, due to the approach curves, disappointed the scientists, but otherwise it was "just the jolly old ticket".

They were after sending a typical train through at full belt to see how the forward pressure waves compared with calculations. We could tell them a thing or two about these pressures, especially in Standedge. If you were standing in a cross-heading while a train walloped through at around sixty-five, you'd find yourself leaning against a gale. But Fortescue and his pal wanted a tight lining to the tunnel with no major escape routes for the air. They selected the single line furthest from the live tunnel, as this just had regular man-size adits through to its mate next door. What they wanted from us was to block up all cross-headings into this adjacent hole. One clown even suggested that we brick them up, but it was agreed that we only needed timber framework and canvas screen coverings. Albert Hughes, the Works Supervisor, organised it, and we immediately began to have cold feet by the look of the first. It flapped about a bit so Albert boosted it with layers of strong roofing felt. "Try that for size!" said Albert – so I did, and hence the injury in the cause of research. The "Cathedral" was fitted with an enormous screen on four by fours with raking timbers backing it up.

We were given a couple of weeks to put all this stuff up, after they'd done a few dummy runs with a loco and coaches. On the day set for the serious tests, we weren't going to be left out, so we set ourselves up in the next tunnel, on the Whickham. This is a small powered trolley capable of carrying eight men and a driver comfortably, or any number you wanted if it was going out at the end of a shift. (I said "comfortably" there – it should be "adequately" as comfort was totally alien to the Whickham trolley.) Given the nod, we set off parallel to the test train, and about five minutes ahead of it, so that we could be at one of the more central cross-headings to get an idea of the effectiveness of our handiwork.

Although small, you could hear the engine on the Whickham coming a mile away. Sat on it you couldn't hear anything but, and it was that old tunnel sensation of a slight puff of draught which puzzled me enough to suggest pulling up. We did this in time to feel another, stronger gust of wind, and I don't suppose any of us were genuinely surprised when the explosion came about twenty yards in front of us. We shot down to the heading to find very little resembling a felt-covered screen, just a kit for one. Canvas strips were more or less in one piece, but the rest looked like Armageddon at Swan Vestas. To some extent we were trapped, and had to heave the mess aside before we could pass. Our journey out was a series of stops to clear our way, since every screen except the one nearest the end had blown up, with varying degrees of devastating distribution.

We found the test train pulled up about a mile outside the tunnel, along with a most unchuffed gang of Fortescues, brassed off because they'd failed to get the results they'd wanted. The loco had failed them by only managing to get up to 55 mph at full thrust, due to the air pressure in front of it. When we told them that our efforts hadn't been a complete success and that one or two leaks might have occurred, they took it really badly, things being worse than they'd thought. Carruthers, who appeared to be the complete optimist, decided to have a re-analysis in The

Station pub to see if the results looked better the right side of a couple of pints, but they didn't.

All was not lost, though, according to later correspondence. From what they'd managed to rescue out of the readings, Farnborough worked out that it would take up to fifteen Deltic locos to push a train through a tunnel as long as the one needed under the Channel. (I'm not sure what that means in power terms, but it sounds a lot.) So our time wasn't wasted after all as it did prove conclusively that it will be forever impossible to build a railway tunnel under the English Channel, so don't believe the rumours you might have heard!

★

Morley Tunnel again, my No. 2 hole, just to record for posterity one of the many feats of Joe Mallon, at one time the PWay Supervisor covering the tunnel. Joe had many claims to fame, including sparring with the great Joe Louis, so he hardly needed to look for further distinction by betting that he could ride his bike through the near two miles of Morley. It was a Sunday morning at the end of a shift. Joe loaded his bike into a wagon, sat on it, and got a lift through to Dewsbury. There was a Steward's Enquiry as to whether this was a valid riding record, and I don't believe any bets were honoured. But I could never understand his determination to defend this achievement, since it paled into insignificance compared to his most prestigious act.

If I were to be asked for a list of things I would most not like to come across in a tunnel, it might on first thoughts run thus:

1. A dead body. This has too often been a discovery by patrolmen (with lamps).
2. A train on the wrong line. Hardly likely, but it would certainly be a nasty surprise.
3. A roof collapse, even a slight one.
4. An elephant. And if I did, then it would immediately hit the No. 1 spot.

This last item would never have occurred to me were it not for Joe's experience. First, the general picture. Morley Station is about a mile from the town centre. The old question of why it wasn't built nearer the town is not simply answered by the preference to build it somewhere near the railway, as Morley Town Hall stands about sixty feet above the railway, almost slap bang over the middle of the tunnel. The platform ends run from the mouth to an area which used to house a large loading dock for animals. In the heyday of the Bertram Mills's travelling circus, much of the stock went by train and transferred to road at Morley for shows in the Leeds/Bradford locality. It was a quiet location, and very little interest would be created locally.

Like all PWay Supervisors, Joe Mallon was used to calls about animals on the track, usually horses or cattle – both of which can derail a train at speed, without doing themselves any favours. But even the unflappable Joe was a shade out of his depth when he got the message that there was an elephant on the line. Circus staff thought they had it cornered at the mouth of the tunnel, but had reckoned without the animal's apparent acceptance that it had just suddenly got dark, and that the darkness seemed to be an escape route. It might not have been scared of tunnels, but all of B Mills's staff were, especially tunnels full of elephant. So Joe arrived on the scene to find the animal several hundred yards inside his tunnel and increasing.

Studied reflection might have suggested going round to the other end, and shooing the elephant back out to Morley, assuming that you can shoo an elephant, but everyone was jumping around wanting immediate action, so Joe lit his lamp and, with two involuntary volunteers, went in after it. He sensed both relief and disappointment in that it didn't seem attracted to their lights, but he admitted later that this hardly helped formulate any plan of action. In fact no grand plan occurred to him at all, he just had an instinct that he needed to get round the back of the thing.

Always a thinker, Joe was struck by a philosophical thought as he got near enough to the elephant to sum up the situation. It was that bit in the Bible about a camel and the eye of a needle. From site tests, Joe realised the truth behind the story, in that the nearer the camel got to the needle, the bigger it grew, as the eye shrank. Having an elephant in a tunnel, it was perfectly clear that the animal had doubled in size, whilst the tunnel had shrunk to half what it used to be. There didn't seem to be much room left between the sides of this small hole, and what had now turned into a mammoth.

It was at the first airshaft, half a mile in, where Joe made his move, one of such military precision that it would have delighted Wellington. Whilst his two comrades disguised themselves as bits of a tunnel, he slipped past the elephant in the momentary gloom just before the daylight of the shaft. His two helpers, now emboldened by Joe's example, and suddenly dubious about being in front of an approaching elephant rather than behind it, followed his example, so that all three were in a position to persuade the animal towards the distant daylight. All went well from there on, except for the delicacy required following any elephant of regular bodily functions in a dark tunnel, let alone one that's a shade nervous. Patience, time, carefully placed feet all contrived to persuade the animal that the light at the end of the tunnel was attractive, along with the large bundles of vegetation placed at the mouth, and after an hour the elephant ambled out, followed by three railwaymen with a combined weight several stone less than when they went in.

I've never had an experience as unnerving as Joe's, but there are less hazardous tricks that tunnels can play. Take Elland Tunnel, for example, for me a wormhole in space. It's only five hundred yards long, between the old stations of Elland and Greetland, yet it shot me through the universe in minutes.

Whenever we had a job at or near Elland, the chainmen and I would travel from Leeds to Huddersfield, and take a bus or car out to site. If we were working around Greetland, on the other hand, it involved taking a train from Leeds in a completely different direction through Bradford to Halifax, with a lift on from there. These were two different worlds to me, with no conscious connection, until one day I actually walked through the tunnel. Coming out at Greetland after only ten minutes' walking from Elland gave me the strangest of feelings, like having travelled in time. For if I ever returned to Huddersfield from Greetland, it would be by way of Bradford and Leeds, a total journey of an hour and a half, whereas I'd just made the connection between these two worlds in a ten-minute stroll. It was like a time-warp tunnel. A shock akin to finding Glasgow on the outskirts of Exeter.

But I had a much more severe mind shock at Thackley Tunnel near Shipley. I was working in there one Saturday night with Kev Smith, out of the Leeds Drawing Office, on a track renewal through the length of the tunnel. It was a hectic night, trying to keep tabs on the two most animated of contract digger drivers, a team called Zen and Leatherbarrow. These two were always asked for by name as they had tunnel excavation work off to a T. After digging themselves in at either end of the train of empty wagons, slightly deeper towards the drains, they set off with their machines tilted, so producing an automatic cross-fall. Kev and I were there to monitor the depth of dig to the designed final track levels. With these two operators, along with another two almost as good, this meant being on the move all night. Around five in the morning, the dig was almost done, so Kev sent me out for a quick break, with him following twenty minutes later.

Midsummer morning daylight met me at the tunnel mouth, and immediately the exhaustion of the night's work lifted. The constant roar of the diggers, dulled by the steam-filled tunnel, still throbbed in my ears, but gradually it disappeared along with the hot tea in the scalding tin mug. Well set up again, I plunged back into the tunnel to relieve Kev, passing him as he made his way out.

Back in the tunnel, walking on the churned-up bed of ballast, I stumbled on towards the trains in an enclosed halo of thick smoke and steam. The only light came from my hand-lamp which barely illuminated the ground at my feet, let alone the surroundings. Everything had closed down, and there was an uncanny silence, while the two locos continued to steam away in the distance. I stopped regularly to look at the bed we'd produced; ash or stone, wet or dry. As I walked on, I realised that I'd underestimated the amount we'd done, at the same time trying to work out exactly how far into the tunnel I was. Suddenly, I was faced with the faint outline of the tunnel mouth and realised that I'd managed to walk right through, passing both trains without even seeing them.

"Forgotten something?" said Kev, as he passed me, walking back into the tunnel. This was a mind-boggling shock for me, since I'd not long since left him at the other end.

I looked around. I was back where I'd started. Somehow I'd managed to get so disorientated by the thick fog in the tunnel that I'd turned completely round at some point and walked back out the same way I'd come in! Such things momentarily blow the mind.

★

"Now thee just stand here, Mike, lad! Ah'm bahn off in a shade further. What ah want thi t'do is watch them three sleepers where ah've shoved them bunce scales under. See they're not shekken out!"

Harry Hanson, on the occasion of my first trip into Standedge. Why the locals had to have their own names for things, when the company provided perfectly adequate ones, beat me. These "bunce scales" were void meters that he'd fitted under the rail at a sleeper. They had a lever set against a scale, registering the movement of the rail downwards as a train passed over, a movement that suggested a void between the sleeper bottom and the ballast. In a short time I'd learnt "tun dish" for oil can, and very reasonably "leckin (leaking) can" for watering can, along with "low ties" for shoes.

The spot Harry had chosen for me was alongside one of the long water troughs placed in the middle of the tracks in all three tunnels, near the Diggle end. This was the only level piece of railway between Manchester and Leeds, hence the unique situation of troughs in a tunnel.

"Just keep thissen squat in t'manoil, and keep thi eye on them theer four sleepers. See if t'rail's jumping abaht in t'chair at all. Ah'm off inter twenty-three tablet to see t'same thing theer."

Anyone unfamiliar with water troughs should know that they were about nine inches deep, six of which were filled with water, with long run ins and outs at either end. Travelling at full speed, the fireman would lower a chute from the tender at a marked point, take up water, and lift the chute out before the trough end.

Harry had acted like a kindly father figure up till then. He'd taken me for my first sight of the canal tunnel, with its inspection boat tied up, about a quarter of a mile in. He'd shown me the foundation stone of the new tunnel, where rumour had it that a gold sovereign had been placed. (I could have found this stone for myself. All the mortar had been gouged out round it to penknife blade depth.) Finally, he was allowing me to assist in his observation work.

Waiting for the approaching train to thunder past, I examined my immediate surroundings, and was interested to see that this bit of tunnel wall was amazingly clean and clear of soot. The seventy-year-old brickwork looked as fresh as the day it had been put in. This was hardly surprising, as it turned out, since when the train did eventually come belting through, picking up water as it passed, it seemed as if a good half of it was thrown out to the sides, and well up the tunnel walls. I can vouch for it drenching everything from rail level up to five feet ten and a half inches.

"We allus do that to young 'uns, comin' in t'oil for t'fust time, like. It's a sort of whadyercallit, intimidation ceremony. Has t'a got very wet?"

Some Exotic Surveys

"Well, I think it's bloody undignified, we'll be a flamin' laughing stock, ah tell thee!"

"There's no other way I can see to do it, Bill," I said. "I've tried everything else. Besides, I thought this might be right up your street."

"Mebee it is of a Sunday morning wi't'grandkids round t'park pool, but not at the end of a station platform wi' aif on Huddersfield watchin' includin' them theer dopey buggers. They'd wet their friggin' sens, that lot." This was the local station gang, noted for their intolerance of individual eccentricities, particularly amongst technical staff and associates.

"OK! There's no need for you to bother, Bill, if you don't want to. I'll have Wilf and Percy along to lend a hand, and I'll be using lookouts from the gang, so they'll be involved too. Don't really need you at all, in fact. You can stay well out of it."

"D'yer imagine that if tha's holdin' a ferret regatta at t'tunnel end, wi' Wilfred and Percival skippin' all ovver, chasin' 'em, and fishin' 'em out at t'end, with Hubert's lads theer tryin' to look as if it's nowt t'do wi' them; d'yer think fer a minnit that ah'm bahn to sit in here and miss it all? No way med, Mike – if tha's determined to stand theer at the bloody hub of Huddersfield lookin' a reet dollop, ah'm havin' a seat in t'stalls!"

All I was trying to do was to trace the routes of various track drains coming out of the two tunnels at Huddersfield Station. Complications were added as tributaries from the old goods yard and overflows from the steam loco water columns joined the delta of drainage, still leaving at least half a dozen freely flowing nomadic drains of uncertain parentage. This sort of problem was just the thing for me. Everything seemed to combine here, the drains merging with station roof gutters, safety escape systems from the nearby warehouse hydraulic wagon lift, plus two which so far as I could make out were running uphill. Amongst them all was a continuous cast-iron pipe that had travelled eight or nine miles from reservoirs up in the Pennines above Standedge Tunnel. Not wanting to miss out on the fun, the Marsden Main, as it was called, decided to shed a percentage of its load as it passed through on its way down to the loco sheds at Hillhouse, a mile further on.

I'd mapped out the visible drainage catch-pits, along with all the pipes running in and out of them, and had tried to discover where each one came from or went to. (A catch-pit is a hollow pit between pipes where any solid material might gather, rather than clog the pipes.) For this I'd studied the local land survey plans, and looked up any old drainage surveys from the past, while trying to put together a comprehensive plan of the overall tunnel-end system. This was supposed to lead me towards drawing up a new all-embracing scheme prior to Elliot Milner submitting a drainage proposal for the next Engineer's Inspection. If I was going to rip up all the existing drains, then it was essential that I didn't leave any of those joining the party high and not so dry when any new layout was completed. When laying a new drainage system, it's best not to come across surprises on the day. Marsden Station comes to mind, but that's another day, another page.

It is inevitable, at this point in the tale, that I refer to my university education and degree in civil engineering, for it is such a qualification that put me so far ahead of the lads on the ground when it came to tracing the paths of the various drains. By virtue of my record I was entrusted with far more-advanced equipment than that at the disposal of the lengthmen. These homespun individuals had to rely on spitting down a drain, and watching the various possible outlets to see where it emerged. I had powers four times as great, five, if you counted the spitting method as one. I had the scientific resources of coloured dyes – four, in fact, and all nicked from the office in Leeds. Such is the power of learning! These were a none too brilliant yellow, a deep carmine red and a violent violet, together with the persistent and fantastic fluorescent green. While the first three would be clear of a system within hours, this mighty green would leave traces that could be detected days later. Thus, in a complex system like the one at the end of Huddersfield Station, once you had made four guesses, using all four dyes, and then tried spitting if nobody was watching, there was nothing for it but to wait a day or two for them to dissipate. Aside from all this, the three weaker colours were relatively hard to detect in the depths of a deep, dark catch-pit anyway, and the red and violet could almost be indistinguishable. A further clue could be available if the surveyor was cursed with a strong sense of smell, which was so in my case. Apart from the obvious, odours of oil leakage or soap could help in the routing, though it was never overwise to follow some smells too far back up the system.

Not far enough away, five-sixths of the station gang had stood watching my artistic efforts with interest. Interviewing them and their ganger, Hubert Rhodes, merely added to the confusion, as it became obvious that they hadn't a clue where any of the waters came from or went to, or cared much, despite a railway lifetime tending to the cleaning and general maintenance of these drains. They felt that they had been more than cooperative. Mr Rhodes himself even momentarily left the sanctuary of their cabin, which was a most unusual event. Hubert's non-involvement with any actual work had long been an accepted principle, that is until Elliot came on the scene as the bright young local Engineer. In this role he had waited for the retirement of the old PWay Supervisor, Dai Reece, who fully supported the ganger's actions (or inactions). Indeed, Mr Reece followed the man's example on many weekend shifts, running jobs from the warmth and comfort of the local gang cabin. There was no resentment from the gang regarding Hubert's non-participation in the workload, simply because he was a wizard at filling in the daily timesheets, and more than made up for the lack of one man by his manipulation of the bonus system.

"That bloke's a genius!" Harry Sykes, the sub-ganger, had once said to me. "He's worth far more to us sat in theer wi' his pencil and the Bonus Book, than ivver he would be aht 'ere. He can show that us five can earn far more bonus for all six on us, than t'next gang along can workin' at full strength. Nay, lad, we leave well alone, an' tha should tell yon Mr Milner that he'll 'ave us ter answer to if he meks Hubert come out an' shovel along of us. He's hexecuteive is Hubert!"

Elliot did eventually get the ganger to step outside now and again, when Jack Senior arrived as the new supervisor. This soon backfired as Hubert took sick leave, readily endorsed by the family doctor, a man who was never left short by virtue of some of his patient's many sidelines in small farming. Meanwhile, the gang continued to prosper, as the daily sheets were ferried up to the Rhodes cottage at Marsden for filling in, even managing to squeeze out some form of bonus for himself, off sick. As to Jack's predecessor, Mr Reece (which is how he was universally known – except by Elliot, who was allowed to address him as Dai), this gentleman's idea of an honest shift supervising a double maintenance gang every second Sunday in Standedge Tunnel was unique. It would start on the Friday with a train ride.

Mr Reece would take an express up to Staleybridge, travelling through the tunnel at speed. He would stand for the four or five minutes it took to complete the three miles of the tunnel next to an open window. There he would reckon to listen for sounds made by the train running over sleepers with voids beneath them, a kind of hollow roar echoing from the tunnel walls. In the pitch dark he would note down where he estimated these faults were and this would form the basis for his Sunday programme of work. All that was sensibly required of him on the day was to take possession of the line and instruct the ganger as to which sections he thought might need repairs. The lads were then sent into the tunnel, while he would spend the rest of the day in the blazing warmth of the extensive tunnel-end cabin complex. This approach to supervision was very much along the lines of the Huddersfield ganger, and a mutual respect existed between the two men for their common approach to responsibility. After all, two Engineers back from Elliot, and it was accepted that the incumbent might spend the occasional afternoon having a meeting over eighteen holes and a chaser, which rather formulated managerial guidelines through the ranks.

I'm a scientist at heart, with a conviction that every problem has a solution, and that every solution is capable of throwing up several more problems. When I was being pestered to submit papers to the Institution of Civil Engineers (ICE), in order to attain full membership, I used this as being part of my philosophy. Our Chief Civil Engineer at the time turned his nose up at it, saying that such thinking was all right for a Women's Institute (WI) talk, but was no line to take with the august body of examiners at the ICE. Thinking this over, I decided that the WI would do for me, and evermore dismissed attempts to shake me into doing what I ought – writing insincere bollocks to please a bunch of dull old farts. So in pursuing my beliefs about problems, I became known as a bit of an innovator, a constructive dreamer, and follower of lateral thought – or as Bill put it more than once "a bit of a barmy bugger at times". This was why his comments about what others might think, at Huddersfield Tunnel end, left me cold.

Yet what Bill might baulk at being seen doing in public didn't affect his willingness to drop helpful suggestions as to what I might be seen doing. So we'd exhausted the coloured dyes, the spit, and Bill's contribution of tipping the entire contents of the hole-punching machine into one of the drains (this was when Bill made the discovery that, in the main, confetti sank rather than floated). I also found him happy to watch me trying some of his other ideas, such as emptying the liquor from a jar of pickled onions into one pit, and seeing where the smell came out; he even helped when dignity allowed, by hitting pipe ends with a hammer, for me to dash about trying to locate a responsive outlet. All this did was to make sure his punched paper holes stayed sunk by covering them in bits of broken pipe end. On the other hand he decided to keep his distance while Percy, Wilf and I tried calling down the pipes to each other.

Bill was never too sure in himself as to whether any suggestion he came up with was a wind-up on his part, or actually something of use. Obviously his intention was to get me going, but he was always afraid that he could possibly be proving helpful. One such occasion was him turning up one Monday morning with a bucketful of tadpoles.

"Ah thought as 'ow tha could mebee colour 'em up somehow, with paint or summat. Then tha could dump 'em in one catch-pit, and see weer they come out, like!"

At which his head would drop to one side, with his eyes twinkling over a mock-serious mouth, half-wondering whether he might have come up with something useful. I told him he hadn't, and went on to elaborate on the sort of brain necessary to keep giving birth to the sort of ideas he was forever dropping in, while he tried desperately to look hurt, this with a face that was gagging to grin. Nevertheless he had provided the germ of an idea, which we were now discussing. (This was where we came in – with me enthusiastic and Bill fearing for his local reputation and dignity.)

Toy boats was what I'd come up with. Here was proof, if ever I'd needed it, that three years of intensive study, including fluid dynamics and structural design, resulting in a two-one B.Tech. in Civil Engineering was not time wasted. It wasn't long before Bill became a willing bonsai shipbuilder, and was helping test out matchbox trays, carved bits of sleepers and slices of a balsa model aeroplane kit. They were fitted out with matchstick masts and an array of individually decorated sails. Bill was now full of it, up to but not beyond the point of putting it all into effect. He could see no personal gain in terms of respect hanging down drain catch-pits launching little boats under the gaze of the five cynical tunnel-end men and a selection of the population of Huddersfield.

I was personally geed up by a "they laughed at Newton" attitude, Bill going along with this as far as they might be referring to Bobby Newton, star of *Workers' Playtime*, but not when I went on to explain that I was talking about some bloke who made up rules about not falling off the world and ripe apples not dropping upwards.

"If you're goin' to carry on wi' that as an argument, I'll go bring in Harry Hanson as arbitrator, interlectoral stuff's more up his street," threatened Bill. "I reckon this here's work for technical men, not clerical operatives like what I am, so tha can wait till Wilf or Percy's ower 'ere. Let them watch thee playing battleships down drain oils. At least they don't have to live 'ere afterwards!"

I launched out on a different tack. Get the lads involved, rather than having them looking on and busting themselves trying to think up daft remarks. I cleared this with Jack Senior, and started on the more difficult job of persuading the station gang. At first a reaction along Bill's lines prevailed; "over dead bodies" being a condition stipulated. They too had people to whom they would rather not expose themselves while indulging in this pioneering work. It might produce medals, accolades, and Nobel prizes for contributions to drainage engineering, but more immediately it'd be sure to make them look a right set of doylums in the club come Friday night. I indulged in diplomatic skills way beyond my position, and went in to negotiate with Hubert Rhodes. Ten minutes scanning the little blue book of legitimate bonus enhancements proved it could be a handy little money interceptor, so startlingly enthusiastic zeal erupted, and the job was on. Now unfettered by reputational fears, Bill also fell into line with a horrifyingly cheerful eagerness.

Every possible drainage junction and catch-pit was revealed and opened up, many still with trapped clots of green fluorescence. There was one which had not so far shown up in my investigations, whose presence I'd only suspected; solid brick, eight feet deep and equipped with a ladder. Water was trickling in from five different directions, and the sump was coloured with the inevitable green dye. One by one the little balsa boats – with paperclip keels and a wild variety of mast materials conjured up from butchered Christmas decorations – were launched, with me keeping a complex record of the boats' trimmings, using equivalent tinsel snips pasted in my survey book. (Bill had offered to match it all with a pretty pink bow for the cover, with a maroon tassel as bookmark. My invitation for him to stick his bow and tassel in a more mundane setting induced a mock sulk lasting all of five minutes.) It was then that I discovered the trick of rejuvenation.

Get a few men together, persuade them that it is necessary to do something which appears superficially childish, and within minutes they'll be jumping around like excited playschool undergraduates.

Water, and things in it, moves very slowly through drains under normal conditions. I'd once spent an extremely pleasant afternoon waiting for my ubiquitous green dye to pass under four tracks and show up in one of two culverts on the other side of the railway. In a long warm hour I'd collected a catalogue of culvert wildlife observations before the merest hints of bright green unfolded in the next twenty minutes to become an overall spread of brilliant colour, and there was absolutely nothing I could do to speed up the process. Modern techniques, such as tiny TV cameras thrusting their way through the pipes, have spoiled all that by now, no doubt, and taken with it the wealth of thinking time which is in such short supply today.

Not that things were quiet, or peaceful, or even barely sensible between the platform ends and the tunnels at Huddersfield that day. Catch-pits weren't far apart, compared to my idyllic culverts, and in no time my developing bunch of overexcited buffoons were yelling out colours, logos, and other identifying details. It wasn't long before I cottoned on to the fact that money was changing hands. What boat would appear first, where it would turn up, along with places and non-arrivals by dinnertime. One of the gang, Shrapnel Bert, was so heavily involved that the characteristic stammer which gave him his name, was at a peak. Normally placid and quietly spoken, at times of passion Bert would shatter into staccato incoherency. Bets were being won and lost as he screamed out "Ber, ber, ber brown!" or "Blue!", "Grere, grer, grer, grey!" or "Green!" "Yer, yer, yer, yours has sunk, Frankie!"

"If ivver theer's a fire," Bill commented, as he stood by me translating the runners and places, "and it's Bert what finds it, God help us all!"

I'd picked my day carefully. Elliot Milner was on two days' leave. Though in his time a first-class surveyor and draughtsman, Elliot could be – how you might say – restricted in his use of imaginative methodology. In other words, if he'd come across his senior (only) technical assistant belly-down between tracks, head and arms sunk deep into a drainage catch-pit, launching a frivolously decorated mini-flotilla, he might not have understood. Don't get me wrong – he was more than happy, weeks later, with the resulting complex runs of coloured lines all over a plan of the tunnel-end drainage, but he would still have been a bit iffy about the methods used.

Tiny boats were appearing all over, some in most unlikely places, and a brilliant confusion of routes started to map out in my survey book. The gambling aspect only strengthened my trust in the bawling and shrieking around me – money drove potential winners to double-check all results. Bill's inevitable additions of doctored biros as miniature submarines, beer mats masquerading as aircraft carriers, and damaged polystyrene purporting to be icebergs contributed little, but added to the colour of announcements of declared finishers. Growing apathy on his part, as results began to dry up, combined with the abject failure of his oil tanker, which bore a striking resemblance to a tennis racket handle, led to his return to the harbour of his office and his tea mug.

When Bill returned three-quarters of an hour later, with a bottle of Lambs Navy which he'd filled with water and added a fairly convincing mix of the red and violet dyes, he found events drawing to a conclusion. I had a full survey book, and a hopefully comprehensive catalogue of arrivals at the large brick pit that we'd decided was the main outfall. I had to climb down this, trusting a distinctly dodgy-looking ladder of rust, in order to re-marshal my small navy. Many, however, had been sadly lost in action. My resultant plan of the various runs, drawn up over the following day, was enhanced by each confirmed route being designated a separate coloured pencil. Bill, examining the finished result, suggested sending a copy to Crown Decorating Materials, to have it copied up as wallpaper.

Out of all this a fairly comprehensive new system was devised and submitted for the following year's renewals programme. I was surprised to find myself commended for the details within my plans by the Engineer, but I decided that the innovatory methods of my survey technique were irrelevant, and best kept quiet.

Many years after I'd left Huddersfield, I was still called upon to comment on any schemes or difficulties that arose on the old Area. Nine years was an excessively long time to spend gaining an intimate knowledge of a relatively small section of the railway system, albeit well over a hundred track miles, but it was true to claim that there wasn't a thirty-yard stretch where I hadn't done something or other. So I was often asked about past findings.

Perhaps twenty years had elapsed when I was called in to chat over the drainage system at the tunnel end of the platforms at Huddersfield, there being some evidence of blockage within.

Developments in technology had made leaps and bounds during those years. I was listened to with a deal of respect, as I ran over my old plans, before being treated to "the most peculiar pictures" from the drains, picked up by special closed-circuit TV cameras, which could propel themselves along within. I looked on with envy as the clear pictures unfolded, clearly and effortlessly showing up minor collapses, cracks, and identifiable rubbish part blocking the way, until – "This is the bit, Mike! We couldn't get the camera through any further. What d'yer reckon, eh? Looks like a *Blue Peter* mock-up of a nasty battle at sea in Nelson's day! Couldn't you swear that that looks just like a load of mashed-up little boats?"

★

When we finally got down to doing the drainage renewal work at the tunnel end two years later, an interesting little incident cropped up illustrating the man-management skills needed by the supervisory staff to counter the artfulness of the workforce. Having a maze of tracks running into the platforms, with connections from one to the other, there wasn't much room left between them for BR standard pre-cast concrete catch-pits. So lots of purpose-shaped brick ones had to be built to fit into the various spots where a pit was thought to be needed. This was the job of our local Works Supervisor. Ken Oxley was now in the chair at Huddersfield, a relaxed man, not too troubled by the world, mid-forties, wiry build with wavy blond hair, and fit. A light twin-tubed pipe was a permanent fixture and fitting in one corner of his mouth, with the other generally set in the upward curl of a grin. Ken had to battle against his naturally calm disposition to introduce some harder discipline into his crafts-men, who had grown with the philosophy that no job was so small that it couldn't fill a day. One such artisan was Jack Watling, working on building the catch-pits, and producing some very indifferent results. Jack claimed undisclosed personal circumstances as an excuse, and whatever these might be they tended to move him to overindulgence in the evenings, such that it was clearly affecting his work for most of the next day. Ken, basically soft, was desperately trying to pull the bloke together, spurred on by Elliot Milner's refusal to accept some of the finished results.

Ken turned up one morning during the building work and found Jack deep in his latest pit. It was obvious that his head was receiving messages of extreme discomfort every time he bent down to lay a brick, with the result that the developing catch-pit looked more like a cement-stained pile of bricks than anything vaguely organised.

It started from a clear rectangular base, missing one corner due to the track layout. It passed through several indefinable geometric disasters, before finishing up disguised as a remotely recognisable ellipse. During this journey from the base's horizontal plane, it progressed upwards with the various layers of brick fixed in uncoordinated Mexican waves, before it struggled to the surface. Here judicious variations of mortar thickness brought it back to something close to a level, albeit a result that favoured one end particularly.

"This here's got to be t'last straw," said Ken to the two pink dots set in the white sea of Jack's face, which was looking up at him. "It just won't do, Jack. Thurs not one brick in line wi' another, and t'walls are bulgin' in an' out. Tek it down, start agen, and ah'll look at it in t'mornin'. If thurs no improvement, you're headin' down t'road. Ah'm sorry, burrit's not me, it's yon Milner; he just won't stand for it!"

Next morning the catch-pit had been completely rebuilt back to level with the ground. Ken's first thoughts were that it was absolutely appalling, but on reflection decided it wasn't as good as that. Jack was leaning heavily at regular intervals, and drinking copious amounts of water. Ken simply had no choice and suspended him on the spot, pending discussions with Elliot.

"Can you hold on a sec, please, Ken?" pleaded the sad case. "Ah knaw it's not good, in fact ah knaw it's downright bloody awful, but ah've a load o' bother at home, and ah couldn't tek the heave ho right now!"

"It's no good, Jack," went on Ken, quite against his nature, "but I've nivver seen owt built worse than this. I'll get hung if I let it pass."

"Tell you what, then," said Jack, grasping at a straw, "if ah c'n show thee a worse 'un, wot you've nivver said nowt abaht, will tha gius another chance?"

"I might," said Ken, desperate for some reason not to go through with his threat. "Wheerabahts is it?"

"Foller me," said Jack, and set off for the far end of the station, just before the point where the lines reached the long viaduct. Three minutes' walk, or five if you were working with Jack's head on. He bent down and lifted a couple of short timbers, revealing a truly distressed catch-pit that could only be described as a stiff arrangement of bricks.

"That's bloody horrific," Ken said. "I've got to hand it to you, yours is bad but it ain't nearly as bad as that 'un. Fair enough, get thissen home, get some rest and keep off the juice tonight. You can have another stab at it tomorrow."

They were both of them grateful for this outcome, and they walked back along the platform towards the tunnel together. Ken could not come to terms with what he'd seen.

"D'yer know who built that one, then?" he asked Jack. Then with a sudden attack of fear, "It weren't one of our lads, was it?"

"'Fraid so," said Jack. "It were me!"

★

Wilf and Percy, though escaping the maritime surveying episode, were unfortunately involved in too many of my inventive surveying techniques. They would return strongly to basics, questioning every move or suggestion that I made, trying to come to terms with doing things, however straightforward, that they may never have been asked to do before. They would readily quote their experiences "surveying sods at Wyke" as an example.

Six days before Christmas part of the embankment at Wyke near Bradford decided to part company with the rest of the railway. It started with the patrolman spotting a crack running along the middle of the "six-foot" space between the two tracks. He immediately closed the line and set off rabbits running in from all directions. Elliot and I met up with the Bradford PWay Supervisor, Dennis Durand, who had brought along a volunteer gang on the off-chance that immediate repairs could be carried out. Representatives of all other interests were turning up to formulate a chaos of priorities. Elliot needed to keep the line shut for safety, operating staff needed it reopening in some form, telecommunication people wanted to protect their precious trackside cables, Dennis needed to work out whether he should send men home to rest, in order to return that night. Just a crack in the afternoon became a chasm by night as the ground slipped away from beneath one track. Surveys the next day showed the embankment to be moving in a near-perfect circle, dropping at the top, and bulging near the foot. All the usual repairs and reconstruction work were carried out over the following days, and I finally left site for home at four o'clock in the late afternoon of Christmas Eve. Sheet piling through the slip circle halted the movement, stone replaced the lost banking and a normal service was restored. But no one had found out why it had all happened.

Not a Christmas person, once the kids had unwrapped their parcels, I got to wondering. As a result, on the bright, crisp New Year's Day I returned to site, together with Wilf and Percy. We were driven there by Bill, who fondly imagined that that was to be his role for the day. Working on a ghost of a theory dug out of one of my old textbooks, I had them all mark out a lattice in the fields, either side of the railway embankment around the area of the slip. I then had a bemused team line each other up so that ground-level measurements could be taken at the intersection of the grid lines. So intent was I on a result, that tricks like pushing the levelling staff down rabbit holes or perching it on mole hills were met with my equivalent of a snarl. After four hours of concentrated work I arranged for the others to be back in their homes by three, thus forming yet another brick in the wall of future cooperation.

From the readings, I drew out a contour map of the two fields, not in fifty-foot intervals like the office ordnance maps, but in tenths of a foot. As the plan neared completion, a distinct valley appeared running straight across the line of the railway, marking a watercourse, long gone underground before the embankment had been constructed. Yet to the eye, both fields still looked plain, gently sloping and dull. It was apparent that the late stream had run directly through the position of the slip, and clearly revealed the cause – movement of sub-surface water. Cut-off drains were dug and the stream diverted. Only a full explanation of what I was trying to do persuaded the two chainmen that they weren't just dancing among the daisies for nothing, and the survey had been completed with no more than a menacing threat of "tha'd better be reet!"

Reactions were not always so peaceful; downright hostility could break out at times, such as on the occasion when Elliot wanted a similar exercise to be done near Stanningley Tunnel. There was evidence that the steep bankings were liable to slipping, and he wanted me to design cut backs, with loading on the embankment toes in the form of a large step in the slopes. He left me with the job of explaining this to Wilf and Percy, who had both dealt with Elliot as a surveyor, and were not slow to comment to his face if they felt that they were being mucked about. All three of us were far from excited about the days which followed spent setting up a level on one in three slopes, managing two readings before having to reposition, and having nothing better than Percy's boot toe as temporary reference points between set-ups. My attempts to jolly them along by observing that the sheep and cows they often saw on the steeply inclined fields around Marsden seemed to cope, led to a furious debate that mealtime. Percy was deeply convinced by what one of the farmer's up that way had told him, about evolution having developed Pennine cattle with legs on one side a good six inches shorter than the other. He argued this to be true, and proved it by the way all the cattle were facing the same way. We successfully completed the Stanningley job despite these difficulties, but only because we were all as fed up with it as each other.

This marked a high in my book for the cooperation I received from volatile chainmen, but I drew the line at involving them in a very private form of survey, one that I pioneered on the Leeds District, and which would have evoked new levels of derision, had Wilf and Percy been in attendance. True, there was one practising this art on the adjacent York patch, and doing it quite openly, using official railway equipment, but I pursued it secretly and alone, and with equipment I had made myself. It was months after discovering the ability before I came out, confided in Bill, and returned to the slip site at Wyke, finally showing Bill that he too had the mystic power of finding drains and watercourses by dousing. For we both found that the stream that had taken so long to trace by levelling was instantly exposed by water divining.

My discovery of the art took place in my own garden, using a coat hanger cut in two, each half bent like an "L", and supported in empty biro cases. I knew of the existence of underground streams, but not where they were. Having mapped three at the back of the house, I persuaded a doubtful wife to do likewise, without telling her where I had discovered them. We were both quite mystified by the fact that she too managed to locate all three streams, and exactly where I had. I was convinced, but a convinced water diviner can become a very lonely person.

A chance remark to Eddy Stapleton had led to exhaustive testing in the yard outside the offices at Huddersfield, never really proving anything, since I kept "finding" the lavatory drain run, which we both knew was there anyway. Anything else I "discovered" could not be proven since that would mean digging up the yard. It was only after Eddy, who had a delightfully simple faith in my abilities, persuaded me to help him in the station sidings that proof could be given, with the result that the already convinced Bill still generously branded me as a witch.

Eddy had been given a fairly straightforward job of designing some drainage for the sidings, easy up to the point where he had to locate some existing outfall for the collected waters. Local men and the older supervisors swore to the existence of a culvert passing under the small yard, but knew not where precisely. Eddy prevailed on me to attempt to locate it by divining – and in daylight! Which is why I was to be seen walking self-consciously up and down the sidings, with Eddy dancing alongside, marking on the rails each twitch of the coat-hanger halves. Bill and some of the gang watched on. Despite having discovered that he too could do it, Bill kept face with the lads by crossing himself with the sign of the cross every time my rods swung and Eddy marked another spot on the railhead. Yet they all had to admit that when looked at broadly, the marks did line up right across the yard. Eddy, still having far more faith than me – his reputed harridan superior – hired excavating machinery for the coming Sunday, along with a gang, spending upwards of £10,000 on the strength of a twisting coat hanger. But he had the sewer fully exposed for all to see on the Monday morning, and a complete solution to the problems.

News of this filtered back to Leeds, and not via Elliot, who had been appalled when he discovered that he had risked all that money on a sorcerer's whim, regardless of the result, and he was not going to let the hierarchy at Divisional Office know that he was so trusting. However they did find out, and I was forced into demonstrations in the Drawing Office on my next visit. Here the audience were more or less content for me to "find" the large office teapot full of water, placed on the floor, despite the fact that I tripped over it on a couple of passes. All tried to emulate me, and some sort of succeeded. Meanwhile, the population of coat hangers began to fall off alarmingly, an animal usually remarkable for its ability to multiply within the wardrobes of the world.

So I had at last fully come out, but was I ready to try the high board yet?

Suppose, for a moment, the sceptics of the world unite, and constitute an International Institute for Dedicated Doubters, then it has to be established at the centre of gravity of real Yorkshire-men, which is Dewsbury. If they then should hold a World Conference on the Major Concerns of the Sceptic in Today's Society, then the third item on the agenda, following debates on "Martian Society" and "The Complete Loch Ness Angler", would be the subject of Water Divining. Should they want a Life President and Grand Master of the Order of St Thomas the Doubter, then they need look no further than John Midgley, Pedantic and Extremely Practical PWay Engineer, formerly attached to the District Civil Engineers at York.

It is then the action of a naive and foolhardy individual, to introduce said Midge to the art of water divining in Dewsbury Station, watched over by a dozen or so of the local town-folk waiting on the two platforms, all carrying the same expression of sad resentment that the authorities do not have a tighter control on who is and who is not released back into society.

To illustrate the suspicious scepticism of the area, take a pub in Dewsbury, with a publican wishing to stimulate a seasonal spirit. He might try advertising the Landlord's Special Offer. Dewsbury Man would then enquire as to exactly what form the Landlord's Special took. He would be told that it was a composite ticket for a pie, a pint and half an hour round the back with the most attractive barmaid – for the all-inclusive price of £1.75. Dewsbury Man would ponder this, weighing it up carefully in his mind, and then ask, "Whose pies are they?"

In later years, John Midgley and I were to be thrown together to mastermind, plan and carry out major projects. John had a broader experience than me, but with me having the longer service record. There was enough common ground and opinions to make us a credible team together. Had John been present at the Drawing Office demonstration of dousing he probably would not have bothered to take notice, for if he had, he would have been quick to point out the stupidity of trying to locate a teapot using two bits of wire, when the thing was there for all to see.

We had been called in at Dewsbury to investigate a regular flooding problem, suspected to originate from an underground stream. Having tramped up the formation and back through the very wide space between platforms which once carried four tracks, we both agreed about there being a stream, but not as to where it was exactly.

Lying on the track side were a number of six-foot lengths of signalling bonding wire. This is a very strong, five-millimetre-thick wire used to carry track circuit currents across any joints in the track. It is to coat-hanger wire what a telegraph pole is to a bamboo support.

"Right, clever bugger," said Midge, picking up two of the metal rods. "Ah've been hearing as to how brilliant you are at finding watter with coat hangers; just stand back and watch a champion! How do you get going?"

"Not with them things for a start off, John," I advised. "They're far too big and heavy. Have you ever done it before, then?"

"Nope," said John, "but if you can do it, I'll be buggered if I can't. Now then, how does it work?"

"Haven't a clue," I began, only to be shouted down.

"Look, if you want to keep it to yourself, be like that. For as long as I've known you, you've not been able to tell me nowt I didn't already know, and there's still a lot I can tackle that you've no idea about, yet they reckon you're more important nor me. It's fust time I've asked you owt, and you can't, or won't tell me!"

All this was, to a large extent, true. I was where I was, in relation to John, on the basis of a longer experience, which was a paramount consideration on the railway. I had, however, known John long enough by then, and watched him at work sufficiently to realise that it was unfair to compare anyone with John Midgley. In my opinion, John was the finest permanent way engineer I had ever come across in my thirty years on the railway, but I would never have told him so. On the other hand, I knew that I had it over John in areas such as diplomacy, technical reporting and in what he would call "bullshitting", but which I was pleased to see as communication. It all led to an uneasy rivalry on his part, something which did not surface in me, because I knew that if John had the choice of weapons, then he would win every time.

In the present situation I could see everything stacked against me. John had selected materials which were many times heavier and longer than anything I had ever tried before. John had never done any divining, and did not at all believe in it. He was, however, keen to learn he might be, and did not take advice or instruction from anyone he regarded as inferior. Additionally, John would have walked naked between the platforms carrying a bunch of roses if it happened to be the way to achieve a particular result. If we were to try divining for the stream, I wanted solitude, darkness and a complete absence of humanity, particularly the sort you found in Dewsbury. However, I knew that I was going to have to do it.

"You want two pieces, about two and a half feet long, bent into Ls, and slotted onto two tubes, like pen holders," I explained.

"Well," said Midge, "you've got two pieces, about six foot long, no way of cutting them, and no tubes, so you'll have to make do! Here." With which he bent the last foot of each rod at right angles, using the rail as an anvil. "No, on second thoughts, just tell us what t'do next! I'll show thee you can't have it all your own way!"

Well beaten, I explained to him that he must not grip the rods, while he holds them out in front of him, and try and keep them about a foot apart and level.

"Right!" said John, obviously certain in his own mind that if someone like me could do it, then he certainly ought to be able to copy me, else it was just a trick. "Come on, then!" With which he marched off up through the platforms.

Suddenly, to my complete amazement, I saw the rods swing violently across each other.

"Bloody hell fire!" exclaimed John, "You might have warned me it hurts!"

"You've done it!" I said. "You've only bloody managed it!"

"Course I have! If you can do it... but, how does it work?"

I didn't know, of course, which lowered me still further in Midge's estimation. A keen mechanic, it was in his nature to need to know how anything he handled worked. I was also wondering what John had meant about it hurting. With the satisfaction of success, he was now perfectly happy to hand over the rods, and I retraced his steps over the discovered stream. I was startled to discover the force which the rods exerted, giving the palms of my hands a burning sensation as they twisted within my gentle grasp.

Meanwhile, from the platforms on either side: "Ay oop, lads, dust'a know t'wheels 'ave come off thi barrow?"

"Are them things loaded?"

"Do they know you're out, lads? Is theer a phone number what ah should ring?" Overriding all this derision, and totally ignoring it, was the now enthusiastic John Midgley, driving a new toy, but completely in the dark as to how. Charging up and down the tracks, and then the platforms themselves, he kept finding traces of goodness knows what below. Hopeful passengers were now becoming steadily more alarmed as this lunatic in their midst was driving through them, two lances pointing straight ahead, elbowing them aside as he went, with just the occasional "Ay up!" or "Sorry!" Approaching one lady from behind, John found his rods swirling wildly; she was greeted by, "Never mind, luv, only fifteen minutes to Leeds, and you can always go on the train!" She heard this and he said it, but it meant different things to each of them.

Back in Leeds, I was by mutual agreement pushed into the

background. It was now John Midgley who gave impromptu demonstrations of the douser's art. He found teapots, kettles, a concealed half bottle of whisky, the toilets, a dead mouse, all the radiators and heating pipes and some undisclosed run of something buried under the floor. At home, Mrs Midgley, with little initial interest in her husband's new-found skill, was rapidly increasing the depth of her apathy, as he found that there were drains running away from the house, water supplies coming in, trees where the dog had last had a pee, and the fishpond in the garden. Their dog was becoming paranoid, forever seeing bossman approaching it with two rods pointing out in front, reckoning to work out if it was time to take it for a walk.

Midge's fixation was only cured when I insisted on calling in the York Area lad, Dave Carter, custodian of the official railway brass dousing rods that were encased in a veneered dovetailed carrying case, to check on some vital watercourses at Guiseley. Both John and I had found them, but I wanted to know more. Dave came over from York, momentarily unsettled to find that the world sloped alarmingly outside the flat earth of his home base. His skills in the notoriously poor drainage area of the Vale of York were invaluable, and he could not at first understand how anyone with a tilting landscape could ever have a drainage problem, other than what to do with it when it got to the bottom of a hill. I contented myself by just showing Dave the site, whereas Midge had to have a go with the posh executive equipment, only managing to reproduce what we already knew. However, Dave fared somewhat better.

Walking up and down several times, the rods positively dancing in his hands, he eventually agreed on the position of the water courses, but went on to predict the precise depth they were at, whether they were free-flowing streams or in pipes, and exactly what material the pipe was made of. He also located and described two gas mains. Subsequent digging the following Sunday, on Dave's evidence, was able to be carried out by machine to within a foot of his predicted depths, and then by shovel, locating the stated delicate earthenware, and in addition the two extremely sensitive gas mains. When all this was pointed out to John and me on the Monday, I showed satisfaction at the savings in manpower afforded by being able to confidently predict depths, while John ignored the whole thing, settling for one of his disgruntled explosions when trying to hang his coat up in the lockers, discovering that "someone had nicked all the bleeding coat hangers".

★

Why I had been against the brave idea behind the twistector (a device which must be gone into another day), I could not say. It was just instinct. I didn't like the thing, and could see all sorts of problems; Elliot just accused me of being a Luddite, a reactionary and a regressive traditionalist, to add to my famed pessimism. I was hurt by all this as I had always regarded myself as merely a realist, and was stung to remind Elliot of some of my great and innovative actions in lateral thinking, particularly with regard to the experiment of setting out alignments by teapot.

"Setting out" is a term covering the transference of information from a drawing to the ground. It is usually a straightforward business, as long as the surveyor has worked out the equipment necessary in any particular situation, and the designer has some practical experience. I can quote many instances where a lack of this had led to my calling on headquarters at York, to allow the person concerned to gain that experience by "coming and trying for himself!" One such was for a stretch of completely new railway, where the York draughtsman had presented a datum measurement of 103 feet from an established baseline. On this occasion I settled for asking headquarters to send through a 103-foot tape-measure. I then redesigned the entire new line, cuttings and drains, and set out my scheme. This I found ironic in that the totally impractical HQ dreamer was awarded his professional qualifications, in part due to his design, which he still fondly believes was used.

Returning to the teapot.

"We've a bit of a problem, Eddy!"

This was towards the back end of Eddy's time at Huddersfield, and a much-developed young engineer had evolved from the timid beastie of twelve months before. I accept some responsibility for this, but the cooperation that the lad had inspired in the chainmen, added to his respect for the trackmen and supervisors, with the hardening up which living with Bill Boyes produced, had more than just contributed.

Eddy asked the nature of the problem. It was during the period when my schemes for the major realignments of the two remaining tracks up the Colne Valley were being executed, and the relaying supervisors in Leeds were seeking some idea of the position of the final centre line of the new railway. Normally, this would involve hammering wood pegs in the old track formation left by the removal of the Fast Lines. I had once sent Eddy out to set out two hundred yards in this way, and he had returned with Wilf and Percy after three hours of trying to drive pegs into the concrete solidity of the old base.

"That weren't appreciated," Wilf made perfectly clear. "If you've ever tried plantin' rhubarb in a runway, tha might've had some idea what tha were askin'!"

"Have you managed, though?" I asked unadvisedly.

In deleting expletives here, it results in reducing a two-minute reply to "No!" So hammering pegs deep into the old formation was not an option, especially as they were talking about a two-mile stretch here! It was Eddy who started the flow of inspiration, by rooting around in one of the sheds outside the office, looking for some item of equipment which Jack Senior swore was there. Being a thorough lad, he had to practically empty the hut before he found what he was looking for, but was interested to discover in the course of his exploration a few tins of paint, under some sacking. He brought one in for inspection.

Eddy was a little cautious of old tins of paint for reasons that will be revealed on a future page. What was left of the label revealed nothing. But a trickle of rather vivid colour down one edge gave some indication. Eddy had thought it a good idea to use it for marking out the new track centre line, but was shouted down by the assembled company based on the idea of laboriously painting a two-mile line on rough stone.

Eddy retreated to sulk. But it was the very obvious aspect of the paint that suggested to me a novel method for setting out the two miles of track between Longwood and Slaithwaite, up the valley.

My initial idea was to run a line of cheap paint along the centre line of the proposed alignment, though now having the (very) cheap paint, it was a little later before I fully worked out the operation. Elementary to the task was the necessity to safely open the tins. Experience had discovered that old paint could be temperamental. After a few failures, each one reducing by one the number of people prepared to ever help us out again, the think tank that was Bill and myself, devised a system which eventually opened the remaining tins at a relatively safe distance. Nearest to success was the Works resident blacksmith, in his shop under the viaduct arches. Bill had him drill a small hole in the lid to release any pressure.

I had the rest of the operation sorted out in my mind, but would need help. I could only confide in Bill who agreed with me that it would be best to keep Elliot Milner in the dark, as the car was involved in an unorthodox manner. It was a credit to our powers of persuasion of a suspicious Eddy, who eventually agreed to help, on the promise that he would at all times be inside the car, and the paint would not. Finally, a day was spent tapping two miles of wooden pegs into the hard surface of the old formation, enough for them to just stand up. This was fine for the length of their tapered points, but any permanence was impossible. Eddy was intrigued that the pegs were placed two feet off the centre line, but queries were answered by a gentle, "You really don't want to know!"

He was further intrigued as Bill made adjustments to the front bumper of the car, wedging a broom handle behind it, the same two feet off centre, and right in the driver's line of sight, before decorating it with strips of sacking. All this was removed before Elliot should see it. And so up to site.

Eddy's stipulation that he and the paint should not coincide in any way was beginning to backfire on him. He was firmly confined to the car, whilst Bill and I reinstated the pole and sacking, before disappearing round the back. With the boot lid in the open position he could see nothing, and this fulfilled the intentions of the other two precisely. After ten minutes Bill returned to the driving seat and instructed Eddy to warn him of the approach of any trains on the line adjacent to them. The next bit he just did not believe. Without waiting for me, or closing the boot, Bill set off, deliberately driving down the line of pegs and destroying a full day's work, but not the car – the sacking seeing to that. Every few hundred yards Bill would sound the horn, stop, get out and fiddle with something in the boot. He would then return and drive on, repeating the operation until they reached the end of the line, every peg now lying flattened. And still there was no sign of me!

Had Eddy been a by-stander he would have observed an equally eccentric scene. A car being driven slowly down the side of the railway, with a broom handle fastened to its front bumper and its boot wide open. He would also have noticed an uncomfortable-looking character leaning out of the boot, pouring a steady stream of violent scarlet paint from an old enamel teapot onto the ground behind the car, producing a long and fairly even line of colour, right at the proposed track centre.

Saturday Nights

Duggie Lomax was bounding about like a thing possessed. "I'n't this great, Mike? I can do with this. Brilliant! And we get paid!"

This was his first real Saturday-night job, and it was obvious that he hadn't deviated from his usual Saturday evening before it. These were the days when having a drink was frowned on but only drinking on duty was forbidden. In fact most of the lads' pickup points before a Saturday-night job were at pub corners. Duggie had got himself well prepared for a night of new delights; he was in that euphoric state between the last drink, and the first reaction, except, up to tonight, that reaction would have been for him cushioned by sleep. All the other lads, experienced as they were, had got themselves outside little more than a couple of pints, and were approaching the night's work in a slightly less dour way than they otherwise might have. Duggie, though, was bounding around like Tigger, friends with everyone, and spouting poetic enthusiasm about the twinkling stars, the disappearing house lights, and the lengthening run of gas flares lighting up the job ahead. Duggie was in love with everyone, and everything.

Not me, though. Saturday-night work spoiled my entire weekend. From waking Saturday morning, through checking I'd got all that I'd need, to not overdoing the day, and attempting a few hours' sleep in the early evening when my whole being is urging me to be out in the garden with a couple of bottles, before telly and bed. Coming home on Sunday morning, I'd be feeling way past sleep, but incapable of doing anything of worth, up to the evening meal and a heavy night of recovery. Monday would pass fairly well, but Tuesday would be zombie day. By Thursday there'd be a full recovery, in time to attend site meetings for the next Saturday-night's job. A week of nights I could adjust to, but the sudden change from days to a long night out in the open, returning immediately back to day shifts, was never easy.

This particular Saturday, when I had Duggie with me, gaining experience before going solo, had been a particularly trying one. A baking hot July day, with evening heat, open windows, and summer noise. Kids trying their best to communicate with another galaxy without artificial aids. Some invisible bloke attempting to cut down an oak tree using his basic, one speed, beginner's model Black and Decker. Three women talking, but not listening – the one with the laugh from hell suddenly getting the point of the "special red brick with a gold stripe running right round it" story. With all this combining in a lullaby for the chronically deaf, I managed no more than a light doze. However, by the time I was getting out of the gang bus around eleven, with the last glimmers of daylight on the horizon, and the temperature down to something acceptable, my spirits were on the up. Barely four hours before daylight, and a job virtually complete from my standpoint. Such nights, at such a time of year, just got better as they went on, peaking at around three when the first glow appeared in the morning's south-eastern sky. Not for Duggie, though.

This life and soul had leapt from the bus and into the cabin for the traditional mashing, to then serenade the bemused gang, who had instantly become his best mates, with a very personal version of "O Sole Mio" (which started on the lines of "Arse 'Ole Me Only, I'm Funny That Way") before descending into depths of depravity that hardly gave the Drawing Office representation a good name among the gang lads.

"Isee wi' thee, Mike? What's 'e here for? What's he on? Duzzuz after 'ave a friggin' cabaret now, to gerrus in t'mood, like? 'Cos ah could manage nicely wi'out Mario Bloody Lanza, theer."

But it couldn't last. Three o'clock found Duggie sat out on the banking, attracting a comprehensive layer of dew, with his head in his hands, begging all heaven to stop these nerks around him banging away at the rails and fastenings, and stating on solemn oath that never ever, in whatever be left of his life to come, would he let another drop pass his lips, honest to God. Which was a pity, because I'd thoroughly enjoyed myself, even if I was spending more time out on the job than usual. And that mainly for the benefit of this shivering bundle of spent humanity.

De-stressing continuous welded rail jobs, like this, were the best. With no use of engineer's trains, you generally got off to a prompt start, rather than a three-hour wait for everything to get itself to site in the correct order. In fact, I'd begun to organise these jobs exceptionally well, from my point of view, when they involved my own patch of the Huddersfield Area. All necessary preliminaries would be done on the Friday, with the point at which I wanted the rails cut clearly marked. A gang bus would collect up the lads around eleven, and drop them on site to get started. It would then come over to pick me up at my door, and get me there by the time the rails had been cut as marked, and lifted up onto rollers. One of our trusted gangers would have placed my rail thermometers in the places I'd marked, so I was ready to pile in immediately I arrived, making reference datum marks at various points along the six hundred yards or so of free rail. Now that we'd got hydraulic pumping gear to stretch the rails, the technical involvement had been drastically reduced from the old days of trundling trolleys of rail heaters up and down the track. Today we only had to work out from the temperature readings of the thermometers placed on the foot of the rails, the induced stress needed to bring them up to a virtual temperature of 21°C, so that they'd be stress-free when that temperature actually prevailed. A calculated gap was made at the point where we'd first cut the rails, and the pumps were set up to pull the two rail ends together for welding.

All that was then required of me was to check that the elongation of the rails was evenly distributed throughout, and wait for two successful welds to be made. My driver, who'd been taking his prescribed rest, would then run me back home for four, returning in time to pick up the lads after they'd finished fixing down the rails again. I was quite happy to be paid for the four hours, the lads got all that was coming to them, and the bus driver considered his duties as money for old rope. Everybody happy, and a job properly carried out.

For Duggie's inauguration I'd purposely done it from cold, arranging to be on site from beginning to end in order to take him through it step by step. I wouldn't say that this had been a complete success, as my early marking up and explanations had been met with an impatient, "Yeh, yeh, yehs; OK, Mike, what's next? This is fantastic, i'n't it? This is the life," before he broke into a contrived chorus of "I love to go a-stressing track, at midnight, in the dark. Seven pints of Tetleys best – oh isn't this a lark!" All of which left the workforce distinctly unimpressed.

When it came to my favourite bit of the night, the tapping of the weld, when white-hot fusion takes place as the molten material flows into the preformed housing around the two rail ends, Duggie was going through his breast-beating of self-reproach. He'd paid no real attention while I'd tried to interest him in checking the extensions, and open hostility erupted as the lads started hammering the rail clips home again.

A summer night's de-stressing could be almost enjoyable. Whatever the time of year, the sight of each man's lamp as they moved away into the blackness had a Disney-style effect, with them bobbing along, completely out of synch, yet all moving in the same direction. But on a summer night this would be set against the faint glow along the skyline, and the day's oppressive heat would by then have given way to a wholly fresher feeling – one of fully contented comfort. On summer nights, you could forget that there was any other time of year.

Such as this next one in mid-January, for example.

I'd managed some sleep that evening and arrived cold but alert at the site cabin to find it filled with humanity, smoke from coal, wood and tobacco, snores and sweat. For the fire would be going.

A lineside cabin's fire was never anything short of a furnace. Generally contained within an old black range, with an oven at the side, these fires went deep, and could be piled high in coal, way up the back. On weekdays, the youngest member of the gang would be nominated to turn up early enough for a blaze to be well on its way to inferno status before the cabin was full, and there could be no excuse for the kettle not to be both boiling and untouchable by a quarter past seven, balanced on the grid in front of the flames. So, when a Saturday night was centred on a particular cabin, with visitors from other gangs, it would be a matter of honour to see that the stove was fired with an unusual vigour.

A million miles away from the balmy summer breeze, and fading light, I approached the cabin alongside Harry Hanson,

Supervisor. In the light of our lamps sleet was flashing past and bitterly cold needles spiked any exposed flesh. The cabin was heaving – built for six or seven, you could guarantee at least a dozen within. Gaslight tossed a soft radiance through the murky windows, and a red glow surrounded the couple of feet of chimney pipe standing clear of the bubbling tar-timbered roof.

"You'll have a job getting them out of there, Harry!"

"Thee wait and see. When ah say out, it's out! They knaw as 'ow ah mean it!"

Not quite expecting "Good evening, my willing team. Behold, 'tis time to take up the task before us", I was still startled by Harry flinging open the door with a "Gerrout 'ere, tha lazy boogers, tha's 'ere t'wark, not sit round knittin' and drinkin' friggin' tea! Thee, thee, thee an' thee – bars. Yor two, shovels. Harold! Get thi dets (warning track detonators – Ed) dahn. Frank, Joe, Cairo, Midneet, wi' me. Barney, thee see to t'fire, an' see t'kettle's full, then dahn to t'crossing wi' thi 'ammer in five minnits!"

So with a silent "Hey ho!" the far from willing fragmented team eased their separate bodies from the close confines of their mates, the padded plank seats and eventually the cabin itself. Passing through the heat lock with an 80°F differential, they moved off into the darkness, the wind, and the piercing sleet. I could see steam rising from the backs of the coat collars in front of me, until these outer layers took on the ambience of the Arctic night.

After half an hour, during which time Harry had got each man down to his allotted task, he looked round sensing that he was short-handed.

"Weer's Barney? Has tha seen Barney? Frankie, get thissen back an' liven t'bugger up. Ah want thi both back dahn 'ere, ten minnits sharp!"

With which Frankie happily trotted back to the warmth, on a mission impossible – that of talking Barney out of the melting down within to the pelting down without. Twenty minutes passed before Harry realised that he was now two bodies short.

"Weer the bloody hell 'ave they got to? Mike! Tha's doin' nowt. Go seek t'buggers aht, theer's a good lad!"

Strictly speaking, Harry had no right to give me instructions, but as my initial work was done, I'd no objection to taking a rest, and perhaps a drink of tea, so long as I could work out how they managed to pick up a near-molten kettle and take it to the cup. I walked back with wind assistance, for the first time not noticing the piercing ice pricks on my face. I found the cabin much as we'd left it, but now with sparks dancing skywards from the dull-red glow of the chimney. Inside, Barney and Frankie were laid out along the side benches, dead to the world. No amount of reasoning or prodding made any impact, as my lack of any authority was silently, but implicitly, made clear, so I could do no more than return to Harry and report failure.

"Tha what! Thee cum wi' me, lad! Ah'll show thee how to shift them idle buggers!"

An air of alarm seemed to shoot among the workforce. "Aw, nay, Harry, not the bloody stove! We've t'go back theer afore long! Lay off, Harry, don't do owt drastic! Just sign 'em off! We'll cover for 'em!"

But Harry was determined in whatever method of persuasion he was to adopt, both feared and suspected by the lads, so I made the stumbling return journey to the cabin, trying to keep up with a very disturbed and determined supervisor. I'd no idea what he had in mind as a way of raising the sleeping beauties, but I couldn't see a lingering kiss figuring largely in his plans. Harry kicked open the door. "Get thi' bloody arses aht 'ere now!" No reaction. "Right! If that's the way tha wants it!"

With that, Harry marched in, flung open the range door at the side of the fire, and to my utter amazement unbuttoned his trousers and peed directly into the baking hot oven. Steam rose in clouds, Harry backed off and out of the cabin, slamming the door and turning the key. In the time it took for him to readjust his flies, there arose a muffled screaming within and a pounding on the door. Harry unlocked it, and two retching bodies shot out into the very fresh air.

"Reet! Chuck some watter ower it an' get thissens dahn theer wi' t'rest. Tha's both docked an hour!"

★

I always felt that there was some injustice in the fact that I got paid the same in winter as in summer. Take the simple job of de-stressing, above, so pleasant in summer, even a relief to be out in the cool of nights sandwiched between scorching hot days, when there's no escape. In winter things are the other way round. However unpleasant the day might have been, you could guarantee that the night would be many times worse.

We'd a stretch of experimental rail fastenings at Gledholt, a mile out of Huddersfield. As can sometimes happen, "experimental" was a euphemism for "obviously useless from the start" in this case. A similarly complicated fastening had come to one of our Chief Civil Engineers in a dream, presumably featuring George Stephenson coming down a golden staircase with the new idea worked in gold, and lying on a velvet cushion. It was adopted with only murmurings of doubt. Such was the awe this fellow was held in that they actually named the clip after him. Again, what could be put together on the experimental bench was murder when blended with minus temperatures and a blizzard. The ones at Gledholt had seriously less hold on the rail than the emerging perfection of the Pandrol clip, and they were made up of many small components, making the design of a special tool to install and remove them essential. This in itself became more difficult each time it was done as it wore away a section of the concrete sleeper. Since these fastenings were experimental, we were called upon to check the stresses in them twice a year at first, each time being in effect a re-stressing operation. One such night fell in January, and it was cold!

So cold that the mercury in my rail thermometers suffered a severe bout of shyness, and clung tenaciously to the comfort of the bulb at the base. This reserve spread among the men, and increased as the night wore on. Having forced itself up to the 14°F mark, the mercury persuaded itself that it had overachieved, and slunk back towards the security of its reservoir as the night passed. Flurries of snow, in a dry powder form, hardly added much to the layer of ice which covered everything, but where they settled on bare flesh, they melted, ran to a prominence, and almost instantly froze again. Each track fastening point had two clips and four pieces of plastic insulation and packing to take out and lay aside. Fiddly, to say the least, and it all had to be handled with frost-affected fingers, now joining the black of the night. When it came to replacing them we found that the minuscule amount of warmth gained from our fingers had transferred to each component and momentarily melted the ice where they lay, before quickly freezing again and attaching them solidly to the concrete sleeper ends. The job overran well into daylight, and it was afternoon before we reopened to traffic, having had to seek out new components as replacements.

It was all a waste of time, as it turned out. Experimental readings were based on the continued effectiveness of the original fastenings, most of which we'd needed to replace, and the temperature was so cold that we found we'd actually lost stress in the rails when we at last managed to weld up the gap. On the following day, with fingers still itching from the night's ravages, and with open cuts around my thumbnails weeping all day, I penned a report much on the lines laid out here, but with the added benefit of not having to rely on memory for a description of the pain that I was in from handling the bits and pieces – it was only just beginning to wear off as I wrote in a script worse than usual. I contrived to bleed, just a little, over unimportant bits of the paper. Years later, I had the belated contentment of discovering that my agonised writing had been sent on upwards, along with a typed translation, as our Engineer felt that the penning itself betrayed so graphically the hopelessness and agony experienced in handling the new clip fastenings. As a result, no more were ever used on the Region.

These clips only went to underline the beauty of the final Pandrol line of clips, now seen almost throughout the railway system in their various guises. Not only are they the most effective of fastenings for grip, they are also undeniable things of beauty as a piece of sculpture, and I would much prefer to gaze at one in a glass case were it to be presented in opposition, say, to a stack of bricks or a half sheep. Also, in those bad old days of realistic safety precautions, the Pandrol's main selling point was that you knocked it out with a track hammer, and later knocked it back in the same way. Arguments later prevailed from the Health and Safety people, applauded by railway tool manufacturers, for the design of yet another special instrument to do this more safely, and once we had a surplus of these, they then went on and invented a machine to do it all instead. Such is progress, and economic survival.

But let me not moan too much about working in all weather, for I have to acknowledge the sympathetic care that my loving company lavished on us as protection against the ravages. Each man was supplied with clothing to defend him and to saturate him in sweat trying to actually move around in it. Overalls, gloves, jackets and wet-weather gear were dolled out and regularly renewed. Supervisors, however, were treated as special, and each received a distinctive dark blue greatcoat. We technical staff... well, we actually got nothing, officially, but there were few who hadn't fiddled something along the way. I was the proud owner of one of the greatcoats. It was Jack Senior's in reality, but Jack was very careful with his tackle, and never worked weekends, so replacement clothing would reach him well ahead of his need for it. Hence my greatcoat.

You wouldn't say that Jack and I were the same build, but so long as I wore a thick pullover and jacket as well, the coat fitted me marginally better than it did Jack. They came in two sizes – "Big" and "Bigger". The first had been modelled on somebody very much akin to Harry Hanson, who managed to look smart at most times, while the larger size was obviously fashioned from the full width of the bale of cloth, with minimal wastage, and would have gone a fair way to accommodating an average gang. I never met anyone who didn't get just a little lost inside one of these coats, and there were plenty of five-foot-nothing supervisors who had to pick up their skirts to cross over rails in the smaller version. They could also suffer the disconcerting effect of turning round inside the coat and finding that it had more or less stayed put. Pockets were placed at a level beyond their arm lengths, and the only way to access them was to crouch until the hem touched the floor, and pocket and hand coincided. Even for this to work, some nifty needlecraft was necessary to reduce the lengths of the sleeves that matched the coat in proportions taken from the mountain gorilla. But it was an undeniably effective garment in one way or another.

Its moment of destiny was during winter sun when it really came into its own; at any other time it had shortcomings. In the morning sun of either spring or autumn it acted as an absorbent blanket of warmth up to midday. After that it became an encumbrance, a nuisance and a portable sauna. But in steady rain it turned treacherous. Many a wet night has begun in relative comfort, the coat beating official waterproofs which attract rain from all directions, collect it in rivulets, which then act as tributaries to the river running from the hem and onto your trousers. None of that with the greatcoat – it just acted as a collector, until around two o'clock, which is everyone's low point. Up to then it just got heavier and heavier with the accumulated rain until it began to ease through the lining to the body beneath. Once that link had been made it steadily drenched you, and took upwards of a week to dry out afterwards. From my experience with the greatcoat I wonder at sheep; why aren't they on their knees during steady rain? Snow wasn't quite as bad, except it would refuse to melt or drop off, gaining extra purchase in the fibres. Eventually, you took on the appearance of a major hazard to moderate-sized shipping. It simply built up to yet another point of collapsing the human stuffing.

Once, on a very cold, but still night, I had been more active than is usual for advisory staff, which was supposed to be our official role, and needed to loosen up for a while to cool down. The coat had one more surprise up its sleeves for me. When I finally managed to ease the two-inch buttons through the two-inch and a very little bit buttonholes, I opened it up to find that the combination of my unusual energy and the intense cold had produced a thin layer of frost on the lining!

In later years, the powers relented, and technical staff began to be issued with more and more clothing, including the most vicious boots imaginable. These were always your size by virtue of the fact that the unsubtlety of the steel toecaps worked towards hacking your toes back to fit.

By then, though, I had become "management" and qualified for a half share in an experimental raincoat. Unlike the old greatcoat, which did have its moments, this high-tech, multi-layered, seven ply, state-of-the-art garment managed to be useless in every climatic state in which I tried it. It remains today, as new, on a peg in the hall.

★

Nowadays, the stressing of the rails up to the equivalent of 21°C is being done by hydraulically stretching them. As ever, progress equals loss of romance and the sense of uncertainty. When I started we did it properly, by actually putting heat into the rail to make it expand as nature intended. Propane heaters mounted in baffles thrust heat into the rails, and the expansion over the next one hundred feet in front measured until it equated to the design temperature, at which point the rails were quickly fastened down again. A perfect imitation of the sun shining from four inches above the rail over ten feet of track in the middle of the night; what could be more natural? And foolproof, too! Well, in all the jobs that I was involved in, using this pure method of reproducing the sun's effect precisely, it never ever worked properly once!

Human error played a small part at all times.

I first met up with the rail-warming tackle at Shipley, under the guidance of one Jumping Joe Davis, a breezy, easy-going character, fairly well up in the Leeds Drawing Office, who tended to bounce about with an enthusiasm born out of a belief that nothing could ever go wrong, and when it did it would only take a jiffy to put right. Whenever I was out with Joe, I couldn't lose the impression that everything was planned, choose what, and that he always had an answer ready for any situation. Possibly the most dangerous of colleagues to ever put your trust in, reliable only in that if there are two choices, he'll take the wrong one, and ever convinced that the best way is the quickest possible one; in short, a raving optimist.

This was not strictly a night job, but a six o'clock start on a very cold dark morning is almost there, and was a necessary event for me to progress to many solo nights in the future. The heating trolley was already set up by the time I got there. It used to be a characteristic of anything developed for the railway, by the railway, that they'd put it together and work with it too closely. Never would they take twenty paces back and take a look at what they'd produced, to consider the effect it had on the very impressionable Great British Public, as they watched us at work on a Sunday morning. What we had here was a platelayer's trolley with two large propane gas cylinders stood upright on it. Fore and aft was what looked like two sets of garden trellis that had blown over, running on small wheels, with lengths of tin channelling curved over the rails. Overall it looked like a half-successful attempt by the *Blue Peter* team to make a sunbed during a glut of toilet rolls and empty Fairy Liquid bottles. It only wanted a broken windscreen and a couple of used exhausts and you could have called it a scrapyard.

"What's that, then, lads?" – local rep of the Great British Public, plus dog, from over the fence as daylight broke.

"Experimental radio link," said Joe, typically, as I was to find out in time. I later had a lot of experience of his skills at digging holes, climbing in, and then digging deeper.

"Oh, aye. And what's it reckon t'do, then?"

"It sends messages by them transmitters over the rails at the front, and receives them through the back ones."

"So why the gas bottles, 'cos ah can tell that's what tha's got theer on t'trolley? Why is t'a warmin' up t'rails like that?"

"That's to get more important messages through easier, electronics move down rails away from the heat faster than if they're cold. You've heard of hot lines?"

"Oh aye. So why's it on a trolley then, to move up and down?"

"That's so that the signals set off in the right direction. There's no point sending a message from here for Carlisle and finding it ending up in Leeds; we've to give it a nudge towards Carlisle at first, y'see."

"Gerraway! So what's t'stop it just goin' off round t'corner and endin' up in Bradford?"

"My young assistant, Mike, here'll explain. I've got to go see that it's set up right. Come down when you're ready, Mike – no rush." With which Joe escaped, leaving me to try and work out an explanation as to how what he'd been putting forward as a communication centre doubled as rail stressing tackle. I explained to our neighbour that Joe was only allowed out into the community on Sundays, and that his attendant nurse was taking five in the cabin. I suggested to him that he pop out later, in a couple of hours, when we'd got it going properly, but the old lad said that he'd settle for "sendin' t'dog down to tek a look, 'cos ah'll get more bloody sense from him than ah'll get from thy dozy mate, theer!"

I settled for telling Joe that I'd given the old fellow his name and work telephone number, and had promised that Joe would send out some leaflet about it to him. Joe seemed a shade upset by this, but he tended to treat me more warily in future. Not that it put him off altogether.

Our gang had unfastened the rails in front of us, and lifted them onto blocks over which they were supposed to slide. We were still in an era when the idea of putting the rails on rollers had yet to be thought up. Railway pioneers were proud and jealous of their skills. They'd invent the wheel only when they were good and ready, and not before, and they certainly wouldn't listen to rumours that someone else had done it already.

"Right, I reckon we're ready, Mike. Now I'm going to turn the gas on to each burner in turn, and I want you to fire the spark gun in them, OK? Right front left first; here goes!"

There was a loud hissing noise from the general direction of the equipment. I was assuming that "Right front left" meant that he was ready for the front burners to his left to be lit up. I fired the small flint pistol he'd given me under the baffle. Nothing happened.

"Sorry, that was back left, right? These tubes are all jumbled. I'll try for the right one now. No, hold on, it's me, I'm getting right and left mixed up from here. Try that set," – pointing. "And listen, why not set light to some paper, the gun might not be sparking enough."

I did as I was told with a handy sheet of newspaper at the lineside, while Joe turned on the gas. We could tell that he'd got it right this time, since the force of its blast blew the blazing paper back up the banking, starting a small grass fire, but failing to light the burners.

"My fault; too much pressure. Tell you what, I'll turn them all on very low, and you just nip round 'em with the paper in turn. No, that must have been too much again. Just hang back a bit, these knobs are a touch keen."

I stood back, examining my wristwatch to see if was fireproof as well as its advertised properties at ten fathoms; I only wondered, since I'd just lost all the hair off my left arm as Joe's enthusiastic blast shot a torch of flame up inside my coat sleeve. I turned to watch my instructor and mentor leaping off and on the trolley, testing the pressure of gas coming from each burner, until he was satisfied, and knew exactly where each tap should be turned to.

"Right you are, Mike, I've got them all on low, try 'em now!"

Propane gas is a funny thing to work with. It's considerably heavier than air. You can't really smell it, because very little rises to the nose, and on a still day it will tend to hang about in a layer, around ankle height. A potentially explosive sheet.

It was a very still cold day, that Sunday morning. I returned to using the official flint-spark starting pistol again. This time there was a satisfyingly loud "Woooof", and the equally pleasing sight of Joe stood aloft on the trolley like Joan of Arc, surrounded by a momentary flash inferno. I'd lost some stray hair poking from under my cap, but Joe, as he stepped off the trolley in a shakily nonchalant manner, looked by his expression to have lost a lot more.

"Did you manage to get through, then?" called a voice from the fence.

This incident put Joe out of sorts for the day. We got beyond the halfway point, marking and checking the expansion over each hundred-foot length to Joe's satisfaction. As I found to be usually the case, we'd one rail moving far better than the other, and Joe had no intention of shutting down one side of the heaters, knowing that we'd have to light them up again later, so he took the illogical decision to overstretch one rail by the amount the other refused to move. It wasn't for me to query his actions, and when he decided that we would take a break I happily went along with it. Once more, he was not going to shut down the heaters, and we could see that there was plenty of gas left, because the frost on the outside of the bottles was over halfway up them, which was a fair indication of the liquid level within.

Only ten minutes later, or maybe twenty, I nipped out to have a look at things, wanting to get on with the job. I was surprised to see that the trolley, the gas and the burners were now a foot up in the air, due to the rails, which were secured fore and aft, having buckled upwards under the intense, and very local heat. In case this was a normal situation, I thought to mention it in a sort of casual manner to Joe, but hadn't intended him spilling his second cup down his front as he grabbed the water carrier to throw any chance of future cups of tea over the rails. The trolley was stuck fast, with the rails having nipped inwards as well, and it took all the gang to push it over this blistering hump. Even though we'd moved on to a quite different section of the fence by now, a familiar voice asked if that was the right wavelength that we'd been trying for.

I was supposed to go solo after two accompanied, and instructional stressing jobs, so, with the rather negative experiences of the first, I needed to get to grips with my second session, but held out no great hopes when I found it was to be with Hugo Langton. Hugo, or Huge, as he was familiarly known, was a most pleasant clown. He was a bit rounded, but this was only made significant by his shortfall in length. It was he who had the small air pistol in the office, firing paper pellets at the tracers' bottoms as they bent erotically over their drawing boards. Great for fun, good for exotic chat, Hugo was feared useless for instruction. I was both right and wrong. Prior discussion at a site meeting, and a rundown of how he was to attack the job between Elland and Brighouse, was truly illuminating. How we actually went about it was a variation based loosely on the theme, at times inspired by panic, but rooted in nonchalance.

We were stuck with one of those worst of all starting times, three in the morning, with no transport laid on. Last trains and buses dumped me at the PWay Office on Elland old station at half past eleven, but even at that time Huge was already there, busy getting himself outside his first mug of tea, and taking an initial plunge into Mrs Huge's snap tin of delight.

"What the hell d'we do for three hours, before we can get started, Hugh?"

"Four, actually. It'll take ages to get line possession, offload the tackle and water the lads. If we keep our heads down in here, we needn't go out until four, soonest."

"So what d'we do, then?"

"Oh, I don't know… we'll fit in a few brews, bit of shut eye, some erudite and enlightening conversation… p'r'aps even a bit of instruction on the finer points of rail stressing. Who've you been out with up to now?"

"Jumping Joe Davis."

"Right, so you now know how to get a job done in the least possible time. Tonight we'll learn how to get the most out of a job, in strictly financial terms. For a start off, not getting any transport has added five hours on straight away, allowing that we left Leeds at ten. I bet you didn't get that much time in on the whole job with Joe. Rushes things too much. Anyway, I'm off to look at the ceiling for a bit. Shut up, and read summat!"

With which my guru for the night lay back on the couch, and slotted a handkerchief under his glasses. Within ten minutes there was no sign of life but for the slight fluttering of the hankie. I couldn't relax like this; I'd be as tight as a Durex on a melon until we actually got going – when I could see progress towards getting back home. It was a long enough night ahead, and I wasn't interested in seeing how much longer we could make the job last. By half past two I'd exhausted every possible way of wasting time, broken by two more negative conversations with Hugh as he rose for another mashing and a pee, before resuming his sleep with a casual expertise. Fortunately the lads started to turn up about then. They were better known to me than Hugh, although it became apparent that they knew of him well enough.

"Don't let him drag it out, Mike. Ah've a pigeon show in Cleckheaton this aft! Ah'm told he's a bugger for takin' his time."

"An' ah'm facin' a withdrawal of conjugglin' rights if ah don't get 'er weshin' machine plumbed in afore tonight; thee see toowit, lad – away by ten, latest, OK?"

"He's supposed to be showing me, tonight. I've no control over him at all, really!"

"Right, then it's dahn to us. OK!"

I couldn't see how, but they all seemed to believe it to be within their reach to get the job done sharper than Hugo's financial ambitions dictated.

We got possession of the line by three thirty, having to wait for the sacred newspaper train to go through, twenty minutes late, and I managed to prise a reluctant Hugh away from his diminishing food mountain. The lads were already well away, unclipping the two rails, and their twinkling dance of Tilley lamps was rounding the first bend in the far distance as a small group of four followed, jacking up the rails and putting the slide blocks under them. A last pair of men were setting up the heating trolley, and needed little help from us – not that they were going to get any offered by Hugh, as it might endanger his plans by speeding the job up too much. It was a cool night, without wind – ideal for stressing, and Hugh saw to the lighting up of the burners. In the dark, as opposed to the early light of my last job at Shipley, he seemed to move effortlessly from propane bottles to flame jets, lighting each easily and quickly with the spark gun, and without what I'd come to believe was the compulsory explosion. For all his "steady away" approach, Hugh had already gained twenty minutes over Joe's performance, and had retained his eyebrows in the process. I thought better of mentioning this to Hugh, as it might well have upset him.

Eventually the unclipping team returned, having unfastened the half-mile as far as the distant adjustment switches, which adjoined the old jointed track beyond. We were away.

Once more I found that the rail expansions were hit and miss, as we treated each hundred feet in turn, but Hugh worked on the basis of achieving the correct extension in one rail at least, before having the men fasten them down. Again I could see ways of running the job out a bit longer, but true to the lads, and especially myself, I said nothing to Hugh.

These particular clips were a shade more difficult to hammer back than usual, and every sixty feet of the hardwood-timbered track had four more than you'd find on concrete, so the rail-warming team were doing a bit better than the fastening down gang. So much so, that we got a shade too far ahead of them, aided by Hugh's constant singing, and the noise of the burners. Add to this that with long-welded track, the ringing in the rails as the lads hammered back the clips was as loud at thirty feet as three hundred. Ideally, the main gang should be reinstating the rails immediately behind the heating tackle, but we were relying on our little team working alongside the trolley, putting the odd clips in, just to hold the last section at the expansion we'd managed. Hugh was quite untroubled to find that when the hammering stopped, and the lads had all gone for their break, there was some two hundred yards of free rail behind us.

"Right, then, we may as well take five as well."

"Shouldn't we go back to where they've got to with the burners, Hugh?"

"Strictly speaking, yes, but it won't harm; it'll be "reet enough for t'railway'" – an expression I heard at least a hundred times in my career. "We'll just hold on till they catch up." Hugh's instincts for prolonging work did not extend to doing the job twice over.

We joined the lads in the accompanying coach with loco on the opposite line. Intent on their early finish, they didn't stop for long and soon returned to their pinning down. Hugh put aside his tin, leaving four doorsteps of marmalade for later, and emptied his mug. I got up to leave as well.

"Where're you off?"

"I thought we'd be getting cracking again."

"Oh, no. Wait for the lads to catch us up. Take another ten or so."

For once I managed to join the gentle snoring of the horizontal Hugh. (This was a skill I noticed about him, on the nights we occasionally met up in the future. Whatever raw materials he was presented with, he could make a nest out of them, and a fairly comfortable one at that.) I woke suddenly, and found that we'd been down for the best part of three-quarters of an hour. I raised the dead, who showed no great concern over the matter, and even reached to make another cup. It was now the cold light of a misty dawn, and I was alert and fresh, working out quickly that the roles had now been reversed. Our heating trolley stood isolated as the gang had caught us up and passed on with thoughts of pigeons and domestic bliss in mind, and were out of sight round the bend. Hugh was now faced with bringing them back to unfasten again, while we carried on with the heating. He then showed a depth of diplomatic awareness with which I would not have credited him. Against all the rules, he grabbed another sandwich, and decided not to cause upset, but to sort of carry on regardless.

To ease his conscience he fired the burners up to full, and proceeded steadily on towards the gang, having absolutely no effect on the fastened-down rails, other than that there were a few surprised crows who settled to perch briefly on the rails behind us, picking up remnants of his last bits of sandwich, and toasting their feet at the same time.

We passed the gang after a couple of hundred yards or so, and resumed textbook-stressing to a higher temperature on Hugh's argument that it would all roll out over the untreated length in a day or two of traffic, once more declaring that it was "near enough for t'railway"!

Two buses and a train had me back home for one o'clock, a bath and bed. I had to meet Hugh in the Leeds Office next morning to witness him making out the necessary de-stressing form, solemnly declaring that this half-mile of the Up line between Brighouse and Elland had been properly stressed according to the handbook, so help him God.

*

Mention in the Club that you're going on a drainage job tonight, and they start moving away from you immediately. There's perception of only one kind of drain, and they don't want to know you again until you're the right side of two baths and inside a full change of clothing. In reality there's little else more satisfying than a night spent in a ditch, following the rail-mounted trencher, from its initials popularly called the Rag Man's Trumpet for some unknown reason. I would watch fascinated as it released pockets of built-up water trapped for years in the track, freeing it to run into a new drainage system being installed immediately behind me. The water's fresh, relatively clean, and quite smell-free. We were never ever intentionally required to work in nasty stuff like sewage. We got mucky, true; but it was always good clean muck. Until Marsden Station. A job which promised to be a doddle, but then, not everything lives up to its promise in life.

Strictly speaking, I could have left the gang lads to do it by themselves, as the bottom of the trench was to be a steady metre below rail level throughout, and a reliable outfall had already been made, but I went along anyway. A track gradient of something like 1 in 150 provided a good guideline for renewing the old central drain between the platforms, which had become hopelessly blocked with – and this is important – fine, unpolluted, clay. This would, over years, have found its way down from Standedge Tunnel, a mile further up.

My purpose on these jobs was to keep a constant check on the trench depth, and see that the team following up were laying the drain exactly to the measurements I'd designed. It meant spending the whole night in the trench, following closely behind the repetitious crunching of the chain of buckets that was the trencher. The machine hauled itself along by way of a winch and cable run out in front of it. A continuous loop of tooth-faced buckets dug into the forward end of the trench, and carried the spoil up to a conveyor system that in turn, and in theory, deposited the muck in wagons on the adjacent track. This worked under ideal conditions, but any large lumps or small rocks could be thrown clear of the wagons, while excessively wet stuff could try to make the complete journey round the chain, depositing itself on the helmeted technical lad in the trench. At gaps between wagons it could well drop through the space and onto the track, unless watched. The teeth coped well with compacted muck, clay and even solid shale, but tended to come out runner-up when meeting solid rock.

We technical staff were also there to work out a way round any problems which might crop up, such as a sudden appearance of rock, but Marsden was to be a straightforward drain replacement, digging through ground that had been dug out before, even though it might have been many years ago. There were no problems anticipated at all.

While the two supervisors worked towards gaining track possession and setting up the trains, there was little else to do but pass the time in the cabin, with many of the local lads. In Marsden terms it was winter – which up there stretches between September 30 and May 1 – and that meant there had to be a fire in the hearth. It was also night, and that extended the definition of winter to exclude only the second half of July, and the first two weeks of August. Furthermore, a fire wasn't a fire unless it took up the whole space between the grate and the lower projection of the chimney. Creosote was bubbling in the cracks of the door, yet, as one, the men only acknowledged the heat by setting aside the odd cap or scarf, "So as ah'll feel t'benefit when wi've to go aht."

There was a spot of muttering among them, based on their unhappiness about the work we were to do on their beloved length. "Tearin' up a perfictly good drain. Bloody vandalism, an' a waste on good money, 'f ye ask me!"

"But it's blocked solid – there's no water going through it. It's serving no useful purpose."

"Nobbut needs a pull-thro', that pipe's as sound as t'day it were put in."

"You tried a pull-through, and look what happened."

"Wrang engine. It were nobbut ower-powerful. Bloody writhed at it!"

Their answer to a blocked drain, rodding having failed, was to hijack a loco during one of the Sunday possessions in the tunnel. Problem drains – ones that had a tendency towards getting made up with clay – would have a strong wire cable running through them. One end, emerging from a catch-pit, would be wound round the loco buffers, and the other, at the far end of the blockage, would have three massive links of wagon coupling chain attached to it. Every gang had a set of links; they pinched them from trains of wagons stabled in their local sidings overnight. They were hidden away so that innocence could be feigned when the loco and shunter returned to pick up the wagons, finding only half of them moving due to the missing link.

"Bloody kids!" was all they got out of the gang.

I'd seen this drain clearance system used, quite illegally, to great effect, the loco moving steadily away and pulling the cable through the drain with the link on the end forcing a long floppy cylinder of clay to snake out of the catch-pit. It was like toothpaste coming out of the tube when you press for too long. (In fact that's not a bad comparison. I have heard tell of lads in years past using the superfine clays that block some drains as toothpaste, mixed with a bit of jam to make it palatable – which I suppose was a bit counterproductive.)

Anyway, the method failed at Marsden. The powerful loco – over-powerful, as it turned out – pulled so mightily and the blockage resisted so stubbornly, that the ground surged upwards as a shockwave ran along the top, and the drain was pulled to the surface. A lot of covering up had to be done to hide the result.

"Well, ah still think tha's muckin' up a good 'un."

"It was picking nothing up. It's not even a carrier, and the station's swamped with water! You see, when we start digging, we'll loose loads of water from out of t'track."

"It's a Sunday forrus, George, whatever tha sez! Gi'up moanin'."

"And you can clean out a new drain, which is a good bonus. If it's bunged up solid it's no good for you and it's no good for t'railway!"

"Nah, tha's gorra point theer! 'Appen it's an idea after all!"

Then from the shadows well away from the fire: "Well, ah reckon it wain't be as straightforrard as t'a thinks." – Cairo Bill.

"How's t'a mean, Bill?"

"Nivver mind, ah just think tha's bitin' off more than tha can chew, that's all."

Cairo Bill, sixty-something, couldn't read or write – knew which end of a shovel was which, could pick one up at seven on a Sunday morning, and put it down warm at six the same night – capable within his limits and able to put a tinge of apprehension in me.

"What do you know, that we don't, Bill?"

"Nuthin'. Just sayin'."

With this gang, I'd been used as an educated expert on what their chances on the pools were in mathematical terms. I'd been required to explain the basic chemistry of why their kettles furred up, or didn't. I'd produced satisfactory explanations as to why it was warmer in the village than three miles further on up in the Pennines, half a mile nearer the sun. (A problem that they'd understood, unlike the great thinker that was Harry Hanson.) We'd run over the working of the television, and why they couldn't be run on distilled water like their old radios were. (I'd given up on the idea that having the batteries topped up and recharged was what they saw as running on water – and Cairo's assertion that his ran on paraffin just had to be left as one of life's mysteries!) Even the advantages of a washing machine over a posser and peggy tub, or even a stone on the canal bank, had been scientifically looked at. Yet, while they accepted that I might be capable of designing a bridge, could set out a fresh railway curve in a field using a theodolite and string, and could quote formulae and calculations relating to the flow of liquids through pipes of various shapes and sizes, I knew nowt about their drains!

So it was, with poorly disguised smugness, that I stood in the trench an hour later, calf-deep in water satisfyingly oozing from beneath the two tracks. Due to a last-hour hitch, we were having to dig downhill, which meant that any water we released came down with us. This did not worry me too much, as I had now broken into a clearer piece of drain, and it was getting away slowly. But Cairo Bill continued to trouble me. He would keep leaving his allotted task at regular intervals to come and have a look at me down in the trench.

"All reet still, lad?"

"Alright, Bill. Why?"

"As long as tha's all reet." And away back to where he should be.

Around half past two we broke through a nine-inch-diameter earthenware pipe running across the lines. It was bunged up solid, and shouldn't have been there.

"Ahhh," said Bill.

Quarter of an hour later we hit another, by which time the first had started to eject a creeping sausage of the most foul-smelling material imaginable. The second bled much sooner. The third relieved itself immediately, with a loud belch. So suddenly, that I was out of the trench like a rabbit. In all we cut through six foul sewers crossing the railway, now pouring their collective filth into the trench, where I was standing. The night wore on, and got riper by the hour. Even less impressed than me was the pipe-laying team, two wagon-lengths back, and packing pipes to level in this most unhealthy of streams. Cairo Bill had stopped coming over to look, since he could now use other senses. As dawn broke, even flies were turning back and forming picket lines. Very few breakfasts were tackled that morning.

By eight we had connected up to the outfall, and had back-filled with stone ballast over the new pipes, but I was left with a mystery, and with it a problem. Elliot made one of his early Sunday visits. These were accurately timed to coincide with me packing up my things ready for off home. I've put many an extra hour in having to escort the boss through the job, and taking whatever criticism there was coming, from he who had been in a warm bed all night. He was in time to see the broken pipe ends before the trench was back-filled. With daylight, the whole thing was even more worrying as each of the six interceptions coincided with the back doors of a row of six terraced houses way up the hill above the station. Further investigations were left for the next day.

Very often, Elliot would give me a quick lift home when we met up on Sunday mornings. Not today, though, as he said he needed to go a roundabout way back, and I'd be better off in the gang bus as arranged. This had nothing to do with the fact that I'd not escaped the ambience of the night, and had about me the aroma of one who had been mucking out a cowshed in between breaks of relaxing in a pig sty. My boots I decided to just lose.

Next day, bright and early, I caught the train up to Marsden, to be followed later on by Elliot, and Jack Senior. While they were concerned as to the source of the effluent we were picking up, I was more concerned about what was happening to it after we'd given it free passage down our new drain. While on my own, I shook a quantity of fluorescent dye – the violent electric-green type – down the outfall catch-pit, to see if it reappeared anywhere further down the track. There was a water system, the famous Marsden Main, that ran all the way to Huddersfield and fed the loco sheds at Hillhouse, and I was rather concerned that I'd not managed to get into that. The idea of filling the tender of a crack express with the contents of a watered-down cesspit I found intriguing, but unnecessary.

I met up with the gang, tidying up after the Sunday, and made a beeline for Cairo Bill.

"How much d'you know about these sewers, Bill?"

"Nowt, lad. Kem as a complete surprise."

"So why all the interest, then? You were expecting something to turn up all night!"

"Nowt on't sort! Ah jus' felt it in mi watter, that's all!"

"Tha's wastin' thi time wi' Bill," said John Oldroyd, the ganger. "Don't tha think ah've bin onter 'im all mornin' afore tha kem. He knaws summat, that's fer sure, and he's got summat t'do wi'it, but he'll not give. He's bin on this patch all his life. Ah'm nobbut a comer-in, yet ah've bin 'ere fifteen year!"

Later that day, Jack and Elliot visited the cottages above the station, where we suspected the problem came from. Everyone was out at work, except for one exceptionally old, and rather deaf lady.

From an unsatisfactory conversation, heavily weighted on her side, both investigators managed to get little more than a telling off. As soon as she cottoned on that they were the "men from t'Council about t'drains" she laid in something heavy, shouting that it was thirty years since she'd complained, and why had it taken them so long to get here.

They eventually managed to get away, with abuse drifting down behind them, and were intercepted by a lady pulling a shopping trolley up the hill, and about to go into the end house.

"You been upsetting old Ada, then? It'll take weeks to quieten her down, now. What's the trouble?"

Elliot explained, while Jack continued to fend off distant insults and expletive-loaded suggestions, by continually raising his hat to Ada, who seemed to take this as a threatening gesture. Meanwhile, Mrs Sykes was telling Elliot of the troubles they'd had some twenty-five years or so back, when all the drains had seized up over a period of a couple of months, causing the Council to lay a new main sewer along the backs of the houses, and out into the road. Ada had been away when this had been done, and remained convinced that her complaints had gone unattended. So the drains I'd broken through were what was left of an old system, and I'd managed to expose material of a very mature nature – twenty-five years mature, in fact, which accounted for the extraordinary quality of the smell.

Together, the three of us wandered along the length of the drain as far as the outfall. Water was running freely, showing precisely how much the job had needed doing, and how successful the night's work had turned out, but for the bit of trouble. Satisfied that no damage had been done, my two mates were now quite relaxed about everything, while I was still nattering to myself as to where I'd dumped a load of ancient sewage. It was a very pleasant spring afternoon by now.

"I always like this time of year, especially up here," said Jack. "It's the yellow season, when all the broom's out along the bank side, with the gorse not far behind, and there's the wild daffs, down towards the river there. And doesn't everything look fresh? New greens coming through all over, fresh grass against the old black stuff. And that really light green you get as this year's leaves start bursting. I've always been partial to spring colours rather than the rust of autumn. Green as far as you can see, topped with the purple of the heather as you get to the tops.

"Ay up, though! Never seen that before, mind! See theer, yonder, beyond t'canal, in front of that row of cottages... see that small reservoir what they use for washing t'wool in t'mill on t'back of it. Are you with me? Look in that near corner! Can you see t'bloody water turning a bright green? Now weer the buggery is that comin' from?"

Felix

My dad, a dedicated Christian, drilled into me the concept of man's equality with man.

"Just remember, we all come from the same mould... some just turn out mouldier than others."

I wish I'd been able to show him Felix. No one could ever have made a mould that bad – and then used it.

★

I pleaded a lack of job application forms at Huddersfield; I worked on achieving exactly average height and weight for a male so that I wouldn't stand out from the crowd; I never learnt to drive a car as this became an assumed and essential skill in promotional moves; I never spoke out on management training courses; I never handled a typist, tracer or young female clerk in order that I could preserve my terminal dullness; I took work home rather than appear keenly sat at my desk after hours; I only went into dark pubs, and then drank nothing but Guinness, but I was still hounded down, honed for promotion, analysed, interviewed, and assessed. Ladders were placed at my feet. I pleaded ambitional vertigo, but they eventually spiked my pleasantly idyllic dead-end career on the Area out at Huddersfield, and reeled me in to the nerve centre.

For years the Brass had been trying to tempt, cajole and order me back into the Leeds District Office. They'd get me involved in project jobs at Huddersfield, and then in bigger ones playing away from home, all without changing my mind. Then other things conspired, in a short period, to take away the attraction of life out at Huddersfield, where you more or less ran things your own way. First Bill died, following a final heart attack. A year later Elliot moved to the higher profile of the Leeds Area office, and in-between management hit me below the belt with their trump card, mixing up more than my metaphors – they sent Felix Ferris out to be my assistant for a ten-year spell, which, according to the calendar, apparently lasted no longer than twelve months.

Here was the one weakness about the perfection of life at Huddersfield. In a two- or three-man office you were well and truly stuck with the company chosen for you. I'd generally made the best of it, and got along with all the long-termers so far. Fly-by-night management embryos could usually be suffered for their four- or eight-week stays, though they were a varied lot. From limpet eagerness to having a total inability to make intelligent social contact with any other life form but their own kind. I'd spotters, posers, egotists, first-class honours, first-class conners, prats, pillocks, and complete wazzocks. Masterminds, with the drawing ability of a crippled stick insect, and others, with brains like empty Smarties, who could draw at the speed of a fourteenth-century copy monk and share his practical knowledge of railway civil engineering. Somehow I coped – until Felix came along. I had a year of him, sometimes diluted by the addition of one of the degree lads, and sometimes in concentrate form, as when Elliot thoughtlessly and quite selfishly disappeared into hospital for an operation. After that year I'd have agreed to go anywhere, rather than chance another Felix.

Had he lived, Bill might have watered Felix down a bit, but his sense of comic irony made him choose the very day of Felix's arrival to pull his final black joke on me by shunting himself off into the siding of eternal life, leaving me completely on my own with this incomprehensible bulk. Wilf and Percy, the chainmen, tried in their own way to knock the stuffing out of Ferris – but he was so badly packed in the first place that you merely moved it about. I mean, if you hit him in one spot, it would only lead to a bulge somewhere else, and he'd present you with a quite new situation to cope with. He was both naive and amazingly cocky with the chainmen, so that he became their most challenging and potentially improvable patient to date. Bill would have reacted in one of two ways towards this one; either to completely ignore him as of no satisfying prospect, or he'd have put Felix to the sword. It was such a waste; I'd have given anything to see the confrontation. Elliot's long-term absence should normally have led to a substitute from Leeds or York, but due to the upper level's insupportable opinion of my abilities, I was landed with Elliot's job, and far worse, Felix was entrusted with mine.

Felix Ferris cut an unusual figure – no, that's too sharp a phrase. He couldn't cut a tooth. It suggests having a distinct edge, a dependably mappable outline. Felix was perpetually out of focus, a doughy mass, suffering internal tectonic movement. He'd pour himself into chairs, and simply adopt the shape of anything he might lean on. There was probably six feet something of him, if measured along his longest axis, which was about as definable as the dead centre of a mountain range. This convoluted column started with a pair of enormous feet which would fall dead flat on every step, but at a variety of turned-in angles, and it continued upwards in a random manner to end in a wisp of fair icing. We were never able to get a shot of his full height since his frame never managed to align itself all in one go. You could set off upwards with confidence, and some part or something would be positioned off skew, and it'd throw you. He had the most relaxed body shape imaginable; "hourglass" was a description I'd once put to it, like a panda sat on one made of rubber, with about fifty minutes'-worth of sand already run through. Put him in front of one of those distorting mirrors and he'd probably reflect back as Superman. He always carried a hurt, but dignified expression, except when he felt that he'd got one over. Then it would change to a slanting smirk, exaggerated by his circular spectacles, having him take on the appearance of a taxidermist's nightmare – an owl dribbling off its perch. In mental terms, you couldn't actually call Felix thick, he just had a learning curve the radius of the earth. This curve also had many a thousand tangents of enquiry, hinting at a healthy intelligence and an investigative mind, but you can always have too much of a good thing, as anyone spending an hour with Felix, and answering the sixtieth daft query, would agree. No doubt his mother loved him, perhaps because, being so close, she never saw him all in one go, like the world had to.

He was one of the factors changing my life at the time; a situation that my conservatism always rebelled against, and reacted badly to. Felix did move on after a year, to be replaced by one Eric Edwards, a solid dependable lad, good enough to furtively take over the reins as I was slipping gently into the new life in Leeds. It was during the final day's transfer of my gear from Huddersfield, that a truly emotional scene took place as Eric presented me with a carefully collated package of treasures that he'd labelled "The Felix Museum". The entire anthology and accumulation of artefacts had been put together in just the one fortnight of overlap between Felix and Eric, a fortnight which stuck in my memory like hair down a bathplug, if only for the fact that it had been the first time I'd ever seen a man cry. Eric, as he'd neared the end of the two-week period of handover, had come to sit in with me, while I was pretending to be Elliot behind the tomb of a desk, and he poured out the frustration of just one day's work alongside Felix. A day of illogical decisions, irrational behaviour, and with chainmen at the end of their tether.

To be made curator of what was to become the notorious Felix Museum collection showed a close professional bond between the two of us. Items were added in later years as my fame in this honorary position spread to other offices in which Felix had been beached, but restricting this report to just the first fortnight of collation may throw more light on the subject than any amount of descriptive prose.

"The Felix Museum Collection" – compiled by E Edwards, and presented to M Collins on the occasion of his promotion to Leeds.

Exhibit 1 – Ink Bottle:
This is an empty Indian Ink bottle, complete with its rubber dispensing tube and suction cap, for filling up drawing pens. It has been meticulously washed clean – a very difficult and time-consuming procedure with such a permanent mixture. Why? There's so little use for an empty ink bottle and dispenser when you've run out of orphaned hamsters to feed. Besides which, Felix wouldn't have known one end of a hamster from the other, which would have proved equally confusing for the baby.

Exhibit 2 – Plan:
A 36" x 24" drawing, which, according to the title block, was of the boundary of New Pudsey Station car park at a scale of 10 feet:1 inch. It consists of just five lines, with no points of

reference, and looks like the plotted directions on a map of buried treasure. Yet the drawing and survey had taken well over a week to do, another time-consuming procedure.

Exhibit 3 – Eraser:
Electric erasers were rare, and our team at Huddersfield had managed to acquire one. It must have been the last one to be made, since the Leeds Office, who had coincidentally just lost one, couldn't get another from Central Stores. With this spinning eraser, we'd managed to pocket a large stock of purpose-made cylindrical rubbers to fit into its drill chuck. Despite this, the Felix Museum boasts the remains of a carefully pared-down 3" ink rubber, cut to an inch-long cylinder, a quarter of an inch in diameter, to fit the chuck. To have produced this must have been yet another considerable time-consuming job.

Exhibit 4 – Minutes of a site meeting compiled by F Ferris:
A stencilled foolscap of minutes of a meeting held to decide on the procedure for the demolition and tidy clearance of the site of a redundant building. The contractors throughout are referred to as "Messers" Hardwick.

Exhibit 5 – Telephone Message:
"Wring York 3631" (Eric had failed to control his feelings, and had defaced the note by substituting "neck" in pencil.)

Exhibit 5a – Another Telephone Message:
"Ring Keighley": the recipient on return spent a good hour searching through staff based at Keighley, with increasing anger on both sides until Keith Lee rang him for the second time.

Exhibit 6 – Level Book:
In this are recorded Ferris's readings during a level survey, compiled by reading off the chainman's staff as it is placed on targets from a few feet to up to one hundred yards away. Due presumably to the surveyor's eyesight, readings at the remote distance are recorded to within ten centimetres (far too vague), whereas the closest readings are to the nearest millimetre, that is, inclusive of the thickness of any rust on the rail. When translated to the drawing board, such extreme variations in precision are plain daft. To utilise the millimetre readings would require a full-

scale drawing at least – in which case you'd need a sheet of paper ten feet deep and half a mile long.

Exhibit 7 – Letter and Drafts:
From a copy on his file of the finished letter, we gathered that Felix was attempting to compose a note to the Personnel Department, informing them of his success in a recent GCE "O" Level examination, so that his records could be amended, and any appropriate cash awards made. Ten discarded draft letters were recovered from the wastebin, by the devoted Edwards, every one on headed railway letter forms. By using a vague knowledge of geological dating, they could be placed in precise order. What the subject of the exam was may be guessed from the last letter recovered. It is significant. The complete series of drafts is produced below:

   (a) <u>Examination Resutt</u>. (sort of underlined)
       On the 8th June I took (breakdown of inspiration)
   (b) <u>Examination Result</u>. (quicker breakdown, but again underlined)
   (c) Carbon copy of (b)
   (d) Another copy
   (e) Examination Result. (once more the Muse dries up.)
   (f) (Heading obliterated)
   [underneath in rough] Examination Result
   On the 8th June 1971 (one and a half lines obliterated) On the
      26th of this month I sat for my "O" level exam in
      (indecipherable) (obliteration) (obliteration) was informed
      that I had passed with a Grade 5
   (g) Totally blank piece of paper
   (h) Exam Resu (crossed out.)
   (i) (with carbon copy)
<u>Examination Result</u>. (underlined)
On the 26th of this month I was informed that I had passed my
      Examination in "O" level English Lang

Reported *sic* throughout.

★

Felix managed to get everyone's back up at some time or other, even that of PWay Supervisor Jack Senior, the most docile of men. I remember it had been declared Mental Health Week, or some such, so I was in a "look after No. 1" frame of mind when I "loaned" Felix to Jack for "experience". Who it was gained the most experience is debatable, but a day of constant questioning by Felix ensued, about every little detail, even to an automatic "Why?" when Jack announced that he was going to the toilet. He was eventually kicked out into the yard to wash the personnel carrier, a standard BR gang bus; "…and don't forget the roof!" was Jack's parting shot in an attempt to keep him at bay for as long as possible.

As it turned out, the task took Felix the best part of the week to complete, since the bus was in daily use from half past seven until half past three. Yet every afternoon Felix would be there with his bucket, saucepan (for swilling down) and issue BR shammy leather. It was a desperately slow job the way Felix did it, and illuminates the history of the washed-out ink bottle. He'd wash a square foot at a time, and then stand back to study the results. Sometimes it was better than a previous square, sometimes it proved wanting. Either way, Felix would move to balance the overall effect. Of a morning the bemused gang would find their bus with a tidemark moved further along it each day. Friday, in true Felix logic (start at the bottom and work your way up) was devoted to the roof, the first time anyone had bothered with it, the result of which was that Saturday found the bus decked out in dirty streaks running down all sides, but with a clear translucent yellow roof in showroom condition.

"Why is the roof of the bus yellow, and why can you see through it?" was Felix's question next Monday, as he was being told to start all over again because of the filthy black streaks. Jack had little idea, and cared less, but knew that he was forced to answer. Otherwise Felix's kitten with a ball of wool would nag away for ever.

"It's a psychological experiment by Derby Research," he replied – gaining inspiration from a letter he'd just received that morning about some report or other from them (Derby Research being the source of most innovations on the railway). "It's supposed to work on the lads as they go off on a job; gets them thinking it's nice and sunny out there! Gees them up on the poorer mornings."

"What about when they're going on a night job?" was the next wagon on Felix's train of thought. Jack was beaten, and said so. He was sorry he'd started it when a week later the ganger complained about "some bugger pissin' about wi't'bus!" Appearing from nowhere, stuck on the roof panels, were very primary-school-window pictures of smiling moons and fairy stars.

All this was at an early stage in the Felix era, and I was still wondering just how much responsibility I could give this walloper, not having met such outstanding naiveté and literalism before. I dug back in my mind to some of the gullibility tests that Bill and I used to try out on the graduates. The trouble was they all involved Bill to a large extent, so drastic adaptation was called for. In the past I'd nip out of the office, set up a situation, and have Bill observe the subject's responses, so I changed the idea to a kind of Chinese whispers set-up, albeit with just Felix and me playing.

"Just nipping out for ten minutes, Felix. D'yer think you can take messages if they're asking for me or Elliot?"

Felix visibly swelled in various places, and almost sat up straight until nature and gravity regained control. This was his idea of Being in Charge, and it obviously appealed to him. So then I went over to the Works Supervisors' Office and phoned back across to the Drawing Office, via Hilary on the switchboard. She didn't help much, querying my fitness level in not being able to walk to say what I'd got to say, rather than disturb her and her book, so things had to be explained. In the manner of most women, she saw sociological and psychological experiments in researching the reactions of Felix to presented problems as me "acting like a big kid". More time was wasted as I discussed a theory of mine as to the unsurprising lack of female scientists through the ages, and it all got a bit silly. All I was proposing was presenting Felix with a couple of "situations", in what I vainly hoped were disguised accents. I was never over good at this, and my Asian would always develop into Welsh, and vice versa. Still it was only Felix I had to fool, and nature had given me a nine points start.

"Hello," said the attempted Scotsman, sounding more like broad Yorkshire with a terrifying impediment and throat infection. "Is yon The Engineer?"

"No," replied Felix, "he's out, but I'm Mr Ferris, his assistant." This immediately threw the Caledonian tyke, and it took me time to get my head round the idea of Felix as Elliot's deputy.

"Well, Mr Ferret, I wonder if you can help me."

"I'll certainly try," replied a helpful Mr Ferret. "And it's Ferris, actually, Felix Ferris."

"Feel his what?" I thought to have a short bash at "the get them annoyed, and see how they react" routine.

"Can I help you at all?" Annoying tactics either failing or sailing right over the target's head.

"It's possible," continued McMe. "My name's MacIntyre. I'm a scrap contractor and I've been asked to pick up a load of lead at Springwood Junction. Now I've had a look on the map and the easiest way to get my lorry to site is to drive through the tunnel from Huddersfield Station; it's only half a mile, and I've had a wee look at the tunnel mouth and there looks to be room at the side of the track."

"We have recently singled the track through there," replied Felix, displaying good local knowledge, "and I'm sure a lorry would fit OK at the side," – displaying decision making. "Could you make sure you wait until a train has just come through, and then you'll know there won't be another for a while; oh, and put your headlights on, it's very dark in there," – displaying an affinity with the downright obvious. To any reader at all in doubt, the whole idea was unthinkable.

I felt uncomfortable. So daft was the situation, and so helpful the encouragement that I decided Felix must have rumbled me. Nobody, absolutely nobody with a mental age above three weeks, or having five minutes' experience on the railway, could go along with it. I sat back in the deserted Works office and looked around for inspiration. I found myself staring fixedly at the wall and a picture of a young lady wearing a small hankie. She was called April, and she was smiling back at me. In small print to one side of her were the dates for the month of May. This struck a chord, and I tried again, using an outside line, plus my Cornish Farmer and a couple of feet between me and the phone over which I'd hung a BR checked duster – all this in order to get past Hilary, without further interrogation or research into my sanity. However, when she answered, she asked if I was going to be fooling about all afternoon.

Felix answered, "Hello, Civil Engineer's, how can I help you?"

This time my Welsh, third-generation British native Pakistani answered.

"Hello, boyo, is it the Engineer that you are after being, look you?"

"Not quite," said Felix, "but I'm his chief assistant and he's left me in charge. What can I do for you?"

"My name is Mr Dai Evans," (I was now inextricably trapped in my Taffy Patel). "I'm the Headmaster of Honley Grammar School, in the private sector. My ysgol overlooks the railway just before the short tunnel next to Honley Station." (This was pure showmanship. From many trips to Wales, picking up on the more common roadside signs, I'd collected "Ar Werth" – "For Sale", "Araf" – "Slow", and "Ysgol". As I went on, I was attempting credibility suicide by trying to drag the other two words in as well.) "Do you know it?"

"Certainly!" replied Felix, who I was sure hadn't a clue where Honley was, or even what line it was on. "What can we do for you?"

"Well, it's like this," the tiring accent slipping into the safer haven of upper-class twit. "The school is having an Open Day on May 1st, with a May Day theme, nothing political, don't you know... boyo, and all that, and we would very much like to put up a symbolic maypole. Our ideal focal position would be just on our side of the fence at the top of the railway cutting, but I was wondering whether this would infringe any railway rulings. We already have the pole, all sixty feet of it, though two feet would, of course, be stuck in the ground. Could you advise me at all?"

"May I check up on this one, Mr Evans? I'll have to consult the land plans, but in passing I would recommend a pole of sixty feet being planted at least three feet into the ground... speaking as a Civil Engineer."

"Ay, ye may be right, laddie, you're the expert, after all," agreed Mr Evans, suddenly struck down by another linguistic identity crisis. "Incidentally, once it's up, we'll be leaving it up, with the school flag on it. Brilliant red, it is, with the initials of our school motto on it – 'Superior Teaching Our Password'."

"That'll be fine, it should look quite jolly!"

"Excellent, thank you very much! Oh, and your name, please?"

"Mr Ferris. I'll be in touch within the hour, Mr MacIntyre. Yakky Dar!"

The use of the scrap contractor's name, along with pidgin Welsh, confirmed it; Felix was not as daft as he made out. I was dead sure by now that I'd been copped on both counts. So as to preserve some dignity, I raced over to the nearest shop, bought a small book, costly enough to warrant a bag, and went back to the office with superficial proof of a purpose for going out.

I was somewhat flummoxed to find Felix doing the butterfly stroke through the chest of land plans.

"Oh, good," said the erstwhile Assistant Engineer, "could you remind me where Honley is, please?"

"Penistone Line, third stop," I said cautiously, wondering whether it was me that was being wound up now. "Why?"

"Oh, nothing much, just a query we've had in. I'm sure I can manage… oh, and by the way, a scrap man rang, about collecting that lead at Springwood Junction, but it wasn't anything important." He turned to perform a reverse pike into the plan files again, eventually climbing out with the land details around Honley. These he spread out, took measurements, and baffled me completely by settling down to some complex-looking calculations.

I was still unsure of my ground, and felt distinctly edgy, so I had a mashing and retreated to the relative safety of Elliot's office. There, on the extension, I was both dismayed and relieved to intercept a conversation between Felix and Honley Grammar School. This was after I'd caught him ringing Directory Enquiries for the school's number. Whilst I was now fairly reassured that I was still several streets, if not towns, ahead of the lad, the discussion that followed between Mr Felix Ferris, AMICE (Assmd.), and a confused school secretary, confirmed that he wasn't kidding when displaying his gullibility.

"Honley Grammar School, good morning, the school secretary speaking."

"Hello! Could I speak to Mr Evans, please?"

"Mr Evans? We've no Mr Evans here; have you got the right number? This is Honley Gram—"

"Your headmaster rang me an hour ago, regarding the boundary between us. This is British Rail, the Civil Engineer speaking." And that, I thought to myself, must be the third promotion he's given himself inside an hour!

"Our Head is Mr Sheridan-Hyde…"

"That'll be it, my boy must have misheard." Some hearing defect that, I thought, there's not much difference! And who the hell is this boy supposed to be? Me?

"Are you sure it's Mr Sheridan-Hyde who spoke to you? I do not recall putting a call through."

"Sure! He wanted some information regarding the boundary land between you and the railway."

"We certainly do have such a boundary with the railway. However, I'm afraid that he is not available at the moment, so could you give me a message, please?"

"OK. Would you tell Mr Hyde that Mr Ferris, the British Rail Chief Engineer rang back." (That's it, I thought, there's no further up for him to go, now!) "And regarding the maypole, I have no objections to his proposals, as I've examined the plans and find that should a sixty-foot pole, positioned alongside our joint boundary, fall across the railway cutting at the point he described, it is long enough to be caught by the top of the opposite banking, and remain well clear of traffic. And the flag sounds lovely, tell him. Thank you. Good morning!"

I sat back with a mixture of emotions, swamped by an imagined conversation that would shortly be taking place in the headmaster's office at Honley Grammar School, thankful that the busy Directory Enquiries would be unable to trace this Ferris character, Chief Engineer of Everything To Do With Railways in Huddersfield, should Honley Grammar pursue the matter.

★

As a subject for correction, Felix fair flummoxed the two chainmen, being a one-off in their experience. He simply didn't respond to their basic charm-school tactics in the way he was supposed to. They threw the lot at him. Anything subtle he just did as advised, with a sulky expression. Blatantly obvious wind-ups he took on where his chin occasionally made an appearance, shooting back a sad stare at them that only went to make them feel guilty and uneasy. We had many disturbed dinnertime discussions on how to deal with the lad, on that glorious once-a-week day when Felix was at day-release college. He just didn't fit into either of their "pleasantly thick" or "objectionably superior" categories. He was simply Felix. They'd all get along reasonably, until it came to a bit of leg-pulling, and Felix would put up the pout barriers, and remark on how sorry he felt for them. But he could also get violent when wronged.

Percy came back from town one dinnertime, with his sandwiches and a bit of shopping from the new-style small supermarket across the square. "Ay oop," he announced, "it's suddenly summer! They've got t'first strawberries in at Lodge's, but they don't half cost... what the bloody hell's up wi'im?" This was a reaction to the super-blob of intense high pressure that was Felix, catapulting out of its chair, and sending Percy spinning. Recovering, we all went to the door to see a lazy trail of dust rising to the sky, between us and the yard gates.

"Ah reckon," said Wilf, "as 'ow tha's said summat of interest to t'lad. Ah'd no idea he could shift like that! Ah wonder how long it'll tek for him to stop quivering once he stands still!" This led to one of the usual Felix question symposiums common to times when the subject wasn't around. We shut up abruptly as Felix poured himself back through the door, presumably from Lodge's, judging by the carrier bag bursting with several full punnets of strawberries.

"Ah tek it tha's a bit partial to strawberries, lad," observed Sherlock Wilf. "Gi'us one!"

"Go get your own," replied Mr Congenial, "they cost me a lot of money."

"G'on," tried Percy, "just the one," reaching out to take a choice specimen from the top punnet. He jumped back, shaking his hand after getting a crack from Felix's dessert spoon, which the youth had raided from his drawer. "Ay up, lad, there's no call for that! Ah just wanted the one!"

Felix screamed like a hysterical child, "You can't, you can't! They're mine, mine!" He then backed into a far corner with bag, spoon and enormous dinner plate. There, with a tumbling pyramid of fruit, he sat hunched over the plate, shovelling spoon after spoon straight into a gaping mouth, with no evidence of chewing. Any escaping strawberry would have him leaping on it with a demented whimper, eyes staring in ten directions at once for the slightest movement in the enemy camp. Returning to base he'd hunch up that bit tighter than before, until plate, spoon, dish and mouth disappeared from sight. It was like watching a bulimic vacuum cleaner, just fitted with a new bag.

Percy broke into the high-speed chomping sound: "Bloody hell, lad! When's t'Best Before on 'em? Aif past two?" We three sat transfixed, never having seen this side of Felix before, and we were totally lost as to how to deal with it. Above the rampaging mouth, the nostrils flared and the eyes pressed wide open against the restriction of his glasses, staring fixedly at us, the threat. All the while hand, spoon and eating machinery worked on in mechanical splendour. Barely three minutes passed before the last trace had left the plate and entered the unknown region. We then witnessed a second transformation as the subject relaxed from a defiant glare, put aside his empty plate and superheated spoon, sat back, belched, and took the dominoes out of their drawer, with a "Ready for a game, then?"

This temper didn't really flare again until the following late autumn, when a market crisis led to Lodge's having to ration sugar to two two-pound bags per person. This seemed to have created a panic of world famine proportions in the Ferris household, and went some way to explain Felix's extraordinary figure. Over a two-day period, Felix must have made twenty trips to the shop, and several to another one further up town. Each time he returned with a full ration of sugar from all the shops visited, stashing his spoils away in a large cardboard box, which he had liberated from the PWay store, at the expense of three dozen brush heads. Rather than burying it, and marking it by peeing on the spot, Felix opted for the lesser security of the top of the tall plan cupboards.

With a combination of disgust at this antisocial behaviour and their natural inclinations, Wilf and Percy were obliged, while Felix was out gathering more harvest, to rehouse the odd packet in various boltholes throughout the three offices. It was only when it came to stocktaking at the end of the second day that Felix realised what was happening. After creating a frenzied Felix-shaped hole in the ceiling, he spent the next day scouring every corner of the offices for his lost gold. All this accompanied by a frantic whining as he hardly managed to keep control of the situation. However many bags he recovered, the box never got any fuller.

I tended to stand back from all this, not wanting to interfere with the natural corrective talents of the chainmen. I noticed that sometime into their travels the sugar bags were beginning to leak, and more and more office mice were realising that all their Christmases had come at once. Wary of more violence, Wilf and Percy quit the manoeuvres, and satisfied themselves by systematically going through all the packs and scratting a tiny hole in each, and shoving in minute clippings of propelling pencil lead, mouse-muck length, which should have proved disconcerting when later poured out into the Ferris communal sugar trough. Apart from the fact that they hardly needed my help, I'd decided that to some extent Felix had to be tolerated, since he could become almost useful over the next three weeks or so. Elliot had by now returned to the fold, forcing me into the same office as The Lump, but he was due to go back into hospital for further tests. Felix would once more become my door-to-door chauffeur for the period. There was little point in antagonising him, especially as the lads were doing quite well without me.

Bear with me, for a moment, because you need to know that throughout the years of these chronicles, the great Trans-Pennine M62 motorway was under construction, and Elliot and I would go out on occasional dinnertimes, or make diversions on the way to site inspections, in order to see how the massive earthworks and bridge building was coming on. We were occasionally involved anyway, as works crossed or neared the railway, and although the pair of us were very specialised, we were both all-round civil engineers at heart, and took a general interest in the motorway's progress. Elliot's springtime hospital tests proved the need for a fairly urgent operation, so the following December saw my second, more-extended spell deputising, and of being driven by Felix. It was during this period in charge that I unintentionally found out what it was like to be royalty, courtesy of Felix.

Elliot's first week off coincided with a heavy fall of early snow, starting one day at two o'clock in the afternoon. Darkness was falling around four – nearer three in such conditions, and I decided to make an early start home to escape the worsening weather and avoid the traffic. Naturally the traffic had had precisely the same idea. But I'd reckoned without Felix's resourcefulness. He knew of a roundabout way, which would take us away from the mainstream, and I agreed that three-quarters of an hour moving was better than thirty minutes stood still, so off we went. Spot Mr Gullible!

Twenty minutes out of Huddersfield we were still moving nicely, although visibility was rapidly deteriorating. Felix was virtually steering by chest as he leant forward to peer into the swirling darkness to add at least eighteen inches to his sighting distance. There were frequent stops to clear the windscreen before I noticed the road becoming rather bumpy for a while, but Felix put this down to compacted snow, and drove on. By now I'd become quite impressed by my decision to put my trust in Felix's judgement about the route, as traffic was very light, so light, in fact, as to be nonexistent. Traditional power cuts with the first arrival of snow were presumably to blame for the absence of road lighting, but we pressed on. Suddenly, my natural pessimism flared up, evaporating the short-lived confidence. It could have been Felix's unusual silence which caused it, but the next snow clearance stop had me questioning the excessive width of this quiet minor road Felix had found, and I was just flicking through my geography of the area as to where this runway might be, when the sickening truth hit me. We had pre-empted the Queen, by managing to open up another stretch of the M62 before she got around to it, and what's more, we hadn't a clue as to whether we were pointing towards Hull or Manchester.

Getting onto the motorway works had been a fluke, combined with Felix's never far-off natural incompetence. Getting off, especially as Sod's Law had clicked into gear, so that we were travelling on the wrong carriageway, and in the wrong direction, was a nightmare. Even so, at the end of it, Felix could not see how he could be in any way to blame, and fell into one of his sulks to the detriment of a possible lasting relationship with the first bit of civilisation we came across. For this reason I would like to belatedly apologise to a Mr and Mrs Hartley of Blackley Road near Elland for an incident which occurred one snowy evening in the late sixties, when a six-foot sack of spuds with glasses on knocked them up, and after intense questioning began berating them violently for not being Mr and Mrs Hartley of Blackley Road, much nearer Leeds.

Whenever Felix got a wrong number, which, with his polony fingers working on orders from his fallible brain, was often, it was always implied that it was the wrong number's fault for being such.

After another accusing stare at the Hartleys, Felix returned to the driving seat, and under my strict orders turned round and followed our disappearing tracks back to the official road system.

★

By now, a balanced assessment of this most unbalanced of creatures must have been put to you, the jury, and the sort of emotions he churned up in those around him. In considering our subject, then, along with the stability and sensitivity of his natural reactions, his consideration for others, his absolute predictability, and the finesse with which he carried out the sweeping up of whatever his latest disaster might be, you should be able to gauge the wisdom of creating a cocktail of himself and some dodgy detonators. First, though, Felix's ferret-like nature has to be appreciated.

Felix was a foraging animal; and we all came to realise that the best way to keep him quiet was to give him a cupboard or storage compound to scour. These exercises could prove interesting, such as the day – the once-a-year day – that the cleaners had Jack Senior's carpet up in the PWay Office. In the course of this spring clean they would prize it off the floor, in certain spots with the aid of a shovel, take it out into the yard, and walk up and down on it in the fresh air. After an afternoon's sun it would be brought back in and relayed, turning it through ninety degrees to even out the wear. Felix came across this manoeuvre just the once during his time at Huddersfield.

"What's that?"

"What's what?"

"That, in the floor."

"Dunno," said Jack, "it turns up every year, once a year, when we take the carpet up. Suppose it's some sort of trapdoor or summat."

"What's under it?"

"How should I know? What's usually under a floor in a PWay Office in Huddersfield? A bit more of Huddersfield, I suppose!"

"Please can I have a look, please?"

"Help yourself!"

So, armed with the offered assistance of a knife and fork, Felix started to scratch away around the patch of short boards. As usual, with Felix, progress was slow, but dogged. Jack did have the passing thought that the lad might do a little better if he lent him the chisel and screwdriver he kept at the back of his drawer, but he enjoyed seeing determination too much, and a quiet Felix even more, so he said nothing. These tactics eventually led to Felix pleading for an extension of the carpet-up period, and he was allowed another half day. It was early next afternoon when the boards relented, and Felix revealed a dark hole. It took him little more than five minutes, kneeling on the edge and thrusting his head into the unknown with his bum acting like a marker buoy, to realise that it was dark down there.

Jack suddenly favoured intervention at this point, as he watched Felix preparing to go below with a spluttering Tilley lamp filled with paraffin, a recipe for a fire bomb. He fetched out a large battery hand-lamp that was much safer in these conditions. Head first, Felix slithered amoeba-like through the hole, only to reappear festooned in cobwebs after what had sounded to be a positive contact with a floor. He had found that the cellar had a depth of no more than four feet. Having left his arms and hands below, he could do little to reorganise his appearance, so with a daft grin he dived back into what seemed a satisfactory environment for him.

He was obviously finding things, judging by the muffled whoops or ouches, depending on the nature of the discovery. We followed his progress by means of the thumps on the underside of the floor, and associated cries of anguish. His re-emergence was a bit hampered by our thoughtlessness in putting a large sheet of cardboard over the hole, just to see if the lad had any homing instinct, like seals and ice holes. (We also put a chair over the hole to stop any of us tumbling down, purely on health and safety grounds.)

Muffled curses still managed to escape, turning into a clear cry of triumph as he found the trap followed by an agonised yelp as he found the chair. In a flurry of chair, cardboard, and possibly fifty years of spidery construction, a dishevelled head appeared above ground level, plus one arm, with a hand grasping a tin of something.

"There's boxes and boxes and boxes full of these down here," bubbled Felix, "lots and lots and lots of them... help me out someone."

"Please" might have done the trick, but the company decided to crowd round Felix's head and shoulders to examine his find, leaving the lad in a cruel semi-crouching position, his excitement apparent from his expression as of an egg-bound ostrich.

Harry Hanson, the most senior in age present, recognised the waving tin. "Tha knaws what that is, dun't'a? That's part of us war rations, held for emergency for if t'gangs had to work on bomb damage. What's it say on t'side?"

"Bugger all, there's no label on it; go fetch some more, lad!" With which Felix's head was pushed back through the floor.

Quarter of an hour later, we were all sat round Jack's desk, fending off a throbbing Felix. He was shedding all sorts of bodily collected materials, disturbed after many years of solitude. On the desk, on a plate, was a lump of pale pink meat, assumed to be corned beef. The same dilemma struck us all; here we were, sat on a hoard of free meat, not knowing its edibility rating. Now half past four, Harry settled the issue by saying he'd take a tin home and try it on the wife.

Next day, Harry reported that his beloved had tried the meat, declared it quite nice, if oddly flavoured. It had been three hours later when he returned from the pub, that he was battered with questions about the origins of the "tinned veal" that she'd been given. From this, plus the fact that she'd been off-colour all the previous day anyway (this being full justification for Harry to try out the meat on her in the first place, since "it could 'ardly mek her much wuss nor wot she was already!"), we declared the meat suspect.

We had all the tins excavated, using a now protesting Felix for whom the excitement of the adventure had lost its edge, and they were distributed throughout the lads in the gangs, with the strict instructions that the meat was to be treated only as pet food. This was an unfortunate restriction to impose, since one or two ate such anyway as a matter of course!

Felix, the Marco Polo of dusty sheds and closets, was now fired up with exploratory zeal. He was practically begging Jack to be allowed to rummage through the many cupboards within the PWay Office. This suited us fine, although with every return from the recesses, Felix was adorned in muck and fluff, which he was under orders to shake off out in the yard. Jack came to treat him as just a big feather duster. I couldn't have that – he could never be that useful. Still, the overwhelming argument was that it kept the nuisance quiet for a while. That was until he happened on the detonators.

"What're these, Jack?" Probably the fiftieth occasion Jack had heard this, with minor variations. Between times, whenever he looked up from his desk, he'd see the wriggling Ferris rump, like a big clock face with the hour hand anywhere between four and eight. The remainder of the animal would be buried deep inside a cupboard or large drawer. It looked like a burrowing hippo with piles.

"What do they look like?"

"Well, this one's round and red and old and sort of wrinkly."

Without turning round, Jack did himself no favours by dredging up from nowhere with a deep sigh, "It's a supervisor's foreskin."

"I don't think it is," the query had come from the ample bum, with one waving arm emerging from its side clasping Mystery Object No. 512. Dissatisfied with the response, the dark side of

Felix emerged, glasses akimbo, and with straw hair exploding in all directions. "Why does a supervisor need four skins, anyway," he asked, momentarily diverted.

"More the better," muttered Jack. "You need a hide like a rhino in this job sometimes."

"They look like old detonators to me," continued Felix, "but they're awfully—"

"Ahhhhh... now then... we don't want to be playing with such things as them, do we?" Jack had risen sharply on the word "detonators". He noticed with some slight alarm that the sample that Felix was rubbing and polishing on his jumper was in pretty poor condition, and was actually rusted through. "Just put 'em back, lad, I'll see to 'em later; leave 'em near the front."

Track detonators are quarter-inch-thick discs, about two inches in diameter, with a couple of lead strips fastened to the side. These are there to clamp the device to the head of the rail. Their purpose is to warn of dangers ahead, and they were often used in days of old to enhance signalling at times of thick fog before more sophisticated systems were developed. Heavy train wheels passing over them would cause a cracking explosion, adequate to be clearly heard over the noises within a steam engine cab as well as inside the more enclosed surroundings of a diesel loco. They could also be heard over quite a considerable length of the train, causing many a nervous passenger, terrified of speed in the prevailing thick weather conditions, to have almost terminal palpitations. Explosions were both loud and accompanied by much small shrapnel. Detonators were also brightly colour-coded, to indicate their year of origin, since old ones became unreliable. Very old ones, such as the sample that Felix was waving around, could rust and leak, taking them one stage further on, from unreliable into bloody dangerous.

Fortune would have it that Harry Hanson came in at that moment, following a morning's track walking. "Bloody hell, lad. What's t'a got theer? Them's friggin' far gone... we should get shut on 'em sharp!"

"How do you do that, Harry?"

"Simple, lad, tha—"

"Harry! No! Just leave it..." Jack tried, but tried less than well enough. Harry was not given to deep thinking, and would never have mastered the game of "Consequences" beyond the first fold. To put it to Felix that these dets were in a delicate condition, that they needed to be rendered safe, that this could be by controlled explosion, and that Felix might feel himself fully capable of tackling the task, was not a train of thought Harry could follow beyond the front buffers. Airing his limited knowledge was one of Harry's few intellectual pleasures in life.

"Theer's lots o'ways; sithee, let me get mi coit off, and we'll tek a look, but I reckon them's more than ready for scrappin'!" He heaved off his greatcoat, talking all the while about the problems he'd encountered that morning, and of more importance, how he'd solved them with devastating efficiency, virtually inferring that his superior, Jack, was superfluous. Jack, meanwhile, had given up protesting, and was coming round to the idea of occupying Felix with the controlled destruction of the detonators. In his experience, after all, he had found the lad quite capable of following instructions, so long as those instructions were comprehensive, and he knew Harry well enough to attest to the fact that his conversation was usually overwhelmingly comprehensive.

"Just make sure he knows what he's doing, Harry. Nothing he can't handle, you understand?"

Harry was more than delighted to be invited to ventilate his proficiency, an unusual thing, but once such a concession had been made, he'd turn on an air of exaggerated pomposity. Elliot Milner had returned to work that week from his extended leave, and was holding a senior supervisors' meeting in his office next door, which settled Jack's afternoon plans. This left Harry, who rarely went back out again after dinner, to hold forth to an attentively dribbling Felix on the need for, and methods of achieving the scrapping of old, decaying detonators. The onset of light rain put off any practical demonstrations that afternoon.

Wilf and Percy were over the next day, and Felix was still full of excitement about deadly old decaying detonators, but unable to put into effect any of Harry's lofty advice and instructions yet. As usual the single track of the Ferris mind was chattering away to the beleaguered chainmen about the thing uppermost on his mind, and they were being their usual helpful selves.

"Harry says he's seen men peppered by dets going off when they were too close; they can be very dangerous, you know!" Felix in mid-flight, lecturing to a convention of grandmothers on the subject of sucking eggs.

"George were once nearly finished off by a det," put in Percy.

"What, Chainman George?" At least Percy had halted Felix in his tracks.

"Ay, he'd only been on t'job eighteen months, an' all. I've never seen a bloke so cut up!"

"Was he fatally injured, or anything; or something, or… what?" Felix could never do with the annoying habit some people had of just uttering single sentences.

"Might have been, if his mum had found out."

"?" said Felix's face.

"Tha knaws that signal, aif a mile outside Dewsbury towards Leeds, where t'railway's atop that retaining wall, and there's a house reet up agin it, almost touching t'wall? You can see it theer today, t'bedroom winder's five foot off t'wall top. Well, that were George's spot for fog duty. E'd get bored wi' 'ardly any trains at neet, so he took to chuckin' pebbles at t'winder, an go squat in his hut t'see what 'appened. Nivver saw no one, mainly due to t'fog – just heard t'winder going up an' down, like. So he gets too clever one neet, and he's there wi'a branch tappin' 'Ilkley Moor B'aht 'At' on t'glass. Winder shoots up, 'an this lass hangs out, George tumbles backards… an' they get chatting, like. Afore you know it, he's got t'fog hut laid aht from t'wall top to t'winder sill, and he's in theer, like the daft young bugger 'e were! Throws his coat ower t'bed end an' a det bounces out of t'pocket an' inter t'gas fire. Goes off wi'a reet clatter, brings down aif on t'ceiling, an' brings up t'lass's dad. George is out of t'winder like a scalded cat, his coat follers, he teks another tumble, an' t'fog hut bounces down t'wall inter t'small yard between t'house and t'railroad. Don't remember how he explained it away… summat t'do wi' low flying aircraft and a cow, ah think."

"Well, I nivver did!" said Wilf. "Tha tells a ruddy good tale, Percy Kellet, I'll say that for thee!"

"Bloody true! Go ask Harold Blakey, Mirfield gang; it were 'is daughter and 'is ceiling!"

"Why are they different colours?" Felix had totally lost interest when he realised there was no blood involved, and he certainly couldn't have followed George's reasoning in having to get into the lady's bedroom, just to have a chat.

"They've got to be different colours," said Wilf, winking at me, "else how does t'driver know what they mean? If tha wants 'im to stop, 'cos t'signal's agen him, you crack three red 'uns. A caution's two yellers, and a green one fer if t'lines clear, just to let him know where he is." Thus the gullible lump absorbed for life yet another piece of information which he would be quite incapable of keeping to himself, and would further lower his esteem in the eyes of others when passing it on, while trying to impress.

It was later that afternoon, when the chainmen had set off back to Leeds with another survey almost completed, that Felix found himself at a loose end, and with a box of decaying detonators to hand, along with Harry's guide to controlled explosions. This spelt danger.

It was half an hour later that World War Three erupted in the yard outside. No warnings of thunderclouds or sirens, just a sudden devastating fusillade of rapid-fire explosions rattling the office windows and bringing dust down from the light fittings.

Two trains entering and leaving the station stopped on the spot.

An elderly lady was left lying on the platform, screaming a surrender.

All the pigeons on the station ledges and in the square in front shot off, and stayed away for the next twenty-four hours.

Windows in the adjoining George Hotel were shooting up and heads sticking out, to see nothing but others doing the same all around them. They could none of them pin down the source of the explosions, because they should have been looking over to the small railway yard, at a diesel shunting loco, where two desperately entangled railwaymen were in an emotional frenzy trying to sort out what bodily parts belonged to who.

It was twenty seconds after the stuttering eruptions shattered the peace that the PWay Supervisor's door burst open and fifteen stones of disarranged engine driver tumbled through, closely followed by Horace the Hillhouse shunter who was momentarily arrested by a horizontal shunt pole not coinciding with a vertical door. They were clearly very, very, very upset. Not that the office was a haven of tranquillity. The three of us, Jack, Harry and me, had been more than shaken by the volley of explosions out in the yard. Already, we'd set off on a course directly opposite to that being taken by the visitors. A degree of mayhem followed. In it, the violence of waving, enhanced by the aeronautics of a seven-foot shunting pole with its hooked metal tip flailing the air and furniture, was indistinguishable from a re-enactment of one of the bloodier Civil War skirmishes. Aware of the probability of airborne injury, I took up a position crouching on the floor, which proved safer for me, but added a further complexity for the more upright, to whom I became an additional hazard. In no time they'd all joined me in a thrashing mass on the floor. Desks were thumped. Cupboards kicked. Light fittings swung violently. Both phones were ringing. Work sheets were flying, and flakes of plaster and lumps of fluff were settling over the scene, like the snowstorm in a paperweight. The thirty-second mark added a storming of porters, station inspectors, transport police and Felix, all piling into the office, each trying to assert his own authority. Reporting the conversation and associated language would not prove very illuminating, as it was in the broadest of Yorkshire, cluttered with spectacular but unrelated adjectives, and with voice over voice. For fully two minutes there was total confusion. Later, I managed to boil down the chaos into a simple sad chain of events.

Around three to three thirty, the afternoon daily shunting trip brought wagons up to the station from Hillhouse Yard, a mile away, down at the far end of the viaduct. Today everything went as usual, the wagons were dropped off in the station-bay platform, and the diesel shunter ran into the PWay Yard outside the offices at three forty-five.

During his instruction course the previous day, Harry had told Felix of one of the better ways of destroying dangerously old detonators by exploding them using a shunting loco, in a siding, somewhere away from the main line.

Around three fifteen, Felix took twelve of the rotting

detonators out into the yard, and strapped them at four-inch intervals on the siding nearest to the PWay Office, knowing that the shunter was nearby. He had thought of cracking them one at a time, but realised that this would involve a lot of time and fuel, manoeuvring the loco backwards and forwards. So far corroded were the dets that they virtually blended in with the rusty head of the rail.

A subsequent low-key enquiry discovered a vital omission in Harry Hanson's instructions to the young anarchist – that being the essential of informing people of what you intended to do. Had this course of action been adopted, the driver would not have gone into shock as the world blew up beneath his wheels, he would not in panic have hit every button and lever he could, the loco would not have gone into violent reverse, and the shunter, descending from the cab, would not have been impelled upwards by natural reaction, forwards by the sudden loco reversal, and backwards by several of the driver's misdirected panic lunges. Nor would both have subsequently tumbled over a kneeling Felix who had rushed to the scene to examine the remains, making sure that everything had gone to plan.

Felix was saved from a lynching, and excused the rack, mainly because Jack Senior felt that Harry had some answering to do. Remorse, an unusual manifestation, perhaps confused with an air of injustice, resulted in the lad adopting a hang-dog expression lasting several days. He was eventually allowed to use a brazier at the far end of the offices to explode the remaining detonators one after the other, by dropping them into the flames and then taking cover behind a telegraph pole, five yards away. This, like many other things, I recorded on film from the safety of the water tank, above. From there I was struck by the ridiculous spectacle of this lumbering great figure dashing back and forth from the blaze to his place of safety. Here was this contented ostrich, head in sand, eyes behind a twelve-inch post, perfectly oblivious to the remaining 80% of the rotund lump he called his body hanging out at the edges.

★

Tranquillity, which is people working fairly happily together, returned to the offices. An early spring dinnertime some four weeks later saw me and Felix sat with Jack in front of a fire whose ferocity was scorching the furniture, and providing an early-season tan. Harry was at rest in his peculiar cat-napping position, leaning forward with his forehead resting on one fist placed on top of the other, all supported by the desk top. Felix was fiddling amongst some old files, but keeping relatively quiet. A cloud of smoke belched from the chimney following a gust of March wind.

"I reckon there's a bird nesting up there, or something," said Jack, pulling on a long-expired pipe. "Seen it coming and going recently. Whole chimney wants cleaning, I suppose. I can't recall it ever being done in my time here."

Felix quietly pulled himself together – this was a phrase I'd often read in novels but up to now couldn't visualise. He sauntered out through the door into Elliot's office, and presumably on to the Drawing Office beyond.

"Wet himself, has he?" asked Jack. "Doesn't usually leave without being kicked out!"

We fell back into the gentle conversation a blazing fire inspires.

"Hello!" said Jack. "What's he up to now?"

For there, passing before the window, was the sight of Felix climbing the iron ladder up to the water tank. "You know what, I think he's taken that bird's nest you mentioned on board. Not his norm to go in for exercise like that! Just fancy that, he's off to try and shift it! You never know with that one!" As I said this, another belch of smoke sped across the office. "I wonder what he's going to use to clear it?"

"Oh, bugger!" muttered Harry's fists to themselves. "Bugger, bugger, bugger!"

"You what?" asked Jack, slightly alarmed.

"Oh, nuthin'," replied Harry, rising rather too sharply from his slumbers. He moved rapidly towards the door, and out into the yard.

There was no further conversation.

A sudden scuffling noise in the chimney, was followed by the sight of a dull-red disc bouncing onto the blazing coals, and leaping across the office floor. It hit the far cupboard, and spun like an old penny, before slowing down and tumbling over. By the time the second detonator followed it, Jack and I were out of the door as well. Rolling around for a moment or two, the detonator also wobbled to a rest, only to be followed by another. Outside we met Harry, shouting up at Felix, who was wrapped round the chimney stack. Harry underlined his urgency with a handful of small stones. Jack blazed brighter than the fire. "*Harry?*"

"Yon soft bugger!" as Felix glowered down, before presenting us with a sight not to be forgotten as he turned to descend the ladder. "He's just plain barmy! Ah mebee just mentioned in passin'... well, fact is, ah knaws ah did; abaht as how we used to clear out coked-up cabin chimneys bi droppin' an old detonator dahn 'em inter t'stove fire! But ah nivver thought, in this wide world, as how as anyone could be so bloody daft as to... bloody hell! That went with a wallop di'n't'it!"

A muffled "wooff" came from the direction of the office as the final Felix detonator hit its mark. A blast of grey-black smoke exploded through the open doorway, momentarily obliterating the incredible bulk descending the ladder. As it cleared, accompanied by minor sounds of breakage and rearrangement within the office, Felix was seen to be thoughtfully making his way back up the ladder. He remained up there, and out of sight, until just before the time of his train home.

★

On the plus side, the bird's nest seemed to have been cleared, and the chimney didn't puff out smoke any more. Added to that, there wasn't enough of the carpet left to worry Jack about having it cleaned once a year. His mug, left on the mantelpiece was cracked anyway, though sadly full of freshly brewed tea. But above all, Elliot was moved to put it to the staff training officer that Felix had probably absorbed as much experience of Area life as he could, without adding that the Area had certainly suffered enough experience of Felix!

Saloon, Part 1

With the crowd gone, all the bunting coming down and the instant platform garden going into autumnal overdrive, it just lay there, in regal splendour. Twenty minutes ago it was the Royal Train; now it was little more than a long, sectional, outdated mechanical sausage with 1930s nostalgia oozing from the maroon carriages. For all its purple pomp and aura of untouchable aloofness, it had now been removed from the oasis of splendour, non-centre stage, and dumped in the Fish Dock, by a tiny diesel shunter. Affluent to effluent in one short move. Rescue was in hand, though, by way of the two polished locos that they were now tagging onto it, soon for it to take off and become the Royal Train all over again.

It looked incongruous in the siding amongst the adverts and graffiti of the seventies, where such had been allowed to remain – judged to be well outside HM's sensitive gaze. Decorative enhancements abounded, some intentional – like the advert for Aristoc tights, with its young and very female contortionist part curling up over a phone, and part hoisting six and a half feet of remarkable and unbelievably sheer leg to the almost vertical. Other illustrated literature provided gratis by the amateur bards of Huddersfield, detailed in graphic terms long-forgotten romances, both real and supposed, and the various items of bodily equipment thought necessary to cement such unions. Not what you'd have seen before the War, my dear. Certainly not around the Royal Train! Oh, the blasphemy! Just where are we going?

"Ay up, it's off." It slithered out of the Dock, a disjointed green-headed maroon snake. "Does it kind of do owt for you?... I mean – don't you get this sort of gippy thing, like a hiccup stuck in your throat, or summat? Doesn't it make you feel kind of proud whenever you see something grand like that? British, I mean. All 'Rule, Britannia', first of the few, and fighting on the beaches stuff... I know it sounds daft, and I couldn't give a bugger about what's in it – you know me! But there's this sort of lump, pride, somehow…"

I don't know what it was persuaded me to share my inner emotions with one having the sensitivity of a rat trap.

"Problem: stomach reacts at sight of old railway coaches. Symptoms: starts talking bollocks. Cause: could possibly have summat t'do with a quarter of belly pork he had, half an hour ago."

This was during Vince Bell's time at Huddersfield, the practising cynic, and fly slicer. We watched as the train glided out of the platforms – a second time in life for me, Vince's first. Off to pick up Queenie at some other station, equally decked out like a florist's allotment, and locally sanitised of visual abominations such as Gents and Ladies signs. Again, incongruity shouted at you, as the two scrubbed modern diesel locos hauled it away, instead of the traditional ideal of a couple of belching steam engines.

"No, come on, y'know what I'm on about. I've only dealt with the thing a couple of times. It's a bugger of a job having it around anyway, but you've got to admit, it's a fair sight."

"To me it's got the glamour of a set of matching luggage. It's more of a mobile mothballed museum, t'me. An ana-chron-ism!"

"Is that today's word, then; anachronism? Half past twelve! It's taken you about four hours to work 'Today's Word' in, today! You're slipping!"

"I bet there's a word for that, too – using 'today' twice."

About a month back, Vince, along with a dozen other sponsored young hopefuls, had been interviewed by the Chief Civil Engineer, no less, at York. Among other things, their "basics" had been queried, and the Boss had come up with his annual chestnut that they should all do at least one crossword, and learn and use one new word every day. We'd had some tortuous conversations over the last week or two as a result, and Elliot Milner had twice come through asking Vince what the dickens some messages he'd left for him had meant.

"It's unchroniological and antidilouvier… it's a load of old rubbish, along with the junk it's loaded up with. Christ! It's nowt but a string of old coaches what should have been slung years ago. Lump in your throat? Likely more a pain in the…"

"You've no soul! I bet you'd be like them lads out on t'track that turns their backs on it while it's passing, and lean over t'fence pretending not to notice it. D'you know, I've known some folk, women clerks mostly, who'd kill for a ticket to get an OK to stand for three-quarters of an hour, on a freezing platform, staring at the back of some other woman's daft hat, all for a ten-second snatch of whatever specimen of royalty they're tossing off the train that day."

Emotions on seeing the Royal Train varied a good bit, mixing various proportions of pride, humility, scorn, trepidation and hostility, with indifference (if that is an emotion) beating all. For a lot of the lads, though, just having the thing turn up on their patch automatically created loads of bonus-inspiring sentry jobs, so on balance, the mercenary in them would opt for putting up with it.

"Well, I can tek it or leave it, missen. And admit it, I bet it doesn't whip up half the willies in you that the Glass Carriage does!"

This was true. The Engineer's Inspection Saloon, to give it its official title, was another disturbing train, seen much more often than royalty – perhaps two or three times a year. This one really got the emotions going; in this case Pride, Humility, Scorn, Trepidation or Hostility, but very rarely indifference. It was far less impressive than the carriages of sovereign rule, but in my early days it was just as archaic, and what's more, it carried people who were far more immediately important than the Royal Train. Instead of two great locos and a full train of coaches, it would be made up of an adequate small locomotive and the single observation coach. Along with it came loads of distinctly non-bonus bull work; tidying, scrubbing and window dressing, together with an eruption of trumpeting, paperwork, phoning and blue-arsed flying. Come the day of its visit, and supervisors would appear in full issue gear, carrying a broad selection of the track gauges they were, in theory, supposed to cart about daily (nothing short of a steroid-stuffing gorilla-cum-octopus could manage the complete regulation kit). Whatever else might be selected, cross-levels and rail sidewear gauges were a must. Track patrolmen would suddenly be in possession of incredibly detailed records of their daily walking, listing track faults, train speeding, dumped rubbish and dead dogs, along with action taken (repaired, reported, sorted or buried). Gangs would appear in unnaturally clean uniforms, which screamed of inactivity, along with actually visible high-visibility vests. All this would be complemented by accessories such as effective shovels and picks, with complete handles. Meanwhile, Works staff would be dotted all along the route of the Special, buried in all those niggling jobs, neglected for months. In the same wave of emotion, the technical staff like Vince and me would study the proposed route intently, pick out all the likely stopping-off sites, work out the estimated arrival and departure times at each one and arrange to do some job as far away as possible. For once we would defy tradition and definitely not return to the office for dinner, so avoiding any messages, orders, requests or demands emanating from this travelling circus, which was the Engineer's Inspection Saloon. In any case, in his day, that was Bill's job, and I wouldn't have dreamed of interfering.

"Weer will t'a be if tha's wanted, thee two?"

"Somewhere around Wellhouse Tunnel, but it depends, really."

"Which is t'gainest signal box, if ah needs t'give thee a call?"

"Denby Dale – a mile t'other side of the tunnel… or you could try Penistone, but that's the far end of the viaduct, miles away."

"Could you two buggers've fund anyweer on t'Area weer tha could get any more remote, and less handy?"

"Not so far as we could figure out, Bill, but we're open to any ideas!"

Things would be set on a more positive level in the Supervisor's office, next door.

"Glass coach's about tomorrow," announces Jack Senior to his team. "You knows the drill; every man smart, every man working, and nobody wearing their orange vests round their arses. I'll let you know its timetable, but for God's sake don't rely on it. No one relaxes till it's gone through, OK? Oh," as an afterthought, "and no peeing on the wheels this year if it stops near you. Harry! Make sure Wolstenholme's working up t'Branch for the day, out of the road!" This reflecting an unfortunate incident the previous year involving the Chief's inspection and our local railway anarchist.

Things being as they were, it was very likely that these confrontations with the saloon were the only times that the men on the ground actually saw the District Engineer, for it was He who would be carried along in flamboyant luxury. There were times when circumstances forced me to join the coach, and if I ever got any pleasure out of it, then it would be in occasionally seeing even Himself in a subordinate role. That would be when it was the Chief Civil Engineer who was carrying out the inspection. He definitely tipped the scales in the Relevance and Importance Stakes, when compared with the odd passing trainful of queen or prince. And yet, when it was He who had come down among us, He confounded all by coming over to talk to any trackmen or surveyors He encountered. He provided an unfortunate comparison to the unapproachable aloofness of our local District Engineer, J (Jack) A Lewis, by chatting away pleasantly. Lewis would try to copy him in vain, and it was at one of these events that the penny dropped for me... our Engineer suffered from nothing more than a crippling shyness. One particular Chief, Harold Ormiston, was both welcomed warmly for his "one-of-the-lads" approach and at the same time treated warily on account of his amazing knowledge and powers of recall. Since he'd started life working with the gangs around Leeds, and soared to the ivory towers of Greatness, he had a particular affinity with the West Riding, and an incredible memory for detail. I chanced to overhear him opening out to a group consisting of four different grades, made up of the distant Lewis, an urgent young riser, an indifferent supervisor and the length ganger. The conversation started with the Chief, and ran right along the spectrum of command, or downwards as common parlance would have it.

"I don't quite follow your logic, Jack (Lewis), of extending this drain so far from the problem area."

"It's essential if we're to reach a proven outfall, Mr Ormiston. That's so, Richards (local whiz kid)?"

"Oh indeed, sir. We've made every effort to locate a suitable location, and considered numerous alternatives, even to the extent of a pumped siphon, and we are wholly confident that the scheme proposed will be both effective and financially best advised, aren't we, George (Supervisor)?"

"Ay, whatever it was that tha's just said!"

"And you, Jimmy," (Ormiston to the ganger) "haven't you any ideas how we could shorten the run?"

"Well, ah did have a ninklin' that there were an auld culvert hereabahts, Har... er, Mr Ormistion. 'Bout theer, in fac'. Might come in handy, mebee."

"You know damned well there is, Jim! We once went down it together – ooo, must be twenty-five years ago, now. Seek it out, Jack, it'll halve the costs!"

Ormiston smiled at Lewis, who glowered at Richards, who looked shakenly at George, who curled a lip up at Jimmy, who winked at Ormiston.

I enjoyed the varying effects that the Chief, or District Engineer had on the men on the ground, disregarding the aforementioned Wolstenholme, a disreputable individual who would hurl insults at the saloon as it passed by. (But for the fact that he was an extremely good worker, the man would have been removed long ago, and but for his politics of confrontation he could have been supervisory material.)

You'd get the full range of reactions to the Presences. In the extreme, some looked capable of falling down in worship. The ancient art of cap crunching hung on. Oil-blackened headgear would be tugged off, hair smoothed and some deferential form of salute made. This was most definitely cap-screwing country – "There's trouble up t'junction, Mister Milner!" stuff. If actually spoken to, heads would flop to one side, and answers would be given using one eye, looking down, and half a mouth. They would be peppered with "Sirs", or "Mr Lewis, sir" had they ever met before. Tim Avery, Lewis's successor, was a quite different type of boss, and would actually encourage Jack Senior to stand at his ear, and whisper the men's first names to him. He'd simply ask Fred or Herbert how he was keeping, and Fred or Herbert would float for days. Tim, unlike Lewis, would invite complaints, and actually get some, in a very respectful manner. By just turning to his clerk, or Elliot, with a "We must look into that; make a note," he had a remarkable effect. Whether anything came of it or not (and usually it didn't) the disgruntled ones would remark that "At least he listened; no one else's ever listened before".

On the other hand the Engineer might be met with a sullen silence, and seem to be getting nowhere with his pleasantries. Later, I'd find these same blokes glowing with admiration for the Boss: "No side on him at all, and a proper gentleman!" But there were always the few, who would treat management with a completely relaxed attitude, as if meeting them for a game of darts. Tim Avery was such that he enjoyed all contacts, and encouraged feedback from such as me. (I was considered as having a foot in both camps.) In this role of confidant, it was an everlasting puzzle to me how I came to be "Mike" to all the men on the ground, and at the same time "Mike" to the Engineer, and even to some of the various Chiefs I bumped into. It wasn't the fact that I was addressed with familiarity that intrigued me, but rather that some other status contemporaries weren't. It was like many other things that I didn't understand from my position of being behind my own face; any attitude I might have had was completely natural to me, and I couldn't see how some others could treat the lads on the ground as lesser mortals, and the bosses as deities. Every man working to his full ability is equal – Proverbs, Chapter something or other, Verse thingummy. Anyway, that's the way I see things, and pity those who don't. Apart from anything else, the pay-off's useful and pretty gratifying.

Despite all this, I always had an instinctive reluctance to be anywhere near the Inspection Saloon as it trundled round the Area. But there were times when I simply couldn't avoid the dubious treat of a trip. My first full-scale one was in the top league of a Chief Civil Engineer's Programme Inspection. I was there due to some strategic holiday planning by my boss, Elliot Milner.

Never one for mixing with greatness if I'd the choice, I felt distinctly awkward as I sat at the back of the coach, clutching the obligatory welcoming cup of coffee. I tried to go with the swing and bounce of the speeding coach, as tidal waves swept east and west in the cup. It came with a saucer and a spoon, as well as a handle, which just goes to show what sort of posh company I was in. As the day wore on, I sensed that I was probably regarded as being of very little use, and was being merely tolerated for the duration of the trip. As this began to dawn on me it was initially gratifying, and came as some relief, but as usual when placed in a strange situation, my self-confidence grew in inverse proportion to the number of silly things I did or said. By mid-afternoon I'd managed to wind myself up into a state of indignation about being ignored so much. Caution prevailed, and despite all my prepared information going stale, I managed to keep a hold on my feelings by seeing the day as an experience and a chance to sniff around.

Without doubt, the observation section, at one end of the coach, was the most immediately impressive bit; the throne room as it was, with its definite hierarchy of furniture. Equal in pole position were two high wing-back armchairs, sort of grandad-round-the-fire affairs, one on either side of the coach. These took up most of the width, and a lot of the height of the viewing area, immediately reducing the number of effective observers to two. I'd seen such seating in period dramas on the large screen, where they were placed insignificantly in an acre of living room, in front of the staged representation of a roaring fire. Such seats were designed to focus the radiating heat onto the enclosed body, while casting expanding shadows flickering across the floor and up the distant walls. Two small oases of relative comfort in a dark echoing desert. However, placed in an eight-foot-wide railway coach, they formed an almost total eclipse of the observation facilities.

Behind them were four comparatively subdued armchairs. Certainly lower in status, but still superior to the two ranks of straightforward padded seats, ranged down the coach sides. Yet even they could turn and sneer at the clerical table, with its two very clerical chairs, which completed the seating arrangements. While everything above them was in matching upholstery, these last two, one ups from boxes, definitely knew their functional place.

As for the human line-up, a Chief's Inspection would be in a 2-2-6-1 formation; the Chief, along with the District Engineer, sat up front, backed by the particular Area Engineer for the line being examined at the moment, together with the pushiest, most egotistical brown-nosing article among the rest. (I was averse to this breed, in case you hadn't twigged.) In the six back positions would be other Area Engineers, whose time was yet to come, or who were staying on for the ride, and the odd few stranded PWay Supervisors, now well off their patch, along with a Mike-type, who might be there to expound on one particular job or site. In goal, right at the back, was a clerk. No ordinary clerk, though; this was Sydney Adams.

Sydney was to figure large in life on the Area. While he was aware that he was a clerk, and knew exactly where the position of clerk fell in the engineer's tree of evolution, Sydney, above all, knew that he was Sydney Adams, and that in real terms of power, he was superior to all. He was most annoyingly smug, but even worse than that was the realisation that this smugness was irritatingly justified in his case. Power was not judged by the criteria of pay, but of influence – how much you could change or amend things. In noting down whichever of the Engineer's decisions that happened to suit him, and selectively providing supportive material, Adams was the supreme being.

Measuring around six foot two or three, Sydney appeared to be actually around seven feet tall. He always manoeuvred himself into a position where he could seem to be looking down on you. Nobody could ever claim to be a friend of Sydney's, but equally, nobody would ever openly appear to be an enemy. Treating all colleagues with equal contempt, he demanded respect from all – from management because they relied on him for the information he made his own, and from the "lower orders" because of his influence with management.

"Digestives – if you're lucky." These were the first words Sydney ever spoke to me, if you don't count the grunt that served as an acknowledgement of my presence as I sat down next to him at the lowly table.

"Pardon?" We'd both just been handed our coffees, and he could see I was watching the plate of biscuits travelling spasmodically down the coach.

"You'll always find the top rankers" (and I believed he meant to say that) "grabbing anything that looks like two biscuits stuck together with cream in the middle. Custards first, and then those chocolaty ones. Then that lot" (the various area engineers) "the crunchy ones with raisins. Supervisors can't believe their luck finding some ginger creams left, which they'll proceed to… There you are, see!" One of the said breed was dunking a ginger in his coffee as Sydney spoke, realising on the third plunge that nobody else was doing it, and after the fourth embarrassed automatic reflex dunk, finding that he wasn't either, as he surfaced with only half the biscuit coming up for air.

"By the time it reaches us it's plain digestives, maybe some of them wafery ones that go to nothing or those marked 'NICE', which aren't. Mind, there's never any chocolate-coated ones brought out in the first place – they're usually ambushed by the cook and lookouts – except, of course, for these… here!" And from a fluffy jacket lining out came four chocolate digestives.

"You can tell a man," said Sydney, rather extravagantly performing the biscuit's journey from saucer to mouth, so that anyone could see what he'd won, "by the biscuit he finishes up with, not necessarily by the one he chooses from the plate! Would you like one?"

Down at the other end of the coach was the dining area. Only two armchairs here, of first division design, as opposed to premier, yet still armed-up ornately enough to make the navigation of knives, forks and spoons between plate and mouth slightly hazardous. Elbows often became trapped or critically misdirected by the padded arms. These two chairs were there purely to retain the formality, and also for if this should become the observation end of the coach on a return journey. Beyond these, all the remaining chairs were identical. Once more there was a distinct body packing order, more appropriate since this was where the pecking was done.

Same as at the other end, it was crowned by the two Engineers opposite each other, at the top of a long carved table which ran the full length of the dining area. This item was necessarily so narrow that the diners sitting facing each other had to keep an eye on which was their plate, and which belonged to the trougher opposite. Here again the pushy whiz kids floated towards the top end of the table, while the Mikes and clerks were perfectly happy down at the bottom. World-weary Area Engineers with "only-five-years-or-so-to-do" settled for the middle distance, away from the hot seats, but within the area where dinners were served while still reasonably warm. Any trapped supervisors, who'd spent the day hopping between the loco footplate and the saloon as the train travelled through their patches, now hid amongst the uncomfortable comfort wherever they could. Many avoided the experience altogether by arranging for their gang buses to rove the foreign regions, trying to intercept the train with urgent messages necessitating immediate returns to offices and their soothing sandwiches. This had to be a better option than having to face the confusing battery of knives and forks and elbows on the saloon.

Midway between the two ends of the coach was a functions section; a luggage compartment-cum-guard's cupboard, an ornate lavatory, and a phone box-sized kitchen. Within this area were to be found the train's guard, a lookoutman, who changed at every local boundary line, and the cook. This last was immediately recognisable as being a reincarnation of one of the two messengers from the District Office. These were less than comfortable transformations, as was only too clearly revealed by the varying edibility of their culinary creations. The more experienced saloon diners could be spotted cutting their meat into minute pieces, where first timers cheerfully slotted a slab of the stuff into their mouths, and spent the next five minutes chewing away, at the same time examining every nook and cranny of the coach's ceiling.

Where the idea of using the messengers as impromptu cooks started, I never found out, but whoever it was must never have had to sample the results. You could imagine our then team of two, Arthur and Albert, both turning sixty and deemed suitable for only light duties now, as they found themselves unnaturally seated during their interviews for the posts of Office Messenger. It was a position that traditionally went to a trackman or work-shop man, for some reason or other no longer suited to heavy work. Prior to applying, they would have spotted the following appetising invitation in the weekly vacancies, or escape list, as it was cynically known:

Wanted: Keen male of smart appearance having a good working

knowledge of the civil engineering function. Must have ability to work without supervision, and with tact and discretion. Duties – collect all incoming office mail from station, sort and distribute. Likewise, assemble all outgoing mail and ensure it is directed towards the correct destinations. Act as reception and linkmen to the Civil Engineer's offices.

Incidental duties would emerge as they nervously fingered their strangely clean uniforms. Among other things, it would come out that they'd also be required to serve refreshment for the Engineer and any guests. As Albert once remarked: "A doddle; kick aht a packet o'biscuits and cook up some coffee, nowt to it!" As the interview reached a successful conclusion, the Chief Clerk would casually add, "Oh, and by the way, you'll be required to attend on the Engineer's Inspection Special occasionally as well." Translated, this meant that the now-elated successful candidate suddenly found himself landed with preparing a cooked three-course meal for ten or so, in a particularly confined kitchen in which all four walls could be touched at one time, and all without any official help. Bear in mind that these lads, twenty-five years on the track, working with bars, shovels and picks, were to be suddenly pitched into the catering trade, when the only time that they ever went near the kitchen at home was to make sure the wife hadn't left them.

Most managed to take the view of Arthur and Albert that if a woman could cook, then they were pretty sure that they could. "After all, tha's only got to sling some raw grub inter some pans, bung 'em someweer hot for a while, and then dish it all up, with a bit kept aside for thissen, of course!"

These meals were usually designed by the Programme Clerk, based on the emerging capabilities of each press-ganged chef. They also had to pay vague lip service to any managerial special requests. Such would soon come to recognise the common sense in sticking to the clerk's experienced palate, and the menu in due course became standardised as grilled lamb or pork chops. Soup and coffee shared a basic recipe, and the sweet course tended to revolve around a catering tin of fruit salad, together with an ability to gauge equality in dispensing. Albert once explained to me that this was very like measuring out portions of gravel for the fine packing of sleepers, for which he'd a twenty-year record of competence. Arthur had just once come upon a visiting vegetarian, which he initially took to mean some sort of religion lying between Proddy and Left Footer. He'd had the term explained to his incredulous expression, and as a result came up with a triumphant pyramid of boiled sprouts. This he then completely negated for suitability by adding a volcanic flow of fat-rich gravy from the grill drip tray.

Later in my career, when my appearances on the saloon had become more or less standard due to me landing the job of looking after most future trackwork projects, I would become tired of chops. Fate intervened with the discovery of a former assistant hotel chef who had "got out of the kitchen" and joined the track gangs for a more outdoor life. Gerry was far from unwilling to display his former skills, and the inspired engineer of the time relieved the messengers, and took him on for every future saloon run. While hardly stretching his talents, Gerry revolutionised the galley, and its products, such that already truncated afternoon sessions virtually disintegrated into nodding through the various inspection items, due to the new post-dinner euphoria. Albert and Arthur missed the smuggled chops, that usually lost their appeal anyway, by appearing on the teatime menu at home after they'd already had them for dinner. They missed little else, though.

Larder stocking for each trip was arranged officially by the Programme Clerk, and rearranged unofficially on the day such that all the below-stairs individuals, like the train crew, were also able to enjoy the Engineer's hospitality. However, convention dictated they were not allowed to eat at table. Instead, they did it out of sight, either in the kitchen, out on the grass embankment, or back on the footplate.

All trips kicked off, as I've said, with coffee, served up with a tray of biscuits. The first thing the reluctant chef did on joining his train in the sidings was to set the coffee bubbling away. How long the saloon was delayed before being allowed down into the station affected the degree to which the resulting liquor stripped the surface off your teeth. Our messengers were well versed in dishing up instant coffee, but were ill-equipped to cope with the theory and practice of percolation. I quietly marvelled over the years how the combination of ground coffee bean, hot water and messenger could produce such a wide variety of results. But nothing got the better of Arthur or Albert, and they were both determined to produce something drinkable before they retired. However, as it turned out, the excellent Gerry replaced them before they quite got the grasp.

After the morning's work, dinner would be taken. In earlier years, before prohibition struck, this would be preceded and accompanied by a couple of bottles of Double Diamond. An effort once by a society-mixing ambitious Engineer to refresh the company with wine fell foul of the messengers' social inexperience of such a drink. Any dignity in the occasion was shot to pieces by it being served up in half-pint tankards, on the basis that if it wasn't beer, it must be some kind of foreign cider. Preliminary morning field trials which they had thoughtfully conducted had tended to confirm this theory to them.

Dinnertime was when the Engineer felt he could communicate, in what he saw as a relaxed atmosphere. Dinnertime, however, was also a period of extreme tension for the supervisors, plunged into a most unfamiliar of situations. A forced conviviality at the top of the table aimed towards the bottom would be returned in two- or three- word replies, the first being "Yes", followed by "Sir" or "Mr Lewis", depending on how familiar he who had been addressed felt he could be. The ice at the head of the table was seen to float gently aside as duck-like platitudes drifted through it. At the same time, the supervisors sat beneath glacial cliffs, fidgeting with unyielding shirt collars. These rose like fencing out of their funeral and wedding suits, markedly different from the easy lounge suits which the engineers at the front of the coach changed daily. Universal conviviality died a natural death on all lips, as either end of the table inevitably turned in on themselves.

I would find myself, figuratively speaking, opposite the salt, listening to two differently tuned radios, a managerial one to the left, and the other among the supervisors to the right. Radio 3 one side, Radio 2 the other. A cultural see-saw, neither end really needing any input from me, so I just listened, swapping channels at will, with the two groups occasionally approaching each other on converging tracks.

< Left

"Bumped into HJC over at HQ yesterday. Had RLT and old BM with him. Just back from the Board. Heavy business, according to him. Looks like the '69 Financial Initiative is heading for the fan!

"Writing on the wall, months ago, in my opinion. Many think STL's a reactionary old stick, but he had it right at the Spring Conversazionne. Mark this, I thought at the time – said as much to HJ."

Right >

"Which friggin' fork dust'a use fust? Dust'a think they use one fur soup?" In hissed undertone.

"What's t'a mean, 'For soup'? What chuffin' use is a fork, wi' soup?"

"Ah were jus' thinkin' along t'lines on it happen bein' t'ower lumpy posh sort, tha knaws."

"Bund t'be lumpy wi' yon dealin' wi'it. Could burn corn-flakes, yon Arthur!"

"S'true! Once when ah were on this bloody thing they'd given Albert some Yorkshires t'warm up. Dozy twallop used 'em as beer mats!"

< Left

"Don't you feel the initiative became obscured when PLW introduced an infrastructure reappraisal side issue of parallel fragmentation?"

"Oh, but justifiable, surely. I cannot see fiscal policy and line-side hardware linked on comparable terms, but there has to be a mutual bonding at some point in the broader view."

Right >

"What's he give us these teacakes for? Not much cop, either. See!" Tapping it on the table. "Hard as rock, an' bugger all currants."

"'S meant to be 'ard. S'fresh. S'ard because it's crusty. Ah think as 'ow it's French, like. Tha breks it up an' stirs it in thi soup. 'As t'a nivver etten posh afore, say at a wedding, or summat? That theer's French bread, ah'll be bahnd!"

"Ah'm boogered if ah can parlay owt in French, let alone eat it!"

< Left

"I hardly see it gelling with the Minister's objectives, if we're to take them at face value. He was to have addressed the Board, apparently, but the crisis kept him in Whitehall."

"Extraordinarily convenient, I would hazard. SQN would have had a few salient points to put on his plate, I would have thought. And what of KPC, if he'd been on form?"

Right >

"Theer's a programme on t'telly, Fridays, tells thee all about this table stuff. Eatinquette, or summat. Anyroad, this lass wi' a barrer-load of brocken glass danglin' from her ear 'oles were crackin' on abaht summat or other. Settin' tables, 'an usin' cloths an' such."

"Ah likes a tablecloth what's useful. One what tha c'n read. S'only time ah can catch up on what's bin goin' on!"

"We could manage a game of draughts on thissun if tha' fancies. Does that count as useful?"

< Left

"Dimbleby grilled the Minister on *Panorama* last night. Masterly evasion. I just cannot relate to the politician's approach to practicalities. Goodness knows how it comes across to the men on the ground! They could very easily have gained an impression that the industry could survive with a much-reduced managerial input, believe it or not!"

Right >

"Dids't'a catch t'telly last neet, at all? Thur were some article crackin' on abaht railway management bein' a load of bollocks, from what ah could gather. *Pinnerarma*, or summat... because ar lass fancies that Dimplebury bloke, that's why... anyroad, wi' can't get nowt else on our set yet. Brother-in-law says it's gotta be summat t'do wi't'airiel. Reckons we need one."

< Left

"There was one overwhelming point he managed to put over, I thought, with regard to the intransigence of today's union executive. Dammit! They've all worked in the industry at some time. I cannot understand their philosophy or motivation."

Right >
"Saw a bitta that missen. But ah'd to turn it ower, 'cos there's some pillock in an advert what she's keen on. It's *Panorama*, what it's called, by the way."

< Sudden common ground >

"My word, Jack! Do I gather you watched *Panorama*, last night? Didn't you feel that the Minister rather skirted round the main issues which affect you, me, the men, and the very future of railways as a viable force in transport policy for the future, without clouding the issue with European integration and political interference, or, indeed, reference to the ongoing discourse between management and the union pragmatists?"

"Errumpher... (cough)... definitely, Mr Lewis."

Enthusiasm for full inspections in the afternoon tended to wane, and many an item for viewing would be waived through, or just given a slightly more urgent marking than the previous year. From three o'clock onwards people would tend to fade away after the cup of tea (a marked improvement on the coffee, with the messengers now being on home territory) and more biscuits. This marked the end of an essential attendance, and it was then that I might find myself in one of the main armchairs, having a pleasant and useful conversation with someone very important, who I'd scarcely ever expect to meet otherwise.

★

My first saloon trips were with a steam or small diesel loco stuck onto the single coach. You'd often find that the engine made up the greater part of the train, giving the footplate the feeling that they were running as a light engine. You could tell this by the cavalier accelerations and brakings, which were reflected in the nervous excitement of anything inside which was not fastened down. Inevitably, the saloon grew older, and the National Railway Museum got hungrier with expansion, and the ornate stock was pensioned off to be replaced by a sparsely converted self-propelled two-car diesel unit.

From end to end, the old saloon had been finished off by cabinet makers. This was demonstrated in the delicacy of the veneer panelling. Curtains hung at the windows, the sort that are tied back by loops of matching material and are never meant for pulling to. Ceilings were tastefully ornate, with old company plaques cropping up here and there. Floors were carpeted; practicality had long since ruled out the original thick pile which had matched the surroundings; this had been replaced by serviceable matting inscribed "BR" throughout, but when the museum got hold of it, the coach had its splendour restored with the help of carpeting which must have been recovered from the less accessible areas of some ancient boardroom. If this was authentic, then you could bet that in the old days there was very little stepping out onto the varied splendours offered to the tailored shoe by the creosoted sleepers and ash ballast of the tracks, and that most of the inspecting was done through the coach windows.

Apart from that, the very act of climbing up into the coach from ground level was a fair old effort. This was managed via two sets of pneumatic-folding steps tucked away under the coach's bodywork, which had temperaments all their own. Try to drop them and they'd make inadequate gasping noises, until the poor soul waiting on the ground was persuaded, in embarrassing ignorance, to grovel around and try to spot the cause of the trouble. He'd most likely then be flattened as the steps suddenly sprang to life. Once lowered and they'd frequently refuse to retract, cutting out the braking system, and effectively disabling the train.

District trips were very similar to the Chief's, with the Engineer and his main Assistants in the best seats, Area Engineers, as before, in the second row, but now sharing with any relevant Drawing Office heads. Should there be a Mike on this sort of trip, he'd still be propping up the rear, unless he was one of those pushy articles who sees chances of advancement as being proportional to the number of times your face obscures the Engineer's view. Whatever else I might be there for, I'd keep my ears open, because these were the only occasions when you maybe found something out before the messengers, the chainmen or the typists. It was quite incredible how the hierarchy could talk away on confidential matters, in the same way that the gentry did around the dinner tables of old, assuming that the servants were deaf, or dead north of the neck. On the saloon, for domestic servant, read Mike or clerk. But, I hear the impatient yelping, to what purpose, all this grandiose coachwork, pompous incongruent dining and promotional posturing? What lay behind these inspections?

Rails wear thin with use. On curves the outside rail is set at a higher level than the inner one, for added passenger comfort when cornering. Among other things it suffers wear on the contact face as the wheels of locos and carriages seek it out and try to ride up it. Slow, loaded goods traffic, using the same tracks, bear heavily on the lower rail, and cause it to mushroom out. Metal rusts in weather, but put it under cover, in a damp tunnel for instance, and it can gallop into decay as you watch. For all sorts of reasons, rails and the other steel bits and pieces eventually wear out. Wooden sleepers rot, admittedly slowed down by impregnated preservatives, but hard or softwood, one way or another they eventually lose their strength, and begin to disintegrate. Even the ballast below and around the sleepers has problems. It can become waterlogged, eroded and crushed, depending very much on what it started out as. Whatever its problems, its supportive rating eventually goes up the spout.

On the Works side, bridges show their age through weathering, heavy usage, rusting... oh, for loads of reasons, and they come up for all manner of repairs. All these effects of the material grand reaper happen selectively, and it was part of the Area Engineer's job to spot work beyond his domestic budget, and submit it for repair or replacement. Depending on the location, type and speed of traffic and many other factors, the District Engineer compiled all the submissions of his various Area reps, and placed a considered priority marking on each item. He also had to bring into his calculations the excitability and experience of his engineers, and their various abilities to vaporise over differing degrees of damage. This was the purpose behind his travels in the District Engineer's Saloon, to unify his submissions to headquarters.

Then along came the Chief Civil Engineer, with responsibilities extending the length of the country. Now he had to compare the marked histrionics of all his district engineers and add his own scoring, so that the whole region was treated as one, and money allocated on an overall priority basis.

This marking system was troubled with the same difficulties all such systems experience. It started with a simple Priority Mark of 1 for urgent work, 2 for must be done next year, and so on down to 5, which was simply "defer". Then the inevitable "Oh, my God, just look at this" would appear. Hence the introduction of the 1+. Uncertainty, head-scratching and budgetary caution created the 1-, 2-, 3- marks. Suddenly, out of the blue came a shattering, "Bloody hell fire! How're the buggers staying on track like this? It's flaming shattered!" Hence the "S" for special, almost "now", treatment. Added to all this they might have a stretch, which though only a 3, would suit future strategy for engineering purposes if it could be a 1. Hence the arrival of the 1E mark. All straightforward, but whatever happened to the old 1, 2, 3, 4, 5?

To demonstrate their technical knowledge, long-handled toffee hammers would be used by the group of engineers to clout the rusted rails and fastenings. When reversed, a spike, making up the tail of the hammer, was swung with remarkable skill to dig deep into rotting timbers. This was something I'm sure they all practised in private, out in the wilds somewhere. A green newcomer's hand could fail in a wildly impotent way, testing nothing but fresh air. I can't ever remember falling for this one myself, my inborn pessimism assuring me I'd miss, so I didn't even try. Somehow or other, this hammering, tapping, spearing and gouging confirmed to the educated technical engineer what had been blatantly obvious to the PWay Supervisor, using little more than his eyes and fingernails.

★

Serious stuff – inspections; and by association the saloon would have taken on a perpetual mantle of foreboding and gloom, were it not for the entertainment value it provided when used for the alternative, more light-hearted exercise of length marking. For this, the District Engineer would cobble together a party from his two assistants, and all four Area Engineers, of which Elliot Milner was one. On these trips, each member of the party would be dropped off along a particular line at three-mile intervals, to then walk on to the next dropping-off point, solemnly noting the condition of all the bits and pieces and awarding a mark for the standard of maintenance of the track and surroundings. A repeat run of the saloon would pick each marker up again at the end of their stretch, and so would be compiled a comprehensive survey of a particular line's state of health. This was "Length Marking", which was effectively technical bitching about the mess that a colleague's track was in. While I found myself becoming included on these through default – one of the others dropping out – I managed to actually enjoy them. There was an absence of the continuous tension found on inspections, and as a devotee of the laugh whenever possible, I had these trips down as being full of potential and prat-falls. But this could backfire, as on one memorable excursion, so dire that it stands as a tale on its own, and will crop up later.

On return runs, we'd all be gathered around the observation window, commenting pseudo-intelligently on the feel of the ride (the saloon's suspension was most unforgiving), and the general appearance of the track and surroundings. The poor sod who belonged to this stretch would be making feeble attempts at taking notes, while being tossed from side to side and pitched back and forth. None of the rest helped; rather they'd be digging out as much conditional trivia as they could, at the same time sniggering quietly at the furious scribbling going on behind them. While bowling along together, the Engineer would also throw out generalised wisdom on the overall appearance of the line – his various Assistants continually recycling their lists of excuses as to why it was whatever it was, but how it was to be whatever it was for not much longer.

In my early saloon days, with steam, I had a great problem with much of this. Here they'd be, trailing along in the observation suite with a small steam loco on the front. Generally speaking, half of what you could see was either track or sky, and the rest just steam. Had the balance been constant, something might have been salvaged from the exercise, but in practice the ratio of scenery to steam varied from 100% to zero.

"It's barmy, them pretending that they can make any sort of proper examination." I was complaining to Elliot, after I'd been seconded onto one of the length-marking runs. We'd escaped early, and were now waiting for a direct train back to Huddersfield. Coincidentally I was studying a poster pasted up on the wall outside the porters' room, advertising the railway in the countryside. "It's just like these nutters who go chuffing up the Settle–Carlisle line, conned into believing that it's the most scenic route in the country. I'd to go up to Carlisle once with our lass, and you're surrounded by all these barmpots, jabbering away about fields and hills… and, believe it or not, viaducts! The one place you can't see a viaduct is when you're on it! It's like going to Blackpool because of the tower – mind it's what we do; go up it on account of the top being the only place in Blackpool where you can't see it!"

"They pay our wages, these nutters of yours, Mike."

"Oh, I know that, but they're like in a state of continuous orgasm for the entire trip, purely because of the view. And then, what I was trying to say when I started, that view's apparently made all the more scenic by bunging a steam engine on the front, with the smoke and steam blocking out everything all down one side."

"I suppose it's the romance of steam that does it," said Elliot, vaguely, "a visible combination of manufactured and natural power, the might of machinery in perfect harmony with the savagery of nature."

"You what? Where the hell did that come from?" I asked, quite thrown by such poetic musings from this most unpoetic of men. After all, keep Elliot waiting ten minutes for his mug of tea, and you'd end up with loads of words, without any two of them rhyming. "Was it all your own?"

"As one who's spent all his working life in the atmosphere of steam," Elliot went on, "I would have supposed that such sentiments could trip lightly from the tongue, Mike. But I'm rather surprised that you, especially in the position you're in, didn't think of it yourself."

"How do you mean, 'my position'? What position's that, then?"

Elliot pointed to the wording at the bottom of the poster that I was stood gazing at, and grumbling about.

"...the romance of steam, might of machinery, savagery, yeh, yeh, very good!"

"What's up, didn't you enjoy the trip today, then? You came out of it in hand, mind!"

He was eyeing the baby walker, now stuffed under one arm, which I'd found at the bottom of a rock cutting. I'd come across it during my morning walk, amidst mattresses, broken furniture and assorted non-dustbin-type rubbish. Spots like these could be treasure troves – there was one in particular where the railway runs through a vertical rock cutting, with Gledholt Cricket Club's ground on the top. There used to be a regular fallout from Sunday League fixtures which kept the office cricket team in slightly damaged balls for many a season. This baby walker I'd picked up was in almost perfect nick, just a bit stiff in the wheels. It hadn't done it any harm coming second to a three-piece suite in the race over the fence at the top, and I saw it as being almost ideal for the near-toddler we had back home. I'd tortured myself working out whether it was worth picking up and carrying for the rest of my length, about a mile and a quarter; and then having to brave the company's likely reactions to me hoisting it onto the coach. In this worry I was justified.

"What's up, Mike, was the roundabout bolted down, then?"

"Get tired, did you, Mike? You were lucky to get a lift!"

"Ooo, look, it's Judy Garland – do the song!"

"Your mother's going to be that vexed when she finds she's left the gate open again!" Even the kitchen joined in: "Just what ah need on 'ere – does it keep stuff warm an' all?" This along with a call from the unfazed lookoutman: "Tha'd only t'say an' I could've looked out one more thy size, Mike!"

This last remark I thought was rich, coming from a bloke joining us earlier, to act as lookout for the Engineer. Before climbing aboard, he'd thrown a bloodstained bag on first, with a cheerful "Morning, Gents!"

"What have you there, then, Frank?" Elliot had ventured, knowing the total unpredictability of the man.

"Standard lookout gear, Elliot, whistle, horn, dets, y'know… all t'usual."

"And?" said Elliot.

"Oh, in theer? Well, there's a pheasant and t'best part on two rabbits. Anyone got a paper what they've dun wi'?"

He took the woman's pages of an offered broadsheet. Out of the bag he pulled a perfect-looking pheasant, totally intact, obviously hit in flight. This was laid aside, and onto the opened-out newspaper was tipped "t'best part on two rabbits". These were rabbits in kit form, with more than a possibility that some parts were missing. A bloody, almost unrecognisable mess, but apparently tradable tender in the pub later that evening.

We were breaking in a new Engineer around this time. Tim Avery was the recently appointed successor to the late J A Lewis. I found him a refreshing change from old Lewis, far more down to earth, and much easier to get on with. However, he still saw a distinction between meat for the table and dead animals found on the trackside. He couldn't quite grasp that this heap of dead rabbit(s) was anything but a pair of train-reshuffled corpses; it certainly hadn't reached any stage where it could be described as edible. Meat, for the Tim Averys of this world, came from the butcher's, not from farms and fields and railway lines.

"I can't see how you can take stuff that you find dead on the side of the track home and ask your wife to turn it into dinner; it just looks totally disgusting! Even the bird."

Frank put on his all-knowing expression. "D'yer like pheasant, Mr Avery?"

"Well, yes, very much actually, but I wouldn't—"

"Oh don't worry, Mr Avery, ah wouldn't offer thee this. Thur's a good Sunday lying theer for me an' our lass. Burra bet tha's bin in some posh rest'raunt wi' a chunk o'pheasant at three quid a throw…"

("Ten, actually," Tim muttered quietly aside.)

"…an' tha's theer wi't'rest on 'em spittin' out aif undredweight o' lead shot, wheeras me and t'auld lass are munchin' away wi'out a care in t'world. No shrapnel to avoid when it's bin mown dahn bi'a train, tha knaws, and all fer nowt!" This last bit underlined.

I stuffed my baby walker away in the guard's compartment.

"Dust'a reckon it'll be safe, like?" he asked in a concerned manner. "Ah could see they'd all on 'em got theer eyes on it."

I invited the guard, up to then a total stranger, to "Bog off!" and got a satisfyingly hurt look and a laugh back in return. It was now beginning to dawn on me that up to this point trolley smuggling had been easy; I'd still to get it home, after we'd left the relative privacy of the saloon.

We had the office car parked in Leeds, where we'd met the saloon that morning, so Elliot and I took the express home later that evening, travelling in a first-class compartment by dint of Elliot's status pass. That being the case, I'd no space problem, although the ticket inspector seemed to see some incongruity between the classification of the seating and the very second-hand look of the baby walker, but he let it pass. Besides which, Elliot and I – particularly Elliot – had distanced ourselves from the thing, both giving the impression that we'd found it there when we got on. On the other hand, the ticket barrier at Leeds was a trial. "Not sure you need a ticket, if you've come all the way on that thing, sir!"

Tucked under one arm, the damned trolley started growing and becoming progressively lumpier and more free-ranging, especially when I joined the bus queue. Confined by the sides of the tight shelter I could no longer hold it with any degree of comfort. Naturally, the bus was just about full when it came, and I'd to stand most of the way. It's amazing, and I've noticed this before with parcels on buses; out in the fresh air – no problem, but fitting things into a bus was always well nigh impossible. There wouldn't be enough space between you and the seat in front, or parts of it would be overlapping into the newspaper space of the person sitting next to you. Put it foul of the aisle and it will either worryingly change its shape as items of struggling humanity squeeze past it, or if made of sterner stuff, it will make inroads into anyone trying to get on or off. And that, with it placed at a particularly sensitive latitude, what's more. You could bet on the person sitting next to you needing to go ashore before you, by which time the package would have invariably integrated itself into part of the structure of the bus. What had once been a small wooden baby walker, lying on a dumped settee, was now the size of a platform trolley, with a long unwieldy and unyielding handle. It became the focal point of a growing circle of muttering.

It was still just light enough as I was walking up our street for the neighbour to notice and come out to study the walker. "Good year, but do you know what mileage it's done?" In the unforgiving light of our kitchen, it suddenly looked shabby, bent and slightly revolting. However, it was totally ignored by an excited Thelma as she came bustling through, followed by a very wobbly, but upright, eighteen-month-old offspring.

"What do you think? Started off on his own this morning," she said. "Just let go the settee and he was away. He's been toddling around all afternoon, isn't it marvellous? What's that thing you've got? It's a what? Well, we won't be needing it now, will we? Take it outside, it's filthy!"

★

This chasing all over the place in your own private train might seem a bit o-t-t to some – anyway, that's how I used to see it. Once I'd tried it, though, I knew it was really quite a good idea. Look at it this way; before an inspection Elliot and I could spend several days going round all our items by car. Usually, you could only get from road to railway at bridges or stations (we only had three level crossings on the entire Area, a by-product of the Pennine landscape). So any inspection item could involve a walk of up to a mile to get to it, and another half to walk through. Then you'd to trudge back to the car, unless someone like Bill was handy to run it through to the other end. On the coach you simply travelled from spot to spot.

There'd be the permanent way supervisor riding in the train cab, to make sure that you only pulled up at the worst bit of any item, a spot where he might have already replaced several sleepers, leaving the old ones on the side of the track to show what the rest must be like. Just looking at them wasn't enough for the inspection team, though. What I saw as the decaying remnants of a long dead tree, hollow and rotted through in places, had to be thumped and gored with their inspection hammers, to be followed by much muttering and head shaking before they climbed back inside the saloon. It was often a waste of time since the system was clearly open to abuse.

I'd found that more than one crafty supervisor kept a small stockpile of rotting sleepers, which he would run out year after year to the more borderline items, in order to boost his chances of getting them marked up for renewal. I also worked out that the Chief's clerk, Sydney Adams again, had evolved a secret marking system all of his own, which involved spiking a distinctive pattern in the sleepers at the ends. He could then spot a sleeper the following year that he'd seen before, probably miles away. Then came what he was best at, his need to gently embarrass all the home team, from supervisor through to the District Engineer himself. The invention of cans of spray paint negated this supervisory fiddle, but not before Adams had been headhunted by the District as a valuable man to have on their side.

★

Occasionally, the saloon would take on a one-off role. Like the PR trip up the Colne Valley, with town councillors, the Member of Parliament, and journalists from the local papers and TV, together with Elliot Milner, supervisor Jack Senior, and me. BR were trying to pump up some public interest (and sympathy) for proposals to spend on extensive realignment works for higher speeds on the Trans-Pennine route, now that there was direct competition from the new M62 motorway. There was also the possibility of rebuilding some stations lost under Beeching. I'd done all the proposed curve designs, and was by now firmly linked to project work. The powers couldn't really avoid having me exposed to the scrutiny of all the invited notables, despite any doubts or misgivings Elliot might have. He was there too, partly because of who he was, and also, quite obviously to watch out for me in the presence of the press. I'd a far too relaxed attitude towards officialdom – something that goes hand in hand with a serious lack of ambition. I might have been useful to management on the PR side, but I could sense that there was an element of deep mistrust amongst them as to how I might present myself, and the case, in certain company. I only liked to keep things simple and informal, because in my book informality subdued pomposity. However, my nominal betters seemed to see my sort of informality as unruliness. Around this time, management and I were travelling alongside each other, almost on parallel lines, as they began to accept that I lacked ambition for status, but craved higher-profile jobs. As a result, I tended to say what I felt, but not necessarily what I felt they wanted to hear.

It suited both Elliot and me to join the coach at Leeds that day, so we combined an easy start with an early coffee, spending the half hour to Huddersfield hardening up on what had to be put over to justify the expense of close on a million pounds. Arthur and Albert, the old messengers, had long since retired to lives of perpetual companionship at home, and it was the expert Gerry looking after us – so no worries on that front. For the one and only time, there I was, sat by rights in one of the two deepest armchairs, though I hardly looked the part. Despite thinly cloaked instructions, I had not dug out a suit for the occasion. Had management bothered to enquire of Thelma, she would have advised strongly against it anyway, knowing me capable of exhuming the Al Capone-style wedding suit that her retired 1930s' tailor/grandfather had put together while sat cross-legged on the kitchen table. The cut, particularly in the shoulder area, would have meant me approaching carriage doors sideways; it was, after all, built for a church. Elliot was keeping convention alight with his regulation three-piece charcoal job.

Dignitaries and press piled on at Huddersfield after the saloon had been shunted into a bay platform. Fresh coffee was served, and Elliot presented an overall view of the project, holding a token file in one hand and a charcoal lapel in the other. He came over strongly, trying desperately to set me a rigid agenda to follow before then handing over to me for details. This might seem a situation alien to my claim of inbuilt shyness, but I actually found it OK. So long as I was in control, things were fine – in fact fine bordering enjoyable, me being wrapped in the comfort of many practised ad libs, to suit most questions and comments.

After twenty minutes or so, the hourly express which alternately went to either Liverpool or North Wales pulled in, and the saloon was allowed to follow it up the valley, the idea being that I'd explain the reasons for, and effects of, the various realignments at each location we passed. The politicians seemed to be taking it all in, with their practised expressions of earnest absorption, and the TV crew were contentedly sitting in the loco cab, alongside the driver, filming and chirruping away like excited school kids. I wasn't altogether sure that the press from the local paper were totally caught up in the enthusiasm of the moment, since it was still stuffing itself (and its pockets) with biscuits, while determinedly draining the coffee pot.

As soon as we set off, I was away, managing to keep Elliot's tight-lipped features just outside my line of sight. I could comfortably bet that he'd have his fingers crossed – he'd heard me addressing the influential before. "We'll be singling the track through the Slow Tunnel. Clearances are pretty tight here. So tight, in fact, that the occasional guard's van tends to have its chimney circumcised as it comes through." I heard Elliot's unnecessary throat clearance, but I was on a roll now. "Sleepers are actually cut into the rock floor of this tunnel, and singling will give us a bit of leeway for maintenance. In fact it's so tight in here that the guard often goes through his train asking folk to take a deep breath in while the train is in the tunnel!" I got my satisfaction from the shuffles of relaxation among the crowd, together with Elliot spoiling the dignity of his situation a bit by knocking his empty coffee cup over. Instead of him being a steadying influence, Elliot's visible discomfort issued me with challenges.

Halfway through the tunnel, we had to pull up at a signal. I used the darkness, which always took time to adjust to despite the brilliance of a 40-watt light bulb in the saloon ceiling, to advantage. It nullified any messages from Elliot's eye, so I hauled out our story of when he and I were examining the tunnel roof near the station end, and found a crevice behind a small ledge, high up in the haunches. I'd squeezed through and found a compact chamber, with a brick wall at the end. Next day, I repeated the move in the company of the District Bridge Marker, a lad steeped with dark mystery. He was a completely barmy spare-time potholer, with wild staring eyes peering through a complete circle of undisciplined hair and beard. He looked like a startled rat climbing out of a barber's dustbin. With his experience of black holes he and I ventured further into the opening, and found a small gap in the brickwork. This was widened just enough for the deranged troglodyte to achieve that peculiar satisfaction they seem to gain from struggling through tight spots. Collapsing his body to half its size, he wormed his way through. I could hear exclamations, presumably peculiar to such creatures on finding themselves in a previously unknown cave, decorated with stalactites and the like. But there seemed to be a deeper emotion than you'd expect in his muffled cries, such as, "Bloody hell! I've gone to heaven!" My spot-lamp couldn't give me much idea of what Paradise actually looked like, but I got the message when the explorer returned to the hole, and handed me a couple of bottles of Jubilee Stout. We'd wormed our way into a pub cellar!

As the saloon travelled up the side of the valley, I'd be pointing out the various locations where I planned to slue right across the old formations that, prior to Beeching, had carried four lines, now reduced to two. (This allowed me to lengthen transitions between straights and curves, and I explained how this let me use curvature rules up to their limits, and offer the potential for the highest possible speeds.) I was becoming dreadfully well-behaved, but seeing Elliot settling back in his chair too well, I ventured into a little "Wall of Death" technology, which brought him swiftly back to the edge of his seat. This involved extraordinary superelevations, or cants, of the track, using principles similar to those of the fairground motorcycle entertainment cylinders. I'm afraid my analogies ran riot here, in a manner where fantasy increased in direct proportion to Elliot's brow clutching. At Longwood my design crossed the old station area, onto the newer section of the subsequent viaduct. This would make for a long stretch of straight at Longwood Goods, replacing the dog's back leg and underbelly of two reverse curves.

It was impossible to ignore the old lady who every day brought along her camping chair, thermos and knitting, and sat precisely on the line of the new railway. She never caused any problems, and friendly enquiries never really found out what the attraction was for her. She was generally dismissed as a daft old bat, but she set our group chattering, and I could see that Elliot would have preferred it if she hadn't been pointed out in the first place, especially as the local journalist had decided to take out his biro for the very first time and spoil a virgin page of his notepad. He added more notes as I pointed out that we were passing Joe Harry Ward's bridge, reason for name unknown, and he seemed captivated by my ghost of Linthwaite coal drops, which was why I invented it. Sadly, my Beast of Paddock Tunnel seemed to be a step too far for his confident incredulity.

Through Golcar, the new line was to hug the rising banking to avoid going near the biggest earth slip area I'd ever encountered. You could see it as a dip of a few feet where the old Fast Lines had been, running close alongside the railway that remained. An enormous slip circle was apparent, coming out some sixty feet down the embankment slope as a swollen bulge in the fields below. Boundary walls and a footpath had been taken away with it, now well below their original levels. You could tell that its upper boundary line was the natural break between solid rock cutting and the fill used for the second pair of lines in the old four-track days. I still look forward to seeing it move significantly at sometime, though it's now over thirty years since I first came across it, but it made for a good tale of dramas yet to unfold.

From the slip area, my design swung right across into a long straight up to Slaithwaite, where there was the certainty of a new station. Here the MP, Mr Wainwright, (Lib.) asked a far too intelligent question, as to why I would be replacing one straight with another, just ten yards to the side of it. My real reason was that it would make life easier for me while the track relaying went on, but I was in a world of my own by now, and shrugged his question aside, suggesting that passengers would have much better views of the full-flowered gardens which tumbled down from the cliff-hanging houses all the way to the trackside. Mr Wainwright, a true politician, recognised evasion, and laughed before asking a more direct question about Slaithwaite itself, where we were to pull up for a photo call. My pal with the biro and notepad scribbled away furiously.

Elliot dived in at Slaithwaite, and took to chatting up the party. He knew I'd a few too many stories of life and works around this spot up my sleeve, and no doubt thought it was time for *Mikeus*

Interruptus, if only to allow the press ballpoint to cool down. Official snaps taken, we continued on up to Marsden, and through Standedge Tunnel, stabling in a siding off the Goods Loop at Diggle. There we took questions, while Gerry launched his spectacular buffet lunch. Odd councillors were taken outside to be interviewed for television, while the investigative journalist from the local press busied himself with a comprehensive survey of the sandwich fillings.

Elliot and I stayed with the coach through to Leeds, after dropping off the nobs at Huddersfield, on the way back. He appeared to be in a good mood, probably because he'd collared the newshound and engaged him in a long and detailed explanation of the work and its effect on the locals. He'd obviously taken the busy pen racing over the notepad to be an encouraging sign that the lad was getting down the major facts, and was now concentrating on the main issues.

From where I'd been standing, the inadequate cartoon, detailing some of Elliot's less impressive features, which was taking shape at the end of the active pen, did little to convince me that Elliot's eloquent flow was sinking in.

On the following evening, a nice little piece appeared on the TV news magazine, fully justifying the fact-spreading trip, but it was the local newspaper which both Elliot and I found disturbing. It summarised the whole project up, with its eye-catching headline: "A MILLION POUNDS, SO YOU CAN GET A BETTER VIEW OF THE DAFFS!"

★

In a long life, one day can sometimes stand out, every little detail etched in your memory, and seeming almost as long as life itself. The Glass Coach was set up to provide this sort of day, and one such evolved, centring on me and based on the coach. It started out at rock bottom and just went downhill from there, one disaster triggering off another. It wasn't funny at the time... Well, it was, I suppose, but you didn't have to show it. Hence an extra chapter!

Saloon, Part 2

No way did this trip look promising, particularly as Stompy (Bernie) Clark was to be the only messenger available to act as attendant and do the cooking. Albert was on holiday, and Arthur had retired, while Gerry remained undiscovered as yet. In the few weeks before he was to join Arthur in the everlasting bliss of retirement, Albert had been saddled with his most daunting task to date: teaching Stompy to take his place. He said he'd have had a better chance training a dead dog, even if he only managed to get it to lie down! There were problems getting any sort of coordination between Clark, letters and pigeon holes, let alone tea, milk, sugar and cups, so there was nothing about Stompy to inspire any confidence in his ability to cope with cooking for the saloon, especially when you took into account his own confidence that he could! (Regarding the making of tea, saucers were initially brought into the equation, but Stompy wanted to know what the purpose of this stranger to his world was, and nobody could come up with a satisfactory response.)

Stompy was a young lad, very well built, but without the height. (I want an alternative to "well" built. Stompy wasn't moulded "well" at all. He'd been started on, but had never really been finished, the Creator probably having been called away to the phone, or something.) He would stomp along the corridors, with individual parts of his body moving in all compass directions at once, such that the corridor was wholly his, and anyone else had to stand aside. His messenger's uniform was worn in such a way as to convince you that it had been made up from the various cast-offs of three distinctly different people. Each of his main pockets would bulge and fly aside with a life of its own. Just how they came to achieve such detachment could only be appreciated when he occasionally emptied one of them. Out would tumble a miniature tip site of unconnected "souvenirs", as he called the mobile junk yard. Meeting him in the corridor and pressing yourself into the wall as he passed with an ever-cheerful expletive still didn't guarantee safety, as a jacket pocket and contents could be swinging free, to catch you a nasty wallop. Certain missile altitudes can be lethal for a male victim.

In the role of Office Messenger, Stompy could not be rated as a square peg in a round hole. No, he was definitely a round peg, but the round hole was several times bigger than the peg, such that, while slotting in easily, there was plenty of slack, making loads of leeway for mishap. Life was a trial for Stompy, but he was the only person who didn't see it as such. Take, for instance, a fairly straightforward task like making the Engineer's afternoon cup of tea. The journey from tap to table was beset with hurdles. Admittedly, I'm giving a worst-case scenario here, but it's based on many individual observations.

In the corner of the messenger's office-cum-reception was a single gas ring, with a rescued black kettle, minus lid. Several saucers were piled up alongside some cups, upturned on a BR tea towel. This had been clean once, but months of use soaking up the remnants of rinsed cups had reduced the red and blue check pattern to a variable brown, with several fairy rings of fuzzy growth around the edges. This was possibly of no great significance, since Stompy would automatically give each cup a wipe on his uniform sleeve before placing it on a randomly selected unmatching saucer. He grew to accept this last item, purely as a safety net against escaping liquids.

Come the hour of three, and the basic ingredient, water, would be carefully measured into the kettle. This was from a large milkchurn-like vessel that held several gallons, and stood at the side of the radiator. Two examples of Stompy genius: he only had to take the churn to the tap in the Gents about once a fortnight, and by placing it near the radiator, it was always part warmed-up for the gas ring to finish the job. By the end of those two weeks, the water generally became a little cloudy, but was obviously still in a good state, because, if you looked very carefully, you could see it was supporting life in the form of tiny things swimming about in it.

Further small solids entered the reckoning as the open kettle came into play, but no doubt the time taken to mash the tea in the small brown teapot, allowed bits and bobs to settle out. Recognisably brown on the outside, the pot was chimney black within. Proud of his standards of hygiene, Stompy regularly treated it with heavy quantities of Vim scourer, and a Brillo pad that was almost certainly from the first batch that Brillo had ever made. The mixture was then swilled out with an economic amount of his precious water. These "regular" de-cokings Stompy came to refer to as his "spring cleaning", which rather defines "regular".

Now to the recipe. Tea leaves (or the added complication of coffee on special occasions), milk and sugar. All the right things went into producing the steaming cup, but the individual quantities tended to fluctuate, since it was three of one, two of another and one of the last, but Stompy had never really pinned down three, two or one whats or which. No two cups of tea were ever the same, which in itself was some source of comfort to the Engineer, for it was he and his two assistants who were the recipients of Stompy's concoctions.

So then came the journey from messenger's cubicle to the Engineer's door, all of twelve yards. Without fail, the idiosyncrasies of semi-detached bits of the lino-covered floor meant at least one pause to relocate the tea from the saucer back into the cup. (As we've pointed out, the concept of a saucer had come as a revelation to Stompy, and to him its purpose was justified to some extent the first time the lino bit him.) On this short journey, quite a miscellany of incidents might befall the brew. Take the spoon; once again inspired by the lino, it could fly off and land in the fire bucket of sand (fluff, fag ends, pencil shavings, and other things less easily pinned down). Stompy was seen to replace the spoon in the saucer after thoughtfully cleaning off any debris, by dipping it in the tea, and drying it, using his uniform sleeve. Also, when given the added dimension of a free-flowing Stompy head cold, the cup could end up slightly fuller at the end of its journey than when it started out. Stompy did have a hankie (another check duster-cum-tea towel), but it had come without instructions, and the various uses which Stompy put it to did not include wiping rapid fire stalactites off the end of an erupting nose.

One final enhancement would occur at the Engineer's door. Stompy, now aware of the spiteful nature of the lino and therefore steadying the cup with one hand, would be trying to ignore the scalding of his thumb as the tea slopped around it. At this point he might notice the incomplete nature of his earlier rinsing, and spot distinct lip marks on the rim of the cup. This he could see as contravening his code of hygiene, so a quickly licked finger was used to remove the offending blemish. Knock on the door, march in, stumble on carpet, "Tea, Mr Avery!", repeat saucer back into cup routine, place cup with damp saucer directly in front of boss to save him reaching. Lift cup and saucer up again with a "Sorry, Mr Avery!", and perform a final flourish of the hankie to spread the wet, brown ring evenly over the unfortunate document that he had selected as his landing site.

Now in case you've ever happened to meet Stompy at any time, let me assure you on one thing you might have noticed; Stompy didn't have a speech defect as such, but his rapid fire, tumbling delivery coming from opposing sides of his mouth with alternate phrases, tended to induce a hearing deficiency in others. Words did form intelligible sentences, but might emerge in a random order. This effect was exaggerated by excitement or indignation. When I tentatively questioned him about his culinary skills, after news of the proposed saloon trip had leaked out, Stompy had replied with a scrambled, but amazing confidence, in thoroughly unconvincing detail. He still lived at home with his mother, and was fully provided for. I quickly worked out that this lad had watched, but never done, and judging by his mastery of other life skills, I reckoned that we had one here who was capable of burning lettuce and overboiling toast, and be contented with the result.

I knew that I was destined to be on this trip, so I quizzed Ozzie Dean, the clerk responsible for organising the saloon and meal, as to the ingredients he proposed to put at Stompy's mercy. This was not done so much for myself as for Elliot Milner, who was also bound to be a member of the party. Elliot unfortunately was jinxed with a stomach quite alien to the rest of his strong constitution, and was therefore very concerned that anything dumped in it was first and foremost digestible. Ozzie was not included on length-marking jaunts (he only being involved in strictly programme work), so as a result he was fairly unconcerned about the make-up of the menu, and was open to ideas. This was where fellow clerk, the newly appointed Elaine Barnes, was brought into the discussions. She was involved in minor catering in her private life, and would have been an ideal choice to do the cooking, were not these still the days where a messenger's job was the job of a messenger, and nobody else's, especially not a female. Demarcation ruled the day.

So, the self-appointed committee came up with vegetable soup from a packet for starters. This would only need mixing correctly, warming and stirring. Spotting the snag in this, Elaine came in early on the morning and did the mixing herself. This was the age before television devoted the bulk of its output to either rearranging people's insides, their houses, or the contents of an infinite larder. What she could do, was either mother's knee cookery, or what she'd taught herself, and she was more than capable of knocking a programme together combining culinary satisfaction with Stompy-proof simplicity.

We fully explained warming and stirring to an increasingly indignant Stompy, who declared himself "Not flickerin' numb, tha knaws!"

Elaine settled for the traditional grilled lamb chops and new potatoes, with a side salad, as being the safest of combinations, along with written instructions – "Of course I can flickerin' read 'em! Tha's beginnin' to gerron mi flickerin' tits, your three." This apart, our *chef-d'œuvre*-in-making did not see his abilities questioned at all as he read through the bit about not baking, boiling or grilling anything that was green. The feast was to be rounded off with cold sweets and cream, which was something else Elaine could put together and deliver on the day. In fact all Stompy had to do was grill chops, boil potatoes, and sling the stuff on the table in the right order, but I still remained gloomy about it all.

Two sets of instructions were given to Stompy (with secret copies to me). One was headed "Train Schedule", prepared by Ozzie. It gave minute details of all the dropping off and picking up mileages for the marking team, along with train timings, turn-round arrangements and stabling instructions. The other set was Elaine's culinary orders.

It was a cracking fine spring morning on the day, with a promise of much the same to follow. Ideal, Elaine remarked, as we set things out in the saloon kitchen. A warming soup after a cool morning's walk, a light main course and a delicate sweet to prepare for the warmth of the afternoon. Her normal optimistic attitude had but the slightest hint of some fraying around the edges, which was enough to send my habitual pessimism ("sense of reality" in my terms) into spin mode. Everything was loaded up, and the two lists of instructions pinned up in the kitchen. Stompy threatened violence as I attempted to show him which list was which, so I left him to it, and took a look around the saloon.

This was my first chance to explore the new inspection coach, a converted two-car diesel multiple unit. It wasn't a patch on the old one for grandeur. All the finery was gone, with the exception of the Engineer's two wing chairs, now filling most of the former first-class compartment, up front. In true railway style, the new dining table was a more conventional width, which was great until you realised that you now had to practically sit outside and eat through the windows. Anyone sitting in any position other than the very foot of the table was now securely trapped. On the plus side, taking the saloon as a whole, with it having two coaches there was now twice as much overall room.

Making up the day's party were the District Engineer, Tim Avery, and his two Assistant DEs, Quentin Vertigans on the PWay side and Owen Smith from the Works. Jack Senior was to walk with Tim, allowing them to have a thorough policy chat in amiable circumstances. Other runners included two of the four Area Assistants, one of which was Elliot, the other being Nick Bailey, a newcomer to the District. The absent two had managed to arrange previous commitments after getting details of the day's activities. One of them was a star at this, but on the way had had to arrange a parental divorce, the remarriages of both, and consequently two more sets of delicate step-grandparents, in order to account for the unusual number of weddings, deaths and funerals which had demanded his presence. This being a length-marking exercise, the party included recruits from the Drawing

Office. Chief Draughtsman, Kye Bevin and his Senior PWay Assistant, Colin Lamb. I completed the team, substituting for one of the missing Area men. (From this point on I was always to be included on length markings for some reason or another.)

Markers were each allocated one of eight three-mile stretches in the morning, covering from just outside Leeds Station to the Marsden end of Standedge Tunnel – a total of twenty-four miles. Kye was to be excluded from the afternoon session, a railway-style concession to his heart condition only allowing him a morning walk. This condition of his often left him tired and emotional after dinner anyway, due to his personally devised regime of midday medication. This left the remaining seven of us to share out the thirteen miles of the Penistone Branch for our post-dinner stroll.

According to the schedule, Kye was to be whipped off by Percy in the office car to his starting point on the outskirts of the Leeds West End complex. From there he was to walk the first three miles, with me dropping off to cover the next section. This meant that my stretch included the full two miles of Morley Tunnel, a source of great amusement to some of the others. My superiors, in rank if not age, were quick to point out that the junior would always be expected to take on the toughest length. One of these "superiors" I could count among my many two-month whiz-kid specials who'd passed through the Huddersfield Office in my time. I was quite content to recall that this particular individual, now treating me as a subordinate, had once made my tea and coffee twice daily, for eight weeks.

As it happened, the prospect of Morley Tunnel suited me down to the ground, relieving me of having to examine such extras as embankments, ditches and fencing, and making the weather, for two-thirds of my walk at least, completely reliable. The loneliness of the long-distance tunnel walker was familiar territory for me, and something I was more than comfortable with. One thing that always nagged at me, whenever I was track walking alone, was safety, and I'd always considered long tunnels like Morley and Standedge the safest of places you could find on the railway.

So, the skies were blue, I'd got what I considered to be a

doddle of a stretch, and Stompy was well under control, thanks to what appeared to be the most detailed sets of instructions imaginable. Prospects were beginning to look distinctly boring.

There was an immediate blip on the catering side, which I laid entirely at Elaine's feet (in thought only – no man in his right mind would criticise her organisational ability to her face!). She had clearly failed in her list of dos and don'ts to distinguish for Stompy the essential difference between coffee grounds and the instant that he served up now and again in the office. Subsequently the company, with the disgruntled exception of Kye, were exposed to a lukewarm suspension of flavoured gravel, which they each dealt with in their own way.

As was always the case on these occasions, the saloon's start was delayed due to the vagaries of the rush-hour traffic, so Kye found that he'd not only missed coffee, but had been walking for half an hour before we actually passed him. As we did this, giving him a friendly wave of encouragement, we were struck by the progress he'd made. I didn't know, until later chatting to Percy, that Kye had got him to drive a good mile further on than he should, relieving the aged one of a third of his portion. Kye had thoughtfully sent Percy back over the missed bit to make sure that there was nothing obvious he should have seen. As the saloon passed him I knew what must be going through his mind – the sad fact that the train would have to complete the round trip from Leeds to Marsden and back before it even set off again to pick him up on its second run.

So I was the first one to actually drop off from the saloon itself, and as I took each of the vertical steps from coach to ground I felt a wave of relief coming over me. I sensed the responsibility of having to idiot-sit the unpredictable Stompy dropping away. Waving off the departing coach, all my troubles went with it. After all, the next time I was to set foot on it, Stompy would have performed his magic, and there'd be a simple, but acceptable meal to relax into.

By the time the saloon arrived at the final dropping-off point, it was running half an hour late, so Tim Avery put another spoke in the wheel of misfortune by giving instructions for it to return to Leeds and make a start on the picking-up run immediately, rather than stick to the forty-five minute wait that Ozzie had scheduled in. As luck would have it, there were no hold-ups on the run back to Leeds, and they managed a quick turnaround before starting out to pick us all up. So Stompy, obeying the last instruction to the letter, managed to set off twenty minutes early on his mission to collect up all his guests for his culinary experience of their lifetimes. What follows I've had to piece together from the various irritable, incredulous and confused conversations with which the rest of the day was peppered.

Now a quick rundown of the normal rules governing length-marking trips.

1. The picking-up run will always be either on time, or as usually happened, up to half an hour later than schedule. (It is at the mercy of any late-running service trains, which must obviously have precedence.)
2. Whatever progress the walker is making, he should always ensure that he is at the agreed picking-up point by the scheduled time. This still allows at least forty minutes per mile for walking and making notes.
3. Despite the driver having a rough idea where he might expect to have to stop, the walkers should always make their presence clear as they see the train approach.
4. Nothing will then go wrong.

★

Kye Bevin had been feeling the one and a half miles he'd so far completed, and had dropped on a lineside cabin, just as the gang were having their mid-morning mashing. He was a well-known figure to the lads on the ground, regularly appearing on site during Sunday track-works, and he often entertained any willing companions to a drink, if their shift ended around opening time. He'd missed coffee, not realising just how fortunate he'd been in this, since "coffee" was a term he would never have applied to Stompy's warm slurry, so he was more than amenable to the call of "Come on in, Kye, old luv, tha looks like tha could do wi'a cuppa." He checked his watch; three-quarters of an hour before any scheduled pickup. Apart from that, he was determined that he'd walked as far as he was going to. He needed to underline the fact that he was not fit for any further hiking after dinner. The lads in the gang were keen to tap him up about any big jobs that might be coming their way soon, since he was known as being the architect of the last major upheaval of the Leeds track layout. This had lined many local Sunday pockets very well. Kye was always willing to chat, and was comfortable with his implied equality with the lads (I'd watched this in Kye, and had deliberately taken it on board myself). After a refill had been downed from the ubiquitous blue-rimmed white enamel mug, with its scalding-hot handle, Kye took another glance at his watch. Twenty minutes by his watch still left before he would be met by the saloon, which by the Rules of Life detailed by Sod was sadly running the same twenty minutes early. The gang were by now making their way back to their point of work a quarter of a mile away, and only recognised the new anonymous Engineer's Saloon as it passed them, seeing as it was now disguised as an ordinary DMU. One of the lads was sent back to the cabin to tell Kye that he'd missed it, and the ganger wandered off to the signal box to arrange some sort of transport for their pal. This they managed, taking Kye on by gang bus to catch up with the saloon, and his dinner, at Marsden. A minor hiccup, but satisfactorily sorted.

★

I still had that warm feeling of relieved responsibility, and was perfectly happy trudging through Morley Tunnel, pausing now and again to take the occasional track cross-level reading with the obligatory five-foot-long gauge that we had to carry on these walks. I was strictly pacing myself, as the designated rendezvous point was in the sunless cutting at the Batley end of the tunnel. This would always be a rather cool spot on a spring morning, and I had no wish to be there for more than ten minutes if I could help it. While still half a mile from the tunnel end, I felt the telltale draught of a light wind on the back of my neck, clear indication of a train approaching from Leeds, behind me. The air in the tunnel was remarkably clean that morning, and I'd been able to pick out my target of the Batley mouth, two miles off, almost as soon as I'd entered the tunnel at Morley. Turning, I could easily make out the headlights of the approaching train, still a minute away, so I walked on to the next refuge built into the tunnel wall, to stand clear. It was with a sinking feeling that I noticed, as I acknowledged the driver's passing horn, the unmistakable features of Stompy pressed hard up against the windscreen.

Being me, I straight away assumed that I'd cocked up on the timing, so I checked the running sheet as best I could, by the light of my jumping hand-lamp in the tunnel's total darkness. I was able to work out that the saloon was running nigh on half an hour early. This, though I didn't realise it at the time, was due to a combination of the early return start, and the minutes gained by not managing to pick Kye Bevin up. Resigned to fate, I marched off to complete an extra mile beyond the tunnel to take me through Ibbotson Rose's cutting and past the signal box, occasionally womanned by the formidable Isobel. I was particularly fed up, since I could foresee the rubbishing I'd get from the others in missing the train, regardless of the fact that I was deep under the centre of Morley at the time it passed me. On the plus side, I found that I was well placed to catch the Manchester stopper at Batley which would take me on to Marsden, but I still balked at the embarrassment of missing half the dinner. Little did I know...

★

Dewsbury Station stood about two-thirds along Owen Smith's allocated stroll. With the best part of an hour left to walk his final mile, Owen decided to take a look at the job his Works team were doing on the Booking Office there. Never one to turn down hospitality, he grabbed at the offered mug of tea. It was a distinct improvement on his usual afternoon cup in the office, what with not having Stompy's thumb, and other adventures, to add to the flavouring. He was quite oblivious of the saloon as it screamed through the station while he sat inside in comfortable ignorance.

★

By now, Stompy had worked out that things weren't happening quite as they should, but he wasn't sure why. The train seemed to be travelling further ahead of time the more people it didn't stop to pick up, and he was having difficulty getting his thoughts together, especially with the dinner to think about as well. He was now to have a slight revival of spirits, as they passed through Thornhill LNW Junction. Here their line joined the tracks of the Calder Valley route, to diverge again three miles further on at Heaton Lodge. With the Calder line taking a longer way round through the Pennines, by about nine miles in fact, compared to the more direct Standedge/Colne Valley one, this dual section had two differing sets of mileposts, with the higher numbered one prevailing. Prior to the junction, the last milepost they'd passed had 32 miles from Manchester stamped on it; following the junction the Calder Valley mileage prevailed. For this reason, Stompy suddenly entered the familiar territory of total confusion, as the mileposts abruptly jumped up to 39, which according to his sheet was somewhere just outside Leeds. Since his instructions told him to pick up Mr Bevin around the 37-milepost, which would be two miles further on, he allowed himself to relax a bit. The fact that the train had been doing around sixty for twenty minutes since leaving Leeds for the second time, along with questions about Kye's stamina, did not stimulate either cell in Stompy's brain.

Between being buried in uncertainty, and his running orders, Stompy was in no position to spot Elliot Milner waving on the trackside. However the driver did give the frantic figure a friendly toot as he flew past, which really bugged Elliot. He was a mile short of his allotted target, but at the same time he was at one end of Mirfield station platform. He continued moodily through the platforms, responding to the toot of another train coming up behind him. Suddenly he was faced with the no-contest dilemma of either walking his last mile on, only to have to walk back in the hope of another train, or jumping on this one, the local Wakefield to Huddersfield stopper. Quarter of an hour later he was walking into his own office, where he set about trying to sort through the confusion of messages that Bill Boyes had been taking from up and down the line. Bill, who'd put two and two together from the fund of information that he'd spent the morning harvesting, was now beside himself with delight at the turmoil unfolding before him. This did not put him in the best of positions to deal with a now furious Elliot, normally a placid man, but known for erupting spectacularly when unreasonably crossed.

Elliot eventually gathered that Kye had been missed, and had managed a lift up to the dining point of Marsden. I'd sent on a message from the infamous signal box at Batley, not on this occasion female territory, to say that I too had been ignored, but would be making my own way on to Marsden. No word from Owen Smith though, who hadn't as yet realised he'd been stranded, and was at that moment blissfully walking between Dewsbury and Ravensthorpe, humming a spring morning song. A query from Central Control wanted to know just what they thought they were playing at, flying through half an hour, nay, nearer three-quarters ahead of time now. Also there were the usual day-to-day problems on his desk, so Elliot, with some little relief at missing the prospect of a maiden dinner from Stompy, decided to stay put, and go for his usual thirty bob's worth at The Princess, planning to rejoin the saloon when it returned to Huddersfield for the afternoon stint up the Penistone Branch. Finally he rang Marsden signal box to explain all that had occurred, for them to pass on to the saloon when it arrived there.

★

By now you won't be at all surprised to find that Elliot's Area Assistant colleague, Nick Bailey, walking the fifth length, was faring no better. Nick was new to this part of the country, and a complete stranger to the Huddersfield Area. This being the case, he had managed to walk straight on at the divergence point of Heaton Lodge Junction. He was now marching confidently up the wrong valley. It was only a chance encounter with a gang, and a cheerful question, accompanied by an unappreciated slap of his thigh, as to how many miles it was to Manchester, that he realised the answer of thirty-six hardly tallied with his pickup point of the 27-milepost. Much mirth and embarrassment later, he began to retrace his steps, happy only in the knowledge that he had plenty of time to spare. Even this sop was to be dashed away from him as he saw the saloon, approaching some four hundred yards away, only to turn sharp left at the junction, towards Huddersfield. A stranger in a strange land, and a proud one at that, he was not going to return to the gang, so he made for the road, and put himself at the mercy of the local bus services, aiming for Huddersfield after a change in Brighouse.

★

Colin Lamb, the Drawing Office PWay boss, now had Huddersfield Station in his sights. He still had the two North and South parallel tunnels at the far end of the station to negotiate before reaching his rendezvous point, but on paper he'd loads of time left to do it. With the possible remodelling of the whole station area, pencilled in for the not too distant future, and for it to be placed under his wing, he sauntered steadily through the station with added interest before starting on an exploration of the tunnel depths, and the junctions at either end.

Stompy, for once, did not shoot through the station, but had the presence of mind to stop the train, get out and try to find out from the PWay Office why everyone seemed to be avoiding him. This was, of course, long before Elliot's arrival, and all he had was Bill and his small pile of messages, which did in part console the lad that it wasn't a total disaster. Sadly, Bill, as usual, was seeing the funnier side of events, and became completely useless. Stompy, now back down to twenty minutes ahead of schedule, set off again, becoming desperate at the likely lack of takers to sample the mysteries of his kitchen. Needless to say, Colin Lamb was examining the track in Huddersfield North Tunnel, as the saloon slipped by through the parallel South hole.

★

If you're still following this, (perhaps a map would have been handy) you'll realise that there was now only one further pickup left. In the clear countryside up near Slaithwaite, with excellent sighting from the cab window, added to the fact that Stompy's eyes were, by now, stuck out like chapel hat pegs in search mode, you will see that the ideal storyline must fail at the last hurdle, and that there could be little chance of him achieving a complete zero.

No. I'm afraid that if Stompy was destined for a place in history, he was to achieve it with honours.

Quentin Vertigans was savouring the views afforded by this penultimate length that clung to the northern slopes of the Colne Valley. Over on the far side he could see occasional blocks of stone houses gripping the steep slopes alongside the A62, with the valley floor devoted to the river, the canal and one mill after another. Flashes of brilliant yellow heralded the appearance of the year's lineside burgeoning broom bushes. He too was quite a bit ahead of schedule, and had decided to take a breather in the newly opened timber-built station at Slaithwaite. He was last there for the opening, three months earlier, two weeks before Christmas, with some character dressed as Santa Claus turning up on the first train to stop there. With this in mind, he'd just been having a look at the platform footings, which consisted of paving slabs supporting four by four timber uprights. He noted that two of them were still badly cracked. This being the legacy from the extraordinary idea of having a dance team perform at the opening, a story which will appear in full in this book's stop press section. Quentin decided to wander round, under the station bridge, to check to see if the car park had settled down. (Patience! This too will be explained later.)

Now distinctly puzzled, what with the mileposts having reverted to Colne Valley readings, Stompy had determined that he would at least pick up one of his targets. He had the train pull up at Slaithwaite Station so that he could get out and look for Quentin, perhaps in one of the shelters, only for the driver to insist that they got moving, as he knew a service train was in close pursuit (with me on it, as it happened). There was no sign of Quentin who was sadly just twenty feet away, under the station bridge.

★

Stompy's arrival with the saloon at Marsden, for the second time that day, was a fairly sombre affair. He brightened up briefly when he saw Kye Bevin coming down the signal box steps. This gave him a momentary surge of hope, since Kye's was the first name on his pickup list, but this didn't gel with the fact that he'd just passed Tim Avery, together with Jack Senior, half a mile back. These two had the distinction of being the first, and only, walkers Stompy had spotted all morning. The pair could now be seen in the distance walking towards the sidings where the train was being shunted, oblivious of the morning's dramas. Any last flickers of hope spluttered and died with Kye's laboured mounting of the saloon steps, accompanied by an illuminating phrase with each pause for breath. Kye was good with words, and once inside the saloon and realising that his sense of injury was not to impress anyone, since they all seemed to be in the same boat, his vocabulary was used beyond any previous limits. Elliot's message was yet to be despatched to the signal box, as he was at that moment just arriving at his office and beginning the process of trying to research the extent of the debacle, with the "help" of a helpless Bill. At the moment when Tim and Jack stepped up into the saloon, to be greeted by Kye Bevin, and no one else, the state of the nation was as follows:

1. Kye had arrived by gang bus, and was bang back on schedule, helped by the saloon having stopped for a short while at Huddersfield.

2. I was just arriving at Marsden by the service train, almost full of apprehension as to the reaction of the others. Situation (7), below, had occurred three miles back, bringing a little sunshine back into my life. Not being spotted in the pitch dark of the tunnel was a pretty reasonable excuse, and the disappearing figure of Quentin Vertigans around Slaithwaite, in full sun, reinforced this. My actual reception of "Thank God someone else's got a bit of gumption!" from Tim Avery of all people, was not just a little pleasing. Added to this the clouds of confusion began to clear as I listened to the coda of Kye's exposé on the new extension to Stompy's range of inabilities.

3. Owen Smith had cheerfully wandered on after the welcome break in Dewsbury Booking Office, and was passing a couple

of the Huddersfield Works lads, busy working on a waiting room door at Ravensthorpe Station. They hailed him as a popular boss, and expressed surprise that he "weren't on t'glass coach what had whipped through aif an hour ago". A phone call to Control confirmed the unwelcome truth, and Owen readily accepted a lift as far as Huddersfield, "in abaht an aif 'our, or so, when wiv done", from the door-knob technicians.

4. Elliot, as we've seen, was busy at his desk, with one hand on his phone, trying to get an overall picture before ringing Marsden box.

5. Nick Bailey, the one who had taken the wrong turning, was just leaving Brighouse on the Huddersfield bus, with no definite plans for the rest of his day.

6. Colin Lamb, after exploring the bowels of Huddersfield, had arrived at his pickup point, and being a slightly impatient man, had immediately rung Huddersfield signal box to see how long he would have to wait. The answer of minus fifteen minutes didn't go down too well. He tramped back to Huddersfield, there joining up with Elliot who was by now calmer, and in a position to introduce Colin to the delights of The Princess's three-course standard. This cheered Colin up no end, since he'd now be able to claim lunch expenses.

7. Quentin Vertigans had returned to Slaithwaite platforms where he sat a long time, dutifully allowing the stopping train to leave without him, assuming the saloon to be on its tail. He was visibly put out on catching sight of me waving to him from the rear non-smoking section as I passed.

8. Tim Avery was muttering in a dangerous way, with only Kye as an audience. Jack was interrogating Stompy and the guard.

Elliot's message duly arrived at Marsden signal box. He'd caught Colin Lamb, and Owen had turned up, rather sadly at the precise moment that the other two were coming back from dinner. Jack Senior rang back, reporting that we were four at Marsden, so between them Elliot and Jack were able to summarise the disaster score sheet as: Marsden 4, Huddersfield 3, Missing 2 – Nick Bailey (wrong turning) and Quentin Vertigans (sat on a seat at Slaithwaite). The latter was retrieved from obscurity after he rang Control from a signal near the station. Field Marshall Avery then decided that the only reliable way to get his troops together was to take the saloon back to Huddersfield, which he did, on the way achieving a first for the day by picking Quentin up en route. All this gave Stompy welcome time to redeem himself by concentrating on the dinner.

I was still feeling pretty chuffed at making the rendezvous at Marsden, and thought to take a look in the kitchen, experience telling me that I might not expect to stay being chuffed for long. Elaine's instructions were fluttering on a pin above the stove and Stompy was intent on stirring a steaming pan of soup. I got no further than the door, partly due to a brisk "Bugger off, thee!", but mainly because the small galley had visibly shrunk by having the undisciplined bulk of Stompy stuffed into it. His resentment was immediate at the interruption, so I went back to my bottle of warm shandy (this now being the top-whack aperitif under the latest railway drink rules). I'd noted smells and steam, so could only rely on this as being evidence of a meal in the making when asked.

"Everything going OK in that department then, Mike?" asked Tim.

"Seems alright, but the lump won't let me help."

"It's not your place to interfere; if he says he's OK, let him be."

And that's how things stood as we made our way back to Huddersfield, Jack having sorted out the return and a handy bay platform for us to stable in over dinner. By the time the saloon reached Huddersfield, Nick Bailey had been dropped off at the town's bus station and had used a badly abused "You Are Here" map to find his way back to the railway station. He'd asked as to the whereabouts of the Civil Engineer's office, where he experienced a slightly emotional reunion, as he met up with one hungry Owen and the adequately stuffed Elliot and Colin. When all were safely gathered back in the saloon, these last two had the decency to look a bit sheepish in their inner comfort, though Tim Avery still insisted that they join the rest of us at the dinner table for the usual chat and stuff. All was now well... up to a point.

I had taken a place at the kitchen end of the table; not to avoid the company, but rather to keep an eye on things, or rather the thing. "Mike," said Tim, "would you mind nipping in and asking young Clark (Stompy) for some butter for these rolls, please. Oh, and get him to move the soup along. Good lad!" I duly did as bidden, only to meet Stompy pounding down the corridor with a bowl in his hand.

"If tha's lookin' for t'butter, ah'm just bringin' it," announced the butler/chef/courier, a little testily, "so tha can just bugger off back!" (Elaine's instructions – No. 12: "When all are sat down, take in butter for rolls".) He breezed into the dining area, and fired off a cheery salvo. "Butter's here, Mr Avery! Rely on me, Mr Avery. Ah'm 'fraid it's a bit runny, Mr Avery. Ah must've had it a bit too near to t'stove, like, Mr Avery!"

Mr Avery sighed, knifed up some of the "runny butter", and discovered the delights of a roll spread with salad cream. A retreating Stompy was sharply recalled, and returned minutes later, after what the state of his hair suggested had been a mining adventure in the large hamper, with a pack of butter, a big grin and no apology. I decided to intervene here to tackle the unwrapping of it and the disposal of the paper, not a thing that Stompy had seen fit to bother with.

It now became clear that Tim Avery had had misgivings about Stompy's abilities in the kitchen all along, but had decided to bow to tradition.

"I'm afraid dinner may be a little unconventional," he announced. "We've only just got Clark passed out in making coffee and tea with hot water." All chuckled to order. "But," he added, on a cheerful note, "I'm assured that he has precise instructions, and the meal is reasonably simple. That's right, is it not, Mike?"

Hello, I thought, Stompy seems to be down to me officially now! I said "Yes" because that was what he wanted to hear, but my natural pessimism (or what, I repeat, in my opinion is a sense of reality) wouldn't bank on it. I noted with interest that by the nature of the various relieved grunts from around the table, it seemed to be confirmed that I was gradually slipping into an official role as liaison officer between table and kitchen. "At least I can tell you that the soup's hot," I told them with certainty. "I've seen it steaming." Quietly to Jack – "Either that or it's on fire!"

Right on cue, the soup started to appear. With two not eating, Tim Avery had officially invited the driver and guard to help see off the meal, though in the respectful situation of "below stairs" with Stompy, in the other carriage. Without knowing it, they took a bit of the heat away from me and were in the unenviable position of acting as tasters. Stompy passed the first bowls along to the head of the table, and trotted off for more. Three more trips, and everyone was served, Jack and me receiving the last two.

"Mm," remarked Tim. "Looks and smells OK, perhaps a bit thinnish maybe. It's a sort of vegetable consommé, I suppose. Everyone else OK?"

Jack and I looked at each other across the table. Our two bowls contained the unsettling sight of soup in a pyramid form. I'd never met damp soup before, and I could see that Jack was leaning towards indifference about it too. I checked my copy of Elaine's instructions. "14: Stir soup all the time it is heating up." I got out a pencil and added "14a: and again, just before you serve it." The party took it all in good part, especially as the vegetable stock that most of them were facing was pretty reasonable. I tried to pass off any embarrassment by eating my plate of "soup" with a knife and fork.

Most of the company were beginning to relax around now, after what, for most, had been a somewhat fraught morning. As for Elliot, he was just looking pleased with himself, being as he was on the outside of The Princess's Reliable, rather than having to take part in this culinary Russian roulette. I, on the other hand, was far from happy. After all, Stompy had bogged up the roll and butter, then the soup, and we'd yet to see the main course.

There was this sound. It started suddenly, coming from the direction of the kitchen, and it was like violently running water. It went no way towards calming me down, especially when it actually turned out to be violently running water. Everyone noticed it, but they all looked anywhere but in the direction it was coming from, as if underlining that whatever it was, it had nothing to do with them. But, there's an inbuilt nature in all, especially men, that when a small stream appears, you're fascinated to see how far it'll go. It puts you in mind of being back in your childhood, when you'd follow a relieving pee up against a street wall with a study of the progress of the resulting rivulets. When we were kids, we used to bet on where it would come to a stop, as it drifted slowly over paving stones, and dashed down the cracks.

All this came back to me as the waters appeared, meandering down the corridor, and steaming too! Tim Avery's "Mike?", snapped out in a combination of apology, demand and implied responsibility, brought me out of the fascination and sent me tumbling towards the kitchen. There I found an agglomeration of cook, driver and guard attempting to stem some unidentifiable flow, thankfully leaving no room for me to get involved. As I waited for one of them to come up for air, my eyes wandered around the kitchen, and fell on the main course plates laid out on the serving surface. Each one was adorned by pieces of decorative black twigs. I knew that Elaine was a stickler for presentation but was surprised that she hadn't let it pass for once, and not added to Stompy's load by making it look good as well as edible. I checked through my copy of her instructions, mainly because the sight of three pairs of boots, occasional flashes of arm and a trio of writhing uniformed bums fell short of the riveting. No mention on the list of trimmings. Then slowly, through rejection and persuasion, the horrifying truth dawned on me. These black twiglets were not black twiglets after all. They were not adornments to the main course – they were the main course.

Torn between the three occasional plumbers and the hopeful diners sat round the table at the other end of the corridor, I felt I'd be in less danger of physical harm with the latter. I turned back, mentally preparing an announcement for the expectant company, but on the way down the corridor I could see their hopeful faces reflected in the windows, and simply lost my nerve again. Completing a double U-turn, I put my head back through the kitchen door to find the threesome now engaged in mopping themselves down, which suggested that the immediate crisis was over. Then I saw the plates of petrified twigs again.

"What the hell are these, Stomp?"

"Them's thi chops," replied the chef, busy rubbing himself down with a whole roll of blue kitchen paper, small pieces curling up and sticking to every damp bit of uniform, "and, if you ask me, I reckon they're nobbut a shade owerdun!"

"Overdone! They're bloody cremated, man! Talk about sacrificial bloody lamb! How the hell've you managed that?"

"Only by followin' t'instructions wi' a precise precision exactly, that's all! Sithee?"

Even the instructions had suffered; one edge of each page was charred and curled up. Stompy explained that when the chops had caught fire a couple of times, he'd held the grill pan a bit too close to the papers as he blew out the flames. I checked item 32: "Put potatoes on to boil for twenty minutes and put the lamb chops to grill for ten".

"These have been on for more than ten bloody minutes, you daft bugger!"

"Ah knaw they flickerin' 'ave! It says purrem on for ten… we was on our way back to Leeds baht then, as I remember…"

"Ten minutes, you moron! Not ten o'frigging clock! For Chrissake! What the hell're we going to dish up now?"

Not surprisingly, Elliot and Jack had joined us during this exchange of views, which had hardly been discreet. Jack picked up one of the pieces of charcoal and tapped it on the edge of the plate. A short crack appeared between the "B" and the "R". "I don't right fancy these," he said, thoughtfully.

"Ay oop, daft bugger," protested the arsonist. "Ah've signed for them flickerin' plates! Ah've enough on wi'out thee smashin' t'flickerin' kitchen oop, an' all!"

"Look," I said, to my mind, displaying outstanding management potential, "get the taties and salad out to them. I'll nip over to Lodge's and get a few tins of corned beef. They… we're going to have cold salad and new potatoes, OK?"

"Fine," said Elliot, who had really no say in the matter. "You'd best look sharp, though, Tim's beginning to get a bit snarly!"

I arrived back with six tins, tossed one to the crew, and tipped the others out onto a serving plate. Grabbing the carving knife and fork, I set off to face the wolves. There was a slight collision with Stompy, racing back to the kitchen to swap a bowl of double cream he'd just taken in for the salad, mistaking it for the well-travelled runny butter. In the dining area explanations had been made, and I was being hailed for a second time for resourcefulness, which I could've well done without. I'd spent four years getting a degree in civil engineering to impress my superiors, not a catering diploma. I carved the meat, passed it round, and we all took up arms together. A slight pause occurred as Stompy piled in with his own plate, scraped up the remains of the corned beef, and plonked himself down at the bottom of the table. This was way out of order, but it was Stompy.

"Ah," said Avery, now prepared for anything, "coming to join us are you, Bernie?" – delivered in as sarcastic a disapproving manner as possible.

"Yes, thank you, Mr Avery, can you pass the butter, please, Mr Avery?" said the unruffled bundle, still liberally decorated with light blue confetti, stuck to the darker parts of his uniform waistcoat. We all watched as he launched himself into a demolition job on the plateful in front of him, then as one we turned to tackle our own. Slowly, an embarrassed murmur rose above the sound of Stompy shovelling fuel down his neck. The potatoes were lukewarm and rock solid.

"How long were you supposed to boil these?" I hissed into the black hole at the side of me.

"Woodenloo munnoose," it replied.

"Twenty minutes?" I translated, hopefully.

Stompy nodded, chewed, gulped, chewed again, gulped, shook his head a bit to work it all down, before opening up the eating machinery. "Twenty minutes I 'ad 'em on, twenty-one acshally. Watter were jus' beginnin' to bubble when ah took 'em out!"

"It was supposed to bubble for twenty minutes, not go from cold, you dozy bugger!"

"Didn't say that. It said to purrem on for twenty minutes. Right, ah'll go an' get t'fancy puddings, now."

There was no doubt about the sweets, they were excellent. Stompy delivered them all from the top of the table down, and trundled back to the kitchen to fetch his own.

A large and violent explosion shook the whole saloon, followed by the long and unmistakable clatter of falling pans, and a very distant "Bugger!" Then, "It's alright, Mr Avery! Nowt t'worry abaht, Mr Avery." I was on my feet like a cold bum touching scalding bath water.

"Mike, Mike... Mike," said Tim Avery, sharply, but quietly, as a pan lid ended its run along the corridor, and settled on the lino in a decelerating spin. "No!... Leave it, just... leave it... Just get on with your dinner." There was the hint of a tear in his eye.

For a number of reasons, the afternoon's session was postponed. Four weeks later, another length-marking run was organised. Tradition went out of the window and Elaine was put on duty in the kitchen. As far as I can remember, we had a choice of prawn cocktail or melon, poached halibut, new potatoes and three veg, with hot lemon meringue pie and cream to follow.

It was a dull affair.

Rules

Sex was rife in my early days of office life.

In the liberated days of old, before sexual harassment was invented, we used to hang up calendars with pictures of young ladies on them. They all appeared to be in some sort of inferred buff, which would have been full skin and fluff but for the precision-covering of some accurately arranged lengths of flimsy material, which combined with frustrating draughts of pinpoint accuracy. As sexual licence relaxed, so did the ladies develop amnesia, to the extent of forgetting to pack their whispies, along with clothing of any sort. They would be retrieving their situations with some creative positioning of the limited resources left to them, that is their arms and hands, though the draughts were retained to bring out their finer points. Occasionally long hair was used to augment their less than adequate hands. Ultimately, along came the butcher's slab shots. Anatomically detailed and so explicit as to turn the honest voyeur artistically vegetarian. A dozen varied hedgehogs, yawning. After twelve months of these, we secretly yearned for the fine silks, drapings and light breezes of yesteryear.

Mucky magazines were available in the messengers' cubicle, kept under lock and key, and for reference only within the confines. Mucky books, in all senses, with yellowing pages falling open at several grubby greys – an incorporated search mechanism. Undulating paw marks ran down the right-hand sides, with top and bottom corners curled and weakened by so much thumbing-through. Any that escaped used to jump drawers around the Drawing Office, in the guise of technical literature, with false brown paper covers such as "Reinforced Constructions" and "Modern Sleepers and Their Ideal Beds". Then to my surprise, there I was, with only nine months under my belt, finding my popularity sky-high through admitting to be a subscriber to *Which?*, and able to obtain an office copy of the bounds-breaking first edition of the Consumer Association's "Birth Control Methods" publication. It arrived in the startling shame of a plain brown envelope, handed over by my mother with a great unasked question, and smuggled to work in an atmosphere of deep guilt, what with having to use public transport, before delivering it like espionage to the intellectual giants of the office. I failed to come to terms with the communal drooling of the delving group that followed, over words and clinical black and white illustrations. Especially so since they had real incomparable sex all around them, served up on a regular basis, and all above board. This was the sensuous sonic combination of woman, stiletto and lino, which surpassed all else in terms of permissible sexual delight.

Sadly, the seventies marked the end of the golden age of linoleum. It was indigenous throughout our Wellington Street high-rise shack. There was never a need to look up as someone came into the office, walking patterns on lino being as individual as speech. Dying out at the same time was the sharpened shoe, and we were to mourn the loss of what we considered to be the sexiest sound ever, the staccato approach of concentrated taps of heel and sole on resonant lino. Emotions rose sky-high with the sound of t-t-t-t-t-t-t-t, the rapid fire tattoo of the delicate five-footer, or the broader t-T-t-T-t-T, which signalled the arrival of nearly two yards of lissom sensuality. What in later years we learnt to call sexual harassment abounded, but there were no sensitive flowers about in those days to point it out to us. All the girls who braved the fifth-floor Drawing Office were fully aware of the heel-lino effect as they emerged from the stairwell, moved into the corridor and crescendoed through the Plan Room and out into the office. What's more, they clearly rejoiced in it! The very cornering was subtly reflected in the slight accent of the outer foot, and evoked swinging *Summer Holiday* skirt and petticoat drifts, an effect acknowledged by the pointed comments and hooting, as the tap-tap-tapping approached, and there was not one of those young ladies not ready with a smart comeback of equal illegality in terms of modern thinking. Had the politically correct not made such a song and dance about it, sexual harassment as a conscious aim would never have evolved, but would have remained a subtle dream, dying away with the demise of office lino.

It was from their exclusive patterns, both rhythmic and stress, that most of the lady clerks acquired individual nicknames. These were equally meaningful to the observers as they were obscure, but pleasantly intriguing, to the nominees. "Scorcher" had a rapid-fire walk and accompanying hiss of stocking tops chafing each other with every step, suggestive of high abrasion, and charred knickers. "Dizzy", derived from "D-C", gave it extra on one foot, so producing an effect that Eric Gaunt exhaustively analysed on his drawing board, with calculations. This theoretical genius that Eric had was sometimes utilised for the benefit of the railway, with many startlingly innovative results. In the case of Dizzy he proposed the theory that her well-amplified chest was favoured to the left, causing one foot to tread more heavily than the other. He went on to illustrate the situation from his position of authority as a former junior bridge designer, and invented the D-C lopsided bra. (Flushed by the interest that his sketches aroused, Eric went on to produce an art nouveau sculpture using a saucepan and a fire bucket. This was immediately censored by Kye Bevin, the floor's Chief, despite an explanation by the artist; Eric being advised, "When you can do it from memory and not just theory, lad, I might then be interested.")

Jayne juggled with her title of "Screwdriver", and privately and proudly thought she'd cracked it. Her heavy heel was followed by a slight squeak as she pivoted on the sole, producing a strangely erotic image, again assisted by model analysis from Eric. She who was simply "Y" had a broad, widespread step, so that was that!

Years later, when political correctness and suppressive legislation were creeping in, fuelled by sad inadequates and the appearance of one female law student grabbing some work experience, we members of the Local Departmental Council were dragged into discussions about boys and girls and their differences, with the open, caring management of the day. Our most dedicated of staff reps was Elaine Barnes on the clerical side, an explosion of personality, which is in reality the basis of sexuality. On a day's seminar dealing with this modern phenomenon of sexual harassment, Elaine soaked it up for so long, before erupting with demands as to where all this was happening, and why wasn't she suffering her share of it.

Elaine was a remarkable girl, perfectly sound on superficial beauty, but with an abundance of glamour in terms of personality. With an amazingly adaptable body, she first turned up in her early twenties, fourteen stone and looking about thirty. Despite this/because of this, she made a great impression on me by landing on my foot during a game of table tennis, sending me to an early bath. She soon moved away to work in York, and we missed the bubbling personality. I next came across this same quality a year or two later, passing a startlingly trim girl in the Hutton House corridor. Automatically smiling, I passed on, only to be hit on the back of the neck with "Oi! Whassup wi' thee then? Too proud to know us now, are you?" I turned to just catch the Cheshire cat remains of a grin, as the slim figure disappeared into one of the offices. It was the crackling of sexual abuse pouring from within that confirmed the return of a transformed Elaine, back to stay. From looking thirty at twenty, Elaine aged such as to appear little more than twenty by the time she actually did reach thirty – this via many ballooning binges and deflating diets. She was forever the queen of sexual harassment, yet she refused to recognise the fact. She could make the most innocent sentence explode by the way she said it, and by the way she said "It!" Almost anything could be said to Elaine, so long as you accepted it back with interest, but try making unwelcome physical contact, and she could return a sharp elbow with pinpoint accuracy. Sexual harassment existed, but never in the overblown terms used in later years. In excess it was known as bullying, and would be simply dealt with by the victim's colleagues, in some way or other.

We didn't see Sexual Harassment coming, but it suddenly got its act together, recruited a band of neutral-gendered female supporters and revealed itself in BR booklet form, and as a new set of *RULES*. These became effective immediately.

"You've to get shut of all those mucky calendars. Now! And I mean now! Any that display any degree of female nudity are out!"

Sydney "*Gauleiter*" Adams, last seen as a Chief Civil Engineer's clerk on the early saloons, now by the late 1980s successfully enticed into the District Office in Leeds. Syd had risen to the awesome height of Chief Clerk, now known as Administration

Assistant, so that he could tell us, as well as the clerks, what to do. He was still not taken with total seriousness, despite occasional demonstrations of uncontrolled fury during office social activities, dinnertime games sessions and the incomprehensible sight of two grown men crying. (See under: cricket – broken stumps, table football – bent bars, puffters – discovery of within.)

"You what, Syd?"

"You heard me. Get 'em down!"

"Somebody's already done that, Syd. Look at August!"

"You can quit fooling, this is serious; there'll be an inspection tomorrow, and anyone that's got one on their wall, in their cupboard, or stuffed up their jumper is on a Form 1!"

This was deadly serious talk, the Form 1 being the first stage of a recorded disciplinary action.

"Come off it, Syd! You're looking at seconds, up here, the calendars you see fit to let us have. You've always kept the best ones for your own office. What the hell're you on about?"

"You'll all be getting official notification in writing from the new Staff Relations people; I'm just passing it on and giving you fair warning. And just for your information, if you must know, I've now got a calendar up in my cell with a picture of two magnificent snow-white English shire horses, working in the rich light of an early autumn morning, with breath steaming from their gargantuan nostrils, against the kaleidoscope of brown, yellow and orange in the background trees, and within the blue skies above, a circus of wheeling seagulls. And these two mighty Trojans, epitomising the sheer power of the gentle giant, have replaced any display of squalid female exposure, and will be stuck up there for the rest of the pillocking year, pulling this buggering, bleeding, crappy old sodding plough! And that's the only frigging picture on it all flaming year! It's all down to these frigging do-gooding bollock-laiden bricked-up women with two warts for tits and one for a brain! Should never have let 'em in t'offices! Should be at home having kids and cleaning windows, or down t'canal washing things! They're causing more frigging trouble than they're worth!" With which Syd made his personal feelings of disgust abundantly clear, while at the same time infringing every aspect of the new rules he was supposed to be implementing.

"Mucky" calendars were an institution. I think I've mentioned old George Stephenson's nail in the back of his office door supporting an enlargement of Lady Hamilton saying "Hello, Sailor!" by way of a strategic bubble. All atop a set of minute numbers placed just below her toes, representing the days of the year 1822. Isambard Kingdom himself was known to have two oil paintings in his office entitled *Great Eastern* and *Great Western*; what do you imagine they were? Boats? Trains? I should think so! What did he mean by "Magnificent creations", "Superb cantilevered decks", "Steaming beauties"? Girlie calendars are the birthright of every junior draughtsman who gets a kick caring for his 6H.

"This sort of thing's OK though, surely, Syd?" Keith Loach pointed to a calendar from one of the leading track equipment firms. Strategically placed machinery and mechanical track-packing plant, each apparently being operated from or serviced by a selection of spectacularly positioned young ladies.

"They've none of 'em got clothes on," said Syd.

"What's these then?" pointing at the white safety helmets doing little to keep them either warm, or adequately covered, or, for that matter, safe both within and beyond the terms of the Health and Safety at Work Act.

"Them's just gimmicks. Come on, explain to me why they're crawling all over this tamper, with only them tin hats on."

"Perhaps they don't want to get grease on their frocks, Syd."

"It comes down, same as all t'rest! What's she supposed to be doing?" Sydney suddenly taken by September. This particular lady was stood with her back to the camera, leaning over a balcony.

"She's examining this track-fastening tool, down here."

"Oh aye, I hadn't noticed that. She's fit, isn't she?"

"So that one stays up, Syd, what with it featuring track tackle?"

"No, it bloody doesn't, it comes down like all the others; and the same goes for that one over there, that one with that daft bitch using a theodolite. How many of you lot'd stand out there bollock-naked playing with one of those?"

"D'yer mean the theodolite, Syd?"

"'Course I bloody do! Get rid of it!"

Sydney Adams made his exit. One thing about Syd, you always knew where you stood with him. We were under no illusions that, at a stroke, one of the foundations of office life was to disappear for good.

Out of a stunned murmur, made up of defiant mutterings, a slight voice emerged from a serious mouth beneath a twinkling pair of eyes: "He didn't say anything about ours!"

"What?"

"Our calendar, that's OK, from what he said. "Female nudity," he said. That seems to make ours OK." With which we meet Yvonne. One of the pleasanter changes over recent reorganisations was an integration of clerks and technical staff on the same floor, compensating a little for the hygienic drabness of Hutton House. Nothing changed as regards behaviour; we still swore, we still blasphemed, we still hung up mucky calendars, and the few girls now in our midst lived with them, in their way.

Yvonne Flynn was one of the younger immigrants, and should perhaps have carried the feminist banner, but her battle, like Elaine's, was fought in her own inimitable way, in this case by erecting, or rather hanging, the most revolting calendar ever seen. It had naked blokes on it! Well, naked if you didn't count damn silly choirboy collars and stupid bow ties, so "naked" stands. We ignored them, as much as we could. It did arouse (every word you use is dodgy when you're in this field!) a certain disbelief in us, because we were faced with things we'd never seen the likes of before. All the blokes were ugly, there was no doubt about that, but the other thing they all had in common was this dangling monstrosity that made them look as if they were about to tie up a ship. Any one of them could have gone to a fancy-dress party as an old-fashioned petrol pump. Lads don't discuss such things, normally, for fear of unequal comparisons, but these attachments could not be ignored, and the question of successful concealment of such objects within normal clothing was downright baffling. We never let Yvonne or the others see us even glance at the thing. But, by crikey, they were revolting!

Nor did we know how the superficially demure Yvonne had got hold of it in the first place (here we go again!). Anyway there it was, and strictly according to Adams's statement, there it could stay. It had been tolerated by us lads, following the vandalising of one of our veterinary operating table calendars by Vera, another clerk, and a splendidly mature lady in her late forties. The object of her wrath was certainly a good one, nothing below a "40D" and the best part of a yard inside leg. Vera had painstakingly gone through all twelve pages, one Saturday morning, tippexing in two-piece bathing costumes. In the process she used up two bottles of fluid, and had to get her husband to pick her up afterwards, because she felt too dizzy for the bus.

"If our art pieces are coming down, so's your abattoir-hung monsters! Fair's fair!"

Yvonne was defiant: "'Female nudity', he said. You can't even pretend that's female nudity, so that's that!" She confided with me much later that she was dying to rip down her portfolio of revolting pendulums, since she'd found them far more repulsive than our nude women. After all, with most of our mechanic-elles doing manly things with motor bikes, pneumatic drills and trackside generators, she shuddered at the thought of what next year's edition of hers might be like, if the same artistic argument was pursued. She feared that her men might well be pictured ironing or vacuuming, or, heaven forbid, making doughnuts and such.

John Midgley had by now warmed to the injustice of the new rule. "What's the problem with our calendars, anyway? Why's Adams suddenly knocking 'em?"

Vera, at five feet four inches, grew to five-six. "It's all part of the new Industrial Relations policy, sexual discrimination and harassment and assault, and such. And, anyway, they're offensive!"

"How can they be? Don't offend me! Do they offend you, Duggie? Keith? Mike? See, they're not offensive?"

"You didn't ask Yvonne!"

"Nowt to do wi'er, she's a girl!"

"Well, it's not a very pleasant sight."

"Pleasant? Pleasant! I happen to think they're the pleasantest sites around. You reckon them trains nipping in and out from behind trees, like on that official calendar up there's pleasanter, d'yer? I know what's up wi' women, they can't do wi' lookin' at summat better nor what they are, that's what! Bloody hell! That one there could sharpen my pencil any day!"

"And I suppose that doesn't apply to you, when you look at that… that… that thing of Yvonne's, well not hers, but that what's on her calendar. How do you square up with that then?"

"S'not normal, that! I've seen smaller back on't farm, on mi'dad's prize bull when it were going for gold, first on t'season. Nobody's tellin' me that there're blokes walking around like that! Bloody hell fire, woman, he's hung like a Reliant Robin!"

"And you're saying that those… things on that woman are normal? How does she stop from toppling over?"

"Ah that's where we can help you there, Vera, love. You see it's all a simple matter of civil engineering and the theory of the balance. They could've designed the Forth Bridge wi' her in mind. Known as the cantilever, having one thing balancing another. Now you may have noticed her bum… Byyyy 'eck… tha could balance a pint on that!"

"And that's another thing not normal! Three, maybe four things not normal!"

"They'd normally do for me! Look, they're never going to look normal to such as you, are they, love? I mean… well, I mean!" Midge obviously felt he'd made his point well and truly, and that it had gone home, allowing for the natural stupidity level of women. He turned and began to move away, his motor beginning to run down. "Should nivver have allowed women up to t'Drawing Office, it's not natural. You get enough of women at home."

I couldn't do with the idea of him winding down too soon; John was an entertainment when he got indignant.

"I noticed when I was there yesterday, that they've set on a girl in t'PWay Drawing Office at York HQ."

"Be another clerk, or a tracer or summat," said John, now obviously losing interest.

"No, I asked, she's doing civil engineering at Hull Uni. And they're getting another in a couple of weeks. I was introduced, because—"

"Girl surveyors! They can't! It's impossible! You can't work along with girls. I mean, they can't do things like lads can, can they? It'd never work. Can tha see 'em bending over drawing boards and such?" John paused to do just that. "Well, they might get 'em in at York, they're puddled ower theer. They wouldn't dare send 'em ower here, where t'real work's done!"

"That's what I'm saying; they introduced me because she is coming over here in a couple of months. Bridge Office, I think they said."

Midge was genuinely mystified. "How the hell can you have women going out surveying? It's not natural; they can't be doing what we can."

"Like?"

"Lots of things (typical of thee, goin' along with it, like – you're as bad as them!)" – meaning university trained – I hoped. "They'd have to be bending down all t'time, taking measurements and such, I mean!" John had a fixation about women bending over. This had been made abundantly clear when we called round his house, one day, for a coffee, and he'd immediately taken me into the garage to show me the workbench he often spoke about.

"Women can, you know, bend, and that," I protested.

"Look, awkward bugger, you know what I'm gettin' at – you can't have birds out on t'track. They walk different – they'd never get up and down bankings. If they did, and you were following 'em… well!"

"Women can wear trousers, you know, Midge."

"Not proper women, they don't! Not at our house, anyway! Anyroad, it's not just that, is it? I mean, there's real problems. They wouldn't be able to shout at t'chainmen same as how we can. They couldn't talk to supervisors on a level. They'd need to wear gloves; you can't work a level with gloves on, can you? Handbags! How about bloody handbags, then, tell me! They all have handbags. I suppose they'll be stuffed with survey books and pencils and rubbers; and hankies for when they start cryin'. And they can't measure things, can't women. Can't handle owt other than a rolled-up six foot for mekkin' frocks. And they don't understand metres, either. You'd have 'em knittin' in t'cabin come dinner, 'stead of cards. And they'd expect a saucer."

As each objection tumbled out, Midge's voice dropped in severity and became quieter, as he listened to himself. The increasing feebleness of his argument was reflected in his voice.

"I know what's really bothering you, John…"

"Alright, I'll tell thi! How the fack can you go for a pee, when you're out? You couldn't just go up agin t'andiest wall wi' one of them stood theer. And what abaht them, an' all? Women are forever peein', and they have to have someone to go with! Bloody hell… they couldn't just… I'm off t'get some fags!" With which the discussion reached a familiar point, as far as discussions with Midge ever went.

A similar problem for John arose some months later, when the then Engineer, Hugh Crossland, tentatively raised the idea of having an office tie designed, for all to wear.

"What about the ladies?" had been an immediate reaction from a dubious management team.

"I'm open to suggestions."

This played on Midge for a while. "He's not having them wearing ties, an' all, is he? What do we want with office ties, anyway? I don't want folk knowing I'm working for this lot, and that's all an office tie's for, i'n't it? So what's the wimmen going to wear, eh? District Engineer bras? District Engineer tights? District Engineer knickers? So who's ever going to tell who they work for? And I'll tell thee this, I wouldn't bet on anyone wanting to search half of this lot to bother trying. Bloody miserable crowd!"

Hugh Crossland, very sensibly, didn't make the wearing of the office tie a rule. As a result, when they were issued, most people wore them. They had to wear a tie, this tie was free, we'll all wear this tie. Hugh understood rules, and how to have them work, simply by not making them directly.

Rules are the foundation and prop of the railway industry. It's own Rule Book rivals the Bible for volume, and beats it on authority, though the sex and violence isn't as good. But where the Lord God Almighty was satisfied with ten rules, and no sub-sections, BR's 1950 number ran to 246, with every month or so bringing another load of sticky-back amendments. With every little incident on the railway involving hurt to humanity or machinery, you could bank on another page being added to the Rule Book. No union could ever properly introduce a work-to-rule, mainly because it would mean doing absolutely nothing at all (which is against the rules), but it would also involve the impossible task of actually reading and taking in the rules right through.

Rule reading was a regular little ceremony, and a rule in itself, when supervisors would sit in the cabins and read out loud a relevant selection from the book to each gang of five or six men. It uncomfortably took me back to nursery school, sat on the floor around a huge and ancient lady teacher of at least one hundred and ten years, who'd read fairy stories of outstanding political incorrectness. The similarity didn't end there; such lady teachers always sat in the same way as our uncomfortable supervisors, hunched over the book, with great tree-trunk legs pointing north-east and north-west. Way back, some of the supervisors had a shade of difficulty with the actual task of reading, and rules would come out from memory in an amazingly basic form.

"Tha mun gerraht o't'way on trains. Tha mun step dahn inter t'cess when one comes. Tha mun not stand on t'other track 'case 'nuther train comes t'other road. Tha mun not leave tools in t'track, specially jacks. Tha mun not work in bad weather; in rain-or-fog-or-fallin'-snow, inter-t'cabin-tha-shall-go. Nah bugger off an' get some wark done!" With which Moses would gather up his tablets of stone and walk on to the next gang.

Rules have become harder to keep with time. Working in a 1920s office, rules would be limited to getting there on time, being smartly dressed, and providing each day one lump of coal for the office stove. Thirty years on and you were presented with the inhibiting black volume, and thirty years after that, where the print stayed the same size, the book's outer dimensions had doubled. Nowadays it has to cope with so many fashionable modern evils.

Looking back to the 1950 Rule Book, it's difficult to find any reference to the famous three Ds (Drink, Drugs and Doing It). Drink features under Rule 3, coming second to a far more heinous offence:

Rule 3: Employees MUST NOT...
3 (iv) waste or wantonly destroy stationery.
3 (v) consume intoxicating liquor while on duty.

See? Down half a dozen pints at dinnertime and it was OK, so long as you didn't go a minute over, or use some scrap paper as a beer mat (3 iv). I've seen loads of attempts to down the six, but only on special occasions, whenever there was something genuine within the office to celebrate. Engagements, weddings, promotion, retirement, boss's birthday, boss's official birthday, anybody's birthday, anybody's mother's or father's birthday, new frock, new haircut, new dog, new cat, release on bail, recovery from serious illness – we once went for a celebratory drink when one of our number found that he had not suffered a heart attack, and the chest pains had come about due to the buckle on a pair of twisted braces becoming engaged with a shirt button. To PS that, Rule 4 did lay down that no one should be drunk on duty, but isn't that rather a comparative term? Besides which, the generous fifty-four minutes allowed at midday hardly lent itself to achieving such tranquillity.

Reference to drugs can't be found in any shape or form in 1950, unless rules regarding the procedure for guards to throw "packages" off moving trains is a lot more subtle than I give the compiler credit for.

As for sex, just one rather alarming mention:

> Rule 145 (b): The screw coupling not in use must be hung on the hook provided.

So from a comparatively relaxed attitude to life when I started on the railway, I finished at a point where dismissal appeared obligatory for possession of a packet of aspirins or a wine gum, and severe disciplinary action would ensue should a zip be accidentally at half mast. Rules were now so tough, and vengeance so dire, that so far as behaviour on the running lines was concerned, there existed more fear of inadvertently disobeying a rule than in actually getting knocked down by a train, which is what many of the more sensible rules were meant to guard against in the first place.

Rules came, were obeyed for a while, and then went the way of all good rules, into an oblivion of semi-compliance.

New offices, new carpets, new mice. "Staff should not eat food at their desks." Fair enough, we went off and ate our food at someone else's desk. Hutton House had a basement, with only one room in it taking in daylight, and that only through a slit of window just below its ceiling. It was not considered habitable, so after housing the plan and print rooms, a locked file room, a small kitchen, and the chainmen, the small space left over was over-printed "Mess room", and the rule became "no eating upstairs in the offices". In practice, the mess room was the exclusive dinnertime haunt of the Staff Section, issuers of the edict, and no one else. They eventually came to claim the room as theirs, and would resent anyone else joining them. They had to eat there, since they'd devised the rule. Apart from any of that, the equation of seventy staff, fifty-four allowed minutes, sixteen chairs, four tables and one kettle did not weigh up at all.

"No newspapers during working hours." A rule only made after some clown was promoted from Headquarters. In common with everyone back at York, come ten o'clock he downs pencil, puts his feet on the desk and gets out his paper to accompany mid-morning tea. We were amazed! It was not a custom at Leeds, and we wouldn't have dreamed of doing any such thing, demonstrating a blatant waste of company time. We were more likely to be found round one another's desks, discussing sport or TV, but not reading a newspaper. Yet when the rule was issued, on paper, with the Engineer's signature at the bottom, we deeply resented it, and for a while made a point of disobeying it until we realised we were missing out on the office gossip.

Rule: "No trivial private phone calls." Any that must be made should be entered on the pad provided. The ever-gorgeous Jayne had the unenviable job of touring the office every Friday morning, examining the telephone call pads, and collecting monies. Mythical names were set against outlandish locations, with an occasional genuine entry by the saintly Stanley Mole – by now reduced to an affable Christian, far away from his wild crusading days. He may have lost his extreme religious fervour, but an angelic honesty remained as a residue and displayed itself on the phone list. With his being the only booked calls not being made by A G Bell to phone number 2 (found unobtainable), or by a Bob Browning to some Barrett female or St Paul to the Ephesians, Jayne took precious little notice of the list, just collected the regular ten pence from Stanley, and left it at that.

Eric Gaunt was confused by this one week. "I've put down a two-minute call to Scarborough, for when I was seeking holiday digs, and she's not even bothered to collect it! Makes you wonder whether it's worth bothering to be honest after all!"

This had been on my section's phone rather than on his, and we'd all watched him do it. His heart-searching and indignation as to the worth of being above board when it came to declaring calls left us unimpressed. Eric's booked "two-minute call" ignored the other four he'd made, and due to his sheer bad luck with the landladies he'd chosen, not one of them speaking in clear Queen's English, the calls had all lasted at least ten minutes each! These communication problems weren't so much of a coincidence since all five calls had actually been made to small hotels on the south coast of France.

House rules abounded, quite apart from the book of rules. One resulted from a negotiated settlement over a raincoat. Following a minor triumph achieved by carefully argued points, we staff representatives on the LDC managed to obtain a sort of parity with the men on the ground over the issuing of wet-weather gear. Raincoats were provided to be used by section heads visiting sites. Sadly, the agreed budget ran to a specific number of coats, which itself broke down to one coat per section. That was unless the section was as small as my Projects Section and Stanley Mole's General Section; there it came down to one coat between the two sections. A week on, week off rota was worked out, with loud complaints from both sides if their week happened to coincide with a spell of fine weather.

Come the appearance of the first prehistoric photocopying facility, and a whole load of new house rules were generated, augmented on a weekly basis to keep up with the ever more inventive uses that were found for the machine. But Chief Clerk, Syd Adams, must have had some information from his counter-parts in other parts of the system, or else he'd a much more fertile mind than we'd ever given him credit for. Some of his initial instructions, copied to every section and one to stick over the machine itself, suggested taboos which we could not even imagine. His edict regarding private copies was grossly misinterpreted – there was us thinking that we couldn't copy any material for our own personal use, to be paid for later, and Sydney meaning something else entirely, in the way of copying privates, which would never have occurred to us in a thousand years (well, at least not until the Christmas parties).

Safety has been, from the moment of making men on the track visible, by far the greatest source of inspiration for the Jehovah of the Rules. By the dawn of the nineties it had become impossible for Man on the Track to stand up, let alone move, if he was to do everything the rules demanded of him. A quite brilliant drawing sent in anonymously from one of the track gangs purported to show a track patrolman fully kitted out in defensive clothing and obligatory tackle. It looked like a tipped skip with bits of humanity sticking out in places.

Bolstered by the success of the ultimate legislation on drink, which had become a total "none at all" situation, we were tied down by rules which started off as sensible and weren't thought satisfactory by the desk-bound draughters until they became silly. Safety boots started it, and steel soles and steel toecaps became compulsory. One of these would stick firmly to track-warning magnets, nearly twisting your ankle, while the other steadily machetted its way into your toes, and all for what? Stepping on nails or having rails fall over on you. Now to be made to wear this gear when walking over a bed of nails, or scrap timber, is sensible; but to have to wear it for a five- or six-mile hike on track is silly, and potentially damaging. But Jehovah saith, "At all times," and therefore so shall it be. John Milton was pretty sound on the matter of safety boots:

> I did but prompt the age to quit their clogs, by the known rules of
> ancient liberty.

Construction sites are notoriously dodgy for having small tools and such falling on you from on high, and safety helmets are sensible. As they are in tunnels and when working under cranes lifting panels of track with lumps of ballast on them. But when there is absolutely nothing above you, why insist on a safety helmet? If Man on the Track sees a rule as being silly, as well as uncomfortable, he will rebel. Rules are needed as a rule, but they must be sensible.

★

All these rules led to a lot of grumbling, but never so loud as when the whistle sounded, quite rightly, on alcohol. It isn't many years ago that I reluctantly gained fame for my Christmas punch, which also fell victim to the ban. The Engineer at the time, working on the principle that he wasn't far off it himself, decided to invite all retired personnel to what became known as the Annual Christmas Codger's Fuddle. Sandwiches and cake were there in plenty, but only to serve to soak up the Collins Punch. I was standing in the wrong position when the volunteering details were handed out: "Mike, you should be good at making the punch." Why, I never found out.

I had to go home and look it up; I'd no idea what punch was. Whisky, I could buy; beer, yes; but could I find suppliers of punch? No. All I found was lots of recipes, so many that I might well have been looking up how to make food. Punch appeared to be little more than a major accident in an off-licence. Perplexed and confused, not to say worried, I applied some analytical thinking, and came up with a basic recipe for the Collins Punch. Ideally it was made up from:

> Spirits (according to contractors' generosity).
> Fruit.
> Lemonade for bulk.
> More spirits.

Experience of my first year at it amended this, adding:

> More lemonade, to spin it out.
> Hidden reserve of more spirits to dilute the extra lemonade.

A variety of surprising additives, as supplied, listed by a few DIY cooks and party buffs, following their exposure to Mark 1 Punch.

Due to a novel, and economic approach by one of our contractors, Year 2 added liquor from the midfield range, of sherry and martini. Liqueur chocolates were either broken in like eggs, or bitten in two by volunteer lady clerks. This paved the way for the odd bottle of cherry brandy and crème de menthe, as available. Bravado, confidence and downright cockiness caused a downturn in Year 3, when a bottle of Pernod was added to the cast list. Everything went cloudy, and the last chance of spotting illicit fortification in the form of foreign bodies was lost. It also marked my first complaint following one of the oldies having some spilt down his trousers. It appeared that when he got home the dog went for him.

By the fourth year end, my punch had settled down to a basic list of specific ingredients in variable quantities, dependent on several factors. It was mixed up in a loaned black plastic bucket, sworn "clean, and only used for wine making". Right from the first it must be acknowledged that alcohol is an antiseptic – this is a vitally important factor, considering its exposure to the atmosphere and the various seasonal and increasingly jovial passing saboteurs. As the day of the festivities proceeded, and the mix was occasionally left unattended, its sanitary element became increasingly significant and important. One of my colleagues, keen on gardening, suggested that we tested the brew's pH value, but the introduced litmus paper disappeared like a digestive in hot tea, adding yet another curiosity to the mix.

Questioned one year, purely out of passing interest, by the Engineer as to the strength of the potion, the bucket supplier brought in his wine-making hydrometer. However, it refused to even float, and just kept falling over. In Year 5 the basic mix was recorded "as built".

So, here, for what it's worth is:

The Recipe:

(Don't try this at home!)

Ingredients:

6 x 2-litre bottles Lemonade (plus 6 more for reserve tank).
1 Bottle Bacardi.
3 litres Martini Rosso.
1 bottle cheap brandy.
6 oranges + 6 lemons, cut up and squeezed. Solids placed in muslin bag, suspended in mixture from a scale ruler fastened to the handle.
Muslin bag (now permanently part of mixture due to deliberate jiggling) plus string and scale ruler.
Marmalade, as back up to fruit and muslin bag (remove from jar first).
Mint, in leaf form. (You can use concentrated mint sauce, but

you mustn't be too sensitive to remarks regarding lawn cuttings).

Pint of cold tea due to some clown refilling emptied whisky bottle.

Core of 2 apples (discovered when emptying out later).

5 tea bags (discovered ditto).

1 biro (added unintentionally while stirring).

Historic traces common to most black plastic buckets.

1 wooden spoon, lost in error halfway through preparation process.

1 plastic retrieval glove, similarly.

Various coins thrown in by the superstitious, regarding the whole thing as kind of wishing-well.

Variable:

Whisky.*

Wine.**

Bitters?***

Assortment of alcohol-seeking missiles.

---

* Whisky. This is an indeterminate amount, which increases proportionally with nerve. It is acquired thus: Go to Stanley Mole, and ask for any spare he might have. Stanley is teetotal, as we have seen previously, but less violently disposed towards it than he used to be. After seeing his immediate staff all right (that is just Kev Smith – Racky Jones being another TT) this should produce two bottles of whisky. Now apply to heads of Bridges, PWay and Works, who will all have received a case each at least; this may produce a further three bottles. Go see the Engineer and his two Assistants (Works and PWay); tell all three that it's not going too well. They will issue three-line whips to section heads to contribute another bottle each. Plus the Engineer, whose idea it all is, will contribute money for another bottle. By now it may be felt wise to use this in reserve along with the back-up lemonade reservoir.

** Wine. This is a chance thing. The Railway Goods Claims Office may have a sale of stock damaged or lost in transit. Given a fair wind, together with an application strategically made as they all go out for their annual office dinner, and you might get a donation of half a dozen bottles. Otherwise use Engineer's donation. On no account discuss colour or vintage. Once added to the main brew, it will not matter anyway. If fussy, add a bottle of Ribena should the donation happen to be predominantly white.

*** Going public like this, I must have had to listen to twenty knowledgeable experts on the making of punch. This could have been reassuring had any two recipes agreed by at least 50%. One recurring feature, however, was something called Angostura Bitters, which none of them could enlarge on. Taking this to be a remote reference to Anglo Bitters, I compromised by adding a bottle each of Tetley's and Sam Smith's, together with one of Old Peculier. It didn't seem to do any harm.

Further instructions: Do not worry that when stirring the mixture, you notice a change from a rasping sound of spoon against the bucket sides to a smooth one – this is normal when using loaned buckets. At some point during the day, transfer half of the mix to a second bucket, and dilute both with whisky. It is always important from this point onwards, that anything done to bucket 1 is also done equally to bucket 2. This is also the stage when attempts should be made to plunge in and remove the larger items of sabotage. Here I must stress the importance of washing your hands – if you don't, it'll be days before you can get rid of the smell. (As a further point of interest, I noticed every year how clean my fingernails were afterwards.)

All this should have made up two bucketfuls, not counting the staff discount of a third bucket squat under the desk. Keep all empty lemonade bottles. These will be needed when the party is over to take home the organised accidental surplus. Be sure to give one of them to each of the three section heads as an insurance against the following year's supplies, and arrange for wife to bring car down when everyone has gone home, to "help clear up".

After just ten years of achieving an agreed perfection, the recipe degenerated due to the prohibition rules, together with an assault on incoming booze and Christmas gift regulations. All the lemonade was still there, together with an amount of grape juice and the intentional solids. Totally missing was intoxicating liquor of any description, along with any enthusiasm on my part.

What went wrong during these ten years?

Things we were not allowed to mention, that's what. These involved: abroad, free, leisure girls, money, drink, large companies, Happy Christmas! and a few members of staff several grades above gang level.

In the good old days you'd fix up to go round a few sites with, say, a road-crane contractor. From this you and the railway would get some fresh angles as to how particular jobs could be tackled, very often at a saving. Given time, there'd be direct honesty on both sides; none of this, "Well, we've got a few options we're looking at", when there's actually no way out other than one of this bloke's cranes, and for his part, if he thought a cheaper option existed, he'd tell you, so strengthening his chances at landing the job, and another later. Benefits to all, and at the end of the morning it'd be, "Are you doing anything for dinner? I think there's a pub near here does a nice bit of steak." An OK from you and you'd be straight in there. As you walked into this pub which he thinks is "around here somewhere", there's a couple of pints on the bar ready and, "Will you be having chips or potatoes with it today, Frank?" You then settled down for another hour, while he put new equipment and ideas to you.

In later years, following a rules explosion, it became advisable to go round in separate cars, so he can't be seen to be giving you the benefit of a lift, and there was no question about a bite to eat, let alone a drink, afterwards.

Companies used to be able to say thanks for all the past year's association. This was in no way, "If I buy you a snack, will you make sure we get the next job?" Come Christmas now, and things have changed drastically. Some contractors, particularly in the bridge business, used to walk in with a dozen and plonk them on the Bridge Assistant's desk "to share round", while another boxful was going straight into his car boot in some station car park. On the PWay side, our main contractor would substantiate personal thanks with an afternoon meal and a session in the local Hilton casino. Here you got the wild mix of experience and snobbery along with novelty and basics. Carl Youngman, formerly on the Area, but brought into the Drawing Office as PWay head following Kye Bevin's retirement, had a very slightly lower opinion of himself and his abilities than he did of God – who was admittedly getting on a bit now, anyway. If ever there was a wine snob, it was Carl, and he would favour the whole group by ordering the most suitable wines for the various meats and puddings. We noticed that choices tended to coincide with top-whack prices, but Carl felt that this only proved his point about his ability to pick the best.

Duggie Lomax, whose wine knowledge was limited to red, white and pink, with a fleeting recollection of some names like Our Vera's Bristols and Purple Nun, would equally demonstrate his restricted knowledge by announcing that he was partial to "a bit of Rosey!"

"We don't drink rosé in surroundings like these, Duggie," Carl would advise in a condescending humour-the-prat kind of voice. "I doubt if they've any in the building!"

"Well, they bloody soon will have!" and while Carl watched in horror, a pint glass was half filled with an equal mix of Brut Champagne and Chateau La Vieille Cure Claret, then nosed with a resonant snort and downed in two.

Small, but significant gifts would follow and enough chips for a controlled afternoon at the tables.

By the time I hung up my T-square, this had been reduced to a diary and a calendar; and a diary, mark you, stipulated by the Rules as being without a pencil! Diaries with pencils down the spine had to be rejected and returned as being beyond the bounds of an acceptable gift. As a matter of fact, it was usually only the pencil that was worth anything, once the diary had surfaced, forgotten after its first wash in a trouser pocket. But because some bunch of eminences had enjoyed a week of European freebies, with complementary wife-substitutes, five hotel nights, all found, and a three-hour trip around a railway machinery supplier's factory – and most importantly, been found out, I couldn't have a pencil in my diary! Still, a rule for one is a rule for all, and we were told that our betters on high were now suffering the gross inconvenience of having diaries without pencils as well!

All this activity was well recorded in the national press, which finally brings me to another rule: on no account may employees talk to the press without our own PR man being present. One of our most respected Area Engineers, a local political figure, well used to talking to the press and being able to say nothing in a maximum of words, was commenting on a derailment on his patch caused by vandals. He was quoted on the front page thus: "This... (precisely describing the method used)... is the perfect way to cause a derailment!" Headquarters were well impressed by such forthright innocence.

I found it a happy pastime talking to the press. While at Huddersfield, R Supards became a regular grass to the local newshounds. It all started with a chance interception of a call to Elliot Milner, which happened to combine with a particularly dull day and Bill Boyes on holiday. While happily using my alter ego, I still insisted on the anonymity of "a railway spokesman", and altered my department to the remote area of Fuel Analysis Assistant, supposedly watching different types of coal burn. I'd provide an innocent knowledge of a steam engine visiting Huddersfield and where it could be best seen, or info on any visiting dignitary or the winner of the best station award, so long as it was Huddersfield. It was in this vein that I let slip the story of a regular passage of nuclear fuel passing through Huddersfield Station. It didn't, but they wanted a story, and were blessed with gullibility by the bucketful.

News had recently broken that there was a booked train somewhere in the country that included a flask of nuclear waste in its cargo. This had the Greens jumping about in fury and prompted my favourite credulous news ace to ring me to try for information on the running of any trains locally which were likely to derail and annihilate the bulk of the Western World, or at least cause damage within the limits of Huddersfield's inner ring road. Strong denials, overemphatically and slightly hysterically on my part, sowed the necessary certainty within my bait. This demanded a bit of a boost, which I organised in the pages of the Skelmanthorpe Bugle and Mart (I've made that name up, so there's no use going fishing!). The letter, in a remote, but handy minor journal was intended as reinforcement.

> Dear Sirs,
> As a keen locothologist and observer of rail transport movements, I would like to bring to your attention the passage of highly dubious goods through Huddersfield, which presents a very real danger to the public. Although I am not myself a scientist, I do have reliable information that radio activity is involved. This is a disgrace, and should be stopped.
> Yours sincerely,
> Laurie Lodaballs

Phone rings: (by now I had my own, as well as an extension from Elliot's).

"Is that Rupert?" By which I immediately knew my caller to be press.

"It is. I take it you've heard?"

Pause. "Heard what?"

"About the rat?"

"No, we've heard nothing about a rat. What's the angle on that?"

"It didn't have bubonic plague after all!"

"I didn't know about a rat, or bubonic plague; I'm not ringing about that. It's the radiation business."

"Oh, the station clock! No, that's been declared safe as well. They reckon the radiation from the luminous paint they've used on the hands is harmless, unless you spend the rest of your life stood under it, staring up!"

"Do you mean to say that you've not heard about the trainload of highly dangerous nuclear material that goes through Huddersfield every week?"

"Oh, that! Yes, I know all about that!"

"So why have you kept it quiet from me? That's real news, that is! We've had to pick it up from that Skelmanthorpe rag! Come on, let's be knowing."

Why we had to have this rule about not talking to the press, when they were so much fun, beat me. It was particularly satisfying if you played hard to get.

"Too sensitive, this one. I can't possibly give you any real details."

"So it's true then?"

"Damn! I shouldn't have said anything. Look, d'yer think you could just forget I said that?"

"No way! This is big! Look, I only need a hint to point me in the right direction. Timings. Just a nudge at what it looks like."

Only that week I had picked up from *New Scientist* magazine that there was a growing certainty that the radioactive gas, radon, was trapped in granite rocks, and was slowly seeping out into the atmosphere. This meant that it might pose a slight threat to people with houses built over it. This was all I needed. Link it to the regular train of granite chippings running from quarry through Huddersfield to Manchester every Tuesday and Thursday, and Bob's your uncle, as they say!

"Look, I will tell you this; it runs through Huddersfield twice a week, around six in the morning, in the Up direction. It looks exactly like a train of stone hoppers."

"You mean to say they've disguised it to fool the public?"

"I've said far more than I should. You're on your own from there… sorry! I'll watch out for the story!" Phone down.

Sure enough, even though it took three weeks, there was the article together with a compelling picture of the train spread across the front page. What the public were shown was a cunningly disguised trainload of stone, concealing a massive flask of nuclear waste. They were told with confidence that should it suffer a mishap, a derailment, a misdirection, causing the flask to crack, then the whole of West Yorkshire would be affected. Hiroshima was mentioned, along with mushroom clouds, together with international condemnation and wide-scale pollution.

What we on the railway saw was a picture of an everyday stone train of granite chippings crossing Huddersfield Viaduct.

★

"It were thee what fed 'em that story abaht a nuclear bomb goin' through Huddersfield, weren't it? Name 'em as you drop 'em, Percy, ah can't tell whether that's a four or a five!"

"How could it be me? What do I know about shifting nuclear waste about? And why should t'papers get hold of me, I'm nowt round here? And since when have I been a spokesman? And who do I know works for the press? Aye, and what'd be in it for me if I did, eh?"

"Ah thought it were thee! Tha'll cop it one day, sure as eggs! Come on, Percy, tha knaws tha can't knock if tha's got a domino what goes. Rules is rules, tha knaws!"

Epilogue

Many memories are of minor short-lived events that don't easily fit into the foregoing chapters. Some have been passed over as lacking interest, but on reflection were worth telling. Episodes which live for the minute or the day and are stuffed into the memory bank to be brought out later when the poor unfortunate hero of the moment shuffles back into your space, now probably occupying some higher calling in life in a remote part of the railway household – hence an Epilogue.

One such hero was Chris Easton, a lad who was with me at Huddersfield as a young trainee, with hopes rather than the expectations of the fortnight rocket visitors who picked up all that there was to know about Area work in those magical ten days. Ten days, that was, unless we could involve them in a weekend as well. The sight of such turning up on a Saturday night for eight hours in a tunnel, dressed in an older coat but carrying the compulsory briefcase and brolly, tended to stun the gang lads for an hour, until some minor crisis called upon the briefcase being placed in the care of the train's guard and the brolly propped up in a tunnel recess near the start of the job (usually never to be seen again). Young Chris was a pleasant enough lad, with enough respect for the chainmen for them to include him in, but enough cheek for them to feel the need of gentle correction. We (Wilf, Percy, Bill and me) felt that Chris was too laid-back and needed jolting a little.

Chris was allowed one day a week off for "day release" at college, the rest of his learning experience taking place on three evenings each week. This, along with Elliot Milner being out visiting remote parts of his Area, gave Bill and me time to think up and arrange minor accidents.

You will recall the construction of the Area Office; three rooms in terrace form with a false ceiling, above which, by some four feet, was the water tank. Within the false ceiling two-foot-square openings housed four narrow strip lights each and plastic covers. By easing two of the fittings up a little, a length of string could be run down the side of the chimneypiece to a position Percy generally took up for his dinner. It ran up through the light fitting, along the underdrawing to the light above Chris's desk. Here, a box filled with French chalk in powder form was attached to the string and critically balanced so that a tug at Percy's end would bring a shower of chalk down on Chris. (French chalk was used to sprinkle over wet ink drawings to act like blotting paper.)

Dinner that day was fish and chips in traditional newspaper. With Chris diving into his portion, sat at his desk, Percy, who was sitting well behind him, took up the slack on the string. This caused the overfull box to release a slight sprinkle of chalk dust that drifted down in a very attractive way, settling on Chris's head and cod. Seeing Chris look up in a little concern, Percy panicked and tugged the string hard. In the space of time that it took the slight shower of chalk to become a potential drift, Chris leapt impressively back, sending his chair shooting towards Percy, who also took evasive action, unfortunately still clutching the string. The result was that the delicately lifted light covering was yanked up and out of its housing, shot downwards and converted Chris's cod and chips into plaice and mash.

Bill, in his position of observation and possible decoy, should Chris have become suspicious, was forced to leave the room far faster than his heart condition should have allowed, only to explode in violent laughter further down the corridor. Chris, who was already thinking up acts of retribution, spoilt the whole effect by quietly picking up his chair, removing the light cover, blowing off most of the chalk, then to resume eating the rearranged fish without comment. Percy, on the other hand, was scrabbling about the fallout area of his cod and chips, and salvaging what he reasonably could, without picking up too much of Huddersfield.

★

Left to ourselves, as we often were, Bill and I had many matters to occupy our minds during those necessary breaks in leaning over the drawing board or going through complex calculations. Eddy

Stapleton was with us, but took very little part in comic initiative or sidelines. He would unnervingly appear to be just watching and learning, though he did have a moment of triumph over the pair of us on one particular internal project.

There were times during the day when a design problem would become impossible and a pause was called for in order to concentrate for a short while on something entirely different. Over the space of a week or two the mouse provided that diversion.

"Ah'm bahn t'catch that damn thing, if it's last thing ah do!" Bill was well fed up with the mouse, which had once more had a go at the Penguin chocolate bars he kept locked in his drawer. It was a fairly bold animal, and would appear from under the large gas heaters either in Elliot's office, or more usually in ours, while we were working.

"Does Stores issue mousetraps?"

"Ay, but we'll be knee-deep in t'little buggers afore they get 'em 'ere. We'll have to cop it usselves."

As with the office dominoes, made from treated hardboard, there was no good reason to go to the expense of a mousetrap if you could make the near equivalent from resources all around you. Admittedly, those resources tended to be a bit on the large side for the matter in hand, hence huge slabs for dominoes and a wide variety of railway materials available to catch and destroy a mouse.

Bill and I discussed the best methods for catching the mouse, but were obviously approaching the matter from quite different directions, and failed to agree on any basics. Eventually it came down, as often happened, to a challenge, arising out of the usual end of discussion remark of, "OK, if tha thinks tha's so bloody clever, we'll all have a go, and let's see who wins!"

We did collaborate on each other's schemes, but with me having a degree in civil engineering, I was streets ahead of Bill in pure engineering theory. Bill's plans were based on daylight manoeuvres as against mine that needed the dead of night, so we could go ahead together. Eddy didn't disclose any ideas, so we counted him as a non-starter.

I began by being subtle. That is, subtle as far as I thought, but without taking into account the fact that the mouse was equipped with a modicum of intelligence. Mouse Elimination Subtle System (MESS for short) Mark 1 consisted of a box with a ramp up onto the top. At the side of the box was a bucket of water, and between the two a ruler cantilevered over the bucket and resting with one end on the box and eight inches along it on the bucket rim – a sort of loose diving board. At the end over the water was the traditional lump of cheese. This was later replaced by some bacon rind, on the advice of a length gang over Halifax way whose cabin was overrun with tame mice. I found this a most disturbing place as the animals would run freely up your trouser legs to get to the sandwich in your hand. It became apparent that there was a basic difference between Halifax and Huddersfield mice and their culinary expectations, with ours completely cold-shouldering the bacon as it had the cheese. I finally tried chocolate. This our mouse liked, but it also liked our calculations in that it knew when the ruler was too precarious to attempt recovery of the Kit Kat. Some nights it ignored it, and some it took the bait without triggering the collapsing diving board. It was then that an awful thought occurred to us. We were paying out more on Kit Kats than the cost of a mousetrap!

Unbaited, but significantly trickier constructions were built, until we overreached ourselves to find the routes that the mouse was expected to take were beginning to baffle even us. Besides this, Elliot began to complain about the "junk" on the Drawing Office floor, and in retrospect we were bound to agree with him, the journey from the door to the drawing board becoming something of a trial.

It was then that things took a more sinister turn. Our mouse took to the idea that all this time we had been playing with it, by setting up a nightly playground and assault course for it to enjoy, and what's more, a different one every night. It decided that we must be friends, so it concluded that it was safe to come out during the day to play with us. That's when the heavy shovels and the chases down the corridor began. Here again we were beginning to upset Elliot, either entertaining guests, on the phone or conducting a meeting. At first he would explain the crashing of shovel to floor as "just the mouse", until the visitors queried as to how big this mouse was to make all that noise. So Bill took charge.

"Ah tek it tha's got to knaw this mouse, like, and fund it's got an IQ of 150, then? Ah reckon it's goin' t'turn out that bright that it'll be tekken bi all them books tha's used, and it'll stop off for a read!"

This followed one of the regular visits of Wilf and Percy, who had spent their dinnertime observing the mouse bobbing in and out of the furniture, and who had had plenty to say about our various mouse diversions over the weeks.

"It's time tha framed thissens, thee two," observed Wilf. "Get thissens a trap for goodness sake, they're nobbut aif a crown!"

"I'd be one and three down, if we did," I told him. "I'll get nowt out of Bill for his share."

"It's cruelty to dumb animals, that's what it is, and no mistake," said Percy.

"We've done nowt cruel to it!" claimed Bill. "Just chased it abaht a bit!"

"I was referring to t'way t'mouse is lakkin abaht wi' thee two," explained Percy. "It should be prosecuted. Theer should be an RSPC Dumb Animals for protecting t'likes of thee two soft boogers!"

"Reet," said Bill, "there'll be no mouse when tha comes again next week! Ah'll beat the little sod, just see!"

Now because Bill was in the office as a clerk-cum-linkman, answering Elliot's phone when he was out, and finding ways to get messages to him, there came a time in the day when all Elliot's incoming letters had been opened and sorted, all the previous day's filing had been done, Elliot's tea or coffee had been made and the newspaper devoured. It was then that Bill came to a loose end, which, with his agile mind, was dangerous.

Bill took to sitting in the Drawing Office, with me trying to work, and just observing with the patience of an Attenborough. It took very little time to confirm that the mouse lived under the large Drugasar gas heater backing onto the chimney, a six-foot-long by twelve inches deep metal cover over a gas burner. First it would stick its whiskers out to check for any of that revolting cheese or bacon rind it had been coming across, and then it would venture out into the middle of the floor, sniffing from side to side as it went.

"What we need is strategy! We're going to set up an ambush! It's simple. Ah'll sit on t'stove top wi' summat heavy, thee park thissen ower theer and give me a signal when it's coming aht. Ah'll let go and at least give t'little booger an 'eadache."

"Something heavy" turned out to be an empty paint tin of industrial size, filled with weighty rail track screws. Bill perched himself centrally on the fire (turned off, if you're wondering) and held the paint tin out at arm's length. Thirty seconds later it was at elbow to wrist length, and thirty seconds later still put down.

"It's no good," said the ambush party, "ah can't hold that aht theer fer long! We need another angle."

This materialised as a sawn-off broom handle stuck under him while sitting on top of the fire, with the paint tin on the free end, ready to be shoved off. Setting this up brought a few tears to Bill's eyes that he was not going to admit to. Eventually, a large cushion between him and the broom handle made for a satisfactory solution. So there we were, a paint tin full of chair screws on the end of a bit of pole with the other end wedged on top of the fire, under a cushion and Bill in that order.

Our furry friend obligingly appeared nose first and moved slowly out from under the fire. It became apparent, after a few attempts, that the mouse heard me shout, "Now!" seconds before Bill could move to push the tin off the end. Greasing the tin handle with point oil improved Bill's reaction time a little, but we caught not so much as a disappearing tail. Meanwhile, what had escaped our notice was what a tin full of chair screws, falling three feet onto a lino floor sounded like from an adjoining room. Elliot came round to kindly let us know. Further trials were conducted when Elliot was out, but suspended when a rather significant depression began to appear in the floor.

In the end it was Eddy who beat it, as it sniffed around where my trap had been in the middle of the floor. We were sat with all the doors flung open trying to attract some fresh air into the over-hot rooms in mid-July. The mouse ambled out and Eddy spotted it. He grabbed the first thing to come to hand, which happened to be the hole-puncher, and slung it at the mouse. The target, no doubt confused by a sudden eruption of confetti, shot out of the door, and was never seen again.

It was several days before Eddy dared mention that it had been his approach that had been the most successful of the three. He'd been with us six months, and he was learning.

"Reckon it'd've deed laffin at thee two, anyway," was Percy's view of things on the lads' next visit.

★

Bill's inventiveness and skills in adaptability often came out best with the wealth of different materials and objects that the railway presented him with. Most of these were strictly speaking only waiting for their turn to be useful to the railway itself, and some were available to him because of the presence of the railway. There are certain spots at the foot of cuttings where the Great General Public mistake the railway tracks as rubbish collection points. Bill once came across an old stone washhouse sink in such a location and immediately saw its possibilities as a garden water feature. All it wanted was the plughole blocking up and a notch cut into the top at the ends for water to run in and out. With the help of his fellow relayers' wagon driver, Tommy Crossland, in what was loosely termed a dinner break, they managed to lift it onto one end. It was very heavy!

Tommy's wagon was a quarter of a mile away at a road crossing, so the only option was to gradually waddle the sink down the side of the track – carrying it was out of the question. It took the pair of them the best part of an hour and a half to laboriously walk the sink down the cess at the lineside, so suffering many amusing comments from passing freight train drivers. As it was in near-perfect condition, Bill was very anxious that it should not be scratched, or worse still, cracked, and so carried some thick sacking material to paddle it over the more stony spots. When not in use the sacking had to be carried around his shoulder, and the dampness seeping from it managed to find its way down inside his overalls and shirt collar.

After a period that was in reality two dinnertimes rolled into one, they reached the crossing and the wagon. Then followed another trying time attempting to get the sink up onto the back of the lorry over the tailgate. This was achieved by ramping two planks up the back of the lorry, and using a rope through the plughole for Tommy to drag it up the plank, with Bill pushing and guiding it from behind. (You will have realised by now that this was during Bill's pre-heart attack days.) More sacking was sought to bed the sink down in on the lorry and it was carefully roped into place to stop it moving during transit. The easiest and most comfortable part of the operation was transporting it to Bill's house nine miles away, where a mug of tea was seen as essential.

Offloading was much the same as loading, only the other way round. Tommy, who had minimal interest in the sink, was more inclined to rush the operation, meaning that Bill, guiding it down the planks, was obliged to take on most of the weight, as well as making sure that its path didn't veer towards the edge of the ramp. It now had to be paddled up Bill's path, round the house, and into the middle of the lawn. Although by then expert in this manoeuvre, it still took them a good twenty minutes, and there they had to leave it, for there was barely enough time for another mashing before they had to report back to base.

Saturday morning, working for once in their own time, the two met up again. Bill dug a hole in the middle of the lawn precisely to the outside dimensions of the sink, and then the final problem was faced of cutting two notches into the ends. With grave doubts about this, Bill helped Tommy carry a rail saw from the lorry to the sink, a long way for an object generally run into position by two men with a trolley. It immediately became obvious that there was no way that the saw could be clamped on the edge of the sink, so it was abandoned. There was nothing for it but to resort to the mallet and stone chisel. Bill very carefully scored out the shape that he wanted to cut out before persuading Tommy that it would be better if he chipped out the pieces himself. Very delicately he applied the chisel to the line he had marked out, and gave it a tentative tap with the mallet. It made no impression. Several more gentle taps proved no better.

"It's no use tickling it," said Tommy, "tha needs t'give it sharper taps. It'll cut along t'line alright, no problem."

"Look!" replied Bill. "We spent t'best part of last Thursday shifting this thing. I'm not bahn t'do owt ower-rash now!"

Bill repeated his tentative tapping of the chisel, still making no noticeable difference to the glazed surface.

"Give us it here!" said Tommy. "We'll be here all day at this rate!" With which he grasped the chisel and mallet from Bill. "Reet! Let t'dog see t'rabbit!" He shaped himself up against the sink and gave the chisel a much sharper tap than Bill had done, still with no result. It was his second tap that was impressively successful. The sink split into two, through the plughole, along the bottom, and up both ends.

"You don't fancy setting it in t'ground sort of V-shaped, dust'a?" said Tommy eventually. Bill said nothing. It was an emotional moment. He seemed to have lost the power of speech.

★

"Batteries not included." The deadening phrase that ruins many a Christmas Day morning. That is unless you're resourceful, ruthless and cavalier with the property of others. Which is where Bill and his relationship with the railway comes to mind.

Bill had acquired for his grandson an electric train set for Christmas. It had been cobbled together from parts given or, as a last resort, bought from friends and workmates. When they had opened all the brown paper bags and unrolled the newspaper packing, he found that he had accumulated one and a quarter circles of track, several straights, a signal, two locomotives, ten coal wagons, a Pullman coach and fourteen guard's vans. At least he could lay out a fairly respectable oval of track, although when all the rolling stock plus one loco were placed on it and connected up, the engine very nearly met up with the last of the guard's vans.

What had not occurred to Bill was that he was short of an actual source of power. His hunter gathering had failed to turn up a mains transformer. He did have some idea as to the required voltage, and appreciated that to put two hundred and forty volts into the system straight from the plug might have a few exciting but undesirable effects. Apart from the locomotives going up in smoke, they could easily be followed by a lounge carpet and a grandson. He worked out that a number of batteries adding up to a voltage close to that required might just make the thing move round a bit. However, this being the era before cameras and their flash guns or TV remote controls, there was not a single battery in the house. Two doors up had a torch, but dismantling it and applying the batteries to the track did nothing.

It was then that a straightforward solution occurred to him. Only a week before he had taken delivery of five boxes of batteries for the local Signal and Telecomm lads in their absence, and had failed to hand them over, purely because he thought that they might come in useful sometime. He knew that nobody would miss them, or that they could not be traced back to him. Somewhere in the system a materials clerk was puzzling over a delivery note signed "Doctor Beeching", so Bill remained anonymous. The S&T lads would merely order some more, so here he was with five boxes of very big batteries.

Now these batteries, although large (about eight inches by two inches square) were of incredibly small voltages, used for some fancy circuitry in either signalling or telecommunications. Bill knew that they could hardly damage the train set, and that enough of them wired in series should at least provide some motion. The fact that he was in Bradford and the batteries were in Huddersfield did not deter him. His Ford Zephyr had a sizeable boot and plenty of room on the back seat, and it being Christmas Day there would be nobody about near the office. So off he set on the twenty-minute journey to his hoard. Now, of course, he always had to consider his dicky heart and the weight of the batteries; to this end he loaded a lumpy sack of dissipating alcohol, known as his son-in-law, into the car with him. An hour later they were back home.

Dinner then interfered with further progress, and it wasn't until mid-afternoon that the wiring up could begin. Bill had thoughtfully added to his load a large drum of fine cable, another trophy that he had liberated from S&T ownership many months earlier. This was so big that they had to roll it up the garden path and into the Christmas-clean lounge. Then, using an industrial-sized reel of insulating tape, whose origin can be left to the now trained imagination, they set about laboriously wiring each battery to its neighbour until they were piled three high and included two rather effective tunnels over the track for most of its length. It was by then time for evening drinks and cake, so the work was suspended until Boxing Day morning.

Construction work was confined to being within the track oval, overflowing to form the tunnels and a couple of bridges. More and more batteries were wired in until a moment of exhilaration when one of the locos reacted slightly to the current. Yet more power was enthusiastically added until the whole train began to move. Or at least they thought it did.

With the high-rise batteries packed into the track centre, and the obstructions caused by the necessary tunnels and bridges, there was but a small window at each side of the layout where you could actually see the train go by. Still, to Bill, this counted as success.

In order to shed a little light on the need for so many batteries, I made some inquiries of an ex-S&T Engineer. If mystery is only appealing to you as long as you don't know the reasons, then jump on as far as the next break in the text marked *. To those who are intrigued as to the apparent need for so many combined sources of power, here it is.

Each battery would be rated at two volts, and was intended to contribute to track circuits in the real live railway. When the circuit was completed by the presence of a train in the section, then the batteries would be within a short circuit, effectively dropping their voltage to something around a tenth of a volt, and Bill's need for the twelve volts in order to make his model railway spring into life meant that it needed some hundred or so units. What my expert added, and Bill had failed to remark on, was that the effective shorting of so many batteries would generate a considerable amount of heat. No doubt Bill put this down to one of his hot flushes that characterised his dicky ticker condition, or just failed to mention it because it suggested an element of negativity when considering his main objective. Whatever, instead of a spectacular model railway set out in mountainous terrain, Bill actually had the novelty of a toy train moving in and out of a modest volcano!

★

Not all of these reminiscences have a humorous angle, either as they progress, or as a punchline is arrived at. Some are concerned with unusual insertions in an otherwise fairly predictable weekly pattern. Mondays were dominated by what was called the "Monday Morning Meeting". These were for all four Area Assistant Engineers, like Elliot Milner, representatives of the track renewals section, the Engineer himself and his two deputies, along with one or two specialised clerks. This meeting was held in the Engineer's personal chambers round a large table on initially comfortable chairs. The MMM was something of a misnomer, as it often edged into the afternoons as well. It was a kind of post-mortem of all that had happened over the weekend, what lessons were to be learnt from any problems that had occurred, to be followed by the integration of plans for the following week and weekend. Then there came the allocation of manpower from a finite collection of Area maintenance staff and the Relayers. The track-relaying jobs took precedence, after which the Area Assistants had to plead, argue and attempt to retain as much of their own resources as possible. Following all this was the weekly allocation of stone trains.

These consisted of trains of stone hoppers numbering ten twenty-ton wagons apiece. The Relayers needed some to top up their weekend work, and the Areas needed them for similar reasons or just to trickle out along various eroded track shoulders. I often had to deputise for Elliot and found this part the most challenging, as all decorum left the room and the atmosphere turned into that of a fish market, with all engineers shouting out their desperately needed requirements. Solomon in the chair made decisions, and each Area Engineer knew despondently that he had to face his various permanent way supervisors that afternoon and virtually recite his failures to satisfy their needs. All that took care of Mondays.

Thursdays were set aside for technical staff to have site meetings for the jobs on which they were to make names for themselves that next weekend. Very often for me these involved tunnels, and long walks to get to the actual location. The rest of the week was filled with surveying, using the chainmen, or at last getting down to some work at the drawing desk. One of these days would be dedicated to Elliot and myself to visit various sites to examine new track or look through sections that most concerned us. Midway through such days we would visit one of Elliot's select chain of cafés to have meals that ate well into my lunchtime expenses of two shillings and ten pence a day.

Life was steady, busy, and fairly predictable on the Area. Then, on Monday, 13 March 1967, along came Bradford roof to provide me with my greatest, most difficult and most potentially dangerous job up to then in my railway career. This was the covering to Bradford Exchange station. It was a mix of iron arches, cross pieces, corrugated cladding and glass, and the condition of some parts of it were giving much concern, particularly as small sections were prone to descend on passengers during high winds, such that the station would close down during exceptional storms. Bradford Exchange was a terminus with ten platforms and the roof was supported on two sets of seventeen massive hundred-foot-span cast-iron arches, each set covering five platforms. In between the arches were cross connections of either simple girders or complex lattice arrangements. In all there were about six hundred individual structures, half of which could be broken down into more constituent parts. We were looking at around twenty thousand sections of cast iron, all of which had to be identified, examined and assessed for strength. At the end of it all explanatory plans and a report had to be produced. A fair old job, and it was down to me to plan, carry out a survey and report on it.

The way it affected me was that I would have to accompany our Area Bridge Inspector, Ted Buckley, on a three-month journey in and out of the various sections of the sixty-five-foot-high arches. Ted was to report to me his assessment of every one of the twenty thousand components, and I was to record and identify their place in the overall structure. Scaffolding was ruled out because of cost and disruption, and the work could not be done from above.

Elliot Milner could be quite an innovator when he chose to be. His solution was a Simon Platform – a cage mounted on two hinged arms, both springing from the back of a large lorry. Such things are commonplace now. You'll generally find them as centrepieces to every second flurry of traffic cones you meet, but it was a fairly new concept then. Ours was a large lorry body with this kind of praying mantis jointed arm, and we had to go as far as Dudley in the Midlands to get hold of it. When in operation the lorry had to be stabilised by rams from body to ground at each corner. All very well, but it would not fit on the station platforms, apart from which we were only permitted to isolate one platform at a time. The answer here was something that could not be considered today, on safety grounds in our Mary Poppins World of Health and Safety. The lorry would park as close to the platform edge as possible, put two rams down on the platform, and the other two on a flat rail wagon alongside. Bearing in mind that the wagon was only held by a handbrake, and had a sprung superstructure that went down when the wagon was severely loaded, the whole thing was most stimulating! If it decided that its brake wasn't fastened down hard enough, it would slide slowly into a more comfortable position, giving us, sixty-five feet up aloft, a new sensation to add to the considerable swaying back and forth over five feet. If its springs, which were heavily depressed on one side, felt like having a bit of a stretch, the small twang below would be amplified into a sudden lurch in the heavens above. Adding to all our problems, we had to cope and thread amongst the lighting. Central to all platforms were rather inflexible trunking runs of it that had to be avoided at all costs.

Ted Buckley was a gentleman. A phlegmatic character, who carried out his job in a steady and organised way. Normally this involved examining a bridge a day, either over or under the tracks, and erecting ladders in the road, or between the passage of trains. Stone arches would be considered from the point of view of examining them for cracks either lengthways or across the arch (these being far more serious than the longitudinal ones). On metal bridges, Ted would work on the components, chipping away years of paint and rust until he could measure the working thickness of bridge material. Hence technical staff could make calculations on the importance of his findings, depending on their location within the structure, and report on the strength or weakness of the whole bridge. I admired Ted for his dedication and attention to detail, but would not have put him down as one able to alter his routine and take on a structure as massive as Bradford Station roof. Moreover, I had to live with Ted for the three months, most of the time confined within a metal basket, sixty-five feet up in the air.

Ted was universal in such a confined situation; beyond Ted there was just more Ted. My view up there was of rust, steam, pigeons, knitted ironwork into the far distance and the muck of ages in one direction, and in three others, the overwhelming proximity of a familiar navy blue suit, with black and charcoal flashes. Unchanged and uncleaned in the twelve years I knew it, the front displayed an overall random pattern of thousands of small tobacco burns.

To add to the ambience of soot and pigeon deposits, was the smell of a most obnoxious black/brown substance, which Ted chewed constantly while up aloft. It was regularly spat out from the cage, to re-enter the earth's atmosphere below, and occasionally decorate the paying public.

"Nowt nor warse nor what t'pigeons are chuckin' at 'em, lad."

In relaxation during breaks, Ted would cut up this rope of shag into fine slices, and attempt to set fire to it in his pipe. This led to yet more scorched air-conditioning down his frontage. I argued with him that he and his pipe had probably contributed significantly to the terminal corrosion of many component parts of the enormous canopy that we were examining. He responded with a request that I stop talking like a silly bugger.

One of the joiners who shared the small mess room had known Ted for thirty years. I got talking to him about this foul tobacco I had to experience daily in one way or another.

"Ted's allus bin a one fer his shag. Managed to gerrit reet through t'War, nobody knew 'ow, burree got it! Landed 'im in bother once or twice, though, specially when he cut 'oil in his gas mask t'shove t'pipe through!"

"I'd have thought that's when he could've chewed the rotten stuff to best advantage, rather than incinerating it."

"As ah recall, he did at fust, burree couldn't remember not to spit, which were a bugger when he'd got t'mask on!"

I had over the years spent the odd day out with Ted as he examined a particularly interesting bridge. I had walked through disused tunnels with bricks falling from the roof alongside Ted, since these were still our responsibility. I had even been lowered down tunnel airshafts with him, with all the attendant rainwater showering out on us.

Ted's home "office" was a small shed all to himself overlooking the buffers of the Penistone Line, with the main Works office behind it. I had been far more concerned than Ted appeared to be when a train of wagons failed to stop at these buffers, rode up over them and completely demolished his domain. He had momentarily nipped out to the lavatory, and I found him ruefully surveying the remains of all his records and notes of years, fretting over the loss of a pen "with only aif t'ink used".

We were required to wear safety helmets. Whereas today you're not allowed anywhere on site without a bump cap, in the sixties it was a novelty. I took to it reluctantly as it was an uncomfortable thing to wear; Ted was simply confused by it. His helmet refused to fit over his cap that was to him the natural way to wear it, and there was a short period of almost rebellion as Ted felt he could not come to love this intrusion in his working practices. On our first trip up on the hydraulic lift, we tested the thing out from the controls in the basket and immediately knew that the safety helmet was essential. Admittedly our first efforts were a little clumsy, sudden and lurching, and there were quite a few rough introductions with the unforgiving cast-iron girders. As we became more adept with the controls, I would acquire a little amusement by edging Ted over to a metal strut and giving him a slight tap on the helmet. This quickly lost its attraction as Ted, unmoved, would turn and look at me and remark, "Dear, dear, lad, that's not clever tha knaws!"

I never got used to the motion. Not so much the swaying of the lift as we moved in and out of the girders, but the motion I suffered as I got off the bus at the bottom of our street each evening. This would last until way after tea, and was amusingly unpleasant. I didn't really feel comfortable until I climbed back into the cage next time.

Days started at eight on site, and finished at half three, this being a sort of compromise between Ted's and my regular hours. We were accommodated in a small smoke-filled mess room in the station office block, used by all the Bradford-based Works staff, a mixture of brickies, plasterers, joiners, plumbers and gas fitters, with one or two labourers. They all dressed in the traditional old suits, heavy boots and cloth caps. Should any one of them be temporarily made up to acting supervisor, the cap would be replaced by a hat.

It was here that I learnt a few things that I had to bring to Elliot's attention.

All these men were issued, from the top office at Huddersfield, with a job to do for the day. Just one job, be it on the area boundary or in Bradford itself. This meant that for the refitting of a door handle, say, at Hebden Bridge, half an hour away, the men concerned would breakfast at base, take a train around eight thirty, mash a tea in the local permanent way cabin or signal box when they got there, mend the handle, dine, and return to Bradford in the early afternoon. Should the ailing handle be at Halifax, there would be no need to set off until ten at the earliest, returning immediately after dinner. However, if the site be Bradford, or near, they would drink tea and read rescued newspapers (there was an agreement with the station staff to collect newspapers from trains terminating at Bradford, and hand any surplus over to the Works lads), wander out of their shelter around eleven and return for dinner, leaving the whole of the afternoon to sit, snooze and smoke. Fortunately, with running a job of this sort of profile, Elliot was a regular visitor, and soon woke to the local customs, saving me the embarrassment of shopping the culprits. I merely tipped him off when an afternoon visit might prove productive.

Needless to say, things changed in no time, and the men found themselves organised and doing twice the work they attempted before. "Bloody Milner" was not a popular caller!

Ted and I had Saturdays off, but worked every Sunday over the concourse area, it being easier to cordon the few passengers off from the danger area. Ted was, amongst many things, a most conscientious worker. He would allow himself a mug of tea while waiting until I arrived (he had personal transport), but we were up in the cradle by eight thirty, allowing ourselves a fifteen-minute mashing around eleven. Tea was scalded from the ever-simmering large heavy kettle, in white metal mugs with rims of dark blue and matching handles. They were impossible to hold, but I had bought one specially before the job started to put me within the pecking order amongst the lads. This was very important. I was taken aboard as a trusty college lad, and my willingness to go up in the lift into the highest trusses gave me no little kudos in the cabin. I had gone to Bradford Institute of Technology (later University) for my education, which was another Brownie point for me. After dinner (thirty minutes on Ted's decision) we would be back up in the clouds, working through until three, giving time for a clean up and a final tea.

This was the era of the demise of the steam locomotive, gradually being replaced by diesel multiple units – nasty little objects in comparison. Both routes out of Bradford Exchange were up extremely steep inclines in railway terms, so steam drivers would release their all as they left the level platforms to attack the slopes. Retrained diesel drivers would take on the same approach as they always had in the past, sending up an explosion of filthy diesel smoke. Steam was definitely better. Whatever, Ted and I were perfectly placed to receive the full benefit of the two exhausts, sometimes augmented by a banking loco at the rear of the train. The roof was used to this kind of abuse, having experienced it for a hundred years or so, and it showed.

Corrugated cladding sheets were attached to the purlins (cross members) by simple cast-iron clips. These proved to be in near-perfect condition along the lower portions of the roof, but became increasingly corroded and ineffective, or even missing in the upper reaches. Wind, steam and rust attacks had destroyed much of their holding power, allowing the sheets to flap in the slightest of winds. Gales were another thing altogether. One particular day a small tornado was centred on Bradford, and by mutual consent, including Elliot's remote acceptance, the storm led to an abandonment of work for the day – or so we thought. When the first cladding sheet – about eight feet by three – came down onto a busy platform, the situation became an emergency. Many other sheets could be seen flapping furiously in the gale, all central to the two arches. For a while the station was closed, bringing Elliot and the Works Assistant from Leeds over with all haste. We were all well placed to watch the second sheet fall; it was a spectacular sight. On becoming detached in the wind, the sheet first acted as a floating sail, drifting back and forth as it came down. About thirty feet up it suddenly flipped and came down edge on with great speed. What impressed and scared us most was that the metal end struck the tarmac surface of the platform and embedded itself so well that the sheet remained in a vertical position.

There was a quick conference. The Station Master and operators desperately wanted at least part of the station back in action; the engineers' main concern was safety. Eventually, Ted and I were taken aside and asked how we felt about going up in the gale and releasing some of the more obviously dangerous cladding sheets, with no pressure being put upon us. Ted might have been asked if he wanted vinegar on his chips, his answer coming readily, as he saw duty calling. I could hardly refuse to accompany him, mainly to assess what was safe and what was not. The supporting rail wagon was hastily moved into position alongside a central platform near the outside glass screen where the danger seemed to be greatest, and we duly went up, me assessing the comparative solidity of my helmet against platform surfacing should it come to fending off sheets in flight. It took a great deal of persuasion in some cases to release the final clip. The idea was to bring the sheets down in the cradle, but once the wind caught the sheet it was ripped from our hands. Others we temporarily wired down as best we could, all the time with one of us fighting the controls as we swung violently from side to side. Probably sooner than we should, we declared ourselves satisfied and descended, to some acclaim it might be added! Although once more I got the medal along with Ted, it was only he who had persuaded me to go up with him, a trip that would not be contemplated nowadays.

There were very few other moments of drama, but some ascents were not without stress. First, on a quiet calm day, the Engineer from Leeds paid us a visit, and decided that for morale-boosting purposes he should also go up aloft. This meant three of us in the cramped cage, with me on the controls, fully aware of the need to keep a fawn-coated, spotless-helmeted boss and briefcase reasonably clean and free from concussion. Ted came up to point out the weakest points – not the actual weakest as they were up in the sixty-five-foot-high central section, but to some more friendly bad points. I had enough room to compare the pristine condition of my superior officer with the mobile heap of oil and soot called Ted. Sir took a few photos, quite unnecessarily as I had been busy enough, between forcing Ted into contact with the roof, to take a lot myself. Anyway, his own pictures proved that he'd been up and seen for himself, which wouldn't do his reputation any harm either. As a result the Chief Civil Engineer himself came over from York, not thankfully for a ride, but to see at first hand some of the specimens that Ted and I had collected.

Three months later it was back to the comparatively mundane existence of the Huddersfield Office, and back to an unmoving earth. It had been one aspect that I never got used to – the continuous swaying which both Ted and I experienced when out of the lift and back on the ground. I was left in complete peace, except from the usual frolics of Bill, to produce the final report. This was to be a thing of splendour, right up my street.

My first job during the whole operation was to devise a recording method so that every single one of the twenty thousand components could be identified. Then the entire structure needed to be surveyed and reproduced on a drawing, these drawings forming a guide to the report. During this period, and my time in the sky with Ted, I was replaced with technical staff out of the Leeds Office. I was even allocated a typist who Elliot brought over, along with machine, to share the office. The finished report is eighty-five foolscap pages long; I say "is" because I proudly allocated myself a copy that I have at my side now. Sadly for technical staff to follow, this report, which had been a joy for me to produce, enjoying the writing as much as I did, has been forever since held up as an example of how reports should be produced. Fame for me, but at the expense of the misery for others having to produce the same on much less exciting subjects.

The question as to what effect all this effort resulted in must occur to the reader. In short, the whole station was pulled down.

Repairs were out of the question and this was an ideal argument for a new station with a modern appearance. All trains were to be DMUs in the very near future, removing the need for running round facilities for steam locos. Our report was the catalyst that eventually led to the Interchange of today, with an accompanying bus station at the side. A faint glimmer of resurrecting a scheme of the 1930s – to build a viaduct across the city centre to join the two Bradford termini of Exchange and Forster Square – appeared on the horizon, but a study group soon put paid to that.

On one fine and sunny day, with little or no wind to speak of, Ted decided that we would tackle a section of the highest central point of one of the arches, where we could poke our heads out through the sizeable smoke vent and survey the landscape of Bradford. It was particularly interesting for me to pick out the new University complex, built on the site of the old Institute of Technology where I had all my civil engineering education. That had now been upgraded to the status of university just five years after I left. As a result, all the diplomas of technology had been reallocated as degrees of Bachelor of Technology. Today, as I contemplated how three years of intense study had made me worthy to move half a mile down the road, to work alongside a man of little learning but having experience that I would never match, there hanging up in the air with fumes all around me and soot accumulating on my hands and face, I felt it somewhat odd that I had turned down the opportunity on that very day to return to my seat of learning to scrub up and suit myself in order to receive my new degree from the hands of Harold Wilson, at that moment no doubt shaking hands with my former colleagues. On the whole, I thought, I'm better off up here with Ted.

*

I have mused over the sharp difference between the years of experience that such as Ted Buckley had, and the resulting depth of knowledge he had compared to me. Obviously my remit was to have a finger in every aspect of railway civil engineering, where Ted concentrated on bridges and old disused tunnels, but I was acutely aware that it would always be wise to consult Ted and his like before shooting off my own opinions. Experience came with the years so that you retired at the peak of your knowledge and usefulness. I, of course, could boast my greater knowledge and experience to such as young Eddy Stapleton, and yet I could, if I wanted, still learn from him.

My knowledge of old tins of paint, for instance, was probably equal to Eddy's, but for a very brief moment Eddy was vastly more experienced on the subject than I was.

We found the unopened tins under some sacking at the back of one of a few old sheds dotted around the engineer's compound at Huddersfield. Jack Senior had had an idea that he'd seen some somewhere, and we were on the lookout for a bright colour to paint track information on the sleepers. This information was usually to indicate the start and finish of transitions from straights into curves and vice versa, and the accompanying changes in the cant – the elevation of the high rail over the inside one of the curve. The cans we had found carried peeling and hardly legible labels on them, and these all seemed to be the same – lime green. From what I could gather this should have been ideal against the black of the sleepers, so we took a couple.

Next day, Percy drove us (Wilf, Eddy and me) up the Colne Valley to a spot near Slaithwaite (pronounced variously as Slathwit, Slowewaite, depending on which side of the valley you were on, or simply Slaythwaite if you were listening to the train announcer in Leeds). Here we were surveying, realigning and working towards higher permissible train speeds, mainly by lengthening the transitions and recanting. Today we were to measure out and mark up the new cants, hence the paint.

It was a bumpy ride up the old formation, but since two of the four tracks had been removed at the insistence of the great Dr Beeching, we had access by car to much more of the railway than the former four tracks had allowed. So we could set down exactly at the curve end to be marked up. The chainmen measured out the transition and I marked the new cants in the web of the rail with our special greasy yellow chalk. We gave Eddy the job of sorting out the paint.

As we finished our setting out we noticed that Eddy was making a real dog's dinner out of simply opening an old paint tin with a heavily corroded lid. A screwdriver would have been ideal, but we were in a screwdriver-free zone. Percy suggested the shovel we always kept in the boot in case of snow. Eddy leapt on it. Holding the tin between his feet, Eddy carefully introduced the shovel blade to the lip of the cover. Nothing happened. Noticeably from a distance, Percy next suggested tapping the lid to loosen any rust. Eddy duly did this, and then went back to prising it off.

Going back to the beginning of this section you will note that I mentioned that for a very brief moment Eddy had a more detailed experience than I did. This was in the field of old tins of paint. Unlike the business of Bill and the multitude of very low-voltage batteries, I have been unable to discover from any expert source why old paint is explosive.

The lid came off violently and executed a neat parabolic curve eight or nine feet into the air. This was closely followed by 90% of the paint. It had mixed rather well on the bumpy ride, so that the colour base had combined with the usual layer of oil. It was a sort of lime green, which was also the colour of the entire frontage of Eddy, petering out over the surrounding countryside, except for a near-perfect silhouette of Eddy on the grass behind him. What instinct had placed the three older members of the team at what now proved to be a safe distance away we began to discuss, soon interrupted by a lime green wailing noise from what had been Eddy. It was now beyond being funny, as we were faced with transporting this work of modern art back to base without transferring too much of the paint to the car interior.

"I think," said Wilf, "we'd be better off drilling a few oils in t'lids afore we try tekkin' another one apart."

On our eventual return we unwrapped the parcel of sacking and newspaper, which was Eddy, out in the yard, watched with interest by Bill who was both intrigued and saddened. Intrigued as to why we had found the need to decorate Eddy, and saddened that he'd missed it. He was further downcast when Elliot softly asked him, in the form of a command, if he would care to take some turps to the few still wet spots of paint within the car, before turning his attention to hosing down Eddy.

★

"We've got a problem!"

I'd heard Elliot's usually hurried stride, turned up a couple of notches, as it came along the corridor from his room to the Drawing Office. A fraction of a second allowed several possible problems to pass through my imagination. Embankment slip, unexpected visit, derailment, out of tea or coffee, track suicide?

None of these.

"We've got a runaway! Outside, quick!"

Elliot opened my outside door onto the yard, jumped out, and stood looking at the station while he explained. A heavy freight train carrying steel girders had slipped out of control on the incline coming down the Colne Valley from Standedge Tunnel. It would be passing through the station in five minutes or so. Or would it? We rapidly reviewed the various points where permanent speed restrictions applied. The train was apparently being held at a steady 50 mph with all brakes applied. The forty limit through Huddersfield Tunnel shouldn't be a problem, but the station's twenty-five on all lines, and twenty round the back, would be. The train, being freight, would be routed round the back.

As we sharply went through the possibilities, madness reigned on the platforms. Waiting passengers were being urgently herded down the steps into the underpass and far from the freight lines. Frantic overexcited announcements on the tannoy were making things worse. The tunnel-end points were the danger point with heavily curved switches in the forty yards between the tunnel and the platforms. There was nothing that could be done. In the space of five long minutes Elliot was leaping back in to the phone and out again to watch. The signal box was on again, shouting the latest situation. The blokes at Central Control were simply hoping for the best, routing other trains away from the path of the runaway. All lines joining the route were stopped by emergency reds. Elliot and I knew that we were in for an almighty crash at the tunnel end. Emergency services were alerted. These were then diverted away from the goods yard where the pile-up would be. Gates were shut. Passengers were eventually directed out onto the station forecourt. Five minutes stretched out to what seemed an hour. Except it didn't, and it was now two. Then we heard the crescendo of a continuous howl from the approaching train. The station was dead. This was the moment of miracles, and a tribute to maintenance. The train appeared out of the tunnel. The howl was now a sickening scream. Wagons squealed madly through the vicious curves. They swayed crazily. Onto the straight at the back of the station followed by the drastic curves at the Leeds end before hitting the viaduct. Then, from a distance of thirty yards, we saw the driver and his mate.

I have never seen frozen fear like it. Both men were wrestling with the brake to no great effect. Both men were as white as possible, discounting death. This was a flash of probably a second. Yet the train kept to the tracks. Smoke billowed from the wheels, even flames at moments. All down the train brakes smoked and screamed.

We didn't exactly relax, but we both seemed to feel the pumping adrenalin ease slightly. There was time to look at the next problem to be encountered.

"Bradley Junction! Come on!"

A brief word to Bill for him to alert the Leeds Office and the Engineer. Also, to see that for the moment the line which the train had taken should be closed, pending the discovery of track damage. Anything else could be comfortably left to Bill who had a very calm head in real crisis.

We set off in the car to follow the train, knowing that we had no chance of overtaking it, just finding where it finally jumped the tracks. Bradley Junction was overdue for renewal, and trains lurched through it as it was. We were not thinking as clearly as we would have liked, because the speed limit over the next three miles was sixty-five, including Bradley. Seeing from the road that nothing had happened here we momentarily sat back.

"Hell!" A rare outburst from Elliot. A sharp curve at the end of the Colne Valley line as it joined the Calder lines had a permanent speed limit of forty which should have been OK, but this was Tuesday after new track had been put down two days earlier and the whole formation disturbed. A temporary and necessary twenty limit had been placed on the curve. It would not be accurately canted yet, and there was a more than likely chance of the most serious of dangers in railway track – that of twists, or sudden changes in cant.

Heaton Lodge Junction was to be the site of the derailment, and our greatest worry was that the gang working on the renewal would not be alert to a train travelling at more than twice the expected speed. We shot off there. We found a gang sat on the trackside in bewilderment and shock. No damage; no derailment; nobody hurt.

"Bloody 'ell!" said the ganger, in place of his usual "Good Morning, Elliot", or "Mr Milner", depending on how long he had known Elliot. "Tha shudev bin 'ere a minute ago! Bloody train come through doin' fifty…" Elliot quickly explained the situation, but the lads finding voice had to tell us of the expressions on the face of the driver. Elliot rang the signal box at Huddersfield from a signal phone, just to find out if our final obstacle of Mirfield Station had been successfully passed, and found it had been. The train was now on Wakefield Area; Elliot's counterpart, alerted by Bill, was now going through the trauma that we were just emerging from.

We returned to Huddersfield at a regular speed, neither of us saying anything. On arrival we found that the train had been so cleverly routed round Healey Mills marshalling yard that it had encountered no problems, as its speed had by then dropped to forty. It had eventually been diverted up the Crigglestone Branch where the slight uphill incline and the near-welded brakes drew it to a halt. Emergency services were waiting at the nearest access, and two very disturbed crewmen were taken to hospital suffering shock.

*

It was always inevitable that the *Leeds District Engineers' Annual Newsletter* would have to turn up in these pages. The intention was that that should be the basis for an entirely different volume, which might still be the case, but the story behind the building of Slaithwaite (for pronunciation see earlier, but the preferred one is Sloughwitt – as in bough of a tree) new station spans both these reminiscences and the catchment area for the Newsletter.

Briefly the Newsletter started in 1976 with four pages intending to combine the good and bad items of non-news that swam within the District Office around Christmas. When it wound up in 1992 it had swollen to thirty-eight pages in length. There was this magical moment for me, as editor, when everyone in the office momentarily hated me, as they read about themselves, and then warmed to some opposite emotion, as someone else's mishaps were resurrected. The Newsletter was a collection of the year's little stories of the staff's individual or collective cock-ups, in many cases greatly elaborated upon, and readily supplied by those hoping for their names to be kept out that year.

Slaithwaite was the site of one of the District's string of new stations, built very, and often too, economically. The platforms were light-timbered affairs, so light that the one at Bramley was blown over the track in a gale without breaking up. It was fortunately spotted by an alert approaching driver. Slaithwaite was such a one. Upright fence posts standing on paving slabs supported a timber decking; a small stone waiting shelter being the only "solid" construction. It was to be opened in early December, in time for the natives of Slaithwaite to travel to the mighty arcades of Huddersfield to do their Christmas shopping, so it was inevitable that some poor soul had to dress up as Santa Claus and be the first to leap off the train onto the new platform. This was the obvious idea. Not so obvious was the use of a dance troupe to entertain the waiting passengers, underlining the yokel image of such.

I think that on the day I was the senior person on the Area, our involvement only being to ensure that the tracks were at an ultimate alignment to set the platform edge to. Eddy and I observed the proceedings from just off the end of the opposite platform. Dignitaries were in place, Marsden signal box informed us over the tannoy that the train was on time and would be with us in ten minutes. This was the cue for the dance to start.

Now the lad at York Headquarters who had designed these station kits had been given a maximum crowd loading to work to, for which previous constructions had proved more than adequate. What the poor unfortunate had not envisaged was that the immobile crowd might ever be replaced by a set of burly dancers stomping in unison. The first cracking sound went fairly unnoticed by the assembled throng, but Eddy and I saw it. One of the paving stones snapped under the unexpected hammer of synchronised boots, causing the fence post support to drop a little. When two or three had gone the same way, a definite unevenness of the platform became obvious. Hurriedly, Marsden was informed and a request went to delay the train. Without unduly worrying the assembly, and more importantly the Mayor and party, one or two of us had a careful look at the bearings and decided that things were reasonably safe for this first train, but quite unsuitable for any more rustic frolics, and that work would have to be done as soon as the crowd dispersed. This part of the tale did not make it into the District Newsletter, since no one on the District was to blame. What did, however, was the car park. This had been constructed in a great hurry by District Works staff, and the soft clay surface had been subjected to heavy rain just before the tarmac had been laid.

I had a peculiar experience, accompanied by the District wit, Dave Holmes, of walking across it with our Works Engineer – the man ultimately responsible for it. As we walked, a gentle bow-wave of tarmac preceded us, whichever direction we took. Needless to say, the car park was immediately shut to traffic, but it didn't prevent an advertisement appearing in the Newsletter, courtesy of Dave, for "Auntie Bessie's Instant Car Park Mix".

★

Life cannot be ever filled with happiness and joy, and if these pages are a true reflection on life with characters, then it too must carry its fair share of grief. Such is one story about Manny Kaisermann, a clerk in the Leeds Offices. (I don't think that Manny's religious leanings need to be expounded on!) At the time of this event I had finally left Huddersfield and was firmly entrenched in Leeds, dealing with all sorts of track projects. I worked for a long period with Dave Holmes as my No. 1 and, by a collection of coincidences, Eddy Stapleton, from those balmy days under the water tank. Eddy had by then spent a lot of time in track renewals and was developing into a very useful man to have in your team.

Dave was perhaps a little less than perfection when it came to working on a job, although there was rarely anything wrong with the outcome. Some projects I allocated straight out to the lads when there was to be a minimum of meetings about the jobs. Meetings with other departments needed skill, diplomacy and experience, and a need to always convince the others' minds that you were in the most important position, and that they had to work round you. Dave would have a job on his books for six months, only tumbling into it in a mad panic about four weeks before it was scheduled to start. Then there would be a frenzy of ordering outside plant and contractors. In between times, he would have a laid-back air of one concentrating on this year's holiday. That said, when Dave did get going the work flowed and any mishaps were expertly covered up.

However, now back to one of the sadder events in my working life, and little Manny. I say little because he hardly troubled any low-flying aircraft at around five foot two. Manny was Jewish, as I implied earlier, but didn't have the flair of urgency that most of his culture did. He had two speeds in life, steady and sat down, and it was in this latter activity that we first noticed a problem, though even his walking took on a new style. He tended more to shuffle along with his toes pointing inwards and his knees almost colliding, but the act of sitting down was proving very difficult and, if possible, would be confined to one cheek or the other.

To every query about his health, Manny would wave his hand back carelessly, and say, "OK," – nothing more. Bolder approaches were made with direct questions of genuine concern.

"Is it your feet, Manny? You're walking queer recently. What's up?"

"Nowt, just a bit of trouble I've got," was all that you could get out of him. Then he had a day off. Ever the honest one, he declared the reason was that his piles had reached a peak of activity, and that he had been given the ultimate cure in the form of a tube of white pasty stuff. "They're bloody sore!" was his comment, and they must have been, since the last time we'd heard him swear was when he'd been offered a potato crisp that had turned out to be smoky bacon flavour.

Actually Manny was a little bit like Morris Yeo from years back, except that Manny was genuinely prone to minor illnesses, which he usually bore with his noble stoicism and a sigh rather than the flat panic of the hypochondriac.

So it had been piles that had been persecuting Manny for weeks, and instead of becoming a figure of fun as he had expected, he found that the full sympathy of all surrounded him. One of us found one of those inflatable rings at home and brought it in, bringing much relief and gratitude from Manny. Unfortunately, one of Manny's jobs was liaising with our main stores at Stanningley. The curator of the stores was an evil little gnome called Johnny Bass, a sort of winding-down job after an arduous career in track welding, which came about because of breathing difficulties. Johnny had an uncontrollable sense of humour that materialised in little brown paper parcels that you might find on your desk, one morning, relating to any minor misfortune you may have suffered. He had within his gift flags, soap, brushes (handles and business ends), toilet paper, scrubbing pads, nails – in fact everything you'd find in a hardware shop. Some unthinking twerp had leaked Manny's troubles up to Johnny, with the result that a feared brown paper parcel turned up on Manny's desk one morning. Johnny's parcels always created interest amongst the rest of us, so we all witnessed poor Manny unwrapping Johnny's "Ultimate Cure For Piles". It was a steel brush, used for scrubbing rust off metal, and a large jar of Swarfega. There was another note inside that asked Manny to pass it on to Dave Holmes, when he'd finished with it, because Dave was suffering a persistent sore throat, and Johnny indicated that this kit was a cure-all. Then came the fatal morning when Manny was over an hour late in.

We feared that the piles had given him so much trouble that he could not even face the rubber ring, but he did appear at about half nine, a very sorry and tormented figure. He refused to sit down, and instead shuffled about the office in obvious violent discomfort, with frequent visits to the Gents along with a box of soft tissues. Pinning him down around eleven, with a mug of tea in his hand, he told his small audience the saddest tale we had ever heard.

That morning he had got up in his usual befuddled state, read for ten minutes in the lavatory before facing the inevitable toilet paper, and the struggle into his bathroom next door. There, facing him under the mirror, was the usual panorama of tubes, pills, bottles and toothbrushes. With auto-pilot switched on, and not working with best efficiency, he massaged his pile ointment into his left shoulder. Fortunately, Preparation H had little adverse effect in this area, but still in his dreamy post-sleep concussion he then picked up the Fiery Jack rheumatism ointment...

As he told the sad story, *Blazing Saddles* came immediately to mind.

★

As I edged what was traditionally referred to as upwards (which I preferred to see as moving across into new fields), I was forced to mix more with management, not appreciating the fact that I too had become "management". What hit me most were changes in what we call "sense of humour". Management to a large extent was composed of people who took themselves far too seriously, and were shaken when humour emerged.

Incidents that struck me as hilarious were not thought universally to be so, depending in what competing department you were from. Take the incident of bridge No. 24A at Kirkstall, within Leeds. Here I was confined in a room at York, after a fractious meeting, with the Electrification Engineer until we reached an agreement between us on two options; to lower the tracks under the bridge (his demand) or to install a dead section of overhead cable such that the electrical equipment could hang closer to the underside of the bridge (mine). Neither of us would give way, and we eventually both collapsed in helpless laughter at the ridiculous situation of two grown men standing in a corner until we behaved ourselves. The Project Manager took this to mean agreement and released us. We both stood our ground, individually producing reports of consequences supported by our superiors, and leaving it to the Project Manager to decide. If the Electrification Engineer were to have his way there was a danger of track flooding and closure for a period. If I prevailed there was a chance that a train might become stranded in the dead section, closing the line until relief came. My position was based on the hundred-year pattern of floods at the bridge from the adjacent River Aire, making it theoretically likely that a flood could occur once every twenty-five years; his was a daily threat.

In the end the daily threat prevailed, though in fairness this decision was made before the fear of global warming consequences had been absorbed. As things worked out I was just three years into retirement when severe floods blocked the Ilkley and Skipton lines at Kirkstall, as I had predicted. I jubilantly took photos from the bridge, and tried to trace Charlie Batty, the Electrification man, to send him an "I told you so!" message. I was thwarted; Charlie had sadly died two years earlier.

*

Returning to normal life and the theme of characters, which is the basis of all this, Ham Shank Frank is worthy of mention. There had to be a reason that on every Friday in summer, full carrier bags would be hanging out of the upstairs windows of the office in Leeds, on the shady side of the building. These were stuffed with pounds of bacon, gammon steaks, bacon chops and joints of ham.

Frank had been a butcher until giving up to become a yard-man at Healey Mills near Wakefield. He never lost touch with his old wholesalers and had unlimited access to pork products – nothing else, just various portions of porcine geography. One Friday he brought in time sheets as usual, and made a casual offer to the clerk he delivered them to that he could lay his hands on some top-quality cheap bacon. Was he interested? The word "cheap" resonates in most clerks' ears, and a small order was put in for the next week.

Using the phrase "lay his hands on" as applied to Frank was rather apt, since he had a noticeable lack of digits. We assumed (we never raised the subject) that Frank was, or had been, ambidextrous as he has an equal number of fingers missing on each hand. Perhaps he gave up the butchering job when he had evened up the losses to each side. Anyway, it wasn't long before

Frank's main purpose in life on Fridays was to bring in the vast orders of pork and ham. Sometimes he even forgot the time sheets and had to go back for them; other return journeys were made on some other pretext when the orders became too big to handle in one go. The goods were spot-on, and the trade went on way after Frank's retirement until a new broom at the top, returning late from dinner, made enquiries about the array of bags hanging from the windows.

It was interesting as a sideline that even Manny Kaisermann made orders, but these were strictly to sell on.

Frank was definitely cash only, but Johnny Bass (supplier of the cure for laryngitis and piles, all in one kit) never sought payment. Johnny had had to stand down from his job in a track-welding team when his heavy smoking left him handicapped with half a lung. There were a few "green card" men like John employed in offices after a life out in the open. Bill Boyes, my Huddersfield mate, was one such following his savage heart attack. I believe that it was a government requirement that a certain percentage of the workforce had to be green carders. As a result, jobs were rather more created for the man than the man being sought out for a job, so that many of them found themselves in boring dead-end occupation, with, in the cases of both John and Bill, a little too much time on their hands.

Johnny's medical sympathies extended to many items when-ever he heard that someone in the Leeds Office had a problem. Amongst these was a carefully wrapped sheet of very coarse sandpaper, as a cure for warts, and an eye-watering broom handle that he had marked down as a cure for constipation. For the newly engaged young lady in the Typing Pool, John sent down a gift-wrapped package, inside which was a single glove – one of those pale rubber sort much used by dentists, doctors and customs officers today, but then to be worn when handling certain substances. To explain the glove, Johnny had enclosed a note to the reddening typist, saying that this was the latest marketing of a handy "packet of five". Johnny's stores at Stanningley were an Aladdin's cave of delights that we would plunder once a year or so, while Johnny made out a requisition to cover whatever items took our fancy. Railway stores worked on the basis that once every employee had acquired a pencil or a rubber for personal use at home, stock would then remain stable. The same went for dusters, chamois leathers, string, Swarfega, brush handles, soap, batteries, gardening gloves, and wire scourers, and so on, ad infinitum. However, you first had to get through Johnny's array of security devices.

There was a guard dog, found on the trackside, twelve inches high, stuffed, with one eye missing. Central to the store's ceiling was a cardboard box hanging from the roof with toilet roll tubes sticking out from all four sides – a very effective security camera according to Johnny, who had at the side of his desk a pickaxe handle labelled "pickpocket deterrent". The heavy wooden outer door had a notice on it saying "Caution – Automatic Door", and John got a certain amount of pleasure from watching lads walk up and down outside his window, trying to make it open. He would then operate a complicated rope and pulley device that opened the door, apparently without aid that caused some consternation as it worked. Johnny also claimed that the shop was alarmed, pointing to a cat suspended from the ceiling (a striking companion to the guard dog). It had a piece of string fastened to the outside door stretching up to, and wrapped round, two tennis balls attached to the underside of the cat.

Should you ask for the time (or if you didn't he would tell you anyway), Johnny had a "clock" on one of the walls. It was in fact an old clock face, fastened upside down, with a complex arrange-ment of nails holding it up. One large peg in the middle stood well out from the face – it was virtually a catalogue of many of the store's bits and pieces – to tell the time Johnny would shine a hand-lamp up at it, and the central peg turned it into a sundial. With the aid of his torch, Johnny would tell you that it was a quarter to four, and that you should hurry up, because he goes home at four. It was always a quarter to four in the stores.

It should be made clear that not all Johnny's decorations were ever up together at one time. There wasn't the room for one thing, then it was only when something new dropped into his hands that his overactive imagination took hold.

For instance, he once installed a fitted kitchen. This was centred around two actual working things: a gas ring and a single tap marked in stamped tape "cold". (Outside in the yard, on the opposite side of the store wall, was a tap mounted to enable wagons and vans to be cleaned. This one was marked "colder".) The kitchen contained a mop handle and bucket labelled "clothes washer", and a matching pair marked "dishwasher". His fridge was a small oil drum, open at the top, with papers clipped round the edge. These turned out to be the latest instructions from the District Office that Johnny claimed would make any blood run cold. His cooker was, or once had been, an actual small oven inside which Johnny had mounted a candle.

There was for a long while a picture frame on the wall, marked "mirror". (The advent of the hand-held embossing machine for stamping out letters onto tape was a godsend to Johnny. He went through a load of tapes before exhausting his imagination.) Instead of an actual sheet of reflecting glass in the frame, there was a full frontal face of Hitler. Long before Freddie Starr produced his ridiculous Hitler costume, Johnny had been dressing in a ground-contacting supervisors' black raincoat, with swastika armbands, and a purloined fire inspector's black peeked cap. To complete the job, he stuck on the trademark moustache, and posed for photos that were distributed on the underground of office life. Next to the "mirror" he had a discarded television set that did have a mirror in it.

His short shelf marked "Bathroom" had an array of pastes, liquids and powders in tins, bottles and packets, all labelled up as the most inappropriate toothpastes, gargles and talcum. Referring back to the wire brush and Swarfega, I must leave Johnny's imaginative use of railway cleaning, abrasives and lubricants to the reader's own imagination. Bottles of varying shapes and sizes, all discarded down embankments, were filled with cold tea to form the inevitable "wine rack".

For a while there was an unidentifiable length of cloth or carpet hung on one wall, under a placard labelled "Bedroom – Keep Out!" Drawing back the cloth, as you were intended to do, revealed a life-size poster of a lady wearing carpet slippers: just carpet slippers.

A sixteen-foot ladder was left in the stores for a while, as painters attended to some of the offices. Immediate action on

Johnny's part, knowing the ladder could be removed at any time, resulted in the rather unsuccessful mounting of a garden ornamental duck on the top, with a label too far away to read, but assuredly marked "pigeon" according to John, which explained the notice at the bottom pointing upwards "To the Loft". A whole bottle of white correction fluid must have been used to supply the droppings at the foot of the ladder.

As new compulsory safety clothing came out, Johnny rigged up a dummy wearing his version of the kit. Oversize wellington boots were marked up as protection against being dropped in it. Disgusting trousers heavily and nauseatingly stained and marked were stuffed into the boots with remarks about them referring casually to the state of being in deep fear. An actual new high-visibility coat topped the trousers adorned with a large variety of gadgets, all allocated to certain safety jobs. Johnny's "taking care" measures encompassed situations way beyond those required by British Rail, such as the large bulldog clip guarding against premature ejaculation, and the clerical wire basket with an added length of string to be used as a chastity belt. A busted football served as a head, with imposing goggles and safety mask. The goggles were standard welders' gear, except these had small birthday cake candles stuck above the eye-holes – "For seeing in the dark" was Johnny's explanation. The whole array was topped off with an upturned coal-scuttle.

Johnny did have limits – points where he felt he might be sailing too close to the wind. Such a situation occurred in his "kitchen" where he had a small row of hooks, easily concealed, and marked up as a "vegetable rack". Under the hooks were photos of various leading Leeds engineers. He was only brought to task once when a near calamity was averted as a poorly sighted audit clerk mistook John's "ejector seat" for the real thing, and nearly sat down. It was a busted clerical chair with the business end of a ballast fork stuck upwards through the seat.

Johnny's retirement was a mixed affair. During the morning he was entertained in the Leeds Divisional Offices with tea and a special retirement cake, spectacularly iced and decorated by our own Lily Tuke, an absolute genius in the art. Returning to Stanningley to sign off for the last time, Johnny was met by the yard's JCB, and in his second-best suit, laid out in the front bucket. The lads did a very uncomfortable lap of honour round all the various shops, ending up by tipping their load out onto a heap of scrap.

★

It beats me, looking back through these pages, why Charlie Lavender hasn't featured before now. Charlie was a one-off, a dreamer with an ambitious imagination. This manifested itself when he would go off into afternoon trances, gazing at something yards behind the clock on the wall above his desk.

"It's no good trying to hypnotise that bloody clock, Charlie! It's not going to go any faster!" This would be a frustrated Dave Holmes, possibly in one of his furious work modes, aggravated by the figure sat staring into space.

Charlie, like the rest of us, would take his turn on the softer Saturday nights of de-stressing continuous welded rail. As with me, he would look forward to the glorious moment when the violently flaming cauldron of weld material was tapped, and the molten glare ran into the gap between the rail ends, before cooling and forming a solid casting. It was a spectacular couple of seconds, with a slightly nervous anticipation of a run through if the mould was less than perfect. In that situation the whole job had to be repeated.

It was the welding that caught Charlie's imagination, and it wasn't long before we found that he had bought himself a full welding kit for home. Every evening, Charlie was up welding anything he could. When he became reasonably proficient at the job, he offered his talents round the office, mending gratings and holes in pans. But this wasn't enough for the bursting pioneer in him, and he began collecting scrap iron, and making things. His first real triumph was a full dining room suite that caused him to have to reinforce the room's floor. The table alone was a slab of cast iron surmounting four iron rods, with the first attempts at some filigree work. Moving chairs in and out was a two-man job, or rather him and his wife together. But anyone invited in to see it came out full of admiration.

Then Charlie got really ambitious – he would build a boat! He explained his project in the office, and passed round his designs. Opinion was divided straight down the middle as to whether the resulting piece of work would actually float, or just sink like a stone. Charlie was not to be put off. Late into the nights he would be in the shed or on the drive, cutting and welding great sheets of iron, with the aid of a home-made A-frame hoist and block and tackle.

There was a full spring, summer and autumn went into the construction before the problem of transportation occurred to him. The office clock was keenly stared at again, and dinnertimes were taken up entirely with sketching and discarding. He finally came up with a road trolley to carry the boat, much to his delight, as it would mean yet more welding and cutting. Charlie here struck lucky. A whole consignment of tubular iron came his way, a new form for him to experiment with. In the end the road vehicle was magnificently long and large, the size of a medium caravan. He thoughtfully constructed it around and under the boat, rather than having the problem later of lifting the boat onto it.

Charlie's work had really caught the public imagination, and the debate raged on as to whether the thing would or would not float. Scale models were produced, one from a solid block of iron that Charlie obligingly hollowed out, and another from a sardine can. Sure enough one floated and the other sunk without any attempt at floating.

At last the great day arrived. Charlie had been allocated a shorter Saturday night, something he usually fought against, leaving him free to make for the coast, Bridlington being the chosen test bed. Weekend work prevailed for most as the more important way of spending it, rather than travelling over to Brid to watch a boat float/sink. Dave Holmes, on the other hand, was just finishing a week's holiday further up the coast, and announced to all except Charlie that he would end up down at Brid to observe and report back – by now a lot of stake money was involved. Dave was allocated the office Polaroid camera to bring back unbiased evidence.

Charlie did not show up on the Monday morning, claiming

bereavement. This convinced the sink faction that they had won. Dave was late in, and was immediately engulfed as his face displayed nothing. "Did it float or didn't it?"

Dave had been at the quayside for about an hour when Charlie turned up and skilfully executed the reverse onto the ramp down into a fairly high tide (a point that Charlie's attention to detail had taken into account), watched with interest by a few of the locals. Down the ramp and into the water. "Well, did it or didn't it?"

"I still don't know whether the boat can float or not," said Dave, "but I can tell you with confidence that Charlie's trailer did!"

★

Health and Safety at Work has become the overpowering main flavour of work on the railways since the early 1990s. This, to introduce a controversial note, is ironic in the extreme as rules of wear and conduct of staff have become so stifling that a worker fully kitted out simply cannot move or do any job safely. Alongside this was the sell-out to private industry that without any doubt made the railways far less safe for the passengers (discuss using one side of the paper only).

It all started with the high visibility (HV) vest, which met a great deal of resistance, followed later by HV coats, and eventually by HV all-in-ones. Track workers found this added layer far more restricting and very hot in summer. Men were disciplined for wearing the vests round their backsides while stripped off in the heat. Great protest erupted over this, with the argument that most work involved bending over, hiding the correctly adorned vest, but making the bum style perfectly visible.

Then came the boots. Safety boots had always been encouraged, but the lads had previously to buy their own from a wide and popular choice of styles. Enter bureaucracy – safety footwear provided free, and only this issue pair will be approved. Naturally, it was the cheapest style available and cut your feet to ribbons. Track workers tended to order two sizes too big and protect themselves with several pairs of socks. In the midst of all this safety mania was Relaying Supervisor Eric Noakes whose priorities in life were – 1. Getting as many Saturday-morning shifts as he could; 2. Producing new and plausible reasons for rail cranes under his control regularly falling over; and 3. Comfort.

Eric for a long time was synonymous with scrap collection and disposal. He and his gang received old track panels from renewal jobs on Monday mornings, stripped them down, cut rails up and arranged for contract collections by lorry. On Saturday nights he would be out with his lads eagerly working as long a shift as he could, often on more than one job. On Friday afternoons both he and his lads were invariably unavailable and undetectable, thus ensuring the need for Saturday-morning shifts to make for a clear yard by Monday. In the event of a Saturday being turned down, Eric would occasionally manage it that the wooden chair keys through a vital bit of point-work at the entrance to his yard were loosened, resulting in a loco suffering a minor derailment, and so securing an emergency call for Eric to get out with his lads and repair the track.

Safety of his staff was certainly there amongst Eric's priorities, probably lying at No. 4, as long as it didn't interfere with 1, 2 or 3. When guessing the weight of a load he was lifting, and the limiting outreach of the crane, Eric would ensure that all the lads were behind the lift and in no danger. Occasionally he got his guesses (or calculations, as he called them) wrong and the crane toppled over. He could never see how wearing a safety vest could prevent this, so he didn't wear one. Similarly, when tackled, he would ask what use a safety helmet would be if a ton of rail fell on him. An exception was that should he see management approaching he would allow the vest to dangle slightly out of his pocket. Issued safety helmets made attractive pots around the cabin door in which were planted flowers of all seasons. His greatest rebellion, with its failure to conform with No. 3, were the boots, hence his habitual use of carpet slippers inside and out in the yard.

Rather than keeping on issuing disciplinary notices, and warning him of safety checks, management grew weary of protecting themselves from such by ensuring that Eric and gang were nowhere to be seen on examination days.

★

Cricket matches between various local hastily assembled teams and whatever could be trawled together out of the Engineer's staff, always brought out character. Bert Glover, keen, but slightly older and slower than some of the lads, always put himself behind the stumps. Bert's stumping techniques were based on his having the protection of gloves, pads and some form of breastplate and placing the handiest of these objects behind the ball. He wore glasses, not the ideal for a wicket-keeper, so he mostly favoured the upright stance. Should the ball land in his gloves, this was taken as a bonus.

Much the same approach was taken by Neville, who, unlike Bert, moved around a lot. He was usually posted on the boundary with due respect to his also wearing glasses. Unfortunately he did not have vision to a standard where he could clearly detect events fifty yards away, so had to be shouted at if the ball was anywhere within his region. He would run from side to side, guided by the helpful advice of his colleagues, until the ball came into view, at which point he would simply hurl himself at it, regardless of where it might strike.

Dave Holmes was a useful fast bowler. Happily the combination of Dave's accuracy and the six-ball over usually meant that, on an average, one ball came within the reach of the batsmen. Being virtually unplayable, chance had it that somewhere within his allocation of two overs a ball was likely to hit the wicket.

Jack Pinder, Works Supervisor, took a wholly relaxed attitude to the game. As a batsman, this often resulted in quite a few runs. Jack's relaxation stretched to always keeping his pipe clenched between his teeth. He was disciplined enough as to refrain from relighting it while at the batting end, for which purpose he always went out with a full box of matches. Once, and only once, did this habit bite back when Jack took a skidder on the hip, but managed to get three leg byes out of it. His partner, facing up to the next ball, was a little put off to see smoke coming out of Jack's pocket as he ended his run at the bowling end. In no time at all the puff of smoke turned into a small inferno as all Jack's matches went up together. Wet grass was stuffed in, but it was inevitable that Jack had to be tumbled to the floor while his trousers were dragged off and beaten in the grass. Undeterred, Jack carried on with crumpled and smouldering trousers back in place, but with rather more of Jack being visible than before.

★

Some characters are more anti-characters than anything else. Folk who shrink from the public gaze and never take part in office events or voice opinions. They are invariably teetotal lest they should lower their guards – I'm really thinking of Orville Jinks. Not a shy man, but one trying to do his job and live his life without making any waves.

Orville first came on the scene as a clerk in the staff section. (You knew what the various departments and people in the office did in those days by means of a clear title: Materials Clerk, Programme Clerk, Stationery Clerk or Staff Clerk. In the 1980s this last section became Personnel for some reason, only to descend to the ridiculous Human Resources tag.) Orville had many particular roles in the Staff Section, but the one that most affected the staff was his job as free ticket issuer. At his time there, staff were allocated five free passes a year, one of which was a "foreign" pass. At one time this meant a trip on another company's railway, but came to mean a journey outside the Region, ours being the North Eastern Region. Passes were all returns and lasted as long as your holiday, being dated by rubber stamp and with the final destination being written in by hand. Under Orville's control his customers soon found that they had as good as got all five allocations as foreign passes due to his unique handwriting. His pen took on the characteristics of having being used by an arthritic chimp. Any destination written in by Orville could pass as many others.

Easiest were Orville's "Bridlington" (a home destination) passing off as "Brighton" (foreign). "Llandúdno" took staff to London if they wished and of course "Newcastle-on-Tyne" easily stood in for Newcastle-under-Lyme. These were simple; but Orville was so undecipherable that almost anywhere on the ticket could get you anywhere on the railway map. There was only the slight problem at the ticket barrier with "What the bloody hell does that say?" A confident response was all that was needed to get you through.

Orville later moved up into the Drawing Office, where he was principally involved with track abandonments. Again, written yardages were none too clear, and many a job was credited with incredible scrap recovery yardages. Brought to his attention, the effect would be to push Orville further back into his shell. He travelled in daily from Bradford on a staff season ticket, on the same train and at the same point on the train of closed compartments. This is how the Blakey girls got to know him.

Blakey's of Armley were known around the world as producers of the seg, a metal stud to be hammered into the heels and toes of boots to give a longer-lasting life – hence "sparking clogs" on the cobblestones. Years before, local John Blakey was striding over Ilkley Moor when he was made to curse as a small piece of metal embedded itself in his new boots. It proved unremovable, and he found the affected heel lasted much longer than its mate. From this came the idea of the seg, and a factory in Armley to make them for the world, and hence the use of local labour, which since the War had been mainly female. Blakey's girls were notorious. They were as rough as they come, many travelling from Armley Moor, next to the factory, down to Holbeck or Leeds. They soon picked out Orville, as their coarse talk would plunge his head deeper into his railway magazine. Orville became a daily target with them, seeing how many could plunge themselves into his compartment. Worst for him was when one of them might perch herself on his knee, carrying on her loud conversation and forcing Orville's nose up against the magazine's central paperclip. Other office lads faced them with no challenge, often making what should have been taken as offensive remarks, but instead sparking off ribald retorts from the girls. No, it was Orville they targeted.

One morning a group of Blakey's night girls picked out Orville, alone but for a colleague from the Drawing Office, ignored but for a curt "Morning".

In they piled and in the ten long minutes it took to get from

Armley to Holbeck, with a signal stop, they carried on a conversation apparently started on the platform, but designed for Orville's ears only.

"Talkin'v changing names, there's a chap in our section what's doin' just that!"

"What? Changin' his name? How's he do that?"

"Bi' summat called a deed poll."

"What's a bollocking dead parrot got to do wi'it?" Orville curls up at the edges.

"No, it's summat legal, or legitimate or summat. Opposite of bastard ah suppose." Orville's fingers dig deep into his magazine.

"Who issit what's changin' his name, anyway?"

"That Jeremiah Itchyarse."

Orville shrivels.

"Not surprised! What's he changin' it to?"

"Joe Itchyarse!"

Peals of screaming laughter, with Orville reduced to a puddle of steaming sweat.

★

My character file seems almost endless, with hopefully plenty more emerging from a possible compilation of the Annual Newsletters. There you will find Chris Metcalfe who bought a terrace house in Rodley backing onto the canal with mooring for his barge, for just £200! The price reflected the fact that the "house" had had a lorry embed itself in the front, demolishing all the façade and the entire roof. Chris worked nights and weekends on rebuilding the house, later selling it on for a massive profit as he moved permanently onto the barge.

Gwyn Macefield, an extraordinary short barrel of a man, not one you would allocate delicacy as a possible description, was officially a member of the Leeds Drawing Office, yet spent most of his life up at Stanningley Shops where he had a gift of a job making the display model of Leeds new combined stations. He drew the job out to extraordinary lengths as the powers played into his hands by deferring the work and altering designs. Not for Gwyn were bought wagons, track and buffers; he made the lot himself from scratch. His model-making made him a dangerous animal when he was called back into Leeds for a spell – he had the speciality of making small guns. Not for bullets, but devastatingly effective with pins at thirty yards.

One romancer in Leeds was Dwain Vallender. Anything that could be done and recorded as showing great human endeavour, Dwain had done it. In his imagination he was all of Billy Liar. He flew in Spitfires, climbed the Eiger over a weekend, and led police to the solution of many baffling crimes. Sadly, these fantasies tumbled over into everyday life, especially when he might be late in for work. Kye Bevin was the recipient of these excuses when late arrival meant almost half the morning missed. Lesser tardiness meant that Kye himself could be beaten at getting in. Reasons for late arrival included a trip round the British coast by jet on which Dwain had been invited, coming in late to Yeadon Airport due to fog over Dewsbury. Then his train was delayed as a woman gave birth to triplets on the seat in front of Dwain, and his knowledge of first aid was so useful to a nurse on the train that she left the last two infants for him to deliver by himself. One that came out at least once a year was his call-out to join the North Yorkshire cave rescue organisation on a mission down Gaping Gill pothole. In the course of me knowing Dwain, his father was mistakenly sentenced to death, his uncle was battling with his conscience as to whether or not reveal that he was really Adolf Hitler and his grandmother was unlucky enough to have died on five separate occasions.

★

My very first day on the railway was at York, assigned to the Bridge Assessment Section in the prefab huts on the old station platforms. Initiation started with an introduction to the Bridge Engineer who had Mike Prime take me down to my desk. During my interview I was told that I would have the privilege of working under Pat Hodgkins, described as the most brilliant of engineers, only held back in life by a speech impediment. I arrived in the office at half past nine, and was introduced by Pat to old Arthur, Brian and again to Mike. This left an empty desk covered in a dust sheet. I found this first day extraordinarily quiet, apart from being assigned the task of colouring up a map of the region – a traditional welcoming job anywhere in any drawing office. The week progressed quietly with a series of people coming to speak behind a closed door to Pat. Nobody seemed to smile, but I took this to be normal. The following Monday, I was in place bright and early trying to impress. Suddenly, about nine, a cheery little man appeared, rosy-cheeked and with a broad Irish accent and I was introduced. Mike Cantillon was his name, and as soon as he had cleared the sheet off his desk, Brian, out of the heavy silence, made a short speech to the effect that the whole office wished to offer their sincere condolences to Mr Cantillon, with the offer of doing anything within their power to help. I was deeply puzzled, and found out at dinnertime from Mike Prime that the weekend prior to my arrival, the Cantillon family had been devastated at the death of their young son aged about eight. He had been in the way as his older sister swung a golf club in the garden. Such was my first day, my first week, and my first meeting with Mike Cantillon, the first of many of irrepressible pleasure, for this man was my first real character.

★

Not enough mention has been made in these pages of two particularly close colleagues, and characters. One of these I vote to be the character of all characters, John Midgley. He doesn't appear much so far because he and I only met up in the 1980s, forming a team to manage the York Station remodelling for the District Engineer, Leeds. John, and I know I repeat myself, was the finest permanent way engineer I ever met, and at the same time the most outrageous character. He will appear in pages yet unplanned in another place.

Dave Holmes was an earlier colleague, though he did briefly overlap John. He was the master of the one-liners and instant repartee. He it was who reported that there had been a derailment of a Germolene tanker in Woolley Tunnel; no one was hurt, but two days later the tunnel mouth healed up. Carefree painting of Leeds Station roof, with suspect protection, was carried out under the supervision of George McHooligan, as he came to be known after this job. Dave congratulated the Area Manager on his choice of colours, and George for producing passengers to match.

Disgusted by the heavy stress placed on a most simple job of installing a single politically important turnout in a goods line at Stourton Yard near Leeds, Dave issued a report on the job:

Timescale: 32 Sundays planned of which 30 are savers, just in case.
Materials: A convoy of stone ballast brought to site in 6 carrier bags.
Plan of Action: Both sleepers to be packed by hand.

The job to be the subject of a paper read to the Permanent Way Institution and illustrated by a slide.

Dave was delicately cruel to some of our slower colleagues, one of whom has already appeared within these pages under an alias. Dave's summary:

BRIAN is an anagram of BRAIN. An anagram is a jumbled mess.

Towards the end of our association, Dave, at the age of forty, was crippled by cancer of the throat, caused by constant smoking. He went to huge lengths planning his future at this time, discovering that it would be of greater benefit to his wife for him to die in service rather than to retire under ill health. He was kept on in my section, and managed to get to work occasionally – once to travel with me to my new office, and new life with John Midgley at York. Dave soon became too ill to come out, and I would visit him at home or make regular phone calls. He was coughing badly on one visit, and a week later I had this conversation with him on the phone:

Me: "How's the coughing, Dave?"

Dave: "Fine, Mike. I've only got the handles to put on and it's finished."

Within the week Dave was dead.

There the story should close, except that this final chapter was started straight after the sudden death of he who will become my main star in the future – John Midgley, aged only fifty-nine.

Printed in the United Kingdom
by Lightning Source UK Ltd.
110671UKS00001B/4-6